Towards the Far Horizons

Towards the Far Horizons

Two Famous American Mountain Men,
Explorers & Trappers

The Personal Narrative of James O. Pattie, of
Kentucky

Timothy Flint

Narrative of the Adventures of Zenas
Leonard 1831–1836

Himself

LEONAUR

Towards the Far Horizons
Two Famous American Mountain Men, Explorers & Trappers
The Personal Narrative of James O. Pattie, of Kentucky
byTimothy Flint
Narrative of the Adventures of Zenas Leonard 1831-1836
by Himself

FIRST EDITION

First published under the titles
The Personal Narrative of James O. Pattie, of Kentucky

and

Narrative of the Adventures of Zenas Leonard 1831-1836

Leonaur is an imprint
of Oakpast Ltd

ISBN: 978-1-78282-387-2 (hardcover)
ISBN: 978-1-78282-388-9 (softcover)

http://www.leonaur.com

Publisher's Notes

The views expressed in this book are not necessarily
those of the publisher.

Contents

The Personal Narrative of James O. Pattie, of Kentucky

Contents

Original Editor's Preface

It has been my fortune to be known as a writer of works of the imagination. I am solicitous that this journal should lose none of its intrinsic interest, from its being supposed that in preparing it for the press, I have drawn from the imagination, either in regard to the incidents or their colouring. For, in the literal truth of the facts, incredible as some of them may appear, my grounds of conviction are my acquaintance with the author, the impossibility of inventing a narrative like the following, the respectability of his relations, the standing which his father sustained, the confidence reposed in him by the Hon. J. S. Johnston, the very respectable senator in congress from Louisiana, who introduced him to me, the concurrent testimony of persons now in this city, who saw him at different points in New Mexico, and the reports, which reached the United States, during the expedition of many of the incidents here recorded.

When my family first arrived at St. Charles' in 1816, the fame of the exploits of his father, as an officer of the rangers, was fresh in the narratives of his associates and fellow soldiers. I have been on the ground, at Cap au Gris, where he was besieged by the Indians. I am not unacquainted with the scenery through which he passed on the Missouri, and I, too, for many years was a sojourner in the prairies.

These circumstances, along with a conviction of the truth of the narrative, tended to give me an interest in it, and to qualify me in some degree to judge of the internal evidences contained in the journal itself, of its entire authenticity. It will be perceived at once, that Mr. Pattie, with Mr. McDuffie, thinks more of action than literature, and is more competent to perform exploits, than blazon them in eloquent periods. My influence upon the narrative regards orthography, and punctuation and the occasional interposition of a topographical illustration, which my acquaintance with the accounts of travellers in

11

New Mexico, and published views of the country have enabled me to furnish.

The reader will award me the confidence of acting in good faith, in regard to drawing nothing from my own thoughts. I have found more call to suppress, than to add, to soften, than to show in stronger relief many of the incidents. Circumstances of suffering, which in many similar narratives have been given in downright plainness of detail, I have been impelled to leave to the reader's imagination, as too revolting to be recorded.

The very texture of the narrative precludes ornament and amplification. The simple record of events as they transpired, painted by the hungry, toil-worn hunter, in the midst of the desert, surrounded by sterility, espying the foot print of the savage, or discerning him couched behind the tree or hillock, or hearing the distant howl of wild beasts, will naturally bear characteristics of stern disregard of embellishment. To alter it, to attempt to embellish it, to divest it of the peculiar impress of the narrator and his circumstances, would be to take from it its keeping, the charm of its simplicity, and its internal marks of truth. In these respects I have been anxious to leave the narrative as I found it.

The journalist seems in these pages a legitimate descendant of those western pioneers, the hunters of Kentucky, a race passing unrecorded from history. The pencil of biography could seize upon no subjects of higher interest. With hearts keenly alive to the impulses of honour and patriotism, and the charities of kindred and friends; they possessed spirits impassable to fear, that no form of suffering or death could daunt; and frames for strength and endurance, as if ribbed with brass and sinewed with steel. For them to traverse wide deserts, climb mountains, swim rivers, grapple with the grizzly bear, and encounter the savage, in a sojourn in the wilderness of years, far from the abodes of civilized men, was but a spirit-stirring and holiday mode of life.

To me, there is a kind of moral sublimity in the contemplation of the adventures and daring of such men. They read a lesson to shrinking and effeminate spirits, the men of soft hands and fashionable life, whose frames the winds of heaven are not allowed to visit too roughly. They tend to re-inspire something of that simplicity of manners, manly hardihood, and Spartan energy and force of character, which formed so conspicuous a part of the nature of the settlers of the western wilderness.

Everyone knows with what intense interest the community perused the adventures of Captain Riley,[1] and other intrepid mariners shipwrecked and enslaved upon distant and barbarous shores. It is far from my thoughts to detract from the intrepidity of American mariners, which is known, wherever the winds blow, or the waves roll; or to depreciate the interest of the recorded narratives of their sufferings. A picture more calculated to arouse American sympathies cannot be presented, than that of a ship's crew, driven by the fierce winds and the mountain waves upon a rock bound shore, and escaping death in the sea, only to encounter captivity from the barbarians on the land. Yet much of the courage, required to encounter these emergencies is passive, counselling only the necessity of submission to events, from which there is no escape, and to which all resistance would be unavailing.

The courage requisite to be put forth in an expedition such as that in which Mr. Pattie and his associates were cast, must be both active and passive, energetic and ever vigilant, and never permitted to shrink, or intermit a moment for years. At one time it is assailed by hordes of yelling savages, and at another, menaced with the horrible death of hunger and thirst in interminable forests, or arid sands. Either position offers perils and sufferings sufficiently appalling. But fewer spirits, I apprehend, are formed to brave those of the field,

Where wilds immeasurably spread,
Seem lengthening as they go.

. . . .than of the ocean, where the mariner either soon finds rest beneath its tumultuous bosom, or joyfully spreads his sails again to the breeze.

---

1. *Accounts of the Wreck of the Commerce*, by James Riley & Archibald Robbins, two accounts by crew members including the one by the ship's master, James Riley is also published by Leonaur.

Introduction

The grandfather of the author of this *Journal*, was born in Caroline county, Virginia, in 1750. Soon after he was turned of twenty-one, he moved to Kentucky, and became an associate with those fearless spirits who first settled in the western forests. To qualify him to meet the dangers and encounter the toils of his new position, he had served in the revolutionary war, and had been brought in hostile contact with the British in their attempt to ascend the river Potomac.

He arrived in Kentucky, in company with twenty emigrant families, in 1781, and settled on the south side of the Kentucky River. The new settlers were beginning to build houses with internal finishing. His pursuit, which was that of a house carpenter, procured him constant employment, but he sometimes diversified it by teaching school. Soon after his arrival, the commencing settlement experienced the severest and most destructive assaults from the Indians. In August, 1782, he was one of the party who marched to the assistance of Bryant's station, and shared in the glory of relieving that place by the memorable defeat of the savages.

Not long afterwards he was called upon by Colonel Logan to join a party led by him against the Indians, who had gained a bloody victory over the Kentuckians at the Blue Licks.[1] He was present on the spot, where the bodies of the slain lay unburied, and assisted in their interment. During his absence on this expedition, Sylvester Pattie, father of the author, was born, August 25, 1782.

In November of the same year, his grandfather was summoned to join a party commanded by Colonel Logan, in an expedition against the Indians at the Shawnee towns, in the limits of the present state of Ohio. They crossed the Ohio just below the mouth of the Licking,

---

1. *Siege of Bryan's Station and the Battle of Blue Licks* by Reuben T. Durrett, Bennett H. Young, Henry T. Stanton & George W. Ranck is also published by Leonaur.

opposite the site of what is now Cincinnati, which was at that time an unbroken forest, without the appearance of a human habitation. They were here joined by General Clark with his troops from the falls of the Ohio, or what is now Louisville. The united force marched to the Indian towns, which they burnt and destroyed.

Returning from this expedition, he resumed his former occupations, witnessing the rapid advance of the country from immigration. When the district, in which he resided, was constituted Bracken County, he was appointed one of the judges of the court of quarter sessions, which office he filled sixteen years, until his place was vacated by an act of the legislature reducing the court to a single judge.

Sylvester Pattie, the father of the author, as was common at that period in Kentucky, married early, having only reached nineteen. He settled near his father's house, and there remained until there began to be a prevalent disposition among the people to move to Missouri. March 14, 1812, he removed to that country, the author being then eight years old. Born and reared amidst the horrors of Indian assaults and incursions, and having lived to see Kentucky entirely free from these dangers, it may seem strange, that he should have chosen to remove a young family to that remote country, then enduring the same horrors of Indian warfare, as Kentucky had experienced twenty-five years before. It was in the midst of the late war with England, which, it is well known, operated to bring the fiercest assaults of savage incursion upon the remote frontiers of Illinois and Missouri.

To repel these incursions, these then territories, called out some companies of rangers, who marched against the Sac and Fox Indians, between the Mississippi and the lakes, who were at that time active in murdering women and children, and burning their habitations during the absence of the male heads of families. When Pattie was appointed lieutenant in one of these companies, he left his family at St. Charles' where he was then residing. It may be imagined, that the condition of his wife was sufficiently lonely, as this village contained but one American family besides her own, and she was unable to converse with its French inhabitants. His company had several skirmishes with the Indians, in each of which it came off successful.

The rangers left him in command of a detachment, in possession of the fort at Cap au Gris. Soon after the main body of the rangers had marched away, the fort was besieged by a body of English and Indians. The besiegers made several attempts to storm the fort, but were repelled by the garrison.—The foe continued the siege for a week, continually firing upon the garrison, who sometimes, though not often, for want of ammunition, returned the fire. Lieutenant Pattie, perceiving no disposition in the enemy to withdraw, and discovering that his ammunition was almost entirely exhausted, deemed it necessary to send a despatch to Bellefontaine, near the point of the junction of the Missouri and Mississippi, where was stationed a considerable American force. He proposed to his command, that a couple of men should make their way through the enemy, cross the Mississippi, and apprize the commander of Bellefontaine of their condition. No one was found willing to risk the attempt, as the besiegers were encamped entirely around them.

Leaving Thomas McNair in command in his place, and putting on the uniform of one of the English soldiers, whom they had killed during one of the attempts to storm the fort, he passed by night safely through the camp of the enemy, and arrived at the point of his destination, a distance of over forty miles: 500 soldiers were immediately dispatched from Bellefontaine to the relief of the besieged at Cap au Gris. As soon as this force reached the fort, the British and Indians decamped, not, however, without leaving many of their lifeless companions behind them.

Lieutenant Pattie remained in command of Cap au Gris, being essentially instrumental in repressing the incursions of the Sacs and Foxes, and disposing them to a treaty of peace, until the close of the war. In 1813 he received his discharge, and returned to his family, with whom he enjoyed domestic happiness in privacy and repose for some years. St. Louis and St. Charles were beginning rapidly to improve; American families were constantly immigrating to these towns.

The timber in their vicinity is not of the best kind for building. Pine could nowhere be obtained in abundance, nearer than on the Gasconade, a stream that enters on the south side of the Missouri, about one hundred and fifty miles up that river. Mr. Pattie, possessing a wandering and adventurous spirit, meditated the idea of removing to this frontier and unpeopled river, to erect mills upon it, and send down pine lumber in rafts to St. Louis, and the adjoining country. He carried his plan into operation, and erected a Saw and Grist Mill upon the Gasconade. It proved a very fortunate speculation, as there was an immediate demand at St. Louis and St. Charles for all the plank the mill could supply.

In this remote wilderness, Mr. Pattie lived in happiness and prosperity, until the mother of the author was attacked by consumption.

Although her husband was, as has been said, strongly endowed with the wandering propensity, he was no less profoundly attached to his family; and in this wild region, the loss of a beloved wife was irreparable. She soon sunk under the disorder, leaving nine young children. Not long after, the youngest died, and was deposited by her side in this far land.

The house, which had been the scene of domestic quiet, cheerfulness and joy, and the hospitable home of the stranger, sojourning in these forests, became dreary and desolate. Mr. Pattie, who had been noted for the buoyancy of his gay spirit, was now silent, dejected, and even inattentive to his business; which, requiring great activity and constant attention, soon ran into disorder.

About this time, remote trapping and trading expeditions up the Missouri, and in the interior of New Mexico began to be much talked of. Mr. Pattie seemed to be interested in these expeditions, which offered much to stir the spirit and excite enterprise. To arouse him from his indolent melancholy, his friends advised him to sell his property, convert it into merchandize and equipments for trapping and hunting, and to join in such an undertaking. To a man born and reared under the circumstances of his early life—one to whom forests, and long rivers, adventures, and distant mountains, presented pictures of familiar and birth day scenes—one, who confided in his rifle, as a sure friend, and who withal, connected dejection and bereavement with his present desolate residence; little was necessary to tempt him to such an enterprise.

In a word, he adopted the project with that undoubting and unshrinking purpose, with which to will is to accomplish. Arrangements were soon made. The children were provided for among his relations. The author was at school; but inheriting the love of a rifle through so many generations, and nursed amid such scenes, he begged so earnestly of his father that he might be allowed to accompany the expedition, that he prevailed. The sad task remained for him to record the incidents of the expedition, and the sufferings and death of his father.

Commencement of the Expedition

I pass by, as unimportant in this *Journal*, all the circumstances of our arrangements for setting out on our expedition; together with my father's sorrow and mine, at leaving the spot where his wife and my mother was buried, the place, which had once been so cheerful, and was now so gloomy to us. We made our purchases at St. Louis. Our company consisted of five persons. We had ten horses packed with traps, trapping utensils, guns, ammunition, knives, tomahawks, provisions, blankets, and some surplus arms, as we anticipated that we should be able to gain some additions to our number by way of recruits, as we proceeded onward. But when the trial came, so formidable seemed the danger, fatigue, distance, and uncertainty of the expedition, that not an individual could be persuaded to share our enterprise.

June 20, 1824, we crossed the Missouri at a small town called Newport, and meandered the river as far as Pilcher's fort, without any incident worthy of record, except that one of our associates, who had become too unwell to travel, was left at Charaton, the remotest village on this frontier of any size. We arrived at Pilcher's fort, on the 13th day of July. There we remained, until the 28th, waiting the arrival of a keel boat from below, that was partly freighted with merchandize for us, with which we intended to trade with the Indians.

On the 28th, our number diminished to four, we set off for a trading establishment eight miles above us on the Missouri, belonging to Pratte, Choteau and Company. In this place centres most of the trade with the Indians on the upper Missouri. Here we met with Sylvester, son of General Pratte, who was on his way to New Mexico, with purposes similar to ours. His company had preceded him, and was on the river Platte waiting for him.

We left this trading establishment for the Council Bluffs, six miles above. When we arrived there, the commanding officer demanded to see our license for trading with the Indians. We informed him, that we neither had any, nor were aware that any was necessary. We were informed, that we could be allowed to ascend the river no higher without one. This dilemma brought our onward progress to a dead stand. We were prompt, however, in making new arrangements. We concluded to sell our surplus arms in exchange for merchandize, and change our direction from the upper Missouri, to New Mexico. One of our number was so much discouraged with our apparent ill success, and so little satisfied with this new project, that he came to the determination to leave our ranks. The remainder, though dispirited by the reduction of our number, determined not to abandon the undertaking. Our invalid having rejoined us, we still numbered four. We remained some time at this beautiful position, the Council Bluffs. I have seen much that is beautiful, interesting and commanding in the wild scenery of nature, but no prospect above, around, and below more so than from this spot. Our object and destination being the same as Mr. Pratte's, we concluded to join his company on the Platte.

We left the Bluffs, July 30th, and encamped the night after our departure on a small stream, called the Elkhorn. We reached it at a point thirty miles S. W. from the Bluffs. The Pawnee Indians sometimes resort upon the banks of this stream. The country is so open and bare of timber, that it was with difficulty we could find sufficient wood to cook with, even on the banks of the river, where wood is found, if at all, in the prairie country.

Early the next morning we commenced our march up the bottoms of the stream, which we continued to ascend, until almost night fall, when we concluded to cross it to a small grove of timber that we descried on the opposite shore, where we encamped for the night, securing our horses with great care, through fear that they would be stolen by the Indians.

In the morning, as we were making arrangements to commence our march, we discovered a large body of Indians, running full speed towards us. When they had arrived within a hundred yards of us, we made signs, that they must halt, or that we should fire upon them. They halted, and we inquired of them, as one of our number spoke their language, to what nation they belonged? They answered the Pawnee. Considering them friendly, we permitted them to approach us. It was on our way, to pass through their town, and we followed them thither. As soon as we arrived at their town, they conducted us to the lodge of their chief, who posted a number of his warriors at the door, and called the rest of his chiefs, accompanied by an interpreter. They formed a circle in the centre of the lodge. The elder chief then lighting a pipe, commenced smoking; the next chief holding the bowl of his pipe.

This mode of smoking differed from that of any Indians we had yet seen. He filled his mouth with the smoke, then puffed it in our bosoms, then on his own, and then upward, as he said, toward the Great Spirit, that he would bestow upon us plenty of fat buffaloes, and all necessary aid on our way. He informed us, that he had two war parties abroad. He gave us a stick curiously painted with characters, I suppose something like hieroglyphics, bidding us, should we see any of his warriors, to give them that stick; in which case they would treat us kindly. The pipe was then passed round, and we each of us gave it two or three light whiffs. We were then treated with fat buffalo meat, and after we had eaten, he gave us counsel in regard to our future course, particularly not to let our horses loose at night. His treatment was altogether paternal.

Next morning we left the village of this hospitable old chief, accompanied by a pilot, dispatched to conduct us to Mr. Pratte's company on the Platte. This is one of the three villages of the Republican Pawnees. It is situated on the little Platte River, in the centre of an extensive prairie plain; having near it a small strip of wood extending from the village to the river. The houses are cone-shaped, like a sugar loaf. The number of lodges may amount to six hundred.

The night after we left this village, we encamped on the banks of a small creek called the Mad Buffalo. Here we could find no wood for cooking, and made our first experiment of the common resort in these wide prairies; that is, we were obliged to collect the dung of the buffalo for that purpose. Having taken our supper, some of us stood guard through the night, while the others slept, according to the advice of the friendly chief. Next morning we commenced our march at early dawn, and by dint of hard travelling through the prairies, we arrived about sunset, on the main Platte, where we joined Mr. Pratte and his company. We felt, and expressed gratitude to the pilot, who, by his knowledge of the country, had conducted us by the shortest and easiest route. We did not forget the substantial expression of our good will, in paying him. He started for his own village the same evening, accompanying us here, and returning, on foot, although he could have had a horse for the journey.

At this encampment, on the banks of the Platte, we remained

four days, during which time we killed some antelopes and deer, and dressed their skins to make us moccasins. Among our arrangements with Mr. Pratte, one was, that my father should take the command of this company, to which proposition my father and our associates consented. The honour of this confidence was probably bestowed upon him, in consequence of most of the company having served under him, as rangers, during the late war. Those who had not, had been acquainted with his services by general report.

In conformity with the general wish, my father immediately entered upon his command, by making out a list of the names of the whole company, and dividing it into four messes; each mess having to furnish two men, to stand guard by reliefs, during the night. The roll was called, and the company was found to be a hundred and sixteen. We had three hundred mules, and some horses. A hundred of them were packed with goods and baggage. The guard was posted as spies, and all the rest were ordered to commence the arrangements of packing for departure. The guard was detached, to keep at some distance from the camp, reconnoitre, and discover if any Indians were lurking in the vicinity. When on the march, the guards were ordered to move on within sight of our flank, and parallel to our line of march. If any Indians were descried, they were to make a signal by raising their hats; or if not in sight of us, to alarm us by a pistol shot. These arrangements gave us a chance always to have some little time to make ready for action.

It may be imagined, that such a caravan made no mean figure, or inconsiderable dust, in moving along the prairies. We started on the morning of the 6th of August, travelling up the main Platte, which at this point is more than a hundred yards wide, very shallow, with a clean sand bottom, and very high banks. It is skirted with a thin belt of cotton-wood and willow trees, from which beautiful prairie plains stretch out indefinitely on either side. We arrived in the evening at a village of the Pawnee Loups. It is larger than the village of the Republican Pawnees, which we had left behind us. The head chief of this village received us in the most affectionate and hospitable manner, supplying us with such provisions as we wanted. He had been all the way from these remote prairies, on a visit to the city of Washington. He informed us, that before he had taken the journey, he had supposed that the white people were a small tribe, like his own, and that he had found them as numberless as the spires of grass on his prairies. The spectacle, however, that had struck him with most astonishment, was bullets as large as his head, and guns of the size of a log of wood. His people cultivate corn, beans, pumpkins and watermelons.

Here we remained five days, during which time Mr. Pratte purchased six hundred buffalo skins, and some horses. A Pawnee war party came in from an expedition against a hostile tribe of whom they had killed and scalped four, and taken twenty horses. We were affected at the sight of a little child, taken captive, whose mother they had killed and scalped. They could not account for bringing in this child, as their warfare is an indiscriminate slaughter, of men, women and children.

A day or two after their arrival, they painted themselves for a celebration of their victory, with great labour and care. The chiefs were dressed in skins of wild animals, with the hair on.—These skins were principally those of the bear, wolf, panther and spotted or ring tailed panther. They wore necklaces of bear's and panther's claws. The braves, as a certain class of the warriors are called, in addition to the dress of the other chiefs, surmounted their heads with a particular feather from a species of eagle, that they call the war eagle. This feather is considered worth the price of ten ordinary horses. None but a brave is permitted to wear it as a badge. A brave, gains his name and reputation as much by cunning and dexterity in stealing and robbing, as by courage and success in murdering.

When by long labour of the *toilette*, they had painted and dressed themselves to their liking, they marched forth in the array of their guns, bows, arrows and war clubs, with all the other appendages of their warfare. They then raised a tall pole, on the top of which were attached the scalps of the foes they had killed. It must be admitted, that they manifested no small degree of genius and inventiveness, in making themselves frightful and horrible. When they began their triumphal yelling, shouting, singing and cutting antic capers, it seemed to us, that a recruit of fiends from the infernal regions could hardly have transcended them in genuine diabolical display. They kept up this infernal din three days. During all this time, the poor little captive child, barely fed to sustain life, lay in sight, bound hand and foot. When their rage at length seemed sated, and exhausted, they took down the pole, and gave the scalps to the women.

We now witnessed a new scene of yells and screams, and infuriated gestures; the actors kicking the scalps about, and throwing them from one to the other with strong expressions of rage and contempt. When they also ceased, in the apparent satisfaction of gratified revenge, the men directed their attention to the little captive. It was removed to the medicine lodge, where the medicine men perform their incantations, and make their offerings to the Great Spirit. We perceived that they were making preparations to burn the child. Alike affected with pity and horror, our party appealed, as one man, to the presiding chief, to spare the child. Our first proposition was to purchase it. It was received by the chief with manifest displeasure. In reply to our strong remonstrances, he gravely asked us, if we, seeing a young rattlesnake in our path, would allow it to move off uninjured, merely because it was too small and feeble to bite?

We undertook to point out the want of resemblance in the circumstances of the comparison, observing that the child, reared among them, would know no other people, and would imbibe their habits and enmities, and become as one of them. The chief replied, that he had made the experiment, and that the captive children, thus spared and raised, had only been instrumental, as soon as they were grown, of bringing them into difficulties. 'It is' said he, 'like taking the eggs of partridges and hatching them; you may raise them ever so carefully in a cage; but once turn them loose, and they show their nature, not only by flying away, but by bringing the wild partridges into your corn fields: eat the eggs, and you have not only the food, but save yourself future trouble.'

We again urged that the child was too small to injure them, and of too little consequence to give them the pleasure of revenge in its destruction. To enforce our arguments, we showed him a roll of red broad cloth, the favourite colour with the Indians. This dazzled and delighted him, and he eagerly asked us, how much we would give him. We insisted upon seeing the child, before we made him an offer. He led us to the lodge, where lay the poor little captive, bound so tight with thongs of rawhide, that the flesh had so swelled over the hard and dried leather, that the strings could no longer be perceived. It was almost famished, having scarcely tasted food for four days, and seemed rather dead than alive. With much difficulty we disengaged its limbs from the thongs, and perceiving that it seemed to revive, we offered him ten yards, of the red cloth. Expatiating upon the trouble and danger of his warriors in the late expedition, he insisted, that the price was too little.

Having the child in our possession, and beginning to be indignant at this union of avarice and cruelty, our company exchanged glances of intelligence. A deep flush suffused the countenance of my father.

'My boys,' said he, 'will you allow these unnatural devils to burn this poor child, or practice extortion upon us, as the price of its ransom?' The vehemence and energy, with which these questions were proposed, had an effect, that may be easily imagined, in kindling the spirits of the rest of us. We carried it by acclamation, to take the child, and let them seek their own redress.

My father again offered the chief ten yards of cloth, which was refused as before. Our remark then was, that we would carry off the child, with, or without ransom, at his choice.—Meanwhile the child was sent to our encampment, and our men ordered to have their arms in readiness, as we had reason to fear that the chief would let loose his warriors upon us, and take the child by force. The old chief looked my father full in the face, with an expression of apparent astonishment. 'Do you think' said he, 'you are strong enough to keep the child by force?'

'We will do it,' answered my father, 'or every man of us die in the attempt, in which case our countrymen will come, and gather up our bones, and avenge our death, by destroying your nation.' The chief replied with well dissembled calmness, that he did not wish to incur the enmity of our people, as he well knew that we were more powerful than they; alleging, beside, that he had made a vow never to kill any more white men; and he added, that if we would give the cloth, and add to it a paper of vermillion, the child should be ours. To this we consented, and the contract was settled.

We immediately started for our encampment, where we were aware our men had been making arrangements for a battle. We had hardly expected, under these circumstances, that the chief would have followed us alone into a camp, where everything appeared hostile. But he went on with us unhesitatingly, until he came to the very edge of it. Observing that our men had made a breast work of the baggage, and stood with their arms leaning against it ready for action, he paused a moment, as if faltering in his purpose to advance. With the peculiar Indian exclamation, he eagerly asked my father, if he had thought that he would fight his friends, the white people, for that little child? The reply was, that we only meant to be ready for them, if they had thought to do so. With a smiling countenance the chief advanced, and took my father's hand exclaiming, that they were good friends. 'Save your powder and lead,' he added, 'to kill buffaloes and your enemies.' So saying he left us for his own lodge.

This tribe is on terms of hostility with two or three of the tribes nearest their hunting grounds. They make their incursions on horseback, and often extend them to the distance of six or seven hundred miles. They chiefly engage on horseback, and their weapons, for the most part, consist of a bow and arrows, a lance and shield, though many of them at present have fire arms. Their commander stations himself in the rear of his warriors, seldom taking a part in the battle, unless he should be himself attacked, which is not often the case. They show no inconsiderable military stratagem in their marches, keeping spies before and behind, and on each flank, at the distance of a few days travel; so that in their open country, it is almost impossible to come upon them by surprise.

The object of their expeditions is quite as often to plunder and steal horses, as to destroy their enemies. Each one is provided with the Spanish noose, to catch horses. They often extend these plundering expeditions as far as the interior of New Mexico. When they have reached the settled country, they lurk about in covert places, until an opportunity presents to seize on their prey. They fall upon the owner of a large establishment of cattle and horses, kill him during the night, or so alarm him as to cause him to fly, and leave his herds and family unprotected; in which case they drive off his horses, and secrete them in the mountains. In these fastnesses of nature they consider them safe; aware that the Mexicans, partly through timidity, and partly through indolence, will not pursue them to any great distance.

We left this village on the 11th of August, taking with us two of its inhabitants, each having a trap to catch, and a hoe to dig the beavers from their burrows. During this day's march we traversed a wide plain, on which we saw no game but antelopes and white wolves. At five in the evening, our front guard gave the preconcerted alarm by firing their pistols, and falling back a few moments afterwards, upon the main body.—We shortly afterwards discovered a large body of Indians on horseback, approaching us at full speed. When they were within hailing distance, we made them a signal to halt: they immediately halted. Surveying us a moment, and discovering us to be whites, one of them came towards us.

We showed him the painted stick given us by the Pawnee Republican chief. He seemed at once to comprehend all that it conveyed, and we were informed, that this was a band of the Republican Pawnee warriors. He carried the stick among them. It passed from hand to hand, and appeared at once to satisfy them in regard to our peaceable intentions, for they continued their march without disturbing us. But our two associate Indians, hearing their yells, as they rode off, took them to be their enemies, from whom they had taken the child. They immediately disappeared, and rejoined us no more. We travelled a few miles further, and encamped for the night on a small stream, called Smoking River. It is a tributary stream of the main Platte. On this stream a famous treaty had been made between the Pawnees and Shienne; and from the friendly smoking of the calumet on this occasion it received its name.

Next morning we made an early start, and marched rapidly all day, in order to reach water at night. We halted at sunset to repose ourselves, and found water for our own drinking, but none for our mules and horses. As soon as the moon arose, we started again, travelling hard all night, and until ten the next morning. At this time we reached a most singular spring fountain, forming a basin four hundred yards in diameter, in the centre of which the water boiled up five or six feet higher, than it was near the circumference. We encamped here, to rest, and feed our mules and horses, the remainder of the day, during which we killed some antelopes, that came here to drink.

Near this place was a high mound, from which the eye swept the whole horizon, as far as it could reach, and on this mound we stationed our guard.

Next morning we commenced the toil of our daily march, pursuing a S. W. course, over the naked plains, reaching a small and, as far as I know, a nameless stream at night, on the borders of which were a few sparse trees, and high grass. Here we encamped for the night. At twelve next day we halted in consequence of a pouring rain, and encamped for the remainder of the day. This was the first point, where we had the long and anxiously expected pleasure of seeing buffaloes. We killed one, after a most animating sport in shooting at it.

Next day we made an early start, as usual, and travelled hard all day over a wide plain, meeting with no other incidents, than the sight of buffaloes, which we did not molest. We saw, in this day's march, neither tree nor rising ground. The plains are covered with a short, fine grass, about four inches high, of such a kind, as to be very injurious to the hoofs of animals, that travel over it. It seems to me, that ours would not have received more injury from travelling over a naked surface of rock. In the evening we reached a small collection of water, beside which we encamped. We had to collect our customary inconvenient substitute for fuel, not only this evening, but the whole distance hence to the mountains.

On the morning of the 17th, we commenced, as usual, our early march, giving orders to our advance guard to kill a buffalo bull, and make *moccasins* for some of our horses, from the skin, their feet having become so tender from the irritation of the sharp grass, as to make them travel with difficulty. This was soon accomplished, furnishing the only incident of this day's travel. We continued the next day to make our way over the same wearying plain, without water or timber, having been obliged to provide more of our horses with buffalo skin *moccasins*. This day we saw numerous herds of buffaloes bulls. It is a singular fact, in the habits of these animals, that during one part of the year, the bulls all range in immense flocks without a cow among them, and all the cows equally without the bulls. The herd, which we now saw, showed an evident disposition to break into our caravan. They seemed to consider our horses and mules, as a herd of their cows. We prevented their doing it, by firing on them, and killing several.

This evening we arrived on one of the forks of the Osage, and encamped. Here we caught a beaver, the first I had ever seen. On the 20th, we started late, and made a short day's travel, encamping by water. Next morning we discovered vast numbers of buffaloes, all running in one direction, as though they were flying from some sort of pursuit. We immediately detached men to reconnoitre and ascertain, whether they were not flying from the Indians. They soon discovered a large body of them in full chase of these animals, and shooting at them with arrows. As their course was directly towards our camp, they were soon distinctly in sight. At this moment one of our men rode towards them, and discharged his gun. This immediately turned their attention from the pursuit of the game, to us. The Indians halted a moment, as if in deliberation, and rode off in another direction with great speed. We regretted that we had taken no measures to ascertain, whether they were friendly or not. In the latter case we had sufficient ground to apprehend, that they would pursue us at a distance, and attack us in the night. We made our arrangements, and resumed our march in haste, travelling with great caution, and posting a strong guard at night.

The next day, in company with another, I kept guard on the right flank. We were both strictly enjoined not to fire on the buffaloes, while discharging this duty. Just before we encamped, which was at four in the afternoon, we discovered a herd of buffalo cows, the first we had seen, and gave notice on our arrival at the camp. Mr. Pratte insisted, that we had mistaken, and said, that we were not yet far enough advanced into the country, to see cows, they generally herding in the most retired depths of the prairies. We were not disposed to contest the point with him, but proposed a bet of a suit of the finest cloth, and to settle the point by killing one of the herd, if the commander would permit us to fire upon it. The bet was accepted, and the permission given. My companion was armed with a musket, and I with a rifle. When we came in sight of the herd, it was approaching a little pond to drink. We concealed ourselves, as they approached, and my companion requested me to take the first fire, as the rifle was surer and closer than the musket. When they were within shooting distance, I levelled one; as soon as it fell, the herd, which consisted of a thousand or more, gathered in crowds around the fallen one. Between us we killed eleven, all proving, according to our word, to be cows. We put our mules in requisition to bring in our ample supply of meat. Mr. Pratte admitted, that the bet was lost, though we declined accepting it.

About ten at night it commenced raining; the rain probably caused us to intermit our caution; for shortly after it began, the Indians attacked our encampment, firing a shower of arrows upon us. We returned their fire at random, as they retreated: they killed two of our horses, and slightly wounded one of our men; we found four Indians killed by our fire, and one wounded. The wounded Indian informed our interpreter, that the Indians, who attacked us, were Arrickarees. We remained encamped here four days, attending our wounded man, and the wounded Indian, who died, however, the second day, and here we buried him.

We left this encampment on the 26th, and through the day met with continued herds of buffaloes and wild horses, which, however, we did not disturb. In the evening we reached a fork of the Platte, called Hyde Park. This stream, formerly noted for beavers, still sustains a few. Here we encamped, set our traps, and caught four beavers. In the morning we began to ascend this stream, and during our progress, we were obliged to keep men in advance, to affrighten the buffaloes and wild horses from our path. They are here in such prodigious numbers, as literally to have eaten down the grass of the prairies.

Here we saw multitudes of prairie dogs. They have large village establishments of burrows, where they live in society. They are sprightly, bold and self important animals, of the size of a Norwegian rat. On the morning of the 28th, our wounded companion was again unable to travel, in consequence of which we were detained at our encampment three days. Not wholly to lose the time, we killed during these three days no buffaloes, of which we saved only the tongues and hump ribs.

On the morning of the 31st, our wounded associate being somewhat recovered, we resumed our march. Ascending the stream, in the course of the day we came upon the dead bodies of two men, so much mangled, and disfigured by the wild beasts, that we could only discover that they were white men. They had been shot by the Indians with arrows, the ground near them being stuck full of arrows. They had been scalped. Our feelings may be imagined, at seeing the mangled bodies of people of our own race in these remote and unpeopled prairies. We consoled ourselves with believing that they died like brave men. We had soon afterwards clear evidence of this fact, for, on surveying the vicinity at the distance of a few hundred yards, we found the bodies of five dead Indians. The ground all around was torn and trampled by horse and footmen. We collected the remains of the two white men, and buried them.

We then ascended the stream a few miles, and encamped. Finding signs of Indians, who could have left the spot but a few hours before, we made no fire for fear of being discovered, and attacked in the night. Sometime after dark, ten of us started up the creek in search of their fires. About four miles from our encampment, we saw them a few hundred yards in advance. Twenty fires were distinctly visible. We counselled with each other, whether to fire on them or not. Our conclusion was, that the most prudent plan was to return, and apprise our companions of what we had seen. In consequence of our information, on our return, sixty men were chosen, headed by my father, who set off in order to surround their camp before daylight. I was one of the number, as I should have little liked to have my father go into battle without me, when it was in my power to accompany him. The remainder were left in charge of our camp, horses, and mules. We had examined our arms and found them in good order.

About midnight we came in sight of their fires, and before three o'clock were posted all around them, without having betrayed ourselves. We were commanded not to fire a gun, until the word was given. As it was still sometime before daylight, we became almost impatient for the command. As an Indian occasionally arose and stood for a moment before the fire, I involuntarily took aim at him with the thought, how easily I could destroy him, but my orders withheld me. Twilight at length came, and the Indians began to arise. They soon discovered two of our men, and instantly raising the war shout, came upon us with great fury. Our men stood firm, until they received the order which was soon given. A well directed and destructive fire now opened on them, which they received, and returned with some firmness. But when we closed in upon them they fled in confusion and dismay.

The action lasted fifteen minutes. Thirty of their dead were left on the field, and we took ten prisoners, whom we compelled to bury the dead. One of our men was wounded, and died the next day. We took our prisoners to our encampment, where we questioned them with regard to the two white men, we had found, and buried the preceding day. They acknowledged, that their party killed them, and assigned as a reason for so doing, that when the white men were asked by the chief to divide their powder and balls with him, they refused. It was then determined by the chief, that they should be killed, and the whole taken. In carrying this purpose into effect, the Indians lost four of their best young men, and obtained but little powder and lead, as a compensation.

We then asked them to what nation they belonged? They answered the Crow. This nation is distinguished for bravery and skill in war. Their bows and arrows were then given them, and they were told, that we never killed defenceless prisoners, but that they must tell their brothers of us, and that we should not have killed any of their nation, had not they killed our white brothers; and if they did so in future, we should kill all we found of them, as we did not fear any number, they could bring against us. They were then allowed to go free, which delighted them, as they probably expected that we should kill them, it being their custom to put all their prisoners to death by the most shocking and cruel tortures. That they may not lose this diabolical pleasure by the escape of their prisoners, they guard them closely day and night. One of them, upon being released, gave my father an eagle's feather, saying, you are a good and brave man, I will never kill another white man.

We pursued our journey on the 1st of September. Our advance was made with great caution, as buffaloes were now seen in immense herds, and the danger from Indians was constant. Wandering tribes of these people subsist on the buffaloes, which traverse the interior of these plains, keeping them constantly in sight.

On the morning of the 2nd, we started early. About ten o'clock we saw a large herd of buffaloes approaching us with great speed. We endeavoured to prevent their running among our pack mules, but it was in vain. They scattered them in every direction over the plain; and although we rode in among the herd, firing on them, we were obliged to follow them an hour, before we could separate them sufficiently to regain our mules. After much labour we collected all, with the exception of one packed with dry goods, which the crowd drove before them. The remainder of the day, half our company were employed as a guard, to prevent a similar occurrence. When we encamped for the night, some time was spent in driving the buffaloes a considerable distance from our camp. But for this precaution, we should have been in danger of losing our horses and mules entirely.

The following morning, we took a S. S. W. course, which led us from the stream, during this day's journey. Nothing occurred worthy of mention, except that we saw a great number of wolves, which had surrounded a small herd of buffalo cows and calves, and killed and eaten several. We dispersed them by firing on them. We judged, that there were at least a thousand. They were large and as white as sheep. Near this point we found water, and encamped for the night.

On the morning of the 4th, a party was sent out to kill some buffalo bulls, and get their skins to make *moccasins* for our horses, which detained us until ten o'clock. We then packed up and travelled six miles. Finding a lake, we encamped for the night. From this spot, we saw one of the most beautiful landscapes, that ever spread out to the eye. As far as the plain was visible in all directions, innumerable herds of wild horses, buffaloes, antelopes, deer, elk, and wolves, fed in their wild and fierce freedom. Here the sun rose, and set, as unobscured from the sight, as on the wastes of ocean. Here we used the last of our salt, and as for bread, we had seen none, since we had left the Pawnee village. I hardly need observe, that these are no small deprivations.

The next day we travelled until evening, nothing occurring, that deserves record. Our encampment was near a beautiful spring, called Bellefontaine, which is visited by the Indians, at some seasons of the year. Near it were some pumpkins, planted by the Indians. I cooked one, but did not find it very palatable: The next day we encamped without water. Late in the evening of the following day we reached a stream, and encamped. As we made our arrangements for the night, we came upon a small party of Indians. They ran off immediately, but we pursued them, caught four, and took them to the camp they had left, a little distant from ours. It contained between twenty and thirty women and children, beside three men. The women were frightened at our approach, and attempted to run. The Indians in our possession said something to them in their own language, that induced them to stop; but it was some time, before they were satisfied, that we intended them no harm. We returned to our camp, and were attending to our mules and horses. Our little Indian boy was playing about the camp, as usual. Suddenly our attention was arrested by loud screams or cries; and looking up, we saw our little boy in the arms of an Indian, whose neck he was closely clasping, as the Indian pressed him to his bosom, kissing him, and crying at the same time.

As we moved towards the spot, the Indian approached us, still holding the child in his arms; and falling on his knees, made us a long speech, which we understood only through his signs. During his speech, he would push the child from him, and then draw it back to him, and point to us. He was the father of this boy, whom we saved from being burnt by the Pawnees. He gave us to understand by his signs, that his child was carried off by his enemies. When the paroxysm of his joy was past, we explained, as well as we could, how we obtained the child. Upon hearing the name Pawnee, he sprang upon his feet, and rushed into his tent. He soon came out, bringing with him two Indian scalps, and his bow and arrows, and insisted, that we should look at the scalps, making signs to tell us, that they were Pawnee scalps, which he took at the time he lost his child.

After he finished this explanation, he would lay the scalps a short distance from him, and shoot his arrows through them, to prove his great enmity to this nation. He then presented my father a pair of leggins and a pipe, both neatly decorated with porcupine quills; and accompanied by his child, withdrew to his tent, for the night. Just as the morning star became visible, we were aroused from our slumbers, by the crying and shouting of the Indians in their tent. We arose, and approached it, to ascertain the cause of the noise. Looking in, we saw the Indians all laying prostrate with their faces to the ground. We remained observing them, until the full light of day came upon them.—They then arose, and placed themselves around the fire. The next movement was to light a pipe, and begin to smoke.

Seeing them blow the smoke first towards the point where the sun arose, and then towards heaven, our curiosity was aroused, to know the meaning of what we had seen. The old chief told us by signs, that they had been thanking the Great Spirit for allowing them to see another day. We then purchased a few beaver skins of them, and left them. Our encampment for the evening of this day, was near a small spring, at the head of which we found a great natural curiosity. A rock sixteen yards in circumference, rises from eighty to ninety feet in height, according to our best judgment, from a surface upon which, in all directions, not

RESCUE OF AN INDIAN CHILD

the smallest particle of rock, not even a pebble can be found. We were unable to reach the top of it, although it was full of holes, in which the hawks and ravens built their nests. We gave the spring the name of Rock Castle spring. On the morning of the 9th, we left this spot, and at night reached the foot of a large dividing ridge, which separates the waters of the Platte from those of the Arkansas. After completing our arrangements for the night, some of us ascended to the top of the ridge, to look out for Indians; but we saw none.

The succeeding morning we crossed the ridge, and came to water in the evening, where we encamped. Here we killed a white bear, which occupied several of us at least an hour. It was constantly in chase of one or another of us, thus withholding us from shooting at it, through fear of wounding each other. This was the first, I had ever seen. His claws were four inches long, and very sharp. He had killed a buffalo bull, eaten a part of it, and buried the remainder. When we came upon him, he was watching the spot, where he had buried it, to keep off the wolves, which literally surrounded him.

On the 11th, we travelled over some hilly ground. In the course of the day, we killed three white bears, the claws of which I saved, they being of considerable value among the Indians, who wear them around the neck, as the distinguishing mark of a brave. Those Indians, who wear this ornament, view those, who do not, as their inferiors. We came to water, and encamped early. I was one of the guard for the night, which was rather cloudy. About the middle of my guard, our horses became uneasy, and in a few moments more, a bear had gotten in among them, and sprung upon one of them.

The others were so much alarmed, that they burst their fastenings, and darted off at full speed. Our camp was soon aroused, and in arms, for defence, although much confused, from not knowing what the enemy was, nor from what direction to expect the attack. Some, however, immediately set off in pursuit of our horses. I still stood at my post, in no little alarm, as I did not know with the rest, if the Indians were around us or not. All around was again stillness, the noise of those in pursuit of the horses being lost in the distance.

Suddenly my attention was arrested, as I gazed in the direction, from which the alarm came, by a noise like that of a struggle at no great distance from me. I espied a hulk, at which I immediately fired. It was the bear devouring a horse, still alive. My shot wounded him. The report of my gun, together with the noise made by the enraged bear, brought our men from the camp, where they awaited a second attack from the unknown enemy in perfect stillness.—Determined to avenge themselves, they now sallied forth, although it was so dark, that an object ten steps in advance could not be seen. The growls of the bear, as he tore up the ground around him with his claws, attracted all in his direction. Some of the men came so near, that the animal saw them, and made towards them. They all fired at him, but did not touch him. All now fled from the furious animal, as he seemed intent on destroying them. In this general flight one of the men was caught.

As he screamed out in his agony, I, happening to have reloaded my gun, ran up to relieve him. Reaching the spot in an instant, I placed the muzzle of my gun against the bear, and discharging it, killed him. Our companion was literally torn in pieces. The flesh on his hip was torn off, leaving the sinews bare, by the teeth of the bear. His side was so wounded in three places, that his breath came through the openings; his head was dreadfully bruised, and his jaw broken. His breath came out from both sides of his windpipe, the animal in his fury having placed his teeth and claws in every part of his body.

No one could have supposed, that there was the slightest possibility of his recovery, through any human means. We remained in our encampment three days, attending upon him, without seeing any change for the worse or better in his situation. He had desired us from the first to leave him, as he considered his case as hopeless as ourselves did. We then concluded to move from our encampment, leaving two men with him, to each of whom we gave one dollar a day, for remaining to take care of him, until he should die, and to bury him decently.

On the 14th we set off, taking, as we believed, a final leave of our poor companion. Our feelings may be imagined, as we left this suffering man to die in this savage region, unfriended and unpitied. We travelled but a few miles before we came to a fine stream and some timber. Concluding that this would be a better place for our unfortunate companion, than the one where he was, we encamped with the intention of sending back for him. We despatched men for him, and began to prepare a shelter for him, should he arrive. This is a fork of Smoke Hill river, which empties into the Platte. We set traps, and caught eight beavers, during the night. Our companions with the wounded man on a litter, reached us about eight o'clock at night.

In the morning we had our painful task of leave taking to go through again. We promised to wait for the two we left behind at the Arkansas River. We travelled all day up this stream.—I counted, in the course of the day, two hundred and twenty white bears. We killed eight, that made an attack upon us; the claws of which I saved. Leaving the stream in the evening we encamped on the plain. A guard of twenty was relieved through the night, to prevent the bears from coming in upon us. Two tried to do it and were killed.

In the morning we began our march as usual: returning to the stream, we travelled until we came to its head. The fountain, which is its source, boils up from the plain, forming a basin two hundred yards in circumference, as clear as crystal, about five feet in depth. Here we killed some wild geese and ducks. After advancing some distance farther we encamped for the night. Buffaloes were not so numerous, during this day's journey, as they had been some time previous, owing, we judged, to the great numbers of white bears.

On the 17th we travelled until sunset, and encamped near water. On the 18th we found no water, but saw great numbers of wild horses and elk. The succeeding morning we set off before light, and encamped at 4 o'clock in the afternoon by a pond, the water of which was too brackish to drink. On the 20th we found water to encamp by. In the course of the day I killed two fat buffalo cows. One of them had a calf, which I thought I would try to catch alive. In order to do so, I concluded it would be well to be free from any unnecessary encumbrances, and accordingly laid aside my shot-pouch, gun and pistols. I expected it would run, but instead of that, when I came within six or eight feet of it, it turned around, and ran upon me, butting me like a ram, until I was knocked flat upon my back.

Every time I attempted to rise, it laid me down again. At last I caught by one of its legs, and stabbed it with my butcher knife, or I believe it would have butted me to death. I made up my mind, that I would never attempt to catch another buffalo calf alive, and also, that I would not tell my companions what a capsizing I had had, although my side did not feel any better for the butting it had received. I packed on my horse as much meat as he could carry, and set out for the camp, which I reached a little after dark. My father was going in search of me, believing me either lost, or killed. He had fired several guns, to let me know the direction of the camp. We travelled steadily on the 21st, and encamped at night on a small branch of the Arkansas. During the day, we had seen large droves of buffaloes running in the same direction, in which we travelled, as though they were pursued. We could, however, see nothing in pursuit. They appeared in the same confusion all night.

On the 22nd, we marched fast all day, the buffaloes still running before us. In the evening we reached the main Arkansas, and encamped. The sky indicating rain, we exerted ourselves, and succeeded in pitching our tents and kindling fires, before the rain began to fall. Our meat was beginning to roast, when we saw some Indians about half a mile distant, looking at us from a hill. We immediately tied our mules and horses. A few minutes after, ten Indians approached us with their guns on their shoulders. This open, undisguised approach made us less suspicious of them, than we should otherwise have been. When they were within a proper distance, they stopped, and called out *Amigo, Amigo*. One of our number understood them, and answered *Amigo*, which is friend, when they came up to us. They were Commanches, and one of them was a chief. Our interpreter understood and spoke their language quite well.

The chief seemed bold, and asked who was our captain? My father was pointed out to him. He then asked us to go and encamp with him, saying that his people and the whites were good friends. My father answered, that we had encamped before we knew where they were, and that if we moved now, we feared that the goods would be wet. The chief said, this was very good; but that, as we now knew where his camp was, we must move to it. To this my father returned, that if it did not rain next morning, we would; but as before, that we did not wish to get the goods wet tonight. The chief then said, in a surly manner, 'you don't intend then to move to my camp tonight?'

My father answered, 'No!'

The chief said he should, or he would come upon us with his men, kill us, and take every thing we had. Upon this my father pushed the chief out of the tent, telling him to send his men as soon as he pleased; that we would kill them, as fast as they came. In reply the chief pointed his finger to the spot, where the sun would be at eight o'clock the next morning, and said, 'If you do not come to my camp, when the sun is there, I will set all my warriors upon you.' He then ran off through the rain to his own camp. We began, immediately, a kind of breastwork, made by chopping off logs, and putting them together. Confidently expecting an attack in the night, we tied our horses and mules in a sink hole between us and the river.

It was now dark. I do not think an eye was closed in our camp that night; but the morning found us unmolested; nor did we see any Indians, before the sun was at the point spoken of. When it had reached it, an army of between six and eight hundred mounted Indians, with their faces painted as black as though they had come from the infernal regions, armed with fuzees and spears and shields appeared before us.

Everything had been done by the Indians to render this show as intimidating as possible. We discharged a couple of guns at them to show that we were not afraid, and were ready to receive them. A part advanced towards us; but one alone, approaching at full speed, threw down his bow and arrows, and sprang in among us, saying in broken English 'Commanches no good, me Iotan, good man.' He gave us to understand, that the Iotan nation was close at hand, and would not let the Commanches hurt us, and then started back. The Commanches fired some shots at us, but from such a distance, that we did not return them. In less than half an hour, we heard a noise like distant thunder. It became more and more distinct, until a band of armed Indians, whom we conjectured to be Iotans, became visible in the distance.

When they had drawn near, they reined up their horses for a moment, and then rushed in between us and Commanches, who charged upon the Iotans. The latter sustained the charge with firmness. The discharge of their fire arms and the clashing of their different weapons, together with their war-yell, and the shrieks of the wounded and dying were fit accompaniments to the savage actors and scene. I do not pretend to describe this deadly combat between two Indian nations; but, as far as I could judge, the contest lasted fifteen minutes. I was too deeply interested in watching the event, to note it particularly. We wished to assist the Iotans, but could not distinguish them from the mass, so closely were the parties engaged.

We withheld our fire through fear of injuring the Iotans, whom we considered our friends. It was not long before we saw, to our great satisfaction, the Commanches dismounted, which was the signal of their entire defeat. The Iotans then left the Commanches, and returned to their women and children, whom they had left some distance behind. They brought them to our camp, and pitched their own tents all around us, except that of the chief, which was placed in the centre with ours. A guard of warriors was then posted around the encampment, and an order given for the wounded Iotans to be brought into the tent of the chief. There were ten, two of whom died before night. A message was now sent to the chief of the Commanches, in obedience to which he came to the Iotan chief.

A council then seemed to be held, and a peace was made, the terms of which were, that the Iotan chief should pay the Commanche chief two horses for every warrior, he had lost in the battle, over the number of Iotans killed. We gave the Iotan chief goods to the amount of one hundred dollars, which pleased him exceedingly. He expressed himself perfectly satisfied with this recompense for the warriors he had lost in our defence. The knowledge, that a party as large as ours was traversing the country, had soon spread in all directions from the reports of Indians, who had met with us, and we became to these savage tribes a matter of interest, as a source of gain to be drawn from us by robbing, kindness or trade.—Our movements were observed. The Commanches determined to possess themselves of their object by force; and the Iotans interfered in our defence, that they might thus gain their point by extortion from friends.

Not a single Commanche was allowed to enter our camp, as arrangements were making for the Iotans to trade with us. All, who had any beaver skins, or dressed deer skins, were sent for. A guard was placed around in a circle, inside of which the skins were thrown down. Each Indian then inquired for the article he wanted. In this way we exchanged with them butcher knives, paint, and powder and ball, for beaver and deer skins, to the amount of fifteen hundred dollars, allowing them what we considered the value of the skins.

The old Commanche chief came to the Iotan chief to ask permission to talk with us, but was forbidden; and we were told not to have any dealings with him. We did not. The Iotan chief then gave us the character of the Commanche chief. He seemed to be thinking some time before he began.

'I know,' said he, 'you must think it strange that I should fight with the Commanches, and then pay them for their warriors killed, over our own number lost, and make peace with them. I will give you my reasons for doing so. Four years ago, this Commanche chief with his followers, went in company with my father, who was a chief, and a few of his followers, in search of buffaloes. After they had killed what they wanted, they divided the meat. The Commanche took all the best of it, leaving the remains for my father. The old man put up with it, and said nothing. On their return, close to this place they met a band of Nabahoes, a nation that had long been at war with ours, and killed a great number of our people. My father wanted to kill them, and began to fire upon them. The Commanches joined the Nabahoes, and together they killed my father and most of his men. He then paid for the lives he had taken, in horses, giving twenty for my father, and four for each warrior. I only give two horses for a warrior. I am now happy. I have killed three times as many of them, as they did of us, and paid less for it. I know they can never get the upper hand of me again.

40

This Commanche chief is a mean man, for whenever he has power, he makes others do as he pleases, or he kills them, and takes all they have. He wanted to act in this way with you; but I do not think he could, for you know how to shoot better than he does; and you would not give up, as long as you had powder and ball and one man alive.'

My father as commander, said, 'his men were all good soldiers, and knew how to get the advantage in fighting; and that we had plenty of ammunition and good guns, and were not in the least afraid of being beaten by them.'

'I think so,' replied the chief; 'But I thank the Great Spirit, that it happened as it did. I have taken revenge for the death of my father, and his people, and gained, I hope, at the same time the love of a good and brave people by defending them.'

We assured him that he had, expressing our thanks for his aid, and regret for those who had been killed in our defence. 'Yes,' said the chief, 'they were brave men; but they loved my father, whom they have now gone to see, where they will have plenty to eat, and drink, without having to fight for it.' These were his thoughts, as near as I can express them.

The Commanche chief made a second application for permission to talk with us, which was now granted. His object in conversing with us, was, as he said, to make friends with us, and induce us to give him some powder and ball. We told him that we would willingly make peace with him; but not give him anything, as we did not break the peace. He had threatened to kill us, and take our property without any provocation from us, and certainly, if any present was necessary, it must come from him. We did not, however, wish any present from him, and would make peace with him, provided he promised never to kill, or try to kill a white man. He answered, that he had neither done it, or intended to do it; that with regard to us, he only sought to frighten us, so that we should come to his camp, before the Iotans came up, whom he knew to be not far distant, in order that he might precede them in trading with us, adding that as he had been so disappointed, he thought we ought to give him a little powder and ball.

Our answer was, that we had no more ammunition to spare; and that we could not depart from our resolution of not purchasing a treaty from him; but we would give him a letter of recommendation to the next company that came in this direction, by means of which he might trade with them, and obtain what he wanted of these articles. He consented to a treaty on these conditions, and lighting his pipes we smoked friends.

He then asked us if we came through the Pawnee village? We answered in the affirmative. His next question was, had they plenty of ammunition? Our reply was again, yes. We were then given to understand, that he was then at war with them, and had been for a number of years, and that he should soon either make peace with them, or have a general engagement. He would prefer peace, as they were at war with the Spaniards, as well as himself. By uniting forces, they could beat the Spaniards, though in case of a treaty or not, he intended to go against the Spaniards, as soon as he should return from the country of the Pawnees. He added, 'I suppose you are friends with the Spaniards, and are now going to trade with them.'

Our commander replied, that we were going to trade with them, but not to fight for them. 'That,' said the chief, 'is what I wanted to know. I do not want war with your people, and should we accidentally kill any of them, you must not declare war against us, as we will pay you for them in horses or beaver skins.'

We did not express our natural feeling, that the life of one man was worth more than all the horses or beaver skins, his nation could bring forth; but told him, that we would not injure his people, unless they did ours, on purpose. He returned, apparently satisfied, to his camp. We were detained here until the fourth of November by our promise of awaiting the arrival of the two men, we had left with our wounded companion. They came, and brought with them his gun and ammunition. He died the fifth day, after we had left him, and was buried as decently, as the circumstances would allow.

On the 5th of November we again set off in company with a party of Iotans. The Arkansas is here wide and shallow, like the Platte; and has wide but thinly timbered bottoms on both sides. Extending from the bottom ten or twelve miles on the south side, are low hills composed principally of sand. We found travelling upon them very fatiguing, particularly as we met with no water. Late in the evening we reached water, and encamped.

The next morning we resumed our journey. We were exceedingly diverted, during the day, to see the Iotan Indians in company with us, chase the buffaloes on horseback. They killed them with their arrows. The force, with which they shoot these arrows, is astonishing. I saw one of them shoot an arrow through a buffalo bull, that had been driven close to our camp. We were again upon level plains, stretching off in all directions beyond the reach of the eye. The few high mounds scattered over them could not but powerfully arrest the curiosity. From the summit of one I again looked down upon innumerable droves of wild animals, dotting the surface, as they seemed to forget their savage natures, and fed, or reposed in peace. I indulged the thoughts natural to such a position and scene. The remembrance of home, with its duties and pleasures, came upon my mind in strong contrast with my actual circumstances.

I was interrupted by the discharge of guns, and the screams and yells of Indians. The Iotans had found six Nabahoes a half a mile from us, and were killing them. Three were killed. The others, being well mounted, made their escape. The Iotans came to our camp with their scalps, leaving their bodies to be eaten by wild animals. My father sent men to bury them. The Iotans danced around these scalps all night, and in the morning took up the bodies, we had buried, and cut them in pieces. They then covered themselves with the skins of bears and panthers, and, taking the hearts of the dead men, cut them into pieces of the size of a mouthful, and laid them upon the ground, and kneeling put their hands on the ground, and crawled around the pieces of hearts, growling as though they were enraged bears, or panthers, ready to spring upon them, and eat them. This is their mode of showing hatred to their enemies. Not relishing such detestable conduct, we so manifested our feelings, that these Indians went to their own camps.

We encamped the evening of the next day near water. Nothing worthy of record occurred during the journey of the four succeeding days, except that we came to a small creek called Simaronee. Here we encamped, and killed some buffaloes, and shod our horses. We travelled up this stream some distance, and left it on the 15th.

On the 16th we encamped on a creek, where we found four gentle mules, which we caught. I could not account for their being there. Nothing of importance occurred in the two last days.

From the 17th to the 20th, we journeyed without interruption. The latter day we came in view of a mountain covered with snow, called Taos mountain. This object awakened in our minds singular but pleasant feelings. On the 23rd we reached its foot. Here Mr. Pratte concealed a part of his goods by burying them in the ground. We were three days crossing this mountain.

On the evening of the 26th, we arrived at a small town in Taos, called St. Ferdinando, situated just at the foot of the mountain on the west side. The *alcalde* asked us for the invoice of our goods, which we showed him, and paid the customary duties on them. This was a man of a swarthy complexion having the appearance of pride and haughtiness. The doorway of the room, we were in, was crowded with men, women and children, who stared at us, as though they had never seen white men before, there being in fact, much to my surprise and disappointment, not one white person among them. I had expected to find no difference between these people and our own, but their language. I was never so mistaken. The men and women were not clothed in our fashion, the former having short pantaloons fastened below the waist with a red belt and buck skin leggins put on three or four times double. A Spanish knife is stuck in by the side of the leg, and a small sword worn by the side. A long jacket or blanket is thrown over, and worn upon the shoulders. They have few fire arms, generally using upon occasions which require them, a bow and spear, and never wear a hat, except when they ride. When on horse back, they face towards the right side of the animal. The saddle, which they use, looks as ours would, with something like an arm chair fastened upon it.

The women wear upon the upper part of the person a garment resembling a shirt, and a short petticoat fastened around the waist with a red or blue belt, and something of the scarf kind wound around their shoulders. Although appearing as poorly, as I have described, they are not destitute of hospitality; for they brought us food, and invited us into their houses to eat, as we walked through the streets.

The first time my father and myself walked through the town together, we were accosted by a woman standing in her own doorway. She made signs for us to come in. When we had entered, she conducted us up a flight of steps into a room neatly whitewashed, and adorned with images of saints, and a crucifix of brass nailed to a wooden cross. She gave us wine, and set before us a dish composed of red pepper, ground and mixed with corn meal, stewed in fat and water. We could not eat it. She then brought forward some *tortillas* and milk. *Tortillas* are a thin cake made of corn and wheat ground between two flat stones by the women. This cake is called in Spanish, *metate*. We remained with her until late in the evening, when the bells began to ring. She and her children knelt down to pray. We left her, and returned. On our way we met a bier with a man upon it, who had been stabbed to death, as he was drinking whiskey.

This town stands on a beautiful plain, surrounded on one side by the Rio del Norte, and on the other by the mountain, of which I have spoken, the summit being covered with perpetual snow.

We set off for Santa Fé on the 1st of November. Our course for

44

the first day led us over broken ground. We passed the night in a small town, called Callacia, built on a small stream, that empties into the del Norte. The country around this place presents but a small portion of level surface.

The next day our path lay over a point of the mountain. We were the whole day crossing. We killed a grey bear, that was exceedingly fat. It had fattened on a nut of the shape and size of a bean, which grows on a tree resembling the pine, called by the Spanish, pinion. We took a great part of the meat with us. We passed the night again in a town called Albukerque.

The following day we passed St. Thomas, a town situated on the bank of the del Norte, which is here a deep and muddy stream, with bottoms from five to six miles wide on both sides. These bottoms sustain numerous herds of cattle. The small huts of the shepherds, who attend to them, were visible here and there. We reached another town called Elgidonis, and stopped for the night. We kept guard around our horses all night, but in the morning four of our mules were gone. We hunted for them until ten o'clock, when two Spaniards came, and asked us, what we would give them, if they would find our mules? We told them to bring the mules, and we would pay them a dollar. They set off, two of our men following them without their knowledge and went into a thicket, where they had tied the mules, and returned with them to us. As may be supposed, we gave them both a good whipping. It seemed at first, that the whole town would rise against us in consequence. But when we related the circumstances fairly to the people, the officer corresponding to our justice of the peace, said, we had done perfectly right, and had the men put in the stocks.

We recommenced our journey, and passed a mission of Indians under the control of an old priest. After crossing a point of the mountain, we reached Santa Fé, on the 5th. This town contains between four and five thousand inhabitants. It is situated on a large plain. A handsome stream runs through it, adding life and beauty to a scene striking and agreeable from the union of amenity and cultivation around, with the distant view of the snow clad mountains. It is pleasant to walk on the flat roofs of the houses in the evening, and look on the town and plain spread below. The houses are low, with flat roofs as I have mentioned. The churches are differently constructed from the other buildings and make a beautiful show. They have a great number of large bells, which, when disturbed, make a noise, that would almost seem sufficient to awaken the dead.

We asked the governor for permission to trap beaver in the River Helay. His reply was that, he did not know if he was allowed by the law to do so; but if upon examination it lay in his power, he would inform us on the morrow, if we would come to his office at 9 o'clock in the morning. According to this request, we went to the place appointed, the succeeding day, which was the 9th of November. We were told by the governor, that he had found nothing, that would justify him, in giving us the legal permission, we desired. We then proposed to him to give us liberty to trap, upon the condition, that we paid him five *per cent* on the beaver we might catch. He said, he would consider this proposition, and give us an answer the next day at the same hour. The thoughts of our hearts were not at all favourable to this person, as we left him.

About ten o'clock at night an express came from the River Pacus, on which the nobles have their country seats and large farming establishments, stating, that a large body of Indians had come upon several families, whom they had either robbed, or murdered. Among the number two Americans had been killed, and the wife of one taken prisoner, in company with four Spanish women, one of whom was daughter of the former governor, displaced because he was an European. The drum and fife and French horn began to sound in a manner, that soon awakened, and alarmed the whole town. The frightened women, and the still more fear-stricken men, joining in a full chorus of screams and cries, ran some to where the drum was beating in the public square, and others to our quarters.

Upon the first sound of alarm we had prepared to repel the enemy, whatever it might be, provided it troubled us. When this group came rushing towards us, the light of the moon enabled us to discern them with sufficient clearness to prevent our doing them any injury. We did not sleep any more that night, for the women, having got the wrong story, as most women do in a case of the kind, told us that the Commanches were in town, killing the people.

We awaited an attack, without, however, hearing any sound of fire arms. Our conclusion was, that they were skulking around, dealing out death in darkness and silence with their arrows; and in the feelings, which were its natural result, the remainder of the night passed. The first light of morning showed us a body of four hundred men ready to mount their horses. At sunrise the governor came to us to ask, if we would aid in the attempt to recapture the prisoners taken by the Commanches, relating to us the real cause of the alarm of the preceding night. We complied readily with his request, as we were desirous of gaining the good will of the people. Our arrangements were soon made, and we set off in company with the troops I have mentioned.

The 12th was spent in travelling. We stopped for the night at St. John's, a small town. On the 13th we reached the spot, where the murders and robbery were committed. Here we took the course the Indians had marked in their retreat, stopping only for refreshments. We pressed on all night, as we found their fires still smoking. At eight on the morning of the 15th, the trail being fresh, we increased our speed, and at twelve came in sight of them, as they advanced toward a low gap in the mountains. We now halted, and counselled together with regard to the next movements. The commander of the Spaniards proposed, that my father should direct the whole proceedings, promising obedience on his own part and that of his troops.

The gap in the mountains, of which I spoke, was made by a stream. The Indians were now entering it. My father formed a plan immediately, and submitted it to the Spanish commander, who promised to aid in carrying it into effect. In conformity to it, the Spaniards were directed to keep in rear of the Indians, without being seen by them. We took a circuitous route, screened from sight by the highland, that lay between us and the Indians, in order to gain unobserved a hollow in advance of them, in which we might remain concealed, until they approached within gunshot of us. Our main object was to surprise them, and not allow them time to kill their captives, should they be still alive. The party in the rear were to close in, upon hearing the report of our guns, and not allow them to return to the plain.

Our plan seemed to assure us success. We succeeded in reaching the hollow, in which we placed ourselves in the form of a half circle, extending from one side of it to the other, our horses being tied behind us. Every man was then ordered to prime, and pick his gun afresh. The right flank was to fire first, the left reserving theirs to give a running fire, that should enable the right to re-load. The Indians, surrounding the prisoners, were to be taken as the first aim, to prevent the immediate murder of them by their captors.

My post was in the centre of the line. We waited an hour and a half behind our screens of rocks and trees, before our enemies made their appearance. The first object, that came in sight, were women without any clothing, driving a large drove of sheep and horses. These were immediately followed by Indians. When the latter were within thirty or forty yards of us, the order to fire was given. The women ran towards us the moment they heard the report of our guns. In doing this they encountered the Indians behind them, and three fell pierced by the spears of these savages. The cry among us now was, 'save the women!' Another young man and myself sprang forward, to rescue the remaining two. My companion fell in the attempt. An Indian had raised his spear, to inflict death upon another of these unfortunate captives, when he received a shot from one of our men, that rendered him incapable of another act of cruelty.

The captives, one of whom was a beautiful young lady, the daughter of the governor before spoken of, both reached me. The gratitude of such captives, so delivered, may be imagined. Fears, thanks and exclamations in Spanish were the natural expression of feeling in such a position. My companions aided me in wrapping blankets around them, for it was quite cold; and making the best arrangements in our power for their comfort and safety. This was all done in less time, than is required to relate it, and we returned to our post.

The Indians stood the second fire, and then retreated. We pursued keeping up a quick fire, expecting every moment to hear the Spaniards in the rear following our example to check them in their retreat; but we could discover the entrance upon the plain, before we heard anything from our Spanish muskets. The Indians then began to yell; but the Spaniards, after one discharge from their fire arms, fled. Being mounted on good horses the Indians did not pursue them, but satisfied as to our numbers, now that we were upon the plain, they rallied, and rushed upon us.

Our commander now ordered us to retreat into the woods, and to find shelter behind trees, and take aim that every shot might tell, as it was of the utmost importance, not to waste ammunition, saying, 'stand resolute, my boys, and we make them repent, if they follow us, although those —— Spaniards have deserted us, when we came to fight for them. We are enough for these —— devils alone.' As they came near us, we gave them a scattering though destructive fire, which they returned bravely, still pressing towards us. It was a serious contest for about ten minutes, after they approached within pistol shot of us. From their yells, one would have thought that the infernal regions were open before them, and that they were about to be plunged in headlong. They finally began to retreat again, and we soon put them completely to flight. The Spaniards, though keeping a safe distance, while this was going forward, saw the state of affairs, and joined us in the pursuit, still taking especial care not to come near enough to the Indians, to hurt them, or receive any injury themselves. After the Indians rallied, we lost ten men, and my father received a slight wound in the shoulder.

We removed our horses and the rescued captives into the plain, and encamped. The Spaniards had killed an Indian already wounded, and were riding over the dead bodies of those on the ground, spearing them and killing any, who still breathed. My father commanded them to desist, or he would fire upon them, and the Spanish officer added his order to the same effect. The latter then demanded of us, the two women, whom we had rescued, with as much assurance, as though himself had been the cause of their deliverance. My father replied, by asking what authority or right he had, to make such a request, when his cowardice withheld him from aiding in their release? The officer became enraged, and said, that he was unable to rally his men, and that he did not consider the captives any safer in our hands than in those of the Indians, as we were not Christians.

This insult, coupled with such a lame apology, only made my father laugh, and reply, that if cowardice constituted a claim to Christianity, himself and his men were prime and undoubted Christians. He added further, that if the rescued women preferred to accompany him, rather than remain, until he should have buried his brave comrades, who fell in their defence, and accept his protection, he had nothing to say. The subjects of our discussion, being present while it took place, decided the point before they were appealed to. The youngest said, that nothing would induce her to leave her deliverers, and that when they were ready to go, she would accompany them, adding, that she should pray hourly for the salvation of those, who had resigned their lives in the preservation of hers. The other expressed herself willing to remain with her, and manifested the same confidence and gratitude. The enraged officer and his men set off on their return to Santa Fé.

The sun was yet an hour from its setting. We availed ourselves of the remaining light to make a breastwork with the timber, that had drifted down the stream, that we might be prepared for the Indians, in case they should return. We finished it, and posted our sentinels by sunset. The governor's daughter now inquired for the individual, who first met her in her flight from the Indians, and so humanely and bravely conducted her out of danger, and provided for her comfort. I cannot describe the gratitude and loveliness, that appeared in her countenance, as she looked on me, when I was pointed out to her. Not attaching any merit to the act, I had performed, and considering it merely as a duty, I did not know how to meet her acknowledgments, and was embarrassed.

On the morning of the 16th we buried our dead. My father's shoulder was a little stiff, and somewhat swollen. We saddled our horses, and began our return journey. I gave up my horse to one of the ladies, and made my way on foot. We drove the sheep, which escaped the balls, before us. Our last look at the ground of our late contest gave a view sufficiently painful to any one, who had a heart; horses and their riders lay side by side. The bodies of robbers surrounded by the objects of their plunder would probably remain, scattered as they were, unburied and exposed to the wild beasts.

We halted in the evening for the refreshment of ourselves and horses. This done, we again set off travelling all night. The sheep giving out, we were obliged to leave them. At twelve next day we reached Pacus. Here we met the father of the youngest of the two ladies accompanied by a great number of Spaniards. The old man was transported almost to frenzy, when he saw his daughter. We remained here for the day. On the morning of the 18th we all set off together, the old governor insisting, that my father and myself must ride in the carriage with him; but we excused ourselves, and rode by the side of it with the interpreter. The father caressed us exceedingly, and said a great many things about me in particular, which I did not think, I deserved.

The next day at two in the afternoon, we arrived at Santa Fé. We were received with a salute, which we returned with our small arms. The governor came in the evening, and invited my father and the interpreter to sup with him. He ordered some fat beeves to be killed for the rest of us. The father of Jacova, for that was the name of the young lady, I had rescued, came, and invited us all to go, and drink coffee at his son-in-law's, who kept a coffee-house. We went, and when we had finished our coffee, the father came, and took me by the hand, and led me up a flight of steps, and into a room, where were his two daughters. As soon as I entered the room, Jacova and her sister both came, and embraced me, this being the universal fashion of interchanging salutations between men and women among these people, even when there is nothing more, than a simple introduction between strangers.

After I had been seated an hour, looking at them, as they made signs, and listening to their conversation, of which I did not understand a syllable, I arose with the intention of returning to my companions for the night. But Jacova, showing me a bed, prepared for me, placed herself between me and the door. I showed her that my

clothes were not clean. She immediately brought me others belonging to her brother-in-law. I wished to be excused from making use
of them, but she seemed so much hurt, that I finally took them, and
reseated myself. She then brought me my leather hunting shirt, which
I had taken off to aid in protecting her from the cold, and begged the
interpreter who was now present, to tell me, that she intended to keep
it, as long as she lived. She then put it on, to prove to me that she was
not ashamed of it.

I went to bed early, and arose, and returned to my companions,
before any of the family were visible. At eight the governor and my
father came to our quarters, and invited us all to dine with him at two
in the afternoon. Accordingly we all dressed in our best, and went at
the appointed time. A band of musicians played during dinner. After it
was finished, and the table removed, a *fandango* was begun. The ladies
flocked in, in great numbers. The instruments, to which the dancers
moved, were a guitar and violin. Six men and six women also added
their voices. Their mode of dancing was a curiosity to me. The women
stood erect, moving their feet slowly, without any spring or motion of
the body, and the men half bent, moved their feet like drum sticks. This
dance is called *ahavave*. I admired another so much, that I attempted
to go through it. It was a waltz, danced to a slow and charming air. It
produces a fine effect, when twenty or thirty perform it together. The
dancing continued, until near morning, when we retired to rest.

At eight the following morning we received a license, allowing us
to trap in different parts of the country. We were now divided into
small parties. Mr. Pratte added three to our original number, they
making the company, to which my father and myself belonged, sev-
en. On the 22nd, we set off. Our course lay down the del Norte to
the Helay, a river never before explored by white people. We left our
goods with a merchant, until we should return in the spring. Our
whole day's journey lay over a handsome plain covered with herds
of the different domestic animals. We reached Picacheh a small town
in the evening. Jacova and her father overtook us here, on their way
home, which was eighty miles distant from Santa Fé.

In the morning we began our journey, together. During the day
we passed several small villages and stopped for the night in one called
St. Philip, situated on the banks of the del Norte, surrounded by large
vineyards. Jacova's father insisted upon our drinking plentifully of the
wine made at this place.

The morning of the 24th saw us again on our journey. Our companion, the old governor, was much amused at seeing us kill wild geese and prairie wolves with our rifles, the latter being abundant in this country. In the evening we reached another small town, called St. Louis. All these inconsiderable villages contain a church. The succeeding day we traversed the same beautiful plain country, which had made our journey so far, delightful. The same multitude of domestic animals still grazed around our path.

On the 27th, we arrived at the residence of Jacova and her father. It was a large and even magnificent building. We remained here until the 30th, receiving the utmost attention and kindness. At our departure, the kind old governor pressed a great many presents upon us; but we refused all, except a horse for each one of us, some flour and dried meat.

Seven hunters coming up with us, who were going in our direction, we concluded to travel with them, as our united strength would better enable us to contend with the hostile Indians, through whose country our course lay. We made our way slowly, descending the river bank, until we reached the last town or settlement in this part of the province, called Socoro. The population of the part of the country, through which we travelled was entirely confined to a chain of settlements along the bottoms of the del Norte, and those of some of the rivers, which empty into it. I did not see, during the whole of this journey, an enclosed field, and not even a garden.

After remaining one day here, in order to recruit our horses, we resumed our course down the river, Dec. 3rd. The bottoms, through which we now passed, were thinly timbered, and the only growth was cotton-wood and willow. We saw great numbers of bears, deer and turkeys. A bear having chased one of our men into the camp, we killed it.

On the 7th we left the del Norte, and took a direct course for the Copper mines. We next travelled from the river over a very mountainous country four days, at the expiration of which time we reached this point of our destination. We were here but one night, and I had not leisure to examine the mode, in which the copper was manufactured. In the morning we hired two Spanish servants to accompany us; and taking a north-west course pursued our journey, until we reached the Helay on the 14th. We found the country the greater part of the two last days hilly and somewhat barren with a growth of pine, live oak, *pinion*, cedar and some small trees, of which I did not know the name. We caught thirty beavers, the first night we encamped on this river.

The next morning, accompanied by another man, I began to ascend the bank of the stream to explore, and ascertain if beaver were to be found still higher, leaving the remainder of the party to trap slowly up, until they should meet us on our return. We threw a pack over our shoulders, containing a part of the beavers, we had killed, as we made our way on foot. The first day we were fatigued by the difficulty of getting through the high grass, which covered the heavily timbered bottom. In the evening we arrived at the foot of mountains, that shut in the river on both sides, and encamped. We saw during the day several bears, but did not disturb them, as they showed no ill feeling towards us.

On the morning of the 13th we started early, and crossed the river, here a beautiful clear stream about thirty yards in width, running over a rocky bottom, and filled with fish. We made but little advance this day, as bluffs came in so close to the river, as to compel us to cross it thirty-six times. We were obliged to scramble along under the cliffs, sometimes upon our hands and knees, through a thick tangle of grape-vines and under-brush. Added to the unpleasantness of this mode of getting along in itself, we did not know, but the next moment would bring us face to face with a bear, which might accost us suddenly. We were rejoiced, when this rough ground gave place again to the level bottom. At night we reached a point, where the river forked, and encamped on the point between the forks. We found here a boiling spring so near the main stream, that the fish caught in the one might be thrown into the other without leaving the spot, where it was taken. In six minutes it would be thoroughly cooked.

The following morning my companion and myself separated, agreeing to meet after four days at this spring. We were each to ascend a fork of the river. The banks of that which fell to my lot, were very brushy, and frequented by numbers of bears, of whom I felt fearful, as I had never before travelled alone in the woods. I walked on with caution until night, and encamped near a pile of drift wood, which I set on fire, thinking thus to frighten any animals that might approach during the night. I placed a spit, with a turkey I had killed upon it, before the fire to roast. After I had eaten my supper I laid down by the side of a log with my gun by my side. I did not fall asleep for some time. I was aroused from slumber by a noise in the leaves, and raising my head saw a panther stretched on the log by which I was lying, within six feet of me. I raised my gun gently to my face, and shot it in the head.

Then springing to my feet, I ran about ten steps, and stopped to reload my gun, not knowing if I had killed the panther or not. Before I had finished loading my gun, I heard the discharge of one on the other fork, as I concluded, the two running parallel with each other, separated only by a narrow ridge. A second discharge quickly followed the first, which led me to suppose, that my comrade was attacked by Indians.

I immediately set out and reached the hot spring by daybreak, where I found my associate also. The report of my gun had awakened him, when he saw a bear standing upon its hind feet within a few yards of him growling. He fired his gun, then his pistol, and retreated, thinking, with regard to me, as I had with regard to him, that I was attacked by Indians. Our conclusion now was, to ascend one of the forks in company, and then cross over, and descend the other. In consequence we resumed the course, I had taken the preceding day. We made two day's journey, without beaver enough to recompense us for our trouble, and then crossed to the east fork, trapping as we went, until we again reached the main stream. Some distance below this, we met those of our party we had left behind, with the exception of the seven, who joined us on the del Norte. They had deserted the expedition, and set off upon their return down the river. We now all hastened on to overtake them, but it was to no purpose. They still kept in advance, trapping clean as they went, so that we even found it difficult to catch enough to eat.

Finding it impossible to come up with them, we ceased to urge our poor horses, as they were much jaded, and tender footed beside, and travelled slowly, catching what beaver we could, and killing some deer, although the latter were scarce, owing, probably to the season of the year. The river here was beautiful, running between banks covered with tall cotton-woods and willows. This bottom extended back a mile on each side. Beyond rose high and rather barren hills.

On the 20th we came to a point, where the river entered a cavern between two mountains. We were compelled to return upon our steps, until we found a low gap in the mountains. We were three day's crossing, and the travelling was both fatiguing and difficult. We found nothing to kill.

On the 23rd we came upon the river, where it emptied into a beautiful plain. We set our traps, but to no purpose, for the beavers were all caught, or alarmed. The river here pursues a west course. We travelled slowly, using every effort to kill something to eat, but without success.

On the morning of the 26th we concluded, that we must kill a horse, as we had eaten nothing for four day's and a half, except the small portion of a hare caught by my dogs, which fell to the lot of each of a party of seven. Before we obtained this, we had become weak in body and mind, complaining, and desponding of our success in search of beaver. Desirous of returning to some settlement, my father encouraged our party to eat some of the horses, and pursue our journey. We were all reluctant to begin to partake of the horse-flesh; and the actual thing without bread or salt was as bad as the anticipation of it. We were somewhat strengthened, however, and hastened on, while our supply lasted, in the hope of either overtaking those in advance of us, or finding another stream yet undiscovered by trappers.

The latter desire was gratified the first of January, 1825. The stream, we discovered, carried as much water as the Helay, heading north. We called it the River St. Francisco. After travelling up its banks about four miles, we encamped, and set all our traps, and killed a couple of fat turkeys. In the morning we examined our traps, and found in them 37 beavers! This success restored our spirits instantaneously. Exhilarating prospects now opened before us, and we pushed on with animation. The banks of this river are for the most part incapable of cultivation being in many places formed of high and rugged mountains. Upon these we saw multitudes of mountain sheep. These animals are not found on level ground, being there slow of foot, but on these cliffs and rocks they are so nimble and expert in jumping from point to point, that no dog or wolf can overtake them.

One of them that we killed had the largest horns, that I ever saw on animals of any description. One of them would hold a gallon of water. Their meat tastes like our mutton. Their hair is short like a deer's, though fine. The French call them the *gros cornes*, from the size of their horns which curl around their ears, like our domestic sheep. These animals are about the size of a large deer. We traced this river to its head, but not without great difficulty, as the cliffs in many places came so near the water's edge, that we were compelled to cross points of the mountain, which fatigued both ourselves and our horses exceedingly.

The right hand fork of this river, and the left of the Helay head in the same mountain, which is covered with snow, and divides its waters from those of Red River. We finished our trapping on this river, on the 14th. We had caught the very considerable number of 250 beavers,

55

and had used and preserved most of the meat, we had killed. On the 19th we arrived on the River Helay, encamped, and buried our furs in a secure position, as we intended to return home by this route.

On the 20th we began to descend the Helay, hoping to find in our descent another beaver stream emptying into it. We had abandoned the hope of rejoining the hunters, that had left us, and been the occasion of our being compelled to feed upon horse flesh. No better was to be expected of us, than that we should take leave to imprecate many a curse upon their heads; and that they might experience no better fate, than to fall into the hands of the savages, or be torn in pieces by the white bears. At the same time, so ready are the hearts of mountain hunters to relent, that I have not a doubt that each man of us would have risked his life to save any one of them from the very fate, we imprecated upon them.

In fact, on the night of the 22nd, four of them, actually half starved, arrived at our camp, declaring, that they had eaten nothing for five days. Notwithstanding our recent curses bestowed upon them, we received them as brothers. They related that the Indians had assaulted and defeated them, robbing them of all their horses, and killing one of their number. Next day the remaining two came in, one of them severely wounded in the head by an Indian arrow. They remained with us two days, during which we attempted to induce them to lead us against the Indians, who had robbed them, that we might assist them to recover what had been robbed from them. No persuasion would induce them to this course. They insisted at the same time, that if we attempted to go on by ourselves, we should share the same fate, which had befallen them.

On the morning of the 25th, we gave them three horses, and as much dried meat as would last them to the mines, distant about 150 miles. Fully impressed, that the Indians would massacre us, they took such a farewell of us, as if never expecting to see us again.

In the evening of the same day, although the weather threatened a storm, we packed up, and began to descend the river. We encamped this night in a huge cavern in the midst of the rocks. About night it began to blow a tempest, and to snow fast. Our horses became impatient under the pelting of the storm, broke their ropes, and disappeared. In the morning, the earth was covered with snow, four or five inches deep. One of our companions accompanied me to search for our horses. We soon came upon their trail, and followed it, until it crossed the river. We found it on the opposite side, and pursued it up a creek, that empties into the Helay on the north shore. We passed a cave at the foot of the cliffs.

At its mouth I remarked, that the bushes were beaten down, as though some animal had been browsing upon them. I was aware, that a bear had entered the cave. We collected some pine knots, split them with our tomahawks, and kindled torches, with which I proposed to my companion, that we should enter the cave together, and shoot the bear. He gave me a decided refusal, notwithstanding I reminded him, that I had, more than once, stood by him in a similar adventure; and notwithstanding I made him sensible, that a bear in a den is by no means so formidable, as when ranging freely in the woods. Finding it impossible to prevail on him to accompany me, I lashed my torch to a stick, and placed it parallel with the gun barrel, so as that I could see the sights on it, and entered the cave. I advanced cautiously onward about twenty yards, seeing nothing.

On a sudden the bear reared himself erect within seven feet of me, and began to growl, and gnash his teeth. I levelled my gun and shot him between the eyes, and began to retreat. Whatever light it may throw upon my courage, I admit, that I was in such a hurry, as to stumble, and extinguish my light. The growling and struggling of the bear did not at all contribute to allay my apprehensions.

On the contrary, I was in such haste to get out of the dark place, thinking the bear just at my heels, that I fell several times on the rocks, by which I cut my limbs, and lost my gun. When I reached the light, my companion declared, and I can believe it, that I was as pale as a corpse. It was some time, before I could summon sufficient courage to re-enter the cavern for my gun. But having re-kindled my light, and borrowed my companion's gun, I entered the cavern again, advanced and listened. All was silent, and I advanced still further, and found my gun, near where I had shot the bear. Here again I paused and listened. I then advanced onward a few strides, where to my great joy I found the animal dead. I returned, and brought my companion in with me. We attempted to drag the carcass from the den, but so great was the size, that we found ourselves wholly unable. We went out, found our horses, and returned to camp for assistance. My father severely repri-manded me for venturing to attack such a dangerous animal in its den, when the failure to kill it outright by the first shot, would have been sure to be followed by my death.

Four of us were detached to the den. We were soon enabled to drag the bear to the light, and by the aid of our beast to take it to camp. It was both the largest and whitest bear I ever saw. The best proof, I can give, of the size and fatness is, that we extracted ten gallons of oil from it. The meat we dried, and put the oil in a trough, which we secured in a deep crevice of a cliff, beyond the reach of animals of prey. We were sensible that it would prove a treasure to us on our return.

On the 28th we resumed our journey, and pushed down the stream to reach a point on the river, where trapping had not been practised. On the 30th, we reached this point, and found the man, that the Indians had killed. They had cut him in quarters, after the fashion of butchers. His head, with the hat on, was stuck on a stake. It was full of the arrows, which they had probably discharged into it, as they had danced around it. We gathered up the parts of the body, and buried them.

At this point we commenced setting our traps. We found the river skirted with very wide bottoms, thick-set with the *musquito* trees, which bear a pod in the shape of a bean, which is exceedingly sweet. It constitutes one of the chief articles of Indian subsistence; and they contrive to prepare from it a very palatable kind of bread, of which we all became very fond. The wild animals also feed upon this pod.

On the 31st we moved our camp ten miles. On the way we noted many fresh traces of Indians, and killed a bear, that attacked us. The river pursues a west course amidst high mountains on each side. We trapped slowly onward, still descending the river, and unmolested by the Indians. On the 8th of February, we reached the mouth of a small river entering the Helay on the north shore. Here we unexpectedly came upon a small party of Indians, that fled at the sight of us, in such consternation and hurry, as to leave all their effects, which consisted of a quantity of the bread mentioned above, and some robes made of rabbit skins. Still more; they left a small child. The child was old enough to distinguish us from its own people, for it opened its little throat, and screamed so lustily, that we feared it would have fits. The poor thing meanwhile made its best efforts to fly from us. We neither plundered nor molested their little store. We bound the child in such a manner, that it could not stray away, and get lost, aware, that after they deemed us sufficiently far off, the parents would return, and take the child away. We thence ascended the small river about four miles, and encamped.

For fear of surprise, and apprehending the return of the savages, that had fled from us, and perhaps in greater force, we secured our camp with a small breast-work. We discovered very little encouragement in regard to our trapping pursuit, for we noted few signs of beavers on this stream. The night passed without bringing us any disturbance. In the morning two of us returned to the Indian camp. The Indians had re-visited it, and removed every thing of value, and what gave us great satisfaction, their child. In proof, that the feelings of human nature are the same everywhere, and that the language of kindness is a universal one; in token of their gratitude, as we understood it, they had suspended a package on a kind of stick, which they had stuck erect. Availing ourselves of their offer, we examined the present, and found it to contain a large dressed buck skin, an article, which we greatly needed for *moccasins*, of which some of us were in pressing want. On the same stick we tied a red handkerchief by way of some return.

We thence continued to travel up this stream four days in succession, with very little incident to diversify our march. We found the banks of this river plentifully timbered with trees of various species, and the land fine for cultivation. On the morning of the 13th, we returned to the Helay, and found on our way, that the Indians had taken the handkerchief, we had left, though none of them had shown any disposition, as we had hoped, to visit us. We named the stream we had left, the deserted fork, on account of having found it destitute of beavers. We thence resumed our course down the Helay, which continues to flow through a most beautiful country. Warned by the frequent traces of fresh Indian footprints, we every night adopted the expedient of enclosing our horses in a pen, feeding them with cotton-wood bark, which we found much better for them than grass.

On the 16th, we advanced to a point, where the river runs between high mountains, in a ravine so narrow, as barely to afford it space to pass. We commenced exploring them to search for a gap, through which we might be able to pass. We continued our expedition, travelling north, until we discovered a branch, that made its way out of the mountains. Up its ravine we ascended to the head of the branch. Its fountains were supplied by an immense snow bank, on the summit of the mountain. With great labour and fatigue we reached this summit, but could descry no plains within the limits of vision. On every side the peaks of ragged and frowning mountains rose above the clouds, affording a prospect of dreariness and desolation, to chill the heart. While we could hear the thunder burst, and see the lightning glare before us, we found an atmosphere so cold, that we were obliged to keep up severe and unremitting exercise, to escape freezing.

We commenced descending the western declivity of the mountains, amidst thick mists and dark clouds, with which they were enveloped. We pitied our horses and mules, that were continually sliding and falling, by which their limbs were strained, and their bodies bruised. To our great joy, we were not long, before we came upon the ravine of a branch, that wound its way through the vast masses of crags and mountains. We were disappointed, however, in our purpose to follow it to the Helay. Before it mingled with that stream, it engulfed itself so deep between the cliffs, that though we heard the dash of the waters in their narrow bed, we could hardly see them.

We were obliged to thread our way, as we might, along the precipice, that constituted the banks of the creek. We were often obliged to unpack our mules and horses, and transport their loads by hand from one precipice to another. We continued wandering among the mountains in this way, until the 23rd. Our provisions were at this time exhausted, and our horses and mules so worn out, that they were utterly unable to proceed further. Thus we were absolutely obliged to lie by two days.

During this time, Allen and myself commenced climbing towards the highest peak of the mountains in our vicinity. It was nightfall, before we gained it. But from it we could distinctly trace the winding path of the river in several places; and what was still more cheering, could see smokes arising from several Indian camps. To meet even enemies, was more tolerable, than thus miserably to perish with hunger and cold in the mountains. Our report on our return animated the despair of our companions. On the morning of the 25th we resumed our painful efforts to reach the river. On the 28th, to our great joy, we once more found ourselves on its banks. A party of Indians, encamped there, fled at our approach. But fortunately they left a little mush prepared from the seeds of grass.

Without scruple we devoured it with appetites truly ravenous. In the morning we took ten beavers in our traps, and Allen was detached with me to clear away a path, through which the pack horses might pass. We were obliged to cross the river twelve times in the course of a single day. We still discovered the fresh footprints of Indians, who had deserted their camps, and fled before us. We were continually apprehensive, that they would fire their arrows upon us, or overwhelm us with rocks, let loose upon us from the summits of the high cliffs, directly under which we were obliged to pass.

The third day, after we had left our company, I shot a wild goose in the river. The report of my gun raised the screams of women and children. Too much alarmed to stop for my game, I mounted my horse, and rode toward them, with a view to convince them, or in some way, to show them, that we intended them no harm. We discovered them ahead of us, climbing the mountains, the men in advance of the women, and all fleeing at the top of their speed.

As soon as they saw us, they turned, and let fly a few arrows at us, one of which would have despatched my companion, had he not been infinitely dextrous in dodging. Hungry and fatigued and by no means in the best humour, my companion returned them abundance of curses for their arrows. From words he was proceeding to deeds, and would undoubtedly have shot one of them, had I not caught his gun, and made him sensible of the madness of such a deed. It was clearly our wisdom to convince them, that we had no inclination to injure them. Some of them were clad in robes of rabbit skins, part of which they shed, in their hurry to clamber over the rocks.

Finding ourselves unable to overtake them, we returned to their camp, to discover if they had left anything that we could eat. At no great distance from their camp, we observed a mound of fresh earth, in appearance like one of our coal kilns. Considering it improbable, that the Indians would be engaged in burning coal, we opened the mound, and found it to contain a sort of vegetable that had the appearance of herbage, which seemed to be baking in the ground, to prepare it for eating. I afterwards ascertained, that it was a vegetable, called by the Spanish, *mascal*, (probably *maguey*.) The Indians prepare it in this way, so as to make a kind of whiskey of it, tasting like crab-apple cider. The vegetable grows in great abundance on these mountains.

Next day we came to the point, where the river discharges its waters from the mountains on to the plains. We thence returned, and rejoined our company, that had been making their way onward behind us. March 3rd, we trapped along down a small stream, that empties into the Helay on the south side, having its head in a south west direction. It being very remarkable for the number of its beavers, we gave it the name of Beaver river. At this place we collected 200 skins; and on the 10th continued to descend the Helay, until the 20th, when we turned back with as much fur, as our beasts could pack. As yet we had experienced no molestation from the Indians, although they were frequently descried skulking after us, and gathering up the pieces of meat, we had thrown away. On the morning of the 20th we were all prepared for an early start, and my father, by way of precaution, bade us all discharge our guns at the word of command, and then re-load them afresh, that we might, in case of emergency, be sure of our fire. We were directed to form in a line, take aim, and at the word, fire at a tree.

We gave sufficient proofs, that we were no strangers to the rifle, for every ball had lodged close to the centre of our mark. But the report of our guns was answered by the yell of more than an hundred savages, above us on the mountains. We immediately marched out from under the mountains on to the plains, and beckoned them to come down, by every demonstration of friendship in our power. Nothing seemed to offer stronger enticement, than to hold out to them our red cloth. This we did, but without effect, for they either understood us not, or were reluctant to try our friendship. Leaving one of our number to watch their deportment, and to note if they followed us, we resumed our march. It would have been a great object to us to have been able to banish their suspicions, and make a treaty with them. But we could draw from them no demonstrations, but those of fear and surprise.

On the 25th we returned to Beaver River, and dug up the furs that we had buried, or *cached*, as the phrase is, and concluded to ascend it, trapping towards its head, whence we purposed to cross over to the Helay above the mountains, where we had suffered so much in crossing. About six miles up the stream, we stopped to set our traps, three being selected to remain behind in the camp to dry the skins, my father to make a pen for the horses, and I to guard them, while they were turned loose to feed in the grass. We had pitched our camp near the bank of the river, in a thick grove of timber, extending about a hundred yards in width. Behind the timber was a narrow plain of about the same width, and still further on was a high hill, to which I repaired, to watch my horses, and descry whatever might pass in the distance. Immediately back of the hill I discovered a small lake, by the noise made by the ducks and geese in it.

Looking more attentively, I remarked what gave me much more satisfaction, that is to say, three beaver lodges. I returned, and made my father acquainted with my discovery. The party despatched to set traps had returned. My father informed them of my discovery, and told them to set traps in the little lake.

As we passed towards the lake, we observed the horses and mules all crowded together. At first we concluded that they collected together in this way, because they had fed enough. We soon discovered, that it was owing to another cause. I had put down my gun, and stepped into the water, to prepare a bed for my trap, while the others were busy in preparing theirs. Instantly the Indians raised a yell, and the quick report of guns ensued. This noise was almost drowned in the fierce shouts that followed, succeeded by a shower of arrows falling among us like hail. As we ran for the camp leaving all the horses in their power, we saw six Indians stealthily following our trail, as though they were tracking a deer. They occasionally stopped, raised themselves, and surveyed everything around them. We concealed ourselves behind a large cotton-wood tree, and waited until they came within a hundred yards of us. Each of us selected a separate Indian for a mark, and our signal to fire together was to be a whistle. The sign was given, and we fired together. My mark fell dead, and my companions' severely wounded. The other Indians seized their dead and wounded companions, and fled.

We now rejoined our company, who were busily occupied in dodging the arrows, that came in a shower from the summit of the hill, where I had stationed myself to watch our horses. Discovering that they were too far from us, to be reached by our bullets, we retreated to the timber, in hopes to draw them down to the plain. But they had had too ample proofs of our being marksmen, to think of returning down to our level, and were satisfied to remain yelling, and letting fly their arrows at random. We found cause both for regret and joy; regret, that our horses were in their power, and joy, that their unprovoked attack had been defeated with loss to themselves, and none to us.

At length they ceased yelling, and disappeared. We, on our part, set ourselves busily to work to fortify our camp for the night. Meanwhile our savage enemy devised a plan, which, but for the circumspection of my father, would have enabled them to destroy us. They divided themselves into two parties, the one party mounted on horses, stolen from us, and so arranged as to induce the belief, that they constituted the whole party. They expected that we would pursue them, to recover our horses. As soon as we should be drawn out from behind our fortification, they had a reserve party, on foot, who were to rush in, between us and our camp, and thus, between two fires, cut us all off together. It so happened, that I had retired a little distance from the camp, in the direction of the ambush party on foot. I met them, and they raised a general yell.

My father, supposing me surrounded, ran in the direction of the yell, to aid me. He, too, came in direct contact with the foot party, who let fly a shower of arrows at him, from which nothing but good providence preserved him. He returned the fire with his gun and pistols, by which he killed two of them, and the report of which immediately brought his companions to his side. The contest was a warm one for a few minutes, when the Indians fled. This affair commenced about three in the afternoon; and the Indians made their final retreat at five; and the succeeding night passed without further molestation from them.

In the morning of the 26th, we despatched two of our men to bring our traps and furs. We had no longer any way of conveying them with us, for the Indians had taken all our horses. We, however, in the late contest, had taken four of theirs, left behind in the haste of their retreat. As our companions were returning to camp with the traps, which they had taken up to bury, they discovered the Indians, sliding along insidiously towards our camp. We were all engaged in eating our breakfast in entire confidence. Our men cried out to us, that the enemy was close upon us. We sprang to our arms. The Indians instantly fled to the top of the hill, which we had named Battle-hill. In a few minutes they were all paraded on the horses and mules stolen from us. They instantly began to banter us in Spanish to come up to them. One of our number who could speak Spanish, asked them to what nation they belonged? They answered, *Eiotaro*. In return, they asked us, who we were? We answered *Americans*.

Hearing this, they stood in apparent surprise and astonishment for some moments. They then replied, that they had thought us too brave and too good marksmen, to be Spaniards; that they were sorry for what they had done, under the mistake of supposing us Spaniards. They declared themselves ready to make a treaty with us, provided that we would return the four horses, we had taken from them, and bring them up the hill, where they promised us they would restore us our own horses in exchange. We were at once impressed, that the proposal was a mere trick, to induce us to place ourselves in their power. We therefore answered their proposal by another, which was, that they should bring down our horses, and leave them by the pen, where they had taken them, and we in return would let their horses loose, and make friendship with them. They treated our proposal with laughter, which would have convinced us, had we doubted it before, that their only purpose had been to ensnare us. We accordingly faced them, and fired upon them, which induced them to clear themselves most expeditiously.

We proceeded to bury our furs; and having packed our four horses with provisions and two traps, we commenced our march. Having travelled about ten miles, we encamped in a thicket without kindling a fire, and kept a strict guard all night. Next morning we made an early march, still along the banks of the river. Its banks are still plentifully timbered with cotton-wood and willow. The bottoms on each side afford a fine soil for cultivation. From these bottoms the hills rise to an enormous height, and their summits are covered with perpetual snow. In these bottoms are great numbers of wild hogs, of a species entirely different from our domestic swine.

They are fox-coloured, with their navel on their back, towards the back part of their bodies. The hoof of their hind feet has but one dew-claw, and they yield an odour not less offensive than our pole-cat. Their figure and head are not unlike our swine, except that their tail resembles that of a bear. We measured one of their tusks, of a size so enormous, that I am afraid to commit my credibility, by giving the dimensions. They remain undisturbed by man and other animals, whether through fear or on account of their offensive odour, I am unable to say. That they have no fear of man, and that they are exceedingly ferocious, I can bear testimony myself. I have many times been obliged to climb trees to escape their tusks. We killed a great many, but could never bring ourselves to eat them.

The country presents the aspect of having been once settled at some remote period of the past. Great quantities of broken pottery are scattered over the ground, and there are distinct traces of ditches and stone walls, some of them as high as a man's breast, with very broad foundations. A species of tree, which I had never seen before, here arrested my attention. It grows to the height of forty or fifty feet. The top is cone shaped, and almost without foliage. The bark resembles that of the prickly pear; and the body is covered with thorns. I have seen some three feet in diameter at the root, and throwing up twelve distinct shafts.

On the 29th, we made our last encampment on this river, intending to return to it no more, except for our furs. We set our two traps for the last time, and caught a beaver in each.—We skinned the animals, and prepared the skins to hold water, through fear, that we might find none on our unknown route through the mountains to the Helay, from which we judged ourselves distant two hundred miles. Our provisions were all spoiled. We had nothing to carry with us to satisfy hunger, but the bodies of the two beavers which we had caught, the night before. We had nothing to sustain us in this disconsolate march, but our trust in providence; for we could not but foresee hunger, fatigue and pain, as the inevitable attendants upon our journey. To increase the depression of our spirits, our *moccasins* were worn out, our feet sore and tender, and the route full of sharp rocks.

On the 31st, we reached the top of the mountain, and fed upon the last meat of our beavers. We met with no traces of game. What distressed me most of all was, to perceive my father, who had already passed the meridian of his days, sinking with fatigue and weakness. On the morning of the first of April, we commenced descending the mountain, from the side of which we could discern a plain before us, which, however, it required two severe days travel to reach. During these two days we had nothing either to eat or drink. In descending from these icy mountains, we were surprised to find how warm it was on the plains. On reaching them I killed an antelope, of which we drank the warm blood; and however revolting the recital may be, to us it was refreshing, tasting like fresh milk. The meat we put upon our horses, and travelled on until twelve o'clock, before we found water.

Here we encamped the remainder of the day, to rest, and refresh ourselves. The signs of antelopes were abundant, and the appearances were, that they came to the water to drink; from which we inferred, that there was no other drinking place in the vicinity. Some of our hunters went out in pursuit of the antelopes. From the numbers of these animals, we called the place *Antelope Plain*. The land lies very handsomely, and is a rich, black soil, with heavily timbered groves in the vicinity.

On the morning of the 3rd, though exceedingly stiff and sore, we resumed our march, and reaching the opposite side of the plain, encamped at a spring, that ran from the mountain. Next day we ascended this mountain to its summit, which we found covered with iron ore. At a distance we saw a smoke on our course. We were aware that it was the smoke of an Indian camp, and we pushed on towards it. In the evening we reached the smoke, but found it deserted of Indians. All this day's march was along a country abundant in minerals. In several places we saw lead and copper ore. I picked up a small parcel of ore, which I put in my shot-pouch, which was proved afterward to be an ore of silver. The misfortune of this region is, that there is no water near these mineral hills.

We commenced our morning march half dead with thirst, and pushed on with the eagerness inspired by that tormenting appetite. Late in the evening we found a little water, for our own drinking, in the bottom of a rock. Not a drop remained for our four horses, that evidently showed a thirst no less devouring than ours. Their feet were all bleeding, and the moment we paused to rest ourselves, the weary companions of our journey instantly laid down. It went still more to my heart, to see my two faithful dogs, which had followed me all the way from my father's house, where there was always *bread enough and to spare*, looking to me with an expression, which a hunter in the desert only can understand, as though begging food and water. Full gladly would I have explained to them, that the sterile wilderness gave me no means of supplying their wants.

We had scarcely commenced the next morning's march, when, at a little distance from our course, we saw a smoke. Supposing it an Indian camp, we immediately concluded to attack it. Adopting their own policy, we slipped onward in silence and concealment, until we were close by it. We found the persons women and children. Having no disposition to harm them, we fired a gun over their heads, which caused them instantly to fly at the extent of their speed. Hunger knows no laws; and we availed ourselves of their provision, which proved to be *mascal*, and grass seed, of which we made mush. Scanty as this nutriment was, it was sufficient to sustain life.

We commenced an early march on the 6th, and were obliged to move slowly, as we were bare-footed, and the mountains rough and steep. We found them either wholly barren, or only covered with a stinted growth of pine and cedar, live oak and barbary bushes. On the 8th, our provisions were entirely exhausted, and so having nothing to eat, we felt the less need of water. Our destitute and forlorn condition goaded us on, so that we reached the Helay on the 12th. We immediately began to search for traces of beavers, where to set our traps, but found none. On the morning of the 13th, we killed a raven, which we cooked for seven men. It was unsavoury flesh in itself, and would hardly have afforded a meal for one hungry man.

The miserable condition of our company may be imagined, when seven hungry men, who had not eaten a full meal for ten days, were all obliged to breakfast on this nauseous bird. We were all weak and emaciated. But I was young and able to bear hardships. My heart only ached for my poor father who was reduced to a mere skeleton. We moved on slowly and painfully, until evening, when we encamped. On my return from setting our two traps, I killed a buzzard, which, disagreeable as it was, we cooked for supper. In the morning of the 18th, I found one of the traps had caught an otter.

This served for breakfast and supper. It seemed the means of our present salvation, for my father had become so weak, that he could no longer travel. We therefore encamped early, and three of us went out to hunt deer among the hills. But in this sad emergency we could find none. When we returned, my father had prepared lots, that we should draw, to determine who of us should kill one of the dogs. I refused through fear that the lot would fall to me. These faithful companions of our sufferings were so dear to me, that I felt as though I could not allow them to be killed to save my own life; though to save my father, I was aware that it was a duty to allow it to be done.

We lay here until the 18th, my father finding the flesh of the dog both sweet, nutritive and strengthening. On the 18th, he was again able to travel; and on the 20th, we arrived at Bear Creek, where we hid the bears oil, which we found unmolested. We lay here two days, during which time we killed four deer and some turkeys. The venison we dried, and cased the skin of one of the deer, in which to carry our oil. We commenced an early march on the 23rd, and on the 25th reached the River San Francisco, where we found our buried furs all safe. I suffered exceedingly from the soreness of my feet, giving me great pain and fever at night. We made from our raw deer skins a very tolerable substitute for shoes. The adoption of this important expedient enabled us to push on, so that we reached the Copper mines on the 29th.

The Spaniards seemed exceedingly rejoiced, and welcomed us home, as though we were of their own nation, religion and kindred. They assured us, that they had no expectation ever to see us again. The superintendent of the mines, especially, who appeared to me a gentleman of the highest order, received us with particular kindness, and supplied all our pressing wants. Here we remained, to rest and recruit ourselves, until the 2nd of May. My father then advised me to travel to Santa Fé, to get some of our goods, and purchase a new supply of horses, with which to return, and bring in our furs. I had a horse, which we had taken from the Indians, shod with copper shoes, and in company with four of my companions, and the superintendent of the mines, I started for Santa Fé.

The superintendent assured us, that he would gladly have furnished us horses; but the Apache Indians had recently made an incursion upon his establishment, stealing all his horses, and killing three men, that were herding them. This circumstance had suspended the working of the mines. Besides he was unable to procure the necessary coal, with which to work them, because the Apaches waylaid the colliers, and killed them, as often as they attempted to make coal.

We arrived at the house of the governor on the 12th. Jacova, his daughter, received us with the utmost affection; and shed tears on observing me so ill; as I was in fact reduced by starvation and fatigue, to skin and bone. Beings in a more wretched plight she could not often have an opportunity to see. My hair hung matted and uncombed. My head was surmounted with an old straw hat. My legs were fitted with leather leggins, and my body arrayed in a leather hunting shirt, and no want of dirt about any part of the whole. My companions did not shame me, in comparison, by being better clad. But all these repulsive circumstances notwithstanding, we were welcomed by the governor and Jacova, as kindly, as if we had been clad in a manner worthy of their establishment.

We rested ourselves here three days. I had left my more decent apparel in the care of Jacova, when we started from the house into the wilderness on our trapping expedition. She had had my clothes prepared in perfect order. I once more dressed myself decently, and spared to my companions all my clothes that fitted them. We all had our hair trimmed. All this had much improved our appearance. When we started on the 15th, the old gentleman gave each of us a good horse, enabling us to travel at our ease.

On the 18th we arrived at Santa Fé, where we immediately met some of our former companions. It hardly need be added, that the joy of this recognition was great and mutual. We found Mr. Pratte ill in bed. He expressed himself delighted to see me, and was still more desirous to see my father. He informed me, that four of the company that he had detached to trap, had been defeated by the Indians, and the majority of them killed. He had, also, despaired of ever seeing us again. I took a part of my goods, and started back to the mines on the 21st. None of my companions were willing to accompany me on account of the great apprehended danger from the Indians between this place and the mines. In consequence, I hired a man to go with me, and having purchased what horses I wanted, we two travelled on in company. I would have preferred to have purchased my horses of the old governor. But I knew that his noble nature would impel him to give them to me, and felt reluctant to incur such an obligation. When I left his house, he insisted on my receiving a gold chain, in token of the perpetual remembrance of his daughter. I saw no pretext for refusing it, and as I received it, she assured me that she should always make mention of my father and me in her prayers.

I left this hospitable place on the 24th, taking all my clothes with me, except the hunting shirt, which I had worn in the battle with the Commanches. This she desired to retain, insisting, that she wished to preserve this memorial to the day of her death. We arrived at the mines the first day of June, having experienced no molestation from the Indians. We continued here, making arrangements for our expedition to bring in the furs, until the 6th. The good natured commander gave us provisions to last us to the point where our furs were buried, and back again. Still more, he armed ten of his labourers, and detached them to accompany us. The company consisted of four Americans, the man hired at Santa Fé, and the commander's ten men, fifteen in all.

We left the mines on the 7th, and reached Battle-hill on Beaver River on the 22nd. I need not attempt to describe my feelings, for no description could paint them, when I found the furs all gone, and perceived that the Indians had discovered them and taken them away. All that, for which we had hazarded ourselves, and suffered every thing but death, was gone. The whole fruit of our long, toilsome and dangerous expedition was lost, and all my golden hopes of prosperity and comfort vanished like a dream. I tried to convince myself, that repining was of no use, and we started for the river San Francisco on the 29th. Here we found the small quantity buried there, our whole compensation for a year's toil, misery and danger. We met no Indians either going or returning.

We arrived at the mines the 8th of July, and after having rested two days proposed to start for Santa Fé. The commander, Don Juan Unis, requested us to remain with him two or three months, to guard his workmen from the Indians, while pursuing their employment in the woods. He offered, as a compensation, a dollar a day. We consented to stay, though without accepting the wages. We should have considered ourselves ungrateful, after all the kindness, he had rendered us at the hour of our greatest need, either to have refused the request, or to have accepted a compensation. Consequently we made our arrangements to stay.

We passed our time most pleasantly in hunting deer and bears, of which there were great numbers in the vicinity. We had no other duties to perform, than to walk round in the vicinity of the workmen, or sit by and see them work. Most of my time was spent with Don Juan, who kindly under took to teach me to speak Spanish. Of him, having no other person with whom to converse, I learned the language easily, and rapidly. One month of our engagement passed off without any molestation from the Indians. But on the first day of August, while three of us were hunting deer, we discovered the trail of six Indians approaching the mines. We followed the trail, and within about a mile from the mines, we came up with them. They fled, and we pursued close at their heels. Gaining upon them, one of them dodged us, into the head of a hollow. We surrounded him.

As soon as he saw that we had discovered him, and that escape was impossible, he sprung on his feet, threw away his bow and arrows, and begged us most submissively not to shoot him. One of our men made up to him, while the other man and myself stood with our guns cocked, and raised to our faces, ready to shoot him, if he made the least motion towards his bow. But he remained perfectly still, crossing his hands, that we might tie them. Having done it, we drove him on before us.

We had advanced about a hundred yards from the point where we took him, when he pointed out to us a hollow tree, intimating that there was another Indian concealed there. We bade him instruct his companion to make no resistance, and to surrender himself, or we would kill him. He explained our words to his companion in the tree. He immediately came forth from his concealment with his bow, and we tied his hands in the same way as the other's. We marched them before us to the mines, where we put them in prison. The Spaniards, exasperated with their recent cruelties and murders, would have killed them. We insisted that they should be spared, and they remained in prison until the next morning.

We then brought them out of prison, conversed with them, and showed them how closely we could fire. We instructed one of them to tell his chief to come in, accompanied by all his warriors, to make peace. We retained one of the prisoners as a hostage, assuring the other, that if his chief did not come in to make peace, we would put the hostage to death. In regard to the mode of making it, we engaged, that only four of our men should meet them at a hollow, half a mile from the mine. We enjoined it on him to bring them there within the term of four days. We readily discovered by the tranquil countenance of our hostage, that he had no apprehensions that they would not come in.

Afterwards, by way of precaution, my father put in requisition all the arms he could find in the vicinity of the mines, with which he armed thirty Spaniards. He then ordered a trench dug, at a hundred yard's distance from the point designated for the Indians to occupy. This trench was to be occupied by our armed men, during the time of the treaty, in case, that if the Indians should be insolent or menacing, these men might be at hand to overawe them, or aid us, according to circumstances.

On the 5th, we repaired to the place designated, and in a short time, the Indians to the number of 80, came in sight. We had prepared a pipe, tobacco, and a council fire, and had spread a blanket, on which the chief might sit down. As soon as they came near us, they threw down their arms. The four chiefs came up to us, and we all sat down on the blanket. We commenced discussing the subject, for which they were convened. We asked them, if they were ready to make a peace with us; and if not what were the objections? They replied, that they had no objections to a peace with the Americans, but would never make one with the Spaniards. When we asked their reasons, they answered that they had been long at war with the Spaniards, and that a great many murders had been mutually inflicted on either side.

They admitted, that they had taken a great many horses from the Spaniards, but indignantly alleged, that a large party of their people had come in to make peace with the Spaniards, of which they pretended to be very desirous; that with such pretexts, they had decoyed the party within their walls, and then commenced butchering them like a flock of sheep. The very few who had escaped, had taken an unalterable resolution never to make peace with them. 'In pursuance,' they continued, 'of our purposes of revenge, great numbers of our nation went in among the Spaniards, and were baptized. There they remain faithful spies for us, informing us when and where there were favourable opportunities to kill, and plunder our enemies.'

We told them in reply, that if they really felt disposed to be at peace with the Americans, these mines were now working jointly by us and the Spaniards; that it was wrong in them to revenge the crimes of the guilty upon the innocent, and that these Spaniards had taken no part in the cowardly and cruel butchery, of which they had spoken; and that if they would not be peaceable, and allow us to work the mines unmolested, the Americans would consider them at war, and would raise a sufficient body of men to pursue them to their lurking places in the mountains; that they had good evidence that our people could travel in the woods and among the mountains, as well as themselves; and that we could shoot a great deal better than either they or the Spaniards, and that we had no cowards among us, but true men, who had no fear and would keep their word.

The chiefs answered, that if the mines belonged to the Americans, they would promise never to disturb the people that worked them. We left them, therefore, to infer that the mines belonged to us, and took them at their word. We then lit the pipe, and all the Indians gathered in a circle round the fire. The four chiefs, each in succession made a long speech, in which we could often distinguish the terms Americans, and Espanola. The men listened with profound attention, occasionally sanctioning what was said by a nod of the head. We then commenced smoking, and the pipe passed twice round the circle.

They then dug a hole in the ground in the centre of the circle, and each one spat in it. They then filled it up with earth, danced round it, and stuck their arrows in the little mound. They then gathered a large pile of stones over it, and painted themselves red. Such are their ceremonies of making peace. All the forms of the ceremony were familiar to us, except the pile of stones, and spitting in the hole they had dug, which are not practised by the Indians on the American frontiers. We asked them the meaning of the spitting. They said, that they did it in token of spitting out all their spite and revenge, and burying their anger under the ground.

It was two o'clock before all these ceremonies were finished. We then showed them our reserve force in the trench. They evinced great alarm to see their enemies the Spaniards so close to them, and all ready for action. We explained to them, that we intended to be in good faith, if they were; and that these men were posted there, only in case they showed a disposition to violence. Their fears vanished and tranquillity returned to their countenances. The chiefs laughed, and said to each other, these Americans know how to fight, and make peace too. But were they to fight us, they would have to get a company entirely of their own people; for that if they took any Spaniards into their company, they would be sure to desert them in the time of action.

We thence all marched to the mines, where we killed three beeves to feed the Indians. After they had eaten, and were in excellent humour, the head chief made a present to my father, of ten miles square of a tract of land lying on a river about three miles from the mines. It was very favourable for cultivation, and the Spaniards had several times attempted to make a crop of grain upon it; but the Indians had as often either killed the cultivators, or destroyed the grain. My father informed them, that though the land might be his, he should be obliged to employ Spaniards to cultivate it for him; and that, having made the land his, they must consider these cultivators his people, and not molest them.

With a look of great firmness, the chief said 'that he was a man of truth, and had given his word, and that we should find that nothing belonging to the mines would be disturbed, for that he never would allow the treaty to be violated.' He went on to add, 'that he wanted to be at peace with us, because he had discovered, that the Americans never showed any disposition to kill, except in battle; that they had had a proof of this in our not killing the two prisoners we had taken; but had sent one of them to invite his people to come in, and make peace with us, and that he took pleasure in making known to us, that they were good people too, and had no wish to injure men that did not disturb or injure them.'

All this farce of bringing the Indians to terms of peace with this establishment was of infinite service to the Spaniards, though of none to us; for we neither had any interest in the mines, nor intended to stay there much longer. But we were glad to oblige Don Juan who had been so great a benefactor to us. He, on his part, was most thankful to us; for he could now work the mines without any risk of losing men or cattle. He could now raise his own grain, which he had hitherto been obliged to pack 200 miles, not without having many of those engaged in bringing it, either killed or robbed. The Indians now had so much changed their deportment as to bring in horses or cows, that they found astray from the mines. They regularly brought in deer and turkeys to sell, which Don Juan, to keep alive their friendship, purchased, whether he needed the articles or not. Every day more or less Indians came into the settlement to go and hunt deer and bears with us. They were astonished at the closeness of our shooting; and nothing seemed to delight them so much, as our telling them, we would learn them to shoot our guns. My father had the honour to be denominated in their language, *the big Captain.*

Don Juan, apprehending that the truce with the Indians would last no longer than while we staid, and that after our departure, the Indians would resume their former habits of robbery and murder, was desirous to retain us as long as possible. We agreed to stay until December, when our plan was to commence another trapping expedition on the Helay, following it down to its mouth. With every disposition on the part of Don Juan to render our stay agreeable, the time passed away pleasantly. On the 16th of September, the priest, to whose diocese the mines belonged, made a visit to the mines, to release the spirits of those who had died since his last visit, from purgatory, and to make Christians by baptising the little persons who had been born in the same time.

This old priest, out of a reverend regard to his own person, had fled from this settlement at the commencement of the Indian disturbances; and had not returned until now, when the Indians had made peace. A body of Indians happened to be in, when the priest came. We were exceedingly amused with the interview between the priest and an Indian chief, who, from having had one of his hands bitten off by a bear, was called *Mocho Mano*. The priest asked the one handed chief, why he did not offer himself for baptism? Mocho remained silent for some time, as if ruminating an answer. He then said, 'the Apache chief is a very big rogue now. Should he get his crown sprinkled with holy water, it would either do him no good at all, or if it had any effect, would make him a greater rogue; for that the priests, who made the water holy, and then went sprinkling it about among the people for money, were the biggest rogues of all.' This made the priest as angry as it made us merry.

When we had done laughing, Mocho asked us, how we baptised among our people? I answered that we had two ways of performing it; but that one way was, to plunge the baptised person under water. He replied promptly, 'now there is some sense in that;' adding that when a great quantity of rain fell from the clouds, it made the grass grow; but that it seemed to him that sprinkling a few drops of water amounted to nothing.

The priest, meanwhile, prophesied, that the peace between the Spaniards and Indians would be of very short duration. On the 18th, he left the mines, and returned to the place whence he had come. On the 20th, we started with some Indian guides to see a mountain of salt, that they assured us existed in their country. We travelled a northerly course through a heavily timbered country, the trees chiefly of pine and live oak. We killed a great number of bears and deer on the first day; and on account of their reverence for my father, they treated me as if I had been a prince. On the second we arrived at the salt hill, which is about one hundred miles north of the mines. The hill is about a quarter of a mile in length, and on the front side of it is the salt bluff, eight or ten feet in thickness. It has the appearance of a black rock, divided from the earthy matters, with which the salt is mixed.

What was to me the most curious circumstance of the whole, was to see a fresh water spring boiling up within twenty feet from the salt bluff, which is a detached and solitary hill, rising out of a valley, which is of the richest and blackest soil, and heavily timbered with oak, ash and black walnut. I remained here two days, during which I killed fifteen deer, that came to lick salt.

An Indian woman of our company dressed all my deer skins, and we loaded two mules with the salt, and started back to the mines, where we arrived the first of October. Nothing could have been more seasonable or acceptable to Don Juan, than the salt we brought with us. Having mentioned these mines so often, perhaps it may not be amiss, to give a few details respecting them. Within the circumference of three miles, there is a mine of copper, gold and silver, and beside, a cliff of load stone. The silver mine is not worked, as not being so profitable, as either the copper or gold mines.

We remained here to the last of December, when the settlement was visited by a company of French trappers, who were bound for Red River. We immediately made preparations to return with them, which again revived the apprehensions of Don Juan, that the Indians would break in upon the settlement as soon as we were gone, and again put an end to the working of the mines. To detain us effectually, he proposed to rent the mines to us for five years, at a thousand dollars a year. He was willing to furnish provisions for the first year *gratis*, and pay us for all the improvements we should make on the establishment. We could not but be aware, that this was an excellent offer. My father accepted it. The writings were drawn, and my father rented the establishment on his own account, selecting such partners as he chose.

I, meanwhile, felt within me an irresistible propensity to resume the employment of trapping. I had a desire, which I can hardly describe, to see more of this strange and new country. My father suffered greatly in the view of my parting with him, and attempted to dissuade me from it. He strongly painted the dangers of the route, and represented to me, that I should not find these Frenchmen like my own country people, for companions. All was unavailing to change my fixed purpose, and we left the mines, January 2nd, 1826.

We travelled down the River Helay, of which I have formerly given a description, as far as the point where we had left it for Battle-hill. Here, although we saw fresh Indian signs, we met with no Indians. Where we encamped for the night, there were arrows sticking in the ground. We made an early start on the 16th, and at evening came upon the selfsame party of Indians, that had robbed us of our horses, the year past. Some of them had on articles of my father's clothes, that he had left where we buried our furs. They had made our beaver skins into robes, which we now purchased of them. While this bargain was transacting, I observed one of the Indians mounted on the self same horse, on which my father had travelled from the States. My blood instantly boiled within me, and, presenting my gun at him, I ordered him instantly to dismount. He immediately did as I bade him, and at once a trepidation and alarm ran through the whole party. They were but twenty men, and they were encumbered with women and children. We were thirteen, well mounted and armed. The chief of the party came to me, and asked me, if I knew this horse? I answered, that I did, and that it was mine.

He asked me again, if we were the party, whose horses and furs they had taken the year before? I answered, that I was one of them, and that if he did not cause my furs and horses to be delivered up to me, we would kill them all on the spot. He immediately brought me 150 skins and three horses, observing, that they had been famished, and had eaten the rest, and that he hoped this would satisfy me, for that in the battle they had suffered more than we, he having lost ten men, and we having taken from them four horses with their saddles and bridles. I observed to him in reply, that he must remember that they were the aggressors, and had provoked the quarrel, in having robbed us of our horses, and attempting to kill us. He admitted that they were the aggressors, in beginning the quarrel, but added, by way of apology, that they had thought us Spaniards, not knowing that we were Americans; but that now, when he knew us, he was willing to make peace, and be in perpetual friendship. On this we lit the pipe of peace, and smoked friends. I gave him some red cloth, with which he was delighted. I then asked him about the different nations, through which our route would lead us? He named four nations, with names, as he pronounced them, sufficiently barbarous. All these nations he described as bad, treacherous and quarrelsome.

Though it was late in the evening, we resumed our march, until we had reached the point where the river runs between mountains, and where I had turned back the year before. There is here little timber, beside *musqueto*-wood, which stands thick. We passed through the country of the first two tribes, which the Indian chief had described to us, without meeting an individual of them. On the 25th, we arrived at an Indian village situated on the south bank of the river. Almost all the inhabitants of this village speak Spanish, for it is situated only three days journey from a Spanish fort in the province of Sonora, through which province this river runs. The Indians seemed disposed to be friendly to us.

They are to a considerable degree cultivators, raising wheat, corn and cotton, which they manufacture into cloths. We left this village on the 25th, and on the 28th in the evening arrived at the Papa-war village, the inhabitants of which came running to meet us, with their faces painted, and their bows and arrows in their hands. We were alarmed at these hostile appearances, and halted. We told them that we were friends, at which they threw down their arms, laughing the while, and showing by their countenances that they were aware that we were frightened.

We entered the village, and the French began to manifest their uncontrollable curiosity, by strolling about in every direction. I noted several crowds of Indians, collected in gangs, and talking earnestly. I called the leader of my French companions, and informed him that I did not like these movements of the Indians, and was fearful that they were laying a plan to cut us all up. He laughed at my fears, telling me I was a coward. I replied, that I did not think that to be cautious, and on our guard, was to show cowardice, and that I still thought it best for us to start off. At this he became angry, and told me that I might go when I pleased, and that he would go when he was ready.

I then spoke to a Frenchman of our number, that I had known for a long time in Missouri; I proposed to him to join me, and we would leave the village and encamp by ourselves. He consented, and we went out of the village to the distance of about 400 yards, under the pretext of going there to feed our horses. When the sun was about half an hour high, I observed the French captain coming out towards us, accompanied by a great number of Indians, all armed with bows and arrows. This confirmed me in my conviction that they intended us no good. Expressing my apprehensions to my French companion, he observed in his peculiar style of English, that the captain was too proud and headstrong, to allow him to receive instruction from any one, for that he thought nobody knew any thing but himself.

Agreeing that we had best take care of ourselves, we made us a fire, and commenced our arrangements for spending the night. We took care not to unsaddle our horses, but to be in readiness to be off at a moment's warning. Our French captain came and encamped within a hundred yards of us, accompanied by not less than a hundred Indi-ans. They were all exceedingly officious in helping the party unpack their mules; and in persuading the captain, that there was no danger in turning them all loose, they promised that they would guard them with their own horses. This proposal delighted the lazy Frenchmen, who hated to go through the details of preparing for encampment, and had a particular dislike to standing guard in the night. The Indian chief then proposed to the captain to stack their arms against a tree, that stood close by. To this also, under a kind of spell of infatuation he consented. The Indian chief took a rope, and tied the arms fast to a tree.

As I saw this, I told the captain that it seemed to me no mark of their being friendly, for them to retain their own arms, and persuade us to putting ours out of our power, and that one, who had known Indians, ought to be better acquainted with their character, than to encamp with them, without his men having their own arms in their hand. On this he flew into a most violent passion, calling me, with a curse added to the epithet, a coward, wishing to God that he had never taken me with him, to dishearten his men, and render them insubordinate. Being remarkable neither for forbearance, or failing to pay a debt of hard words, I gave him as good as he sent, telling him, among other things no ways flattering, that he was a liar and a fool, for that none other than a fool would disarm his men, and go to sleep in the midst of armed savages in the woods.

To this he replied, that he would not allow me to travel any longer in his company. I answered that I was not only willing, but desirous to leave him, for that I considered myself safer in my own single keeping, than under the escort of such a captain, and that I estimated him only to have sense enough to lead people to destruction.

He still continued to mutter harsh language in reply, as I returned to my own camp. It being now dusk, we prepared, and ate our supper. We had just finished it, when the head chief of the village came to invite us to take our supper with them, adding, by way of inducement, that they had brought some fine pumpkins to camp, and had cooked them for the white people. We told him, we had taken supper; and the more he insisted, the more resolutely we refused. Like the French captain, he began to abuse us, telling us we had bad hearts. We told him, that when with such people, we chose rather to trust to our heads than our hearts. He then asked us to let some of his warriors come and sleep with us, and share our blankets, alleging, as a reason for the request, that the nights were cold, and his warriors too poor to buy blankets. We told him, that he could easily see that we were poor also, and were no ways abundantly supplied with blankets, and that we should not allow them to sleep with us. He then marched off to the French camp, evidently sulky and in bad temper. While roundly rating us to the French captain, he gave as a reason why we ought not to sleep by ourselves, that we were in danger of being killed in the night by another tribe of Indians, with whom he was at war.

The captain, apparently more calm, came to us, and told us, that our conduct was both imprudent and improper, in not conciliating the Indians by consenting to eat with them, or allowing them to sleep with us. My temper not having been at all sweetened by anything that had occurred since we fell out, I told him, that if he had a fancy to eat, or sleep with these Indians, I had neither power nor the will to control him; but that, being determined, that neither he nor they should sleep with me, he had better go about his business, and not disturb me with useless importunity. At this he began again to abuse and revile me, to which I made no return. At length, having exhausted his stock of epithets, he returned to his camp.

As soon as we were by ourselves, we began to cut grass for our horses, not intending either to unsaddle, or let them loose for the night. My companion and myself were alike convinced, that some catastrophe was in reserve from the Indians, and seeing no chance of defending ourselves against an odds of more than twenty to one, we concluded, as soon as all should be silent in the camp, to fly. We packed our mules so as to leave none of our effects behind, and kept awake. We remained thus, until near midnight, when we heard a fierce whistle, which we instantly understood to be the signal for an attack on the French camp. But a moment ensued, before we heard the clashing of war clubs, followed by the shrieks and heavy groans of the dying French, mingled with the louder and more horrible yells of these treacherous and blood thirsty savages. A moment afterwards, we heard a party of them making towards us. To convince them that they could not butcher us in our defenceless sleep, we fired upon them. This caused them to retreat. Convinced that we had no time to lose, we mounted our horses, and fled at the extent of our speed. We heard a single gun discharged in the Indian camp, which we supposed the act of an Indian, who had killed the owner.

We took our direction towards a high mountain on the south side of the river, and pushed for it as fast as we thought our horses could endure to be driven. We reached the mountain at day break, and made our way about three miles up a creek, that issued from the mountain. Here we stopped to refresh our horses, and let them feed, and take food ourselves. The passage of the creek was along a kind of crevice of the mountain, and we were strongly convinced that the Indians would not follow upon our trail further than the entrance to the mountain. One of us ascended a high ridge, to survey whatever might be within view. My companion, having passed nearly an hour in the survey, returned to me, and said he saw something on the plain approaching us. I ascended with him to the same place, and plainly perceived something black approaching us.

Having watched it for some time, I thought it a bear. At length it reached a tree on the plain, and ascended it. We were then convinced, that it was no Indian, but a bear searching food. We could see the smokes arising from the Indian town, and had no doubt, that the savages were dancing at the moment around the scalps of the unfortunate Frenchmen, who had fallen the victims of their indolence and rash confidence in these faithless people. All anger for their abuse of me for my timely advice was swallowed up in pity for their fate. But yesterday these people were the merriest of the merry. What were they now? Waiting a few moments, we saw the supposed bear descend the tree, and advance directly to the branch on which we were encamped. We had observed that the water of this branch, almost immediately upon touching the plain, was lost in the arid sand, and gave no other evidence of its existence, than a few green trees. In a moment we saw buttons glitter on this object from the reflected glare of the sun's rays. We were undeceived in regard to our bear, and now supposed it an Indian, decorated with a coat of the unfortunate Frenchmen. We concluded to allow him to approach close enough to satisfy our doubts, before we fired upon him.

We lay still, until he came within fair rifle distance, when to our astonishment, we discovered it to be the French captain! We instantly made ourselves known from our perch. He uttered an exclamation of joy, and fell prostrate on the earth. Fatigue and thirst had brought him to death's door. We raised him, and carried him to our camp. He was wounded in the head and face with many and deep wounds, the swelling of which had given him fever. I happened to have with me some salve, which my father gave me when I left the mines. I dressed his wounds. Having taken food, and sated his thirst, hope returned to him. So great was his change in a few hours, that he was able to move off with us that evening. In his present miserable and forlorn condition, I exercised too much humanity and forbearance to think of adverting to our quarrel of the preceding evening.

Probably estimating my forbearance aright, he himself led to the subject. He observed in a tone apparently of deep compunction, that if he had had the good sense and good temper to have listened to my apprehensions and cautions, both he and his people might have been now gaily riding over the prairies. Oppressed with mixed feelings, I hardly knew what reply to make, and only remarked, that it was too late now to lament over what was unchangeable, and that the will of God had been done.

After a silence of some time, he resumed the conversation, and related all the particulars of the terrible disaster, that had come to his knowledge. His own escape he owed to retaining a pocket pistol, when the rest of their arms were stacked. This he fired at an Indian approaching him, who fell, and thus enabled him to fly; not, however, until he had received a number of severe wounds from their clubs. I had not the heart to hear him relate what became of the rest of his comrades. I could easily divine that the treacherous savages had murdered everyone. Feelings of deep and burning revenge arose in my bosom, and I longed for nothing so much as to meet with these monsters on any thing like terms of equality. About sunset we could distinctly discern the river bottom about five miles distant from us.

When it became dark, we descried three fires close together, which we judged to be those of savages in pursuit of us. Like some white people, the Indians never forgive any persons that they have outraged and injured. We halted, and took counsel, what was to be done. We concluded that my companion and myself should leave our wounded companion to take care of the horses, and go and reconnoitre the camp, in which were these fires, and discover the number of the Indians, and if it was great, to see how we could be most likely to pass them unobserved. When we had arrived close to the fires, we discovered a considerable number of horses tied, and only two men guarding them. We crawled still closer, to be able to discern their exact number and situation.

In this way we arrived within fifty yards of their camp, and could see no one, but the two, anywhere in the distance. We concluded, that all the rest of the company were asleep in some place out of our view. We presumed it would not be long before some of them would awake, it being now ten at night. Our intention was to take aim at them, as they should pass between us and their fire, and drop them both together. We could distinctly hear them speaking about their horses. At length one of them called to the other, in English, to go and wake their relief guards. Words would poorly express my feelings, at hearing these beloved sounds. I sprang from my crouching posture, and ran towards them.

They were just ready to shoot me, when I cried *a friend, a friend!* One of them exclaimed, 'where in God's name did you spring from. You seem to have come out of the earth.' The surprise and joy upon mutual recognition was great on both sides. I gave him a brief sketch of the recent catastrophe of our company, as we followed them to camp. The company was all roused and gathered round us, eagerly listening to the recital of our recent disaster. At hearing my sad story, they expressed the hearty sorrow of good and true men, and joined us in purposes of vengeance against the Indians.

We were now thirty-two in all. We fired twelve guns, a signal which the wounded captain heard and understood, for he immediately joined us. We waited impatiently for the morning. As soon as it was bright dawn, we all formed under a genuine American leader, who could be entirely relied upon. His orders were, that twenty should march in front of the pack horses, and twelve behind. In the evening we encamped within five miles of the Indian village, and made no fires. In the morning of the 31st, we examined all our arms, and twenty-six of us started to attack the village. When we had arrived close to it, we discovered most fortunately, what we considered the dry bed of a creek, though we afterwards discovered it to be the old bed of the river, that had very high banks, and ran within a hundred yards of the village.

In this bed we all formed ourselves securely and at our leisure, and marched quite near to the verge of the village without being discovered. Every man posted himself in readiness to fire. Two of our men were then ordered to show themselves on the top of the bank. They were immediately discovered by the Indians, who considered them, I imagine, a couple of the Frenchmen that they had failed to kill. They raised the yell, and ran towards the two persons, who instantly dropped down under the bank. There must have been at least 200 in pursuit. They were in a moment close on the bank. In order to prevent the escape of the two men, they spread into a kind of circle to surround them. This brought the whole body abreast of us. We allowed them to approach within twenty yards, when we gave them our fire. They commenced a precipitate retreat, we loading and firing as fast as was in our power. They made no pause in their village, but ran off, men, women and children, towards a mountain distant 700 yards from their village.

In less than ten minutes, the village was so completely evacuated, that not a human being was to be found, save one poor old blind and deaf Indian, who sat eating his mush as unconcernedly as if all had been tranquil in the village. We did not molest him.

We appropriated to our own use whatever we found in the village that we judged would be of any service to us. We then set fire to their *wigwams*, and returned to our camp. They were paid a bloody price for their treachery, for 110 of them were slain. At twelve we returned to the village in a body, and retook all the horses of the Frenchmen, that they had killed. We then undertook the sad duty of burying the remains of the unfortunate Frenchmen. A sight more horrible to behold, I have never seen. They were literally cut in pieces, and fragments of their bodies scattered in every direction, round which the monsters had danced, and yelled. We then descended the river about a mile below the village, to the point where it enters the Helay from the north. It affords as much water at this point as the Helay.

In the morning of the 1st of February, we began to ascend Black River. We found it to abound with beavers. It is a most beautiful stream, bounded on each side with high and rich bottoms. We travelled up this stream to the point where it forks in the mountains; that is to say, about 80 miles from its mouth. Here our company divided, a part ascending one fork, and a part the other. The left fork heads due north, and the right fork north east. It was my lot to ascend the latter. It heads in mountains covered with snow, near the head of the left hand fork of the San Francisco.

On the 16th, we all met again at the junction of the forks. The other division found that their fork headed in snow covered mountains, as they supposed near the waters of Red River. They had also met a tribe of Indians, who called themselves *Mokee*. They found them no ways disposed to hostility. From their deportment it would seem as if they had never seen white people before. At the report of a gun they fell prostrate on the ground. They knew no other weapon of war than a sling, and with this they had so much dexterity and power, that they were able to bring down a deer at the distance of 100 yards.

We thence returned down the Helay, which is here about 200 yards wide, with heavily timbered bottoms. We trapped its whole course, from where we met it, to its junction with Red river. The point of junction is inhabited by a tribe of Indians called Umene. Here we encamped for the night. On the morning of the 26th, a great many of these Indians crossed the river to our camp, and brought us dried beans, for which we paid them with red cloth, with which they were delighted beyond measure, tearing it into ribbands, and tying it round their arms and legs; for if the truth must be told, they were as naked as Adam and Eve in their birthday suit. They were the stoutest men, with the finest forms I ever saw, well proportioned, and as straight as an arrow. They contrive, however, to inflict upon their children an artificial deformity. They flatten their heads, by pressing a board upon their tender scalps, which they bind fast by a ligature. This board is so large and light, that I have seen women, when swimming the river with their children, towing them after them by a string, which they held in their mouth. The little things neither suffered nor complained, but floated behind their mothers like ducks.

At twelve we started up Red River, which is between two and three hundred yards wide, a deep, bold stream, and the water at this point entirely clear. The bottoms are a mile in general width, with exceedingly high, barren cliffs. The timber of the bottoms is very heavy, and the grass rank and high. Near the river are many small lakes, which abound in beavers.

March 1st we came among a tribe of Indians, called Cocomarecopper. At sight of us they deserted their *wigwams*, one and all, and fled to the mountains, leaving all their effects at our discretion. Of course we did not meddle with any thing. Their corn was knee high. We took care not to let our horses injure it, but marched as fast as we could from their village, to deprive them of their homes in as little time as possible. About four miles above the town we encamped, and set our traps. About twelve next day it began to rain, and we pitched our tents.

We had scarce kindled our fires, when 100 Indians came to our camp, all painted red in token of amity. They asked fire, and when we had given it, they went about 20 yards from us, and as the rain had been heavy and the air cool, they made a great fire, round which they all huddled. We gave them the bodies of six large fat beavers, which they cooked by digging holes in the ground, at the bottom of which they kindled fires, and on the fires threw the beavers which they covered with dirt. This dainty, thus prepared they greedily devoured, entrails and all. Next morning, fearful that our guns might have experienced inconvenience from the rain, we fired them off to load them afresh. They were amazed and alarmed, to see us make, what they called thunder and lightning. They were still more startled, to see the bullet holes in the tree, at which we had aimed.

We made signs to them, that one ball would pass through the body of two men. Some of our men had brought with them some scalps of the Papawars, the name of the tribe where our French captain lost his company. They informed us that they were at war with that tribe, and begged some of the scalps to dance round. They were given them, and they began to cut their horrid antics about it.

Our traps had taken thirty beavers the last night. We gave them the meat of twenty, with which present they were delighted, their gratitude inducing them to manifest affection to us. They ate and danced all day and most of the night. On the morning of the 3rd, they left us, returning to their camps. We resumed our march, and on the 6th arrived at another village of Indians called Mohawa. When we approached their village, they were exceedingly alarmed. We marched directly through their village, the women and children screaming, and hiding themselves in their huts. We encamped about three miles above the village. We had scarcely made our arrangements for the night, when 100 of these Indians followed us.

The chief was a dark and sulky looking savage, and he made signs that he wanted us to give him a horse. We made as prompt signs of refusal. He replied to this, by pointing first to the river, and then at the furs we had taken, intimating, that the river, with all it contained, belonged to him; and that we ought to pay him for what we had taken, by giving him a horse. When he was again refused, he raised himself erect, with a stern and fierce air, and discharged his arrow into the tree, at the same time raising his hand to his mouth, and making their peculiar yell. Our captain made no other reply, than by raising his gun and shooting the arrow, as it still stuck in the tree, in two. The chief seemed bewildered with this mark of close marksmanship, and started off with his men. We had no small apprehensions of a night attack from these Indians. We erected a hasty fortification with logs and skins, but sufficiently high and thick, to arrest their arrows in case of attack. The night, contrary to our fears, passed without interruption from them.

On the morning of the 7th, the chief returned on horse back, and in the same sulky tone again demanded a horse. The captain bade him be off, in a language and with a tone alike understood by all people. He started off on full gallop, and as he passed one of our horses, that was tied a few yards from the camp, he fired a spear through the animal. He had not the pleasure to exult in his revenge for more than fifty yards, before he fell pierced by four bullets. We could not doubt, that the Indians would attempt to revenge the death of their chief. After due consideration, we saw no better place in which to await their attack, than the one we now occupied. On the rear we were defended by the river, and in front by an open prairie. We made a complete breastwork, and posted spies in the limbs of the tall trees, to descry the Indians, if any approached us, while still at a distance. No Indians approached us through the day, and at night a heavy rain commenced falling. We posted sentinels, and secured our horses under the river bank. We kindled no fires, and we passed the night without annoyance.

But at daybreak, they let fly at us a shower of arrows. Of these we took no notice. Perhaps, thinking us intimidated, they then raised the war whoop, and made a charge upon us. At the distance of 150 yards we gave them a volley of rifle balls. This brought them to a halt, and a moment after to a retreat, more rapid than their advance had been. We sallied out after them, and gave them the second round, which induced all, that were not forever stopped, to fly at the top of their speed. We had killed sixteen of their number. We returned to our camp, packed, and started, having made a determination not to allow any more Indians to enter our camp. This affair happened on the 9th.

We pushed on as rapidly as possible, fearful that these red children of the desert, who appear to inherit an equal hatred of all whites, would follow us, and attack us in the night. With timely warning we had no fear of them by day, but the affair of the destruction of the French company, proved that they might become formidable foes by night. To prevent, as far as might be, such accidents, we raised a fortification round our camp every night, until we considered ourselves out of their reach, which was on the evening of the 12th. This evening we erected no breastwork, placed no other guard than one person to watch our horses, and threw ourselves in careless security round our fires. We had taken very little rest for four nights, and being exceedingly drowsy, we had scarcely laid ourselves down, before we were sound asleep. The Indians had still followed us, too far off to be seen by day, but had probably surveyed our camp each night.

At about 11 o'clock this night, they poured upon us a shower of arrows, by which they killed two men, and wounded two more; and what was most provoking, fled so rapidly that we could not even give them a round. One of the slain was in bed with me. My own hunting shirt had two arrows in it, and my blanket was pinned fast to the ground by arrows. There were sixteen arrows discharged into my bed. We extinguished our fires, and it may easily be imagined, slept no more that night.

In the morning, eighteen of us started in pursuit of them, leaving the rest of the company to keep camp and bury our dead. We soon came upon their trail, and reached them late in the evening. They were encamped, and making their supper from the body of a horse. They got sight of us before we were within shooting distance, and fled. We put spurs to our horses, and overtook them just as they were entering a thicket. Having every advantage, we killed a greater part of them, it being a division of the band that had attacked us. We suspended those that we had killed upon the trees, and left their bodies to dangle in terror to the rest, and as a proof, how we retaliated aggression. We then returned to our company, who had each received sufficient warning not to encamp in the territories of hostile Indians without raising a breast-work round the camp. Red River at this point bears a north course, and affords an abundance of the finest lands. We killed plenty of mountain sheep and deer, though no bears. We continued our march until the 16th, without seeing any Indians.

On that day we came upon a small party, of whom the men fled, leaving a single woman. Seeing herself in our power, she began to beat her breast, and cry *Cowera, Cowera*; from which we gathered, that she belonged to that tribe. We treated her kindly, and travelled on. On the 23rd, we came to a village of the Shuena Indians. As we approached it, they came out and began to fire arrows upon us. We gave them in return a round of rifle balls. In the excitement of an attack, we laughed heartily to see these sons of the desert dodge, and skulk away half bent, as though the heavens were falling upon them. From their manner we inferred, that they were in fact wholly unacquainted with white people, or at least they never before heard the report of a gun.

The whole establishment dispersed to the mountains, and we marched through the village without seeing any inhabitants, except the bodies of those we had killed. We had received more than one lesson of caution, and we moved on with great circumspection. But so much of our time was taken up in defence and attacks, and fortifying our camps, that we had little leisure to trap. In order that our grand object should not be wholly defeated, we divided our men into two companies, the one to trap and the other to keep guard. This expedient at once rendered our trapping very productive. We discovered little change in the face of the country. The course of the river still north, flowing through a rich valley, skirted with high mountains, the summits of which were white with snow.

On the 25th we reached a small stream, emptying into Red River through the east bank, up which we detached three men, each carrying a trap, to discover if beavers abounded in that stream. They were to return the next day, while we were engaged in shoeing our horses. The next day elapsed, but none returned.

We became anxious about their fate; and on the 27th, started to see what had become of them. At mid-day we found their bodies cut in pieces, and spitted before a great fire, after the same fashion which is used in roasting beaver. The Indians who had murdered them, saw us as we came on, and fled to the mountains, so that we had no chance of avenging the death of our unfortunate companions. We gathered the fragments of their bodies together and buried them. With sadness in our hearts, and dejection on our countenances, we returned to our camp, struck our tents, and marched on. The temperature in this region is rather severe, and we were wretchedly clad to encounter the cold.

On the 28th, we reached a point of the river where the mountains shut in so close upon its shores, that we were compelled to climb a mountain, and travel along the acclivity, the river still in sight, and at an immense depth beneath us.—Through this whole distance, which we judged to be, as the river meanders, 100 leagues, we had snow from a foot to eighteen inches deep. The river bluffs on the opposite shore, were never more than a mile from us. It is perhaps, this very long and formidable range of mountains, which has caused, that this country of Red River, has not been more explored, at least by the American people. A march more gloomy and heart-wearing, to people hungry, poorly clad, and mourning the loss of their companions, cannot be imagined. Our horses had picked a little herbage, and had subsisted on the bark of shrubs. Our provisions were running low, and we expected every hour to see our horses entirely give out.

April 10th, we arrived where the river emerges from these horrid mountains, which so cage it up, as to deprive all human beings of the ability to descend to its banks, and make use of its waters. No mortal has the power of describing the pleasure I felt, when I could once more reach the banks of the river.—Our traps, by furnishing us beavers, soon enabled us to renew our stock of provisions. We likewise killed plenty of elk, and dressed their skins for clothing. On the 13th we reached another part of the river, emptying into the main river from the north. Up this we all trapped two days. During this excursion we met a band of hostile Indians, who attacked us with an unavailing discharge of arrows, of whom we killed four.

On the 15th, we returned to the banks of Red River, which is here a clear beautiful stream. We moved very slowly, for our beasts were too lean and worn down, to allow us to do otherwise. On the 16th we met with a large party of the Shoshonees, a tribe of Indians famous for the extent of their wanderings, and for the number of white people they had killed, by pretending friendship to them, until they found them disarmed, or asleep. One of our company could speak their language, from having been a prisoner among them for a year. They were warmly clad with buffalo robes, and they had muskets, which we knew they must have taken from the white people. We demanded of them to give up the firearms, which they refused.

On this we gave them our fire, and they fled to the mountains, leaving their women and children in our power.—We had no disposition to molest them. We learned from these women, that they had recently destroyed a company of French hunters on the head waters of the Platte. We found six of their yet fresh scalps, which so exasperated us, that we hardly refrained from killing the women. We took from them all the beaver skins which they had taken from the slain French, and five of their mules, and added to our provisions their stock of dried buffalo meat. We had killed eight of their men, and we mortified the women excessively, by compelling them to exchange the scalps of the unfortunate Frenchmen for those of their own people.

We resumed our march, and ascended the river to the point where it forked again, neither fork being more than from twenty-five to thirty yards wide. On the 19th, we began to ascend the right hand fork, which pursues a N. E. course. On the 23rd, we arrived at the chief village of the Nabahoes, a tribe that we knew to be friendly to the whites. We enquired of them, if we could cross the Rocky Mountains best at the head of this fork or the other; and they informed us, that the mountains were impassable, except by following the left hand fork. Knowing that they were at war with the Shoshonee, we let them know how many of them we had killed. With this they were delighted, and gave us eight horses, one for each man we had slain. They sent with us, moreover, ten Indians to point out to us the route, in which to cross the mountains.

On the 25th, we started up the left hand fork, and arrived on the 30th, in the country of the Pewee tribe, who are friendly to the Nabahoes. Their chief village is situated within two days' travel of the low gap, at which we were to cross the mountains, at which gap we arrived on the first of May. The crossing was a work, the difficulty of which may be imagined from the nature of the case and the character of the mountains.—The passage occupied six days, during which we had to pass along compact drifts of snow, higher than a man on horseback. The narrow path through these drifts is made by the frequent passing of buffaloes, of which we found many dead bodies in the way. We had to pack cotton-wood bark on the horses for their own eating, and the wood necessary to make fires for our cooking. Nothing is to be seen among these mountains, but bare peaks and perpetual snow. Everyone knows, that these mountains divide between the Atlantic and Pacific Oceans. At the point where we crossed them, they run in a direction a little north of west, and south of east, further than the eye can reach.

On the 7th, we struck the south fork of the Platte, near Long's Peak, and descended it five days. We then struck across the plain to the main Platte, on which we arrived on the 16th. In descending it we found the beavers scarce, for all these rivers had been thoroughly trapped. The river is skirted with only a few small willows, and the country is open prairie, entirely destitute of trees. We saw immense droves of elk, buffaloes, and white bears, which haunt the buffalo range to prey upon those noble animals. We had the merriest sport imaginable, in chasing the buffaloes over these perfectly level plains, and shooting them with the arrows we had taken from the Indians we had killed. I have killed myself, and seen others kill a buffalo, with a single shot of an arrow. The bows are made with ribs of buffaloes, and drive the arrows with prodigious force.

On the 20th, we left this river and started for the Big Horn, a fork of the Yellow Stone, itself a considerable river of the Missouri. We reached the Big Horn on the 31st, and found but few beavers. June 2nd, we struck over towards the main Yellow Stone, and on the 3rd entered the country of the Flat Heads, who were entirely friendly. We purchased some furs of them. They are Indians of exceedingly handsome forms, were it not for the horrid deformity of their heads, which are transversely from ear to ear but a few inches in diameter, and in the other direction monstrous, giving them the appearance of wearing a military cap with all its plumage. This plumage is furnished by their matted tresses of hair, painted and skewered up to a high point. This monstrosity is occasioned by binding two pieces of board on each side of the head of the newborn infant, which is kept secure with bandages, until the child is three years old, at which time the head bones have acquired a firmness to retain their then shape during life.

On the 11th, we reached the Yellow Stone, and ascended it to its head; and thence crossed the ridges of the Rocky Mountains to Clarke's Fork of the Columbia. But all these streams had been so much trapped, as to yield but few beavers. Clarke's Fork is a hundred yards wide, a bold, clear, pleasant stream, remarkable for the number and excellence of its fish, and most beautiful country of fertile land on its shores. We ascended this river to its head, which is in Long's Peak, near the head waters of the Platte. We thence struck our course for the head waters of the Arkansas, on which we arrived July 1st.

Here we met a band of the Grasshopper Indians, who derive their name from gathering grasshoppers, drying them, and pulverising them, with the meal of which they make mush and bread; and this is their chief article of food. They are so little improved, as not even to have furnished themselves with the means of killing buffaloes. At sight of us, these poor two-legged animals, dodged into the high grass like so many partridges.

We marched up this stream, trapping for the few beavers which it afforded. Its banks are scantily timbered, being only skirted with a few willows. On the 5th, we met a war party of the Black Foot Indians, all well mounted. As soon as they saw us, they came fiercely upon us, yelling as though the spirit of darkness had loaned them the voices of all his tenants. We dismounted, and as soon as they were within shooting distance, we gave them our fire, which they promptly returned. The contest was fierce for something more than 20 minutes, a part of the time not more than 50 yards apart. They then retreated, and we mounted our horses, and gave them chase, though unavailingly, for their horses were as fleet as the wind, compared with ours.

We soon desisted from so useless a pursuit, and returned to the battle ground. We found sixteen Blackfeet dead, and with infinite anguish, counted four of our own companions weltering in their blood. We buried them with sorrowful hearts, and eyes full of tears. Ah! Among those who live at home, surrounded by numerous relations and friends, in the midst of repose, plenty and security, when one of the number droops, and dies with sickness or age, his removal leaves a chasm that is not filled for years. Think how we must have mourned these brave men, who had shared so many dangers, and on whose courage and aid we had every day relied for protection.

Here on these remote plains, far from their friends, they had fallen by the bloody arrow or spear of these red, barbarous Ishmaelites of the desert, but neither unwept nor unrevenged. Having performed the sad task of depositing the bodies of these once warm hearted friends in the clay, we ascended to the head of this river, and crossed the mountain that separates its waters from those of the Rio del Norte, which river we struck on the 20th. We began to descend it, and on the 23rd met a band of the Nabahoes, who accompanied us quite to their chief village. It will be seen, that all these streams upon which we have been trapping, rise from sources which interlock with each other, and the same range of peaks at very short distances from each other. These form the heads of Red River of the east, and the Colorado of the west, Rio del Norte, Arkansas, Platte, Yellow Stone, Missouri and Columbia. The village of these Indians is distant 50 miles from the Rio del Norte. We remained at it two days, and rested our horses, and refreshed ourselves.

This tribe some years since had been at war with the Spanish, during which they plundered them of great numbers of horses, mules and cattle, which caused that they had now large stocks of these animals, together with flocks of sheep. They raise a great abundance of grain, and manufacture their wool much better than the Spanish. On the first of August we arrived at Santa Fé, with a fine amount of furs. Here disaster awaited us. The governor, on the pretext that we had trapped without a license from him, robbed us of all our furs. We were excessively provoked, and had it not been from a sense of duty to our own beloved country, we would have redressed our wrongs, and retaken our furs with our own arms.

Here I remained until the 18th, disposing of a part of my goods, and reserving the remainder for a trip which I contemplated to the province of Sonora. I had the pleasure once more of receiving the affectionate greeting of Jacova, who gave me the most earnest counsels to quit this dangerous and rambling way of life, and settle myself down in a house of my own. I thanked her for her kindness and good counsel, and promised to follow it, after rambling another year in the wilderness.—Thence I went to the mines, where I had the inexpressible satisfaction again to embrace my dear father, whom I found in perfect health, and making money rapidly. I remained there three days, and, accompanied with one servant, arrived in Hanas on the first of September. This is a small town situated in the province of Biscay, between the province of Sonora and New Mexico, in a direction S. W. from the copper mines.

The country is generally of that character, denominated in Kentucky, barren. The soil is level and black. These people raise a great quantity of stock, such as horses, cows, sheep and goats. Their farming implements are clumsy and indifferent. They use oxen entirely in their agriculture. Their ploughs are a straight piece of timber, five feet long and eight inches thick, mortised for two other pieces of timber, one to be fitted to the beam, by which the oxen draw, and another to the handle, by which the man holds the plough. The point that divides the soil, is of wood, and hewed sloping to such a point, that a hollow piece of iron is fastened on it at the end. This is one inch thick, and three inches broad at top, and slopes also to a point.

Their hoes, axes and other tools are equally indifferent; and they are precisely in such a predicament, as might be expected of a people who have no saw mills, no labour saving machinery, and do every thing by dint of hard labour, and are withal very indolent and unenterprising.

I amused myself at times with an old man, who daily fell in my way, who was at once rich and to the last degree a miser; and yet devotedly attached to the priests, who were alone able to get a little money out of him. He often spoke to me about the unsafeness of my religion. Instead of meeting his remarks with an argument, I generally affronted him at once, and then diverted myself with his ways of showing his anger. I told him that his priest treated him as the Spanish hostlers do their horses. He asked me to explain the comparison. I observed, 'you know how the hostler in the first place throws his lasso over the mule's neck. That secures the body of the beast. Next the animal is blindfolded. That hinders his seeing where he is led. Next step he binds the saddle safe and fast. Then the holy father rigs his heels with spurs. Next come spur and lash, and the animal is now restive to no purpose. There is no shaking off the rider. On he goes, till the animal under him dies, and both go to hell together!'

At this he flew into such a violent rage, as to run at me with his knife. I dodged out of his way, and appeased him by convincing him that I was in jest. The rich, in their way of living, unite singular contrasts of magnificence and meanness. For instance, they have few of the useful articles of our dining and tea sets, but a great deal of massive silver plate, and each guest a silver fork and spoon. The dining room is contiguous to the kitchen. A window is thrown open, and the cook hands a large dish through the window to a servant, who bears it to the table. The entertainer helps himself first, and passes the dish round to all the guests. Then another and another is brought on, often to the number of sixteen.

All are savoured so strong with garlic and red pepper, that an American at first cannot eat them. The meat is boiled to such a consistency that a spoon manages it better than a knife. At the close of the dinner they bring in wine and cigars, and they sit and smoke and drink wine until drowsiness steals upon them, and they go to bed for their *siesta*. They sleep until three in the afternoon, at which time the church bell tolls. They rise, take a cup of chocolate, and handle the wine freely. This short affair over, they return and sit down on the shaded side of the house, and chatter like so many geese till night, when they divide, a part to mass, and a part to the card table, where I have seen the poor, betting their shirts, hats and shoes. The village contains 700 souls.

On the 6th, I departed from this town, travelling a west course through a most beautiful country, the plains of which were covered with domestic animals running wild. On the 8th I arrived at the foot of the mountain, that divides the province of Sonora from Biscay. I slept at a country seat, where they were making whiskey of a kind of plantain, of which I have spoken before, which they called *mascal* (maguey). Here were assembled great numbers of Spaniards and Indians. They were soon drunk, and as a matter of course, fighting with knives and clubs. In the morning, two Spaniards and one Indian were found dead. Late in the morning, a file of soldiers arrived, and took the suspected murderers to prison.

In the morning I commenced climbing the mountain before me, and in the evening arrived at a small town in Sonora, called Barbisca; situated on the bank of a most beautiful little stream, called Iago, which discharges itself into the Pacific ocean, near the harbour of Ymus. Its banks are not much timbered, nor is the soil uncommonly good. The morning of the 9th was a great religious festival, or famous Saint's day, which collected a vast crowd of people. After breakfast and mass, the image of the virgin Mary was paraded round the public square in solemn procession, during which there was a constant crash of cannon and small arms. Then an old priest headed a procession, bearing the image of Christ, nailed to a cross.

After these images were returned to their church, they brought into a square enclosure, strongly fenced for that purpose, a wild bull, which they threw down, tied and sharpened its horns. The tops of the houses were all covered with people to see the spectacle that was performing. The bull was covered with red cloth, and two men entered the enclosure, each holding in the right hand a bundle of sky rockets, and in the left a red handkerchief. The rockets were lashed to a stick a foot long, in the end of which was a small nail, a half an inch long, with a beard at the end, like that of a fish hook. They then untied the fierce animal. No sooner was he on his feet, than he sprang at one of his assailants, who avoided his attack, by dextrously slipping aside, and as the animal darted by him, stuck in his neck two small rockets, one on each side.

The other assailant then gave a sharp whistle to draw the infuriated animal upon him. The bull snorted and dashed at him. He dodged the animal in the same manner, as the other had done, and left sticking in his forehead, as he passed, a garland of artificial flowers, made of paper, beautifully cut and painted, and large enough to cover his whole forehead. In this way they kept alternately driving him this way and that, sticking rockets in him as he dashed by them, until he was covered with eight or ten, clinging to his neck and shoulders. They then touched the crackers with a lighted match. Words would not paint the bull's expressions of rage and terror, as he bounded round the enclosure, covered with fire, and the rockets every moment discharging like fire arms.

After this, a man entered with a small sword. The bull bellowed and darted at him. As the bull dropped his head to toss him, he set his feet upon the horns, and in a twinkling, thrust his sword between the shoulder blades, so as to touch the spinal marrow. The animal dropped as dead as a stone. The drum and fife then struck up, as a signal for the horsemen to come and carry off the dead animal, and bring in a fresh one. All this was conducted with incredible dispatch. In this way seven bulls were successively tortured to death, by footmen.

After this, four men entered on horseback, equipped with spears in the shape of a trowel, and a handle four feet long. With this spear in the one hand, and a noose in the other, they galloped round the bull. The bull immediately made at the horsemen passing him, who moved just at such a pace, as not to allow the bull to toss the horse. The horseman then couched his spear backwards, so as to lay it on the bull's neck. The bull instantly reared and tossed, and in the act forced the spear between his fore shoulders, so as to hit the spinal marrow. If the spear is laid rightly, and the animal makes his accustomed motions, he drops instantly dead. But to do this requires infinite dexterity and fearlessness. If the man be clumsy, or of weak-nerves, he is apt to fail in couching the spear right, in which case, as a matter of course, the horse is gored, and it is ten to one that the man is slain. In this way fourteen bulls were killed, and with them, five horses and one man, during this festival. At night commenced gambling and card playing, and both as fiercely pursued as the bull fighting. This great feast lasted three days, during which, as the people were in a very purchasable humour, I sold a number of hundred dollar's worth of my goods.

On the morning of the 12th, I left this place, and in the evening arrived at a small town called Vassarac, and remained there one day. The country in the vicinity is well timbered and very hilly. The woods are full of wild cattle and horses. On the 13th, I travelled through a fine rich country, abounding with cattle, and arrived in the evening at a town called Tepac, situated on a small creek, near a mountain, in which there is a gold mine worked by the Iago Indians, a nation formerly under the protection of an old priest. He attempted to practice some new imposition upon them, and they killed him some years ago. On this the Spaniards made war upon them, and the conflict was continued some years. They lost the best and bravest of their men, and the remnant were obliged to submit to such terms as the Spaniards saw fit to impose. They were either condemned to the mines, or to raise food for those who wrought them.

I remained in this town three days, and purchased gold in bars and lumps of the Indians, at the rate of ten dollars per ounce. The diggings seldom exceed twenty feet in depth. Most of the gold is found on the surface after hard rains. Their mode of extracting the gold from the earth with which it is mixed, or the stone in which it is imbedded, is this. The stone is pulverised or ground, still keeping the matter wet. It is carefully mixed with mercury, and kneaded with the hands, until the water is separated from the mass, and the mercury is perfectly incorporated with it. This process is repeated, until the water runs off perfectly clear. They then grind or triturate the mass anew until all the particles of earthy matter are washed away.

The remaining matter is amalgam, of the colour of silver, and the consistency of mush. They then put it into a wet deer skin, and strain the mercury by pressure through the pores of the skin. The gold is left, still retaining enough mercury to give it the colour of silver. The coarse way of managing it afterwards, is to put it in the fire, and evaporate all the mercury from it, and it is then pure virgin gold. There is a more artificial way of managing it, by which the mercury is saved.

This province would be among the richest of the Mexican country, if it were inhabited by an enlightened, enterprising and industrious people. Nothing can exceed the indolence of the actual inhabitants. The only point, in which I ever saw them display any activity, is in throwing the lasso, and in horsemanship. In this I judge, they surpass all other people. Their great business and common pursuit, is in noosing and taming wild horses and cattle.

On the 15th, I left this place and travelled through a country well timbered and watered, though the land is too broken to be cultivated, and in the evening arrived in a town called Varguacha. This is a place miserably poor, the people being both badly fed and clothed. But their indolence alone is in fault. The land in the immediate vicinity of the town is good, and the woods teem with wild cattle. But they are too lazy to provide more meat than will serve them from day to day. On the 17th I continued my course through a beautiful country, thinly settled by civilized Indians, who raise sugar cane and abundance of stock. They are obviously more enterprising and industrious than the Spaniards. Approaching the shore of the great Pacific, I found the country more level and better settled. Some rich and noble sugar farms lay in my view.

On the 22nd I arrived in Patoka, which is a considerable town, and the capital of this province. It is two day's travel hence to Ymus. The people here seemed to me more enlightened, and to have a higher air of civilization than any I had seen in the whole country. It probably results from the intercourse they have with foreigners, from their vicinity to the Pacific. Most of them are dressed in the stile of the American people. Their houses are much better furnished, and the farmers are supplied with superior farming utensils, compared with any thing I saw in the interior. The chief manufactures are soap and sugar, the latter of an inferior quality, I imagine, in consequence of the clumsy mode of manufacturing it. From the port of Ymus they also export considerable quantities of tallow and hides, for which the farmers are repaid in merchandize at an enormous advance. A great many horses and mules are driven from the interior to this port. Many also are taken to the American states. The price of mules in this province is from three to four dollars a head.

I remained here until I had disposed of all my goods. On the 26th, I left this town, and travelled on to Port Ymus, at which I arrived on the 28th, and first saw the waters of the vast Pacific. I spent a day here on board an American ship, the master of which was surprised at the account I gave of myself, and would hardly believe that I had travelled to this place from the United States. I was equally amazed at hearing him relate the disasters which had befallen him at sea. On the 29th, I left this port, and travelled a N. W. course, through a country full of inhabitants, and abounding in every species of fruit. Snow never falls, although the general temperature is not so warm but that woollen garments may be worn. To add to its advantages, it is very healthy. On the 7th of October, I arrived at a town called Oposard. The population amounts to about 8000 souls.

I here became acquainted with one of my own countrymen, married to a Spanish woman. He informed me, that he had been in this country thirty years, eight of which he had spent in prison. The sufferings he endured from the Spaniards were incredible; and I internally shuddered, as he related, lest I, in travelling through the country might fall into similar misfortunes. As some palliation of their cruelty, he observed, that he was made prisoner at the period when the revolution was just commencing in that country. At that time the Inquisition was still in force, and committed many a poor mortal to the flames, for his alleged heresy. He assured me, that he should have met the same fate, had he not become a member of their church. He afterwards married a lady, who had gained his affections by being kind to him in prison.

I remained with this man two days, and on the third resumed my journey, travelling an easterly course, and part of the time over a very rough country. I met no inhabitants, but Indians, who were uniformly friendly. On the 10th, I arrived at the mines of Carrocha, which were in the province of Chihuahua, situated between two mountains, and considered the richest silver mines in New Mexico. There are about 800 miners working this mine, and they have advanced under ground at least half a mile. On the 12th, I started for the capital, and reached it on the 16th, passing over great tracts of good and bad land, all untilled, and most of it an uninhabited wilderness. This city is the next largest in New Mexico. It is the largest and handsomest town I had ever seen, though the buildings are not so neat and well arranged as in our country. The roofs are flat, the walls well painted, and the streets kept very clean. Here they smelt and manufacture copper and silver, and several other metals. They have also a mint. The terms of their currency are very different from ours. They count eight *rials*, or sixteen four pence half pennies, to the dollar. Their merchandize is packed from Ymus, or Mexico.

I have heard much talk about the splendid churches in this city. It is for others, who think much of such immense buildings, wrung from the labours of the poor, to describe them. For my part, having said it is a large and clean town, I present a result of their institutions and manners, which I considered the more important sort of information. During a stay of only three days here, ten dead bodies were brought into town, of persons who had been murdered in the night. Part of the number were supposed to have been killed on account of having been known to carry a great deal of money with them, and part to have had a quarrel about some abandoned women. This last is a most common occasion of night murders, the people being still more addicted to jealousy, and under still less restraints of law, than in old Spain, in the cities of which, assassinations from this cause are notoriously frequent.

I asked my informant touching these matters, if there was no police in the city? He answered, that the forms of the law were complete, and that they had a numerous guard, and that it was quite as likely they committed the murders themselves, as not. I came to the same conclusion, for in a small and regular city like this, it was impossible that so many guards, parading the streets by night, should not be aware of the commission of such deeds, and acquainted with the perpetrators. No inquest of any sort was held over the bodies. They were, however, paraded through the streets to beg money to pay the priests for performing funeral rites at their burial. This excited in me still more disgust, than the murders. I expressed myself in consequence, with so much freedom, in regard to this sort of miserable imposition, as to give great offence to my host, who, like most of the people, was rigidly devoted to the religion of the church.

On the evening of 16th, I left this city, and travelled through a fine country, thickly inhabited by shepherds, who live in small towns, and possess a vast abundance of stock. It is well watered, but thinly timbered. The most magnificent part of the spectacle is presented in the lofty snow covered mountains, that rise far in the distance, and have their summits lost in the clouds, glistening in indescribable brilliance in the rays of the rising and setting sun.

The road at this time was deemed to be full of robbers, and very dangerous. I was so fortunate as to meet with none. On the 18th, I arrived at a small town, called San Bueneventura, which is surrounded with a wall. In fact, most of the considerable villages are walled. They are called in Spanish, *presidio*, the English of which is, a garrison. In the forenoon, I crossed a small river called Rio Grande, and travelled down this stream all day, the banks of which were thickly settled, and in high cultivation, with wheat, corn and barley. On the 22nd, I arrived at a village called Casas Grandes, or the Great Houses.

On the 23rd, I pursued an east course towards Passo del Norte, situated on the banks of the Rio del Norte. I travelled over a very rough country with some high mountains, inhabited by a wandering tribe of the Apache Indians, that live by seizing their opportunities for robbery and murder among the Spaniards, riding off upon the stolen horses, to the obscure and almost inaccessible fastnesses of their mountains, where they subsist upon the stolen horseflesh.

I know not, whether to call the Passo del Norte, a settlement or a town. It is in fact a kind of continued village, extending eight miles on the river. Fronting this large group of houses, is a nursery of the fruit trees, of almost all countries and climes. It has a length of eight miles and a breadth of nearly three. I was struck with the magnificent vineyards of this place, from which are made great quantities of delicious wine. The wheat fields were equally beautiful, and the wheat of a kind I never saw before, the stalks generally yielding two heads each. The land is exceedingly rich, and its fertility increased by irrigation.

On the 28th, I started for the Copper mines, wrought by my father. This day my course led me up the del Norte, the bottoms of which are exceedingly rich. At a very short distance from the Passo, I began to come in contact with grey bears, and other wild animals. At a very little distance on either side are high and ragged mountains, entirely sterile of all vegetation. I had no encounter with the bears, save in one instance. A bear exceedingly hungry, as I suppose, came upon my horses as I was resting them at mid-day, and made at one of them. I repaid him for his impudence by shooting him through the brain. I made a most delicious dinner of the choice parts of his flesh. My servant would not touch it, his repugnance being shared by great numbers in his condition. It is founded on the notion, that the bear is a sort of degenerated man, and especially, that the entrails are exactly like those of human beings.

On the 30th, I struck off from the del Norte, and took my course for the Copper mines directly over the mountains, among which we toiled onward, subsisting by what we packed with us, or the product of the rifle, until the 11th of November, when I had once more the satisfaction of embracing my father at the Copper mines. He was in perfect health, and delighted to see me again. He urged me so earnestly to remain with him, though a stationary life was not exactly to my taste, that I consented from a sense of filial duty, and to avoid importunity. I remained here until the first of December, amusing myself sometimes by hunting, and sometimes by working in the gold mine, an employment in which I took much pleasure.

In a hunting excursion with a companion who was an American,

101

he one morning saw fit to start out of bed, and commence his hunt while I was yet asleep in bed. He had scarcely advanced a league, before he killed a deer on the top of a high ridge. He was so inadvertent, as to commence skinning the animal, before he had reloaded his rifle. Thus engaged, he did not perceive a bear with her cubs, which had advanced within a few feet of him. As soon as he saw his approaching companion, without coveting any farther acquaintance, he left deer and rifle, and ran for his life. He stopped not, until he arrived at the mines. The bear fell to work for a meal upon the deer, and did not pursue him. We immediately started back to have the sport of hunting this animal. As we approached the ridge, where he had killed the deer, we discovered the bear descending the ridge towards us. We each of us chose a position, and his was behind a tree, which he could mount, in case he wounded, without killing her.

This most ferocious and terrible animal, the grizzly or grey bear, does not climb at all. I chose my place opposite him, behind a large rock, which happened to be near a precipice, that I had not observed. Our agreement was to wait until she came within 30 yards, and then he was to give her the first fire. He fired, but the powder being damp, his gun made long fire, whence it happened that he shot her too low, the ball passing through the belly, and not a mortal part. She made at him in terrible rage. He sprang up his tree, the bear close at his heels. She commenced biting and scratching the tree, making, as a Kentuckian would phrase it, *the lint fly*. But finding that she could not bite the tree down, and being in an agony of pain, she turned the course of her attack, and came growling and tearing up the bushes before her, towards me.

My companion bade me lie still, and my own purpose was to wait until I could get a close fire. So I waited until the horrible animal was within six feet of me. I took true aim at her head. My gun flashed in the pan. She gave one growl and sprang at me with her mouth open. At two strides I leapt down the unperceived precipice. My jaw bone was split on a sharp rock, on which my chin struck at the bottom. Here I lay senseless. When I regained recollection, I found my companion had bled me with the point of his butcher knife, and was sitting beside me with his hat full of water, bathing my head and face. It was perhaps an hour, before I gained full recollection, so as to be able to walk. My companion had cut a considerable orifice in my arm with his knife, which I deemed rather supererogation; for I judged, that I had bled sufficiently at the chin.

When I had come entirely to myself, my companion proposed that we should finish the campaign with the bear. I, for my part, was satisfied with what had already been done, and proposed to retreat. He was importunate, however, and I consented. We ascended the ridge to where he had seen the bear lie down in the bushes. We fixed our guns so that we thought ourselves sure of their fire. We then climbed two trees, near where the bear was, and made a noise, that brought her out of her lair, and caused her to spring fiercely towards our trees. We fired together, and killed her dead. We then took after the cubs. They were three in number. My companion soon overtook them. They were of the size of the largest raccoons. These imps of the devil turned upon him and made fight. I was in too much pain and weakness to assist him. They put him to all he could do to clear himself of them. He at length got away from them, leaving them masters of the field, and having acquired no more laurels than I, from my combat with my buffalo calf. His legs were deeply bit and scratched, and what was worse, such was the character of the affair, he only got ridicule for his assault of the cubs. I was several weeks in recovering, during which time, I ate neither meat nor bread, being able to swallow nothing but liquids.

The country abounds with these fierce and terrible animals, to a degree, that in some districts they are truly formidable. They get into the cornfields. The owners hear the noise, which they make among the corn, and supposing it occasioned by cows and horses that have broken into the fields, they rise from their beds, and go to drive them out, when instead of finding retreating domestic animals, they are assailed by the grizzly bear. I have been acquainted with several fatal cases of that sort. One of them was a case, that intimately concerned me. Iago, my servant, went out with a man to get a load of wood.

A bear came upon this man and killed him and his ass in the team. A slight flight of snow had fallen. Some Spaniards, who had witnessed the miserable fate of their companion, begged some of us to go and aid them in killing the bear. Four of us joined them. We trailed the bear to its den, which was a crevice in the bluff. We came to the mouth and fired a gun. The animal, confident in his fierceness, came out, and we instantly killed it. This occurred in New Mexico.

This stationary and unruffled sort of life had become unendurable, and with fifteen Americans, we arranged a trapping expedition on the Pacos. My father viewed my rambling propensities with stern displeasure. He had taken in a Spanish superintendent, who acted as clerk. This person had lived in the United States from the age of 18 to 30, and spoke English, French and Spanish. This man arranged the calculations, and kept the accounts of my father's concerns, and had always acted with intelligence and fidelity. The concern was on the whole prosperous; and although I felt deep sorrow to leave my father against his wishes, I had at least the satisfaction to know, that I was of no other use to him, than giving him the pleasure of my society.

On the 7th, our company arrived on the del Norte, and crossed it in the evening to the eastern shore. On the evening of the 8th, we struck the Pacos about twenty miles above its junction with the del Norte. This day's travel was through a wild and precipitous country, inhabited by no human being. We killed plenty of bears and deer, and caught some beavers. On the 9th, we began to ascend the river through a rich and delightful plain, on which are to be seen abundance of deserted sheep folds, and horse pens, where the Spanish *vachers* once kept their stock. The constant incursions of the Indians compelled this peaceful people to desert these fair plains. Their deserted cottages inspired a melancholy feeling. This river runs from N. E. to S. W. and is a clear, beautiful stream, 20 yards wide, with high and dry bottoms of a black and rich soil. The mountains run almost parallel to the river, and at the distance of eight or ten miles. They are thickly covered with noble pine forests, in which aspen trees are intermixed. From their foot gush out many beautiful clear springs. On the whole, this is one of the loveliest regions for farmers that I have ever seen, though no permanent settlements could be made there, until the murderous Indians, who live in the mountains, should be subdued.

We advanced slowly onward, until the 15th, without meeting any Indians. At daybreak of this day, our sentinels apprised us, that savages were at hand. We had just time to take shelter behind the trees, when they began to let their arrows fly at us. We returned them the compliment with balls, and at the first shot a number of them fell. They remained firm and continued to pour in their arrows from every side. We began to find it exceedingly difficult to dodge them, though we gave them some rounds before any one of our men was struck. At length one man was pierced, and they rushed forward to scalp him. I darted from behind my tree to prevent them. I was assailed by a perfect shower of arrows, which I dodged for a moment, and was then struck down by an arrow in the hip. Here I should have been instantly killed, had not my companions made a joint fire at the Indians, who were rushing upon me, by which a number of them were laid dead. But the agony of my pain was insupportable, for the arrow was still

MR. PATTIE WOUNDED BY AN INDIAN ARROW

fast in my hip.

A momentary cessation of their arrows enabled me to draw out the arrow from my hip, and to commence re-loading my gun. I had partly accomplished this, when I received another arrow under my right breast, between the bone and the flesh. This gave me less pain than the other shot, and finding I could not by any effort extract the arrow, I snapped it off, and finished loading my gun. The Indian nearest me fell dead, and I hobbled off, glad to be once more sheltered by a tree. My companions were not slow in making their rifles crack, and in raising mutual cheers of encouragement. The Indians were vastly our superiors in numbers, and we found it convenient to slip under the river bank. We were now completely sheltered from their arrows. After we had gained this security, they stood but a few shots more, before they fled, leaving their dead and wounded at our mercy. Truth is, we were too much exasperated to show mercy, and we cut off the heads of all, indiscriminately.

Our loss was one killed, and two wounded, another beside myself though neither of us dangerously. The Indians had 28 killed. Luckily our horses were on an island in the river, or we should have lost every one of them. Our only loss of property was a few blankets, which they took, as they fled by our camp. During the 20 minutes that the contest lasted, I had a fragment of an arrow fast in my breast, and the spike of the other in my hip. I suffered, it may be imagined, excruciating pain, and still severer pain during the operation of extraction. This operation, one of my companions undertook. He was some minutes in effecting it. The spike could not be entirely extracted from my hip, for being of flint, it had shivered against the bone.

The Indians that attacked us, were a tribe of the Muscallaros, a very warlike people, although they have no other arms except bows and arrows, which are, however, the most powerful weapons of the kind. They are made of an elastic and flexible wood, backed with the sinews of a buffalo or elk. Their arrows are made of a species of reed grass, and are very light, though easily broken. In the end is stuck a hard piece of wood, which is pointed by a spike of flint an inch in length, and a quarter of an inch in width, and ground to the sharpest point. The men, though not tall, are admirably formed, with fine features and a bright complexion inclining to yellow. Their dress is a buckskin belt about the loins, with a shirt and *moccasins* to match. Their long black hair hangs in imbraided masses over their shoulders, in some cases almost extending to the heels. They make a most formidable appearance, when completely painted, and prepared for battle.

On the 16th, having made our arrangements for departure, I applied my father's admirable salve to my two severe wounds, and to my companion's slight wound in the arm, and we both felt able to join our companions in their march. We travelled all this day and the following night a west course, and the following day, without stopping longer than was necessary to take a little food. After this we stopped and rested ourselves and horses all night. I need not attempt to describe the bitter anguish I endured, during this long and uninterrupted ride. It will be only necessary to conceive my situation to form a right conception of it. Our grand object had been to avoid another contest with the Muscallaros. In the evening we fell in with a party of the Nabahoes, who were now out on an expedition against the Muscallaros, who had recently killed one of their people, and against whom they had sworn immediate revenge. We showed the manifest proof of the chastisement they had received from us.

Never had I seen such frantic leaps and gestures of joy. The screams and yells of exultation were such as cannot be imagined. It seemed as though a whole bedlam had broke loose. When we told them that we had lost but one man, their screams became more frantic still. Their medicine man was then called, and he produced an emollient poultice, the materials of which I did not know but the effect was that the anguish of our wounds was at once assuaged. By the application of this same remedy, my wounds were quite healed in a fortnight.

The scalps, which some of our number had taken from the Muscallaros, were soon erected on a pole by the Nabahoes. They immediately commenced the fiercest dancing and singing I had yet seen, which continued without interruption three days and nights. During all this time, we endured a sort of worship from them, particularly the women. They were constantly presenting us with their favourite dishes, served in different ways, with dried berries and sweet vegetables, some of which, to people in our condition, were really agreeable.

In size and complexion these people resemble the Muscallaros, and their bows and arrows are similar; though some of the latter have fire arms, and their dress is much superior.—Part of their dress is of the same kind with that of the former, though the skins are dressed in a more workmanlike manner, and they have plenty of blankets of their own manufacturing, and constituting a much better article than that produced by the Spaniards. They dye the wool of different and bright colours, and stripe them with very neat figures. The women are much handsomer, and have lighter complexions than the men. They are rather small in stature, and modest and reserved in their behaviour. Their dress is chiefly composed of skins made up with no small share of taste; and showily corded at the bottom, forming a kind of belt of beads and porcupine quills.—They are altogether the handsomest women I have seen among the red people, and not inferior in appearance to many Spanish women. Their deportment to our people, was a mixture of kindness and respect.

On the 21st, we started back to the river, accompanied by the whole party of Nabahoes, who assured us that they would guard us during the remainder of our hunt. We returned to the river through a beautiful and level country, most of it well timbered and watered. On our return we killed several bears, the talons of which the Indians took for necklaces. On the 26th, we arrived at our battleground. The view of the bodies of the slain, all torn in pieces by wild beasts, inexpressibly disgusting to us, was equally a spectacle of pleasure to our red friends. We pointed out the grave of our companion. They all walked in solemn procession round it, singing their funeral songs. As they left it, everyone left a present on the grave; some an arrow, others meat, *moccasins*, tobacco, war-feathers, and the like, all articles of value to them. These simple people believe that the spirit of the deceased will have immediate use for them in the life to come.

Viewing their offerings in this light, we could not but be affected with these testimonies of kind feeling to a dead stranger. They then gathered up the remains of their slaughtered enemies, threw them in a heap, and cut a great quantity of wood, which they piled over the remains. They then set fire to the wood. We struck our tents, marched about five miles up the river, set our traps, and encamped for the night. But the Nabahoes danced and yelled through the night to so much effect, as to keep all the beavers shut up in their houses, for, having been recently trapped, they were exceedingly cautious.

On the morning of the 27th, we informed them why we had taken no beavers, and during the following night they were perfectly quiet. We marched onward slowly, trapping as we went, until we reached the Spanish settlements on this river. On New Year's eve, January 1st, 1827, the Spaniards of the place gave a *fandango*, or Spanish ball. All our company were invited to it, and went. We appeared before the *alcalde*, clad not unlike our Indian friends; that is to say, we were dressed in deer skin, with leggins, *moccasins* and hunting shirts, all of this article, with the addition of the customary Indian article of dress around the loins, and this was of red cloth, not an article of which had been washed since we left the Copper Mines.

It may be imagined that we did not cut a particular dandy-like figure, among people, many of whom were rich, and would be considered well dressed any where. Notwithstanding this, it is a strong proof of their politeness, that we were civilly treated by the ladies, and had the pleasure of dancing with the handsomest and richest of them. When the ball broke up, it seemed to be expected of us, that we should each escort a lady home, in whose company we passed the night, and we none of us brought charges of severity against our fair companions.

The *fandango* room was about forty by eighteen or twenty feet, with a brick floor raised four or five feet above the earth. That part of the room in which the ladies sat, was carpeted with carpeting on the benches, for them to sit on. Simple benches were provided for the accommodation of the gentlemen. Four men sang to the music of a violin and guitar. All that chose to dance stood up on the floor, and at the striking up of a certain note of the music, they all commenced clapping their hands. The ladies then advanced, one by one, and stood facing their partners. The dance then changed to a waltz, each man taking his lady rather unceremoniously, and they began to whirl round, keeping true, however, to the music, and increasing the swiftness of their whirling. Many of the movements and figures seemed very easy, though we found they required practise, for we must certainly have made a most laughable appearance in their eyes, in attempting to practise them. Be that as it may, we cut capers with the nimblest, and what we could not say, we managed by squeezes of the hand, and little signs of that sort, and passed the time to a charm.

The village, in which was this ball, is called Perdido, or the lost town, probably from some circumstances in its history. It contains about 500 souls and one church. The bishop was present at this ball, and not only bestowed his worshipful countenance, but *danced before the Lord, like David, with all his might.* The more general custom of the ladies, as far as I observed, is to sit cross legged on the floor like a tailor. They are considerably addicted to the industry of spinning, but the mode has no resemblance to the spinning of our country. For a wheel, they have a straight stick about a foot long, rounded like the head of a spool. In the middle of the stick is a hole, through which the stick is fastened. Their mode of spinning with this very simple instrument reminded me strongly of the sport of my young days, spinning a top, for they give this spinning affair a twirl, and let it run on until it has lost its communicated motion to impart it anew. This shift for a spinning wheel they call *necataro*. They manufacture neither cotton nor wool into cloth, and depend altogether on foreign trade for their clothing. The greatest part of this supply comes over land from the United States.

On the 2nd, we started for San Tepec, through a country generally barren, though abounding in water. We saw plenty of bears, deer and antelope. Some of the first we killed, because we needed their flesh, and others we killed for the same reason that we were often obliged to kill Indians, that is, to mend their rude manners, in fiercely making at us, and to show them that we were not Spaniards, to give them the high sport of seeing us run. We arrived in the above named town on the 5th, and sold our furs. Here I met again some of the companions who came with me in the first instance from the United States. I enquired about others, whom I held in kind remembrance. Some had died by lingering diseases, and others by the fatal ball or arrow, so that out of 116 men, who came from the United States in 1824, there were not more than sixteen alive.

Most of the fallen were as true men, and as brave as ever poised a rifle, and yet in these remote and foreign deserts found not even the benefit of a grave, but left their bodies to be torn by the wild beasts, or mangled by the Indians. When I heard the sad roll of the dead called over, and thought how often I had been in equal danger, I felt grateful to my Almighty Benefactor, that I was alive and in health. A strong perception of the danger of such courses as mine, as shown by the death of these men, came over my mind, and I made a kind of resolution, that I would return to my home, and never venture into the woods again. Among the number of my fallen companions, I ought not to forget the original leader of our company, Mr. Pratte, who died in his prime, of a lingering disease, in this place.

On the 10th, I commenced descending the Del Norte for the Copper Mines, in hopes once more to have the pleasure of embracing my father, and relate to him what I had suffered in body and mind, for neglecting to follow his wise and fatherly counsel. I now travelled slowly and by myself, and on the 12th, arrived at the house of my old friend the governor, who met me at his door, and gave me such an embrace, as to start the blood from my scarcely healed wound. I did not perceive at the moment, that his embrace had produced this effect, and entered the house, where I met Jacova, who received me with a partial embrace, and a manner of constrained politeness. She then sat down by me on the sofa, and began asking me many questions about my adventure since we had parted, often observing that I looked indisposed.

At length she discovered the blood oozing through my waistcoat. She exclaimed, putting her hand on the wound, 'and good reason you have to look so, for you are wounded to death.' The look that accompanied this remark, I may not describe, for I would not be thought vain, and the stern character of my adventures forbids the intermixture of any thing of an entirely different aspect. I was not long, however, in convincing her that my wound was not really dangerous, and that I owed its present bleeding to the friendship of her father, a cause too flattering to be matter of regret.

This drew from me a narrative of the occasion of my wound, which I related in the same simple terms and brief manner in which it is recorded in my journal. A long conversation of questions and replies ensued, of a nature and on subjects not necessary to relate. On the 20th, imploring God that we might meet again, we parted, and I resumed my journey, travelling slowly for my father's residence at the Copper Mines. I paused to rest and amuse myself in several of the small towns on my way. On the 26th, I had the high satisfaction once more to hold the hand of my father, and to find him in health and prosperity, and apparently with nowise abated affection for me, though I had rejected his counsels. This affection seemed to receive a warmer glow, when he heard my determination not to take to the woods again.

I then in return wished to make myself acquainted with the true state of his affairs. He had established a *vacherie* on the River Membry where he kept stock. He had also opened a farm on the land which the old Apache chief had given him, which enabled him to raise grain for the use of his own establishment at the mines. He had actually a supply of grain in advance for the next year. He had made similar improvements upon every thing appertaining to the mines. The result of the whole seemed to be, that he was making money rapidly.

He still retained the Spaniard, of whom I have spoken before, as clerk and superintendent, believing him to be a man of real stability and weight of character, and placing the most entire reliance both upon his capacity and integrity. I was less sanguine, and had my doubts, though having seen no decided facts, upon which to ground them, I did not deem myself justified in honour to impart my doubts to my father.

On the 10th of February, my father requested me, on his account, to take a trip to Alopaz, to purchase for his establishment some wine and whiskey, which articles sell at the mines at a dollar and a half a pint. I started with one servant and six pack mules, each having a couple of small barrels fastened over their saddles, after the manner of our panniers. On the 16th, I reached the place, and purchased my cargo, but the weather was so inclement, that I thought it best not to return until it softened. I became acquainted with an American, married in this place. He was by pursuit a gunsmith, and had been up the upper Missouri with Colonel Henry, and an old and noted trader on that river. The mutual story of what we two had seen and suffered, would probably appear incredible, and beyond the common order of things, to most people, except those who have hunted and trapped in the western parts of this continent, among the mountains and savages, and has nothing upon which to depend, but his own firmness of heart, the defence of his rifle, and the protection of the all present God. To such persons, the incidents which we mutually related, would all seem natural.

I remained here until the 1st of April. Spring in its peculiar splendour and glory in this country, had now wakened the fields and forests into life, and was extending its empire of verdure and flowers higher and higher up the mountains towards their snowy peaks. On this day I commenced my journey of return to the mines, with my servant and my cargo bestowed on my mules. Though the face of the country was all life and beauty, the roads so recently thawed, were exceedingly muddy and heavy. One of my mules in consequence gave out the second day. My servant packed the load of the tired mule upon his riding one, and walked on foot the remainder of the day. During the day we discovered fresh bear tracks in the wood, and my servant advised me to have my gun loaded. At this remark I put my hand in my shot pouch, and found but a single ball, and no lead with which to make more.

At this discovery I saw at once the uselessness of self reproach of my own carelessness and neglect, though it will be easily imagined, what anxiety it created, aware that I had to travel through a long and dreary wilderness, replenished with grizzly bears and hostile Indians. Neither did I dare disclose a particle of what was passing in my mind to my servant, through fear that he would be discouraged, in which case, I knew his first step would be to turn back, and leave me to make the journey alone. It would have been impossible for me to do this, as we were both scarcely able to arrange the affairs of the journey. We advanced cautiously and were unmolested through the day. But I passed a most uncomfortable night through fear of the bears, which, thawed out, were emerging from their winter dens with appetites rendered ravenous by their long winter fast. We and our mules would have furnished them a delicious feast, after the hunger of months. No sleep visited my eyes that night.

At ten o'clock of the 3rd, we met a Spaniard on horse back. I accosted him in the usual terms, and asked if he had met any Indians on his way? He answered that he had, and that there was a body of friendly Apaches encamped near the road, at a distance of a little more than a league. I was delighted with this information, for I supposed I should be able to purchase a horse of them, on which I might mount my servant. While I was reflecting on this thought, my servant proposed to purchase his horse, and offered him a blanket in exchange. He instantly dismounted, took the blanket, and handed over the horse. Happy to see the poor fellow once more comfortably mounted, we bade the easy Spaniard *adieu*, and gaily resumed our journey.

In a short time, according to his information, we saw the Indian camp near the road, from which their smokes were visible. We were solicitous to pass them unobserved and pushed on towards a stopping place, which we might reach at twelve o'clock. Here we stopped to enable our horses to rest, and eat, for the grass was fine. I ordered my servant to spancel the mules, and tether the horse to a shrub by a long rope. My gun reclined upon the packs. We ate a little ourselves, and afterwards I spread my blanket on the grass, close by the horses, and lay down to repose myself, though not intending to go to sleep. But the bright beams of the sun fell upon me in the midst of the green solitude, and I was soon in a profound sleep. A large straw hat on the side of my face shaded my head from the sun.

While enjoying this profound sleep, four of the Apaches came in pursuit of us. It seems our Spaniard had stolen his horse from them, a few hours before. They came upon us in possession of the horse, and supposed me the thief. One of them rode close to me, and made a dart at me with his spear. The stroke was aimed at my neck, and passed through my hat, nailing it to the ground just back of my neck, which the cold steel barely touched. It awakened me, and I sprang to my feet. Four Indians on horseback were around me, and the spear, which had been darted at me, still nailed my hat to the ground. I immediately seized the spear and elevated it towards the Indian, who in turn made his horse spring out of my reach. I called my servant, who had seen the Indians approaching me, and had hidden himself in the bushes. I then sprang to my gun, at the distance of ten or fifteen paces. When I had reached and cocked it, I presented it at an Indian who was unsheathing his fusil.

As soon as he discovered my piece elevated, he threw himself from his horse, fell on his knees, and called for mercy. What surprised me, and arrested my fire, was to hear him call me by my Christian name. I returned my rifle to my shoulder and asked him who he was? He asked me, if I did not know Targuarcha? He smote his breast as he asked the question. The name was familiar. The others dismounted, and gathered round. An understanding ensued. When they learned the manner in which we came by the horse, their countenances were expressive of real sorrow. They had supposed me a Spaniard, as they said, and the thief of their horse. They begged me not to be angry, with a laughable solicitude, offering me the horse as the price of friendship. Above all, they were anxious that I should not relate the affair to my father. They seemed to have an awe of him, resembling that due to the Supreme Being. This awe he had maintained by his steady deportment, and keeping up in their minds the impression, that he always had a large army at command, and was able, and disposed at the first insult, or breach of the treaty on their part, to bring it upon them to their utter destruction.

To all their apologies and kind words and excuses, I answered that I knew them as well as any other man, and that they were not to expect to atone for a dastardly attempt to take my life, and coming within a hair's breadth of taking it, by offering me a present, that I believed that they knew who I was, and only wanted an opportunity, when they could steal upon me unarmed, and kill me, as they had probably committed many other similar murders; that they were ready enough to cry pardon, as soon as they saw me handling my rifle, hoping to catch me asleep again, but that they would henceforward be sure to find me on my guard.

At this the Indian who had darted the spear at me, exclaimed that he loved me as a brother, and would at any occasion risk his life in my defence. I then distinctly recollected him, and that I had been two months with the band, to which he belonged, roving in the woods about the mines. Targuarcha had shown a singular kind of attachment to me, waiting upon me as if I had been his master. I was perfectly convinced that he had thrust his spear at me in absolute ignorance, that it was me. Still I thought it necessary to instil a lesson of caution into them, not to kill any one for an imagined enemy, until they were sure that he was guilty of the supposed wrong. Consequently I dissembled distrust, and told him, that it looked very little like friendship, to dart a spear at the neck of a sleeping man, and that to tell the plain truth, I had as little confidence in him, as a white bear.

At this charge of treachery, he came close to me, and looking affectionately in my face, exclaimed in Spanish, 'if you think me such a traitor, kill me. Here is my breast. Shoot.' At the same time he bared his breast with his hand, with such a profound expression of sorrow in his countenance, as no one was ever yet able to dissemble. I was softened to pity, and told him that I sincerely forgave him, and that I would henceforward consider him my friend, and not inform my father what he had done. They all promised that they would never attempt to kill anyone again, until they knew who it was, and were certain that he was guilty of the crime charged upon him. Here we all shook hands, and perfect confidence was restored.

I now called again for my servant, and after calling till I was hoarse, he at length crawled from behind the bushes, like a frightened turkey or deer, and looking wild with terror. He had the satisfaction of being heartily laughed at, as a person who had deserted his master in the moment of peril. They are not a people to spare the feelings of anyone who proves himself a coward by deserting his place. They bestowed that term upon him without mercy. All his reply was, sullenly to set himself to packing his mules.

Now arose a friendly controversy about the horse, they insisting that I should take it, as the price of our renewed friendship, and I, that I would not take it, except on hire or purchase. They were obstinate in persisting that I should take the horse along with me, and finally promised if I would consent, that they would return to camp and bring their families, and escort me to the mines. To this I consented, though I had first taken the precaution to procure some rifle balls of them. We then resumed our journey, and travelled on without incident till the 5th, when they overtook us, and we travelled on very amicably together, until we reached the Membry, which runs a south course, and is lost in a wide arid plain, after winding its way through prodigious high, craggy mountains. It affords neither fish nor beavers, but has wide and rich bottoms, of which as I have mentioned, they gave my father as much as he chose to cultivate.

From the point where the road crosses this river to the mines, is reckoned 15 miles. Here we met the chief of this band of the Apaches, with a great number of his people. They were all delighted to see us, and not the less so, when they discovered that we had spirituous liquors, of which they are fond to distraction. There was no evading the importunities of the chief to stay all night with him, he promising, if I would that he would go in next day with me to my father. I had scarcely arrived an hour, when I saw the Indian, that had darted his spear at me, come to the chief with shirt laid aside, and his back bare. He handed the chief a stout switch, asking him to whip him.

The chief immediately flayed away about 50 lashes, the blood showing at every stroke. He then asked me, if the thing had been done to my satisfaction? I told him that I had no satisfaction to demand. The chief who had whipped him, was positively ignorant of the crime, for which he had suffered this infliction. But he said, when one of his men begged a flogging, he took it for granted, that it was not for the good deeds of the sufferer, and that he deserved it. When I learned that it was a voluntary penance for his offence to me on the road, I felt really sorry, and made him a present of a quart of whiskey, as an internal unction for the smart of his stripes, a medicine in high esteem among the Indians in such cases.

When we arrived at the mines, the old chief enquired what had been done to me on the road? As soon as he was informed, he sprang up, tore his hair, and seized a gun to shoot the poor culprit. I interposed between them, and convinced him, that Targuarcha had not been really to blame in any thing but his haste, and that if I had really been the thief, he would have done right to kill me, and get back his horse, and that not even my father would have thought the worse of him, but that we should both now like him better, as well as his people, for what had happened.

On the 15th, my father proposed to give me a sum of money, with which to go into the United States to purchase goods for the mines. The labourers much preferred goods, at the customary rate, to money, and the profit at that rate was at least 200 *per cent* on the cost. I was reluctant to do this, for my thoughts still detained me in that country. It was then concluded to send the before mentioned Spanish clerk on the commission, with sufficient money to pay for the goods, consigned to merchants in Santa Fé, to be purchased there, provided a sufficient quantity had recently arrived from the United States to furnish an assortment, and if not, he was recommended to merchants in St. Louis, to make the purchases there.

On the 18th, he started under these orders, under the additional one, that on his arriving at Santa Fé, and learning the state of things there, he should immediately write to the mines to that effect. In the customary order of things, this letter was to be expected in one month from the day he left the mines. After he was departed, he left none behind to doubt his truth and honour, nor was there the least suspicion of him, until the time had elapsed without a letter. A dim surmise began then to grow up, that he had run off with the money. We were still anxiously waiting for intelligence. During this interval I had occupied the place of clerk in his stead. It was now insisted that I should go in search of the villain, who had obtained a good start of a month ahead of us, and 30,000 dollars value in gold bullion to expedite his journey. On the 20th, I started in the search, which I confess seemed hopeless, for he was a man of infinite ingenuity, who could enact Spaniard, which he really was, or Russian, Frenchman or Englishman, as he spoke the languages of these people with fluency. Still I pushed on with full purpose to make diligent and unsparing search.

On the 30th, I arrived at Santa Fé. I made the most anxious and careful enquiry for him, and gave the most accurate descriptions of him there. But no one had seen or heard of such a person. I sorrowfully retraced my steps down the Rio del Norte, now without a doubt of his treachery, and bitterly reflecting on myself for my heedless regard of my father's request. Had I done it, we had both secured an affluence. Now I clearly foresaw poverty and misfortune opening before us in the future. For myself I felt little, as I was young and the world before me; and I felt secure about taking care of myself. My grief was for my father and his companions, who had toiled night and day with unwearied assiduity, to accumulate something for their dear and helpless families, whom they had left in Missouri; and for the love of whom they had ventured into this rough and unsettled country, full of thieves and murderers.

My father in particular, had left a large and motherless family, at a time of life to be wholly unable to take care of themselves, and altogether dependent on him for subsistence. There is no misery like self condemnation; and I suffered it in all its bitterness. The reflections that followed upon learning the full extent of the disaster, which I could but charge in some sense upon myself, came, as such reflections generally come, too late.

I arrived at the Passo del Norte on the 10th of May, and repeated the same descriptions and enquiries to no purpose.—Not a trace remained of him here; and I almost concluded to abandon the search in despair. I could imagine but one more chance. The owner of the mines lived at Chihuahua. As a forlorn hope I concluded to proceed to that city, and inform the governor of our misfortune. So I pushed to Chihuahua, where I arrived on the 23rd.

I found the owner of the mines in too much anxiety and grief of mind on his own account, to be cool enough to listen to the concerns of others. The President of the Mexican republic had issued orders, that all Spaniards born in old Spain, should be expelled from the Mexican country, giving them but a month's notice, in which to settle their affairs and dispose of their property. He being one of that class, had enough to think of on his own account. However, when he heard of our misfortune, he appeared to be concerned. He then touched upon the critical state of his own affairs. Among other things, he said he had all along hoped that my father was able and disposed to purchase those mines. He had, therefore, a motive personal to himself, to make him regret my father's loss and inability to make the purchase. He was now obliged to sell them at any sacrifice, and had but a very short time in which to settle his affairs, and leave the country. He requested me to be ready to start the next day in company with him to the mines.

Early on the 24th, we started with relays of horses and mules. As we travelled very rapidly we arrived at the mines on the 30th, where I found my father and his companions in the utmost anxiety to learn something what had happened to me. When they discovered the owner of the mines, whose name was Don Francisco Pablo de Lagera, they came forth in a body with countenances full of joy. That joy was changed to sadness, as soon as Don Pablo informed them the object of his visit. They perceived in a moment, that nothing now remained for them but to settle their affairs, and search for other situations in the country, or return to the United States in a worse condition than when they left it. My father determined at once not to think of this. Nothing seemed so feasible, and conformable to his pursuits, as a trapping expedition. With the pittance that remained to him, after all demands against the firm were discharged, and the residue according to the articles of agreement divided, he purchased trapping equipments for four persons, himself included. The other three he intended to hire to trap for him.

On the 1st of July, all these matters had been arranged, and my father and myself started for Santa Fé, with a view to join the first company that should start on a trapping expedition from that place. On the 10th, we arrived at Santa Fé, where we remained until the 22nd, when a company of thirty men were about to commence an expedition of that sort down Red river. My father joined this company, and in the name of the companions made application for license of safe transit through the province of Chihuahua, and Sonora, through which runs the Red River, on which we meant to trap. The governor gave us a passport in the following terms:

CUSTOM HOUSE OF THE FRONTIER TOWN OF SANTA FÉ, IN THE
TERRITORY OF NEW MEXICO.
Custom House Certificate.
Allow Sylvester Pattie, to pursue his journey with certain beasts, merchandize and money, in the direction of Chihuahua and Sonora; to enter in beasts and money an amount equal to this invoice, in whatsoever place he shall appear, according to the rules of the Custom House, on his passage; and finally let him return this permit to the government of this city in days. Do this under the established penalties.
Given at Santa Fé, in New Mexico.

Ramon Attren
September 22nd, 1827.

On the 23rd, my father was chosen captain or commander of the company, and we started on our expedition. We retraced our steps down the del Norte, and by the mines to the river Helay, on which we arrived on the 6th of October, and began to descend it, setting our traps as we went, near our camp, whenever we saw signs of beavers. But our stay on this stream was short, for it had been trapped so often, that there were but few beavers remaining, and those few were exceedingly shy. We therefore pushed on to some place where they might be more abundant, and less shy. We left this river on the 12th, and on the 15th reached Beaver River. Here we found them in considerable numbers, and we concluded to proceed in a south course, and trap the river in its downward course.

But to prevent the disagreement and insubordination which are apt to spring up in these associations, my father drew articles of agreement, purporting that we should trap in partnership, and that the first one who should show an open purpose to separate from the company, or desert it, should be shot dead; and that if anyone should disobey orders, he should be tried by a jury of our number, and if found guilty should be fined fifty dollars, to be paid in fur. To this instrument we all agreed, and signed our names.

The necessity of some such compact had been abundantly discovered in the course of our experience. Men bound only by their own will and sense of right, to the duties of such a sort of partnership are certain to grow restless, and to form smaller clans, disposed to dislike and separate from each other, in parties of one by one to three by three. They thus expose themselves to be cut up in detail by the savages, who comprehend all their movements, and are ever watchful for an opportunity to show their hatred of the whites to be fixed and inextinguishable. The following are some of the more common causes of separation: Men of incompatible tempers and habits are brought together; and such expeditions call out innumerable occasions to try this disagreement of character. Men, hungry, naked, fatigued, and in constant jeopardy, are apt to be ill-tempered, especially when they arrive at camp, and instead of being allowed to throw themselves on the ground, and sleep, have hard duties of cooking, and keeping guard, and making breast-works assigned them. But the grand difficulty is the following.

In a considerable company, half its numbers can catch as many beavers as all. But the half that keep guard, and cook, perform duties as necessary and important to the whole concern, as the others. It always happens too, in these expeditions, that there are some infinitely more dextrous and skilful in trapping and hunting than others. These capabilities are soon brought to light. The expert know each other, and feel a certain superiority over the inexpert. They know that three or four such, by themselves, will take as many beavers as a promiscuous company of thirty, and in fact, all that a stream affords. A perception of their own comparative importance, a keen sense of self interest, which sharpens in the desert, the mere love of roving in the wild license of the forest, and a capacity to become hardened by these scenes to a perfect callousness to all fear and sense of danger, until it actually comes; such passions are sufficient to thicken causes of separation among such companions in the events of every day.

Sad experience has made me acquainted with all these causes of disunion and dissolution of such companies. I have learned them by wounds and sufferings, by toil and danger of every sort, by wandering about in the wild and desolate mountains, alone and half starved, merely because two or three bad men had divided our company, strong and sufficient to themselves in union, but miserable, and exposed to almost certain ruin in separation. Made painfully acquainted with all these facts by experience, my father adopted this expedient in the hope that it would be something like a remedy for them.

But notwithstanding this, and the prudence and energy of my father's character, disunion soon began to spring up in our small party. Almost on the outset of our expedition, we began to suffer greatly for want of provisions. We were first compelled to kill and eat our dogs, and then six of our horses. This to me was the most cruel task of all. To think of waiting for the night to kill and eat the poor horse that had borne us over deserts and mountains, as hungry as ourselves, and strongly and faithfully attached to us, was no easy task to the heart of a Kentucky hunter. One evening, after a hard day's travel, my saddle horse was selected by lot to be killed. The poor animal stood saddled and bridled before us, and it fell to my lot to kill it. I loved this horse, and he seemed to have an equal attachment for me. He was remarkably kind to travel, and easy to ride, and spirited too.

When he stood tied in camp among the rest, if I came anywhere near him, he would fall neighing for me. When I held up the bridle towards him, I could see consent and good will in his eye. As I raised my gun to my face, all these recollections rushed to my thoughts. My pulses throbbed, and my eyes grew dim. The animal was gazing at me, with a look of steady kindness, in the face. My head whirled, and was dizzy, and my gun fell. After a moment for recovery, I offered a beaver skin to anyone who would shoot him down. One was soon found at this price, and my horse fell! It so happened that this was the last horse we killed. Well was it for us that we had these surplus horses. Had it been otherwise, we should all have perished with hunger.

It was now the 15th of November, and while the horse flesh lasted, we built a canoe, so that we could trap on both sides of the river; for it is here too broad and deep to be fordable on horseback. One of our number had already been drowned, man and horse, in attempting to swim the river. A canoe is a great advantage, where the beavers are wild; as the trapper can thus set his traps along the shore without leaving his scent upon the ground about it.

On the 17th, our canoe was finished, and another person and myself took some traps in it, and floated down the river by water, while the rest of the company followed along the banks by land. In this way, what with the additional supply which the canoe enabled our traps to furnish, and a chance deer or wolf that Providence sometimes threw in our way, with caution and economy we were tolerably supplied with provisions; and the company travelled on with a good degree of

SHOOTING MR. PATTIE'S HORSE

union and prosperity, until the 26th.

Here the greater part of the company expressed disinclination to following our contemplated route any longer. That is, they conceived the route to the mouth of the Helay, and up Red River of California too long and tedious, and too much exposed to numerous and hostile Indians. They, therefore, determined to quit the Helay, and strike over to Red River by a direct route across the country. My father reminded them of their article. They assured him they did not consider themselves bound by it, and that they were a majority, against which nothing could be said. My father and myself still persevered in following the original plan. Two of the men had been hired on my father's account. He told them he was ready to pay them up to that time, and dismiss them, to go where they chose. They observed, that now that the company had commenced separating, they believed that in a short time, there would be no stronger party together than ours; that they had as good a disposition to risk their lives with us, as with any division of our number, and that they would stay by us to the death. After this speech four others of the company volunteered to remain with us, and we took them in as partners.

On the 27th, we divided the hunt, and all expressing the same regret at the separation, and heartily wishing each other all manner of prosperity, we shook hands and parted! We were now reduced to eight in number. We made the most solemn pledges to stand by each other unto death, and adopted the severest caution, of which we had been too faithfully taught the necessity. We tied our horses every night, and encamped close by them, to prevent their being stolen by the Indians. Their footprints were thick and fresh in our course, and we could see their smokes at no great distance north of us. We were well aware that they were hostile, and watching their opportunity to pounce upon us, and we kept ourselves ready for action, equally day and night. We now took an ample abundance of beavers to supply us with meat, in consequence of our reduced numbers. Our horses also fared well, for we cut plenty of cotton-wood trees, the bark of which serves them for food nearly as well as corn.

We thus travelled on prosperously, until we reached the junction of the Helay with Red River.—Here we found the tribe of Umeas, who had shown themselves very friendly to the company in which I had formerly passed them, which strongly inspired confidence in them at present. Some of them could speak the Spanish language. We made many inquiries of them, our object being to gain information of the distance of the Spanish settlements. We asked them where they obtained the cloth they wore around their loins? They answered, from the Christians on the coast of the California. We asked if there were any Christians living on Red River? They promptly answered, yes. This information afterwards proved a source of error and misfortune to us, though our motive for inquiry at this time was mere curiosity.

It was now the 1st of December; and at mid-day we began to see the imprudence of spending the remainder of the day and the ensuing night with such numbers of Indians, however friendly in appearance. We had a tolerable fund of experience, in regard to the trust we might safely repose in the red skins; and knew that caution is the parent of security. So we packed up, and separated from them. Their town was on the opposite shore of Red River. At our encampment upwards of two hundred of them swam over the river and visited us, all apparently friendly. We allowed but a few of them to approach our camp at a time, and they were obliged to lay aside their arms. In the midst of these multitudes of fierce, naked, swarthy savages, eight of us seemed no more than a little patch of snow on the side of one of the black mountains. We were perfectly aware how critical was our position, and determined to intermit no prudence or caution.

To interpose as great a distance as possible between them and us, we marched that evening sixteen miles, and encamped on the banks of the river. The place of encampment was a prairie, and we drove stakes fast in the earth, to which we tied our horses in the midst of green grass, as high as a man's head, and within ten feet of our own fire. Unhappily we had arrived too late to make a pen for our horses, or a breast work for ourselves. The sky was gloomy. Night and storm were settling upon us, and it was too late to complete these important arrangements. In a short time the storm poured upon us, and the night became so dark that we could not see our hand before us. Apprehensive of an attempt to steal our horses, we posted two sentinels, and the remaining six lay down under our wet blankets, and the pelting of the sky, to such sleep as we might get, still preserving a little fire.

We were scarcely asleep before we were aroused by the snorting of our horses and mules. We all sprang to our arms, and extinguished our little fire. We could not see a foot before us, and we groped about our camp feeling our way among the horses and mules. We could discover nothing; so concluding they might have been frightened by the approach of a bear or some other wild animal, some of us commenced rekindling our fires, and the rest went to sleep. But the Indians had crawled among our horses, and had cut or untied the rope by which each one was bound. The horses were then all loose. They then instantly raised in concert, their fiendish yell. As though heaven and earth were in concert against us, the rain began to pour again, accompanied with howling gusts of wind, and the fiercest gleams of lightning, and crashes of thunder. Terrified alike by the thunder and the Indians, our horses all took to flight, and the Indians repeating yell upon yell, were close at their heels. We sallied out after them, and fired at the noises, though we could see nothing. We pursued with the utmost of our speed to no purpose, for they soon reached the open prairie, where we concluded they were joined by other Indians on horseback, who pushed our horses still faster; and soon the clattering of their heels and the yells of their accursed pursuers began to fade, and become indistinct in our ears.

Our feelings and reflections as we returned to camp were of the gloomiest kind. We were one thousand miles from the point whence we started, and without a single beast to bear either our property or ourselves. The rain had passed. We built us a large fire. As we stood round it we discussed our deplorable condition, and our future alternatives. Something was to be done. We all agreed to the proposition of my father, which was, early in the morning to pursue the trails of our beasts, and if we should overtake the thieves, to retake the horses, or die in the attempt; and that, failing in that, we should return, swim the river, attack their town, and kill as many of the inhabitants as we could; for that it was better to die by these Indians, after we had killed a good number of them, than to starve, or be killed by Indians who had not injured us, and when we could not defend ourselves.

Accordingly, early in the morning of the 2nd, we started on the trail in pursuit of the thieves. We soon arrived at a point where the Indians, departing from the plain, had driven them up a chasm of the mountains. Here they had stopped, and caught them, divided them, and each taken a different route with his plundered horses. We saw in a moment that it was impossible to follow them farther to any purpose. We abandoned the chase, and returned to our camp to execute the second part of our plan. When we arrived there, we stopped for a leisure meal of beaver meat. When we had bestowed ourselves to this dainty resort, a Dutchman with us broke the gloomy silence of our eating, by observing that we had better stuff ourselves to the utmost; for that it would probably, be the last chance we should have at beaver meat.

We all acquiesced in this observation, which though made in jest, promised to be a sober truth, by eating as heartily as possible. When we had finished our meal, which looked so likely to be the last we should enjoy together, we made rafts to which we tied our guns, and pushing them onward before us, we thus swam the river. Having reached the opposite shore, we shouldered our rifles, and steered for the town, at which we arrived about two in the afternoon. We marched up to the numerous assemblage of huts in a manner as reckless and undaunted as though we had nothing to apprehend. In fact, when we arrived at it, we found it to contain not a single living being, except one miserable, blind, deaf, and decrepit old man, not unlike one that I described in a hostile former visit to an Indian village.

Our exasperation of despair inclined us to kill even him. My father forbade. He apparently heard nothing and cared for nothing, as he saw nothing. His head was white with age, and his eyes appeared to have been gouged out. He may have thought himself all the while in the midst of his own people. We discovered a plenty of their kind of food, which consisted chiefly of acorn mush. We then set fire to the village, burning every hut but that which contained the old man. Being built of flags and grass, they were not long in reducing to ashes. We then returned to our camp, re-swimming the river, and reaching the camp before dark.

We could with no certainty divine the cause of their having evacuated their town, though we attributed it to fear of us. The occurrences of the preceding day strengthened us in this impression. While they remained with us, one of our men happened to fire off his gun. As though they never had heard such a noise before, they all fell prostrate on the earth, as though they had all been shot. When they arose, they would all have taken to flight, had we not detained them and quieted their fears.

Our conversation with these Indians of the day before, now recurred to our recollections, and we congratulated ourselves on having been so inquisitive as to obtain the now important information, that there were Spanish settlements on the river below us. Driven from the resource of our horses, we happily turned our thoughts to another. We had all the requisite tools to build canoes, and directly around us was suitable timber of which to make them. It was a pleasant scheme to soothe our dejection, and prevent our lying down to the sleep of despair. But this alternative determined upon, there remained another apprehension sufficient to prevent our enjoying quiet repose. Our fears were, that the unsheltered Indians, horse-stealers and all, would creep upon us in the night, and massacre us all. But the night passed without any disturbance from them.

On the morning of the 3rd, the first business in which we engaged, was to build ourselves a little fort, sufficient for defence against the Indians. This finished, we cut down two trees suitable for canoes, and accomplished these important objects in one day. During this day we kept one man posted in the top of a tall tree, to descry if any Indians were approaching us in the distance. On the morning of the fourth we commenced digging out our canoes, and finished and launched two. These were found insufficient to carry our furs. We continued to prepare, and launch them, until we had eight in the water. By uniting them in pairs by a platform, we were able to embark with all our furs and traps, without any extra burden, except a man and the necessary traps for each canoe. We hid our saddles, hoping to purchase horses at the settlements, and return this way.

We started on the 9th, floating with the current, which bore us downward at the rate of four miles an hour. In the evening we passed the burnt town, the ruins of which still threw up smouldering smoke. We floated about 30 miles, and in the evening encamped in the midst of signs of beavers. We set 40 traps, and in the morning of the 10th caught 36 beavers, an excellent night's hunt. We concluded from this encouraging commencement, to travel slowly, and in hunters' phrase, trap the river clear; that is, take all that could be allured to come to the bait. The river, below its junction with the Helay, is from 2 to 300 yards wide, with high banks, that have dilapidated by falling in. Its course is west, and its timber chiefly cotton-wood, which in the bottoms is lofty and thick set. The bottoms are from six to ten miles wide. The soil is black, and mixed with sand, though the bottoms are subject to inundation in the flush waters of June. This inundation is occasioned by the melting of the snow on the mountains about its head waters.

We now floated pleasantly downward at our leisure, having abundance of the meat of fat beavers. We began in this short prosperity, to forget the loss of our horses, and to consider ourselves quite secure from the Indians. But on the 12th, at mid-day, by mere accident, we happened, some way below us, to discover two Indians perched in a tree near the river bank, with their bows and arrows in readiness, waiting evidently until we should float close by them, to take off some of us with their arrows. We betrayed no signs of having seen them, but sat with our guns ready for a fair shot. When we had floated within a little short of a hundred yards, my father and another of the company gave them a salute, and brought them both tumbling down the branches, reminding us exactly of the fall of a bear or a turkey. They made the earth sound when they struck it. Fearful that they might be part of an ambush, we pulled our canoes to the opposite shore, and some of us climbed trees, from which we could command a view of both shores. We became satisfied that these two were alone, and we crossed over to their bodies.

We discovered that they were of the number that had stolen our horses, by the fact, that they were bound round the waist with some of the hemp ropes with which our horses had been tied. We hung the bodies of the thieves from a tree, with the product of their own thefts. Our thoughts were much relieved by the discovery of this fact, for though none of us felt any particular forbearance towards Indians under any circumstances, it certainly would have pained us to have killed Indians that had never disturbed us. But there could be no compunction for having slain these two thieves, precisely at the moment that they were exulting in the hope of getting a good shot at us. Beside they alarmed our false security, and learned us a lesson to keep nearer the middle of the river.

We continued to float slowly downwards, trapping beavers on our way almost as fast as we could wish. We sometimes brought in 60 in a morning. The river at this point is remarkably circuitous, and has a great number of islands, on which we took beavers. Such was the rapid increase of our furs, that our present crafts in a few days were insufficient to carry them, and we were compelled to stop and make another canoe. We have advanced between 60 and 70 miles from the point where we built the other canoes. We find the timber larger, and not so thick. There are but few wild animals that belong to the country farther up, but some deer, panthers, foxes and wild-cats. Of birds there are great numbers, and many varieties, most of which I have never before seen. We killed some wild geese and pelicans, and likewise an animal not unlike the African leopard, which came into our camp, while we were at work upon the canoe. It was the first we had ever seen.

We finished our canoe on the 17th, and started on the 20th. This day we saw ten Indians on a sand bar, who fled into the woods at the sight of us. We knew them to be different people from those who had stolen our horses, both by their size and their different manner of wearing their hair. The heads of these were shaved close, except a tuft, which they wore on the top of their head, and which they raised erect, as straight as an arrow. The Umeas are of gigantic stature from six to seven feet high. These only average five feet and a half. They go perfectly naked, and have dark complexions, which I imagine is caused by the burning heat of the sun. The weather is as hot here at this time, as I ever experienced. We were all very desirous to have a talk with these Indians, and enquire of them, how near we were to the Spanish settlements; and whether they were immediately on the bank, for we began to be fearful that we had passed them.

Three days passed without our having any opportunity of conversation with them. But early on the morning of the 24th, we found some families yet asleep in their *wigwams*, near the water's edge. Our approach to them was so imperceptible and sudden, that they had no chance to flee. They were apparently frightened to insanity. They surrendered without making any further effort to escape. While they stared at us in terrified astonishment; we made them comprehend that we had no design to kill, or injure them. We offered them meat, and made signs that we wished to smoke with them. They readily comprehended us, and the ghastliness of terror began to pass from their countenances. The women and children were yet screaming as if going into convulsions.

We made signs to the men to have them stop this annoying noise. This we did by putting our hands to our mouths. They immediately uttered something to the women and children which made them still. The pipe was then lit, and smoking commenced. They puffed the smoke towards the sky, pointed thither, and uttered some words, of course unintelligible to us. They then struck themselves on the breast, and afterwards on the forehead. We understood this to be a sort of religious appeal to the Supreme Being, and it showed more like reverence to him, than anything we had yet seen among the Indians; though I have seen none but what admit that there is a master of life, whom they call by a name to that import, or that of Great Spirit.

When the smoking was finished, we began to enquire of them by signs, how far we were from the Spanish settlement? This we effected by drawing an image of a cow and sheep in the sand and then imitating the noise of each kind of domestic animals, that we supposed the Spaniards would have. They appeared to understand us, for they pointed west, and then at our clothes, and then at our naked skin. From this we inferred that they wished to say that farther to the west lived white people, as we were. And this was all we could draw from them on that subject. We then asked them, if they had ever seen white people before? This we effected by stretching open our eyes with our fingers, and pointing to them, and then looking vehemently in that direction, while we pointed west with our fingers. They shook their heads in the negative. Then stretching their own ears, as we had our eyes, striking themselves on the breast, and pointing down the river, they pronounced the word *wechapa*. This we afterwards understood implied, that their chief lived lower down the river, and that they had heard from him, that he had seen these people.

We gave the women some old shirts, and intimated to them as well as we could, that it was the fashion of the women to cover themselves in our country, for these were in a state of the most entire nudity. But they did not seem rightly to comprehend our wish. Many of the women were not over sixteen, and the most perfect figures I have ever seen, perfectly straight and symmetrical, and the hair of some hanging nearly to their heels. The men are exceedingly active, and have bright countenances, and quick apprehension. We gave them more meat, and then started. They followed our course along the bank, until night. As soon as we landed, they were very officious in gathering wood, and performing other offices for us. They showed eager curiosity in examining our arms, and appeared to understand their use.

When my father struck fire with his pistol, they gave a start, evidencing a mixture of astonishment and terror, and then re-examined the pistol, apparently solicitous to discover how the fire was made. My father bade me take my rifle, and shoot a wild goose, that was sitting about in the middle of the river. He then showed them the goose, and pointed at me, as I was creeping to a point where I might take a fair shot. They all gazed with intense curiosity, first at me, and then at the goose, until I fired. At the moment of the report, some fell flat on the ground, and the rest ran for the bushes, as though Satan was behind them. As soon as the fallen had recovered from their amazement, they also fled. Some of our company stopped them, by seizing some, and holding them, and showing them that the goose was dead, and the manner in which it had been killed.

They gradually regained confidence and composure, and called to their companions in the bushes. They also came forth, one by one, and when the nature of the report of the gun had been explained to them, they immediately swam into the river and brought out the goose. When they carried it round and showed it to their companions, carefully pointing out the ball hole in the goose, it is impossible to show more expressive gestures, cries and movements of countenances indicative of wonder and astonishment, than they exhibited. The night which we passed with them, passed away pleasantly, and to the satisfaction of all parties. In the morning their attention and curiosity were again highly excited, when we brought in our beavers, which amounted in number to thirty-six.

After we had finished skinning them, we left the ample supply of food furnished by the bodies of the beavers, in token of our friendship, to these Indians, and floated on. On the 27th, we arrived at the residence of the chief. We perceived that they had made ready for our reception. They had prepared a feast for us by killing a number of fatted dogs. As soon as we landed, the chief came to us, accompanied by two subordinate chiefs. When arrived close to us, he exclaimed, *wechapa*, striking himself on the breast, pointing to our company, and repeating the same phrase. We understood from this, that he wished to know who was our captain? We all pointed to my father, to whom the chief immediately advanced, and affectionately embracing him, invited us to enter his wigwam. We shouldered our rifles, and all followed this venerable looking man to his abode. There he had prepared several earthen dishes, in which the flesh of young and fat dogs was served up, but without salt or bread.

We all sat down. The pipe was lit, and we, and the thirty Indians present began to smoke. While we were smoking, they used many gesticulations and signs, the purport of which we could not make out, though, as they pointed often at us, we supposed we were the subjects of their gestures. The pipe was then taken away, and the chief arose, and stood in the centre of the circle which we formed by the manner in which we all sat around the fire. He then made a long harangue, and as we understood not a word, to us rather a tedious one. We took care to make as many gestures indicative of understanding it, as though we had comprehended every word.

The oration finished, a large dish of the choice dog's flesh was set before us, and signs were made to us to eat. Having learned not to be delicate or disobliging to our savage host, we fell to work upon the ribs of the domestic barkers. When we had eaten to satisfaction, the chief arose, and puffing out his naked belly, and striking it with his hand, very significantly inquired by this sign, if we had eaten enough? When we had answered in the affirmative, by our mode of making signs, he then began to enquire of us, as we understood it, who we were, and from whence we came, and what was our business in that country? All this we interpreted, and replied to by signs as significant as we could imagine. He continued to enquire of us by signs, if we had met with no misfortunes on our journey, calling over the names of several Indian tribes in that part of the country, among which we distinctly recognised the name of the Umeas?

When he mentioned this name, it was with such a lowering brow and fierce countenance as indicated clearly that he was at war with them. We responded to these marks of dislike by an equal show of detestation by making the gesture of seeming desirous to shoot at them, and with the bitterest look of anger that we could assume; making him understand that they had stolen our horses. He made signs of intelligence that he comprehended us, and made us sensible of his deep hatred, by giving us to understand that they had killed many of his people, and taken many more prisoners; and that he had retaliated by killing and taking as many Umeas. He pointed at the same time to two small children, and exclaimed Umea! We pointed at them with our guns, and gave him to understand, that we had killed two of them.

Some of our people had brought their scalps along. We gave them to him, and he, looking first towards us, and then fiercely at them, seemed to ask if these were the scalps of his enemies? To which we replied, yes.—He then seized the hair of the scalps with his teeth, and shook them, precisely as I have seen a dog any small game that it had killed. He then gave such a yell of delight, as collected all his people round him in a moment, and such rejoicing, yelling, and dancing ensued from both men and women, as I shall forbear to attempt to describe. Their deportment on this occasion was in fact much nearer bestial than human. They would leave the dance round the scalps in turn, to come and caress us, and then return and resume their dance.

The remainder of this day and the ensuing night passed in being in some sense compelled to witness this spectacle. In the morning of the 28th, when we brought in the contents of our traps, we found we had taken twenty-eight beavers. When my father enquired this morning anew for the direction of the Spanish settlements, and how far they were distant, we could make out from the signs of the chief no information more exact than this. He still pointed to the west, and then back at us.—He then made a very tolerable imitation of the rolling and breaking of the surf on the sea shore. Below he drew a cow and a sheep. From this we were satisfied that there were Spanish settlements west of us; and our conclusion was, that they could not be very distant.

At mid-day we bade these friendly Indians farewell, and resumed our slow progress of floating slowly down the stream, still setting our traps, whenever we found any indications of beavers. We met with no striking incident, and experienced no molestation until January 1st, 1828. On this day we once more received a shower of arrows from about fifty Indians of a tribe called Pipi, of whom we were cautioned to beware by the friendly Indians we had last left. I forgot at the time to mention the name of that people, when speaking of them, and repeat it now. It is Cocopa. When the Pipi fired upon us, we were floating near the middle of the river. We immediately commenced pulling for the opposite shore, and were soon out of the reach of their arrows, without any individual having been wounded. As soon as our crafts touched the shore, we sprang upon the bank, took fair aim, and showed them the difference between their weapons and ours, by levelling six of them. The remainder fell flat, and began to dodge and skulk on all fours, as though the heavens had been loaded with thunder and mill stones, which were about to rain on them from the clouds.

We re-loaded our guns, and rowed over to the opposite, and now deserted shore. The fallen lay on the sand beach, some of them not yet dead. We found twenty three bows and the complement of arrows, most of them belonging to the fugitives. The bows are six feet in length, and made of a very tough and elastic kind of wood, which the Spaniards call *tarnio*. They polish them down by rubbing them on a rough rock. The arrows are formed of a reed grass, and of the same length with their bows, with a foot of hard wood stuck in the end of the cavity of the reed, and a flint spike fitted on the end of it.—They have very large and erect forms, and black skins. Their long black hair floats in tresses down their backs, and to the termination of each tress is fastened a snail shell. In other respects their dress consists of their birthday suit; in other words, they are perfectly naked.

The river seems here to run upon a high ridge; for we can see from our crafts a great distance back into the country, which is thickly covered with *musquito* and other low and scrubby trees. The land is exceedingly marshy, and is the resort of numerous flocks of swans, and blue cranes. The raccoons are in such numbers, that they cause us to lose a great many beavers, by getting into our traps and being taken instead of the true game. They annoy us too by their squalling when they are taken.

From the junction of the two rivers to this place, I judge to be about a hundred miles. We find the climate exceedingly warm, and the beaver fur, in accommodation to the climate, is becoming short. We conclude, in consequence, that our trapping is becoming of less importance, and that it is our interest to push on faster to reach the settlements. A great many times every day we bring our crafts to shore, and go out to see if we cannot discover the tracks of horses and cattle. On the 18th, we first perceived that we had arrived on the back water of the tide; or rather we first attributed the deadness of the current to the entrance of some inundated river, swollen by the melting of the snow on the mountains. We puzzled our brains with some other theories, to account for the deadness of the current. This became so entirely still, that we began to rig our oars, concluding that instead of our hitherto easy progress of floating gently onward, we had henceforward to make our headway down stream by dint of the machinery of our arms.

We soon were thoroughly enlightened in regard to the slackness of the water. It began to run down again, and with the rapidity of six miles an hour; that is, double the ordinary current of the stream. We were all much surprised, for though I had seen the water of the Pacific at Ymus, none of us had ever felt the influence of the tides, or been in a craft on the ocean waters before. People of the same tribe, upon which we had recently fired, stood upon the shore, and called loudly to us as we passed, to come to land, making signs to us, that the motion of the water would capsize our crafts. They showed a great desire that we might come to shore, we had no doubt, that they might rob and murder us. We preserved such a distance from them, as to be out of the reach of their arrows, and had no intention to fire upon them. Had we wished for a shot, they were quite within rifle distance. We floated on, having had a beautiful evening's run, and did not come to land, until late; we then pitched our camp on a low point of land, unconscious, from our inexperience of the fact, that the water would return, and run up stream again.

We made our canoes fast to some small trees, and all lay down to sleep, except my father, who took the first watch. He soon aroused us, and called on us all to prepare for a gust of wind, and a heavy rain, which he thought betokened by a rushing noise he heard. We realised in a few moments, that it was the returning tide. Still, so strongly impressed were we, that a shower was approaching, that we made all the customary arrangements of preparation, by stretching our blankets to keep out the water from above. But our enemy assailed us from another quarter. Our camp was inundated from the river. We landsmen from the interior, and unaccustomed to such movements of the water, stood contemplating with astonishment the rush of the tide coming in from the sea, in conflict with the current of the river. At the point of conflict rose a high ridge of water, over which came the sea current, combing down like water over a milldam. We all sprang to our canoes, which the rush of the water had almost capsized, though we held the fasts with our hands.

In twenty minutes the place where we lay asleep, and even our fire place was three feet under water, and our blankets were all afloat. We had some vague and general ideas of the nature of the tide, but its particular operations were as much unknown to us, as though we never had heard of it at all. In the consternation of our ignorance, we paddled our crafts, as well as we could, among the timber, not dreaming that in the course of a few hours, the water would fall again. As it was, we gathered up our floating blankets, got into our canoes, and held fast to the brushes, until the water fell again, leaving us and our canoes high and dry. We were now assailed by a new alarm, lest the Indians, taking advantage of this new position in which we were placed, would attack and murder us.

In such apprehensions we passed the night, until the morning shone upon us with a bright and beautiful sun, which enabled us to dry all our wet things, and re-animated us with the confidence which springs from the view of a bright firmament and a free and full survey of our case. When the tide returned we got into our crafts, and descended with it, still expecting to find Spanish settlements. We continued in this way to descend, when the tide ran out, until the 28th, when the surf came up the river so strong that we saw in a moment, that our crafts could not live, if we floated them into this tumultuous commotion of the water.

Here we were placed in a new position, not the least disheartening or trying, among the painful predicaments, in which fortune had placed us. The fierce billows shut us in from below, the river current from above, and murderous savages upon either hand on the shore. We had a rich cargo of furs, a little independence for each one of us, could we have disposed of them, as we had hoped, among the Spanish people, whom we expected to have found here. There were no such settlements.—Every side on which we looked offered an array of danger, famine and death. In this predicament, what were furs to us? Our first thought was to commit our furs to the waters, and attempt to escape with our lives. Our second resolve was to ascend the river as far as we could, bury our furs, and start on foot for some settlement. We saw that the chances were greatly against us, that we should perish in the attempt; for the country yielded little to subsist on, and was full of Indians who are to the last degree savage and murderous, and whom nothing can subdue to kindness and friendship. We had no idea of ever putting ourselves in their power, as long as one of us could fire a pistol, or draw a knife.

We now began to ascend with the tide, when it served us, and lay by when it ran down, until we arrived at the point where it ceased to flow. We then applied our oars, and with the help of setting-poles, and at times the aid of a cordelle, we stemmed the current at the rate of one, and sometimes two miles an hour, until the tenth of February, when we met a great rise of the river, and found the current so strong, that we had no power to stem it in any way. So we concluded to abandon our canoes, come to shore, bury our furs, and make our way across the peninsula to the coast of California, which we thought from the information of the Indians, could not be very distant.

On the 16th, we completed the burying of our furs, and started on foot with our packs on our backs. The contents of these packs were two blankets for each man, a considerable quantity of dried beaver meat, and a rifle with the ammunition. Our first day's journey was through a country to the last degree trying to our strength and patience. It was through the river bottom, which was thick set with low, scrubby brush, interwoven with tall grass, vines and creepers. The making our way through these was excessively slavish and fatiguing. We had a single alleviation. There was plenty of fresh water to drink. We were so fatigued at night, that sleep was irresistible. The weather was warm, and we kindled no fire, through fear of the savages. We started on the morning of the 18th, all complaining much of stiffness and soreness of our limbs. We had been unused to walking for a great length of time; and this commencement was a rude experiment of resuming the habit.

At two in the afternoon, we reached the edge of a large salt plain, which runs parallel with the river. Here we struck a north west course, and travelled the remainder of this hot and fatiguing day without finding any water. We began to suffer severely from thirst. The earth, also, was so loose and sandy, that at every step we sank up to our ankles, the sun beaming down a fierce radiance the while; which made it seem as if the heavens and the earth were on fire. Our tongues became so parched, that not a particle of moisture flowed into our mouths. In this miserable and forlorn condition, abandoned by strength, courage and hope, we found some little alleviation of our misery, when the blaze of the sun was gone, and the cool night enabled us to throw down our weary and exhausted bodies under its dewy shade.

We made an early start in the morning, and pushed on as men, as thirsty as we were, naturally would, in the hope of finding water, until two in the afternoon. What a sight of joy! I have no words to express our delight at the sight of a little lake before us. We sprang greedily to it. The water was salt, too salt to be drank! Not the slightest indication of any other water course, or any omen of fresh water was any where in view. Far in the distance a snow-covered mountain glittered in the sun, and on the opposite shore of this salt lake, and at a distance of three or four miles from it, rose some hills of considerable height. We thought that from the summit of these hills we might possibly discover some water. We gathered dry flags, of which there was a great abundance about us, and made a kind of raft, on which each one of us put his pack, and swam the lake, pushing the little rafts that carried our packs, before us. The lake is about two hundred yards wide, and contains a great variety of fish. In length the lake stretches north and south, bounded on each shore with high, level and well timbered land, though apparently affording no fresh water.

When we reached the west shore of the lake, we saw fresh Indian foot-prints in the sand. This assured us, that there was water at no great distance. One of our company and myself started and ascended the highest peak of the hills in our view. We were not long in descrying a smoke in the south, at the distance of about ten miles. This sight gave us great courage and hope; for we felt assured that there must be water between us and the Indian camp. In a moment we started back with a vigorous step, to inform our companions, who were resting themselves under the shade of a tree. The information reanimated them, as it had us. We all shouldered our packs with a degree of alacrity, and pushed on toward the smoke.—We arrived about three in the afternoon on a small mound, within a quarter of a mile of the Indians. We could distinctly number them, and found them between forty and fifty in number, and their women and children were with them.

Here again was anxious ground of debate, what course we should pursue? should we attempt the long and uncertain course of conciliation, before the accomplishment of which we might perish with thirst? or should we rush among them, and buy the delicious element which we had full in view, at the hazard of our lives? Men as thirsty as we were, would be likely to fix upon the latter alternative, and we did so. We examined our arms to see that we were prepared to attack, or repel, according to circumstances, determined to fire upon them, if they showed either a disposition for fight, or to keep us from the water.

We were within a hundred and fifty yards of them before they perceived us. As soon as they saw us they all fled to the bushes, men, women and children, as though Satan was behind them. We had no disposition to arrest them, but rushed forward to the water, and began to slake our burning thirst. My father immediately cautioned us against drinking too much, pointing out at the same time the hurtful consequences. But men have always proved themselves slow to resist their appetites at the command of their reason. Most of us overloaded our empty stomachs with water, and soon became as sick as death. After vomiting, however, we were relieved. My father told us that we had better stand to our arms; for that the Indians had probably only fled to hide their women and children, and prepare themselves to return and fight us.

Scarcely had he finished these remarks, when we discovered them bearing down upon us, painted as black as a thunder cloud, and yelling like so many fiends. Some of them were armed with clubs, some with bows and arrows. We all arranged ourselves to receive them, behind the top of a large fallen tree. When they were within rifle shot, we made signs to them to halt, or that otherwise we should fire upon them. They comprehended us, halted and ceased yelling, as though they wished to hear what we had to say. We made signs that we were friendly. At this they gazed in apparent confusion of thought, and seemed to be questioning each other, touching the meaning of our signs. These signs we continued to repeat. At length one of them called aloud in Spanish, and asked us who we were? How delightful were these sounds! We answered *Americans*. They repeated the name, asking us if we were friendly and Christians? To these questions we made a ready affirmative.

They then proposed a treaty with us. Nothing could be more agreeable to us. At the same time we perceived that only eight of their people came to us, and the remainder of their company kept back. These eight that seemed to be their chief men, advanced to us, while the rest, with extreme anxiety painted upon their countenances, stood ready for action. We all sat down on the ground, and commenced talking. They enquired with great precision, who we were, whence we came, how we arrived here, what was our object, and whether we had met with any misfortunes? We answered these questions to their satisfaction; and soon the pipe was lit, and we commenced smoking. They then dug a hole in the ground, in which they buried their war axe, and professed to deposite all ill feelings with it. The Indian of their number, who spoke the Spanish language, was a fugitive from the Mission of St. Catherine.—Threatened with the punishment of some misdemeanour, he had fled from the establishment.

After we had finished smoking, they asked us if the remainder of their number might not come and converse with us. This we objected to, unless they would bring their women and children with them. To this order they expressed great reluctance. This reluctance by no means tended to allay our previous jealousy of their pretended friendship. We asked them their reasons for being unwilling to bring their women and children? They answered promptly that they did not feel it safe to put their women and children in our power, until they were more acquainted with us. There seemed reason in this. We observed, that their men might come, provided they would leave their arms behind. To this they readily assented, and called out to their men to come on, leaving their arms behind. A part of them seemingly much delighted, threw down their arms and came on. The remainder equally dissatisfied, wheeled about, and walked moodily away.

The new comers sat down in a circle round us. The pipe was again lit and circled round. Again the terms of the treaty were repeated, and they all expressed their satisfaction with them. They observed, that their head chief was absent, at the distance of two day's journey to the south, that in three or four days he would come and see us, desiring us to remain with them until he should come. Nothing could be more opportune for us, for we were all excessively fatigued, and needed a few days rest. After this they went and brought their women and children, who, like the other Indians we had seen, were all stark naked. At first they were excessively shy of us. This shyness wore off, and in the course of the day changed to an eager curiosity to examine us, and an admiration of our red flannel shirts, and the white skin *under them*; for little show of whiteness was to be seen in our faces. They soon ventured close to us, and with their own hands opened our bosoms, uttering exclamations of curiosity and admiration, especially on feeling the softness of our skins, in comparison of theirs. They certainly seemed to prefer our complexion to theirs, notwithstanding it had not the stamp of their fashion.

At length they made up to one of our companions, who was of a singularly light complexion, fair soft skin, and blue eyes. They wanted him to strip himself naked that they might explore him thoroughly, for they seemed to be doubtful of his being alike white in every part of his body. This, but as mildly as possible, he refused to do. They went off and brought a quantity of dried fish of excellent quality, and presented him. We persuaded him to oblige these curious and good natured women, by giving them a full view of his body. He was persuaded to strip to his skin. This delighted them, and they conversed and laughed among themselves, and they came one by one and stood beside him; so as to compare their bodies with his. After this, as long as we staid, they were constantly occupied in bringing us cooked fish and the vegetables and roots on which they are accustomed to feed.

On the 25th, the head chief came. He was a venerable looking man, whom I judged to be about fifty years old. His countenance was thoughtful and serious, and his hair a little gray. At his return his people greeted him with an acclamation of yells, that made the wild desert echo. The pipe was lit, and we all sat down by him and smoked again. He was a man of but few words, but of sound judgment. After the smoking was finished, he asked us the same questions which had been asked us before. We made him similar answers, adding, that we wanted to travel to the Spanish settlements and purchase horses, upon which we might ride home to our own country, and that we would pay him well if he would send some of his men to guide us to those settlements. He asked us in reply, what we had to give him? We showed him our blankets, and he expressed himself delighted with them, observing at the same time, that he would have preferred to have had red cloth.

On this we pulled off our red shirts and stripped them into small pieces like ribbons, and distributed them among the people. They tied the strips round their legs, arms and heads, and seemed as much overjoyed with these small tatters of worn red flannel, as we should have been, to have brought our furs to a good market among our own people. In giving away our red shirts, we gave away, what in this warm climate was to us wholly unnecessary. To carry our blankets on our backs was a useless burden. We gave two of them to the chief. The two guides that he was to send with us we were to pay after our arrival at the Spanish settlements. These points of contract between us were settled to the mutual satisfaction of all.

We started on the 26th, with our two guides, neither of whom could speak Spanish, and of course we had nothing to do but follow them in silence. We struck off a south west course, which led in the direction of the snow covered mountain, which still loomed up in its brightness before us. Our guides made signs that we should arrive at the foot about midnight, though the distance appeared to us to be too great to be travelled over in so short a time. We were yet to learn, that we should find no water, until we drank that of the melted snow. We perceived, however, that their travelling gait, worn as we were, was more rapid than ours. We pushed on as fast as we could a league further, when we were impeded by a high hill in our way, which was about another league to the summit, and very precipitous and steep. When we reached the top of it we were much exhausted, and began to be thirsty. We could then see the arid salt plain stretching all the way from the foot of this hill to the snow covered mountains.

We thought it inexpedient to enquire of our guides, if there was no water to be found between us and the mountain. It appeared but too probable, that such was the fact. To know it to a certainty, would only tend to unnerve and dishearten us. If there was any, we were aware that we should reach it by travelling no more distance than as if we knew the fact. We found it best to encourage the little hope that remained, and hurried on through the drifted sand, in which we sank up to our ankles at every step. The cloudless sun poured such a blaze upon it, that by the scorching of our feet, it might have seemed almost hot enough to roast eggs in. What with the fierce sun and the scorching sand, and our extreme fatigue, the air seemed soon to have extracted every particle of moisture from our bodies.

In this condition we marched on until nearly the middle of the day, without descrying any indication of water in any quarter. A small shrubby tree stood in our way, affording a tolerable shade. We laid our-selves down to get a few minutes rest. The Indians sternly beckoned us to be up and onward, now for the first time clearly explaining to us, that there was no water until we reached the mountains in view. This unseasonable and yet necessary information, extinguished the last remainder of our hope, and we openly expressed our fears that we should none of us ever reach it.

We attempted to chew tobacco. It would raise no moisture. We took our bullets in our mouths, and moved them round to create a moisture, to relieve our parched throats. We had travelled but a little farther before our tongues had became so dry and swollen, that we could scarcely speak so as to be understood. In this extremity of nature, we should, perhaps, have sunk voluntarily, had not the relief been still in view on the sides of the snow covered mountains. We resorted to one expedient to moisten our lips, tongue and throat, disgusting to relate, and still more disgusting to adopt. In such predicaments it has been found, that nature disburdens people of all conditions of ceremony and disgust. Everything bends to the devouring thirst, and the love of life. The application of this hot and salt liquid seemed rather to enrage than appease the torturing appetite. Though it offered such a semblance of what would satisfy thirst, that we economized every particle.

Our amiable Dutchman was of a sweetness of temper, that was never ruffled, and a calmness and patience that appeared proof against all events. At another time, what laughter would have circulated through our camp, to hear him make merry of this expedient! As it was, even in this horrible condition, a faint smile circulated through our company, as he discussed his substitute for drink. 'Vell, mine poys, *dis* vater of *mein* ish more hotter as hell, *und* as dick as boudden, *und* more zalter as *de* zeas. I can't drink him. For Cod's sake, gif me some of yours, *dat* is more tinner.'

Having availed ourselves to the utmost of this terrible expedient, we marched on in company a few miles further. Two of our companions here gave out, and lay down under the shade of a bush. Their tongues were so swollen, and their eyes so sunk in their heads, that they were a spectacle to behold. We were scarcely able, from the condition of our own mouths, to bid them an articulate farewell. We never expected to see them again, and none of us had much hope of ever reaching the mountain, which still raised its white summit at a great distance from us. It was with difficulty that we were enabled to advance one foot before the other. Our limbs, our powers, even our very resolutions seemed palsied.

A circumstance that added to our distress, was the excessive and dazzling brightness of the sun's rays, so reflected in our eyes from the white sand that we were scarcely able to see our way before us, or in what direction to follow our guides. They, accustomed to go naked, and to traverse these burning deserts, and be unaffected by such trials, appeared to stand the heat and drought, like camels on the Arabian sands. They, however, tried by their looks and gestures to encourage us, and induce us to quicken our pace. But it was to no purpose. However, we still kept moving onward, and had gained a few miles more, when night brought us shelter at least from the insupportable radiance of the sun, and something of coolness and moisture.

But it was so dark, that neither we or our guides could discover the course. We stopped, and made a large fire, that our companions, if yet living, and able to move, might see where we were, and how to direct their own course to reach us. We also fired some guns, which, to our great relief and pleasure, they answered by firing off theirs. We still repeated firing guns at intervals, until they came up with us. They supposed that we had found water, which invigorated their spirits to such a degree, that it aroused them to the effort they had made. When they had arrived, and found that we had reached no water, they appeared to be angry, and to complain that we had disturbed their repose with false hopes, and had hindered their dying in peace. One of them in the recklessness of despair, drew from his package a small phial, half full of laudanum, and drank it off, I suppose in the hope of sleeping himself quietly to death. We all expected it would have that effect.

On the contrary, in a few moments he was exhilarated, like a man in a state of intoxication. He was full of talk, and laughter, and gaiety of heart. He observed, that he had taken it in hopes that it would put him to sleep, never to wake again, but that in fact, it had made him as well, and as fresh, as in the morning when he started; but that if he had imagined that it would prove such a sovereign remedy for thirst, he would cheerfully have shared it with us. We scraped down beneath the burning surface of the sand, until we reached the earth that was a little cool. We then stripped off all our clothing and lay down. Our two Indians, also lay down beside us, covering themselves with their blankets. My father bade me lay on the edge of one of their blankets, so that they could not get up without awakening me. He was fearful that they would arise, and fly from us in the night. I implicitly conformed to my father's wish, for had this event happened, we should all undoubtedly have perished. But the Indians appear to have meditated no such expedient, at any rate, they lay quiet until morning.

As soon as there was light enough to enable us to travel we started, much refreshed by the coolness of the night, and the sleep we had taken. We began our morning march with renewed alacrity. At about ten in the forenoon we arrived at the foot of a sand hill about a half a mile in height, and very steep. The side was composed of loose sand, which gave way under our feet, so that our advancing foot steps would slide back to their former places. This soon exhausted our little remaining strength; though we still made many an unavailing effort to ascend. The sun was now so high, as to beam upon us with the same insufferable radiance of yesterday. The air which we inhaled, seemed to scald our lungs. We at length concluded to travel towards the north, to reach, if we might, some point where the hill was not so steep to ascend.

At two in the afternoon we found a place that was neither so steep nor so high, and we determined here to attempt to cross the hill. With great exertions and infinite difficulty, a part of us gained the summit of the hill; but my father and another of our company, somewhat advanced in years, gave out below, though they made the most persevering efforts to reach the summit of the hill with the rest. Age had stiffened their joints, and laid his palsying hand upon their once active limbs, and vigorous frames. They could endure this dreadful journey no longer. They had become so exhausted by fruitless efforts to climb the hill, that they could no longer drag one foot after the other. They had each so completely abandoned the hope of ever reaching the water, or even gaining the summit of the hill, that they threw themselves on the ground, apparently convinced of their fate, and resigned to die. I instantly determined to remain with my father, be it for life or death. To this determination he would by no means consent, as he remarked it would bring my destruction, without its availing him.

On the contrary, he insisted, that I should go on with the rest, and if I found any water near at hand, that I should return with my powder horn full. In this way he assured me, I might be instrumental in saving my own life, and saving him at the same time. To this I consented, and with much fatigue gained the summit of the hill, where my companions were seated waiting for us. They seemed undetermined, whether to advance onward, or wait for my father, until I related his determination. My purpose was to proceed onward only so far, as that, if the Almighty should enable us to reach water, I might be able to return with a powder horn full to him and Mr. Slover, (for that was the name of the elderly companion that remained with him.)

This resolution was agreed to by all, as a proper one. Being satisfied by our consciences as well as by the reasoning of my father and his companion, that we could render them no service by remaining with them, except to increase their sufferings by a view of ours; and aware, that every moment was precious, we pushed on once more for the mountain. Having descended this hill, we ascended another of the same wearying ascent, and sandy character with the former. We toiled on to the top of it. The Eternal Power, who hears the ravens when they cry, and provideth springs in the wilderness, had had mercy upon us! Imagine my joy at seeing a clear, beautiful running stream of water, just below us at the foot of the hill! Such a blissful sight I had never seen before, and never expect to see again. We all ran down to it, and fell to drinking. In a few moments nothing was to be heard among us, but vomiting and groaning. Notwithstanding our mutual charges to be cautious, we had overcharged our parched stomachs with this cold snow water.

Notwithstanding I was sick myself, I emptied my powder horn of its contents, filled it with water, and accompanied by one companion, who had also filled his powder horn, I returned towards my father and Mr. Slover, his exhausted companion, with a quick step. We found them in the same position in which we had left them, that is, stretched on the sand at full length, under the unclouded blaze of the sun, and both fast asleep; a sleep from which, but for our relief, I believe they would neither of them ever have awakened. Their lips were black, and their parched mouths wide open. Their unmoving posture and their sunken eyes so resembled death, that I ran in a fright to my father, thinking him, for a moment, really dead. But he easily awakened, and drank the refreshing water. My companion at the same time bestowed his horn of water upon Mr. Slover.

In the course of an hour they were both able to climb the hill, and some time before dark we rejoined the remainder of our company. They had kindled a large fire, and all seemed in high spirits. As for our two Indians, they were singing, and dancing, as it seemed to us, in a sort of worship of thankfulness to the Great Spirit, who had led them through so much peril and toil to these refreshing waters. We roasted some of our beaver meat, and took food for the first time in forty-eight hours, that is to say, from the time we left our Indian friends, until we reached this water.

Our Dutchman insisted that the plain over which we passed, should be named the devil's plain, for he insisted, that it was more hotter as hell, and that none but teyvils could live upon it. In fact, it seemed a more fitting abode for fiends, than any living thing that belongs to our world. During our passage across it, we saw not a single bird, nor the track of any quadruped, or in fact any thing that had life, not even a sprig, weed or grass blade, except a single shrubby tree, under which we found a little shade. This shrub, though of some height, resembled a prickly pear, and was covered thick with thorns. The prickly pears were in such abundance, that we were often, dazzled as our eyes were

MESSRS. PATTIE AND SLOVER RESCUED FROM FAMISH

with the sun's brightness, puzzled to find a path so as neither to torment our feet or our bodies with the thorns of these hated natives of the burning sands. This very extensive plain, the Sahara of California, runs north and south, and is bounded on each side by high barren mountains, some of which are covered with perpetual snow.

On the 28th, we travelled up this creek about three miles, and killed a deer, which much delighted our two Indian guides. At this point we encamped for the night. Here are abundance of palm trees and live oaks, and considerable of *mascal*. We remained until the 3rd of March, when we marched up this creek, which heads to the south, forming a low gap in the mountain. On the 7th, we arrived at the point, and found some of the Christian Indians from the Mission of St. Catharine. They were roasting *mascal* and the tender inside heads of the palm trees for food, which, when prepared and cooked after their fashion, becomes a very agreeable food. From these Indians we learned that we were within four days' travel of the mission mentioned above.

Here we concluded to discharge our guides, and travel into the settlement with the Christian Indians. We gave them each a blanket, and they started back to their own people on the morning of the 8th. At the same time we commenced our journey with our new guides, and began to climb the mountain. This is so exceedingly lofty, as to require two days' travel and a half to gain its summit. During this ascent, I severely bruised my heel. We none of us wore anything to shield our feet from the bare and sharp rocks, which composed almost the whole surface of this ascent, but thin deer skin *moccasins*. Obliged to walk on tiptoe, and in extreme anguish, the severe fatigue of scrambling up sharp stones was any thing, rather than agreeable. But I summoned patience and courage to push on until the 12th. My leg then became so swollen and inflamed that it was out of my power to travel farther. The pain was so severe as to create fever.

I lay myself down on the side of a sharp rock, resigning myself to my fate, and determined to make no effort to travel further, until I felt relieved. My companions all joined with my father, in encouraging me to rise, and make an effort to reach the mission, which they represented to be but three miles distant. It was out of the question for me to think of it, and they concluded to go to the settlement, and obtain a horse, and send out for me. I kindled me a fire, for I suffered severe chills. The Indians gave me the strictest caution against allowing myself to go to sleep in their absence. The reason they assigned for their caution was a substantial one. The grizzly bear, they said, was common on these mountains, and would attack and devour me, unless I kept on my guard. I paid little attention to their remarks at the time. But when they were gone, and I was left alone, I examined the priming, and picked the flints of my gun and pistol. I then lay down and slept, until sometime in the early part of the night, when two Indians came out from the settlement, and informed me that the corporal of the guards at St. Catharines wished me to come in.

Being feverish, stiff, sore and withal testy, I gave them and their corporal no very civil words. They said that the corporal only wanted me to come in, because he was afraid the grizzly bears would kill me. I asked them why they did not bring a horse for me? They informed me, that the mission had none at disposal at that time, but that they would carry me on their backs. So I was obliged to avail myself of this strange conveyance, and mounted the back of one of them while the other carried my arms. In this way they carried me in, where I found my companions in a guard house. I was ordered to enter with them by a swarthy looking fellow, who resembled a negro, rather than a white.

I cannot describe the indignation I felt at this revolting breach of humanity to people in suffering, who had thrown themselves on the kindness and protection of these Spaniards. We related the reasons why we had come in after this manner. We showed them our passport, which certified to them, that we were neither robbers, murderers, nor spies. To all this their only reply was, how should they know whether we had come clandestinely, and with improper views, or not? Against this question, proposed by such people, all reasonings were thrown away.—The cowardly and worthless are naturally cruel. We were thrown completely in their power; and instead of that circumstance exciting any generous desires to console and relieve us, their only study seemed to be to vex, degrade, and torment us.

Here we remained a week, living on corn mush, which we received once a day; when a guard of soldiers came to conduct us from this place. This mission is situated in a valley, surrounded by high mountains, with beautiful streams of water flowing from them. The natives raise sufficient corn and wheat to serve for the subsistence of the mission. The mission establishment is built in a quadrangular form; all the houses forming the quadrangle contiguous to each other; and one of the angles is a large church, adjoining which are the habitations of the priests; though at this time there happened to be none belonging to this at home. The number of Indians belonging to the mission at this time, was about five hundred. They were destitute of stock, on account of its having been plundered from them by the free, wild Indians of the desert. The air is very cool and temperate, and hard frosts are not uncommon. This cool temperature of the atmosphere I suppose to be owing to the immediate proximity of the snowy mountains.

On the 18th, we started under the conduct of a file of soldiers, who led us two days' travel, over very high mountains, a south west course, to another mission, called St. Sebastian, situated near the sea coast, in a delightful valley, surrounded, like the other, by lofty mountains, the sides of which present magnificent views of the ocean. This mission contains six hundred souls. This mission establishment, though much richer and neater than the other, is, however, built on a precisely similar plan. Here they have rich vineyards, and raise a great variety of the fruits of almost all climates. They also raise their own supplies of grain, and have a tolerable abundance of stock, both of the larger and smaller kinds.

A sergeant has the whole military command. We found him of a dark and swarthy complexion, though a man of tolerable information. He seemed disposed to conduct towards us with some courtesy and kindness. He saluted us with politeness, conducted us to the guard house, and begged us to content ourselves, as well as we could, until he could make some more satisfactory arrangements for our comfort and convenience. To put him to the proof of his professed kindness, we told him that we were very hungry. They soon had a poor steer killed, that reeled as it walked, and seemed sinking by natural decay. A part of the blue flesh was put boiling in one pot, and a parcel of corn in the other. The whole process reminded me strongly of the arrangements which we make in Kentucky, to prepare a mess for a diseased cow. When this famous feast was cooked, we were marched forth into the yard, in great ceremony, to eat it.

All the men, women and children clustered round us, and stood staring at us while we were eating, as though they had been at a menagerie to see some wild and unknown animals.—When we were fairly seated to our pots, and began to discuss the contents, disgusted alike with the food, with them, and their behaviour, we could not forbear asking them whether they really took us to be human beings, or considered us as brutes? They looked at each other a moment, as if to reflect and frame an answer, and then replied coolly enough, that not being Christians, they considered us little superior to brutes. To this we replied, with a suitable mixture of indignation and scorn, that we considered ourselves better Christians than they were, and that if they did not give us something to eat more befitting men, we would take our guns, live where we pleased, and eat venison and other good things, where we chose.

This was not mere bravado, for, to our astonishment, we were still in possession of our arms. We had made no resistance to their treating us as prisoners, as we considered them nothing more than petty and ignorant officers, whom we supposed to have conducted improperly, from being unacquainted with their duty. We were all confident, that as soon as intelligence of our arrival should reach the commanding officer of this station, and how we had been detained, and treated as prisoners, we should not only be released from prison, but recompensed for our detention.

This determination of ours appeared to alarm them. The information of our menaces, no doubt with their own comments, soon reached the sergeant. He immediately came to see us, while we were yet at our pots, and enquired of us, what was our ground of complaint and dissatisfaction? We pointed to the pots, and asked him if he thought such food becoming the laws of hospitality to such people? He stepped up to the pots, and turning over the contents, and examining them with his fingers, enquired in an angry tone, who had served up such food to us? He added, that it was not fit to give a dog, and that he would punish those who had procured it. He comforted us, by assuring us that we should have something fit to eat cooked for us. We immediately returned quietly to the guard house.

But a short time ensued before he sent us a good dish of fat mutton, and some *tortillas*. This was precisely the thing our appetites craved, and we were not long in making a hearty meal. After we had fed to our satisfaction, he came to visit us, and interrogated us in what manner, and with what views we had visited the country? We went into clear, full and satisfactory details of information in regard to every thing that could have any interest to him, as an officer; and told him that our object was to purchase horses, on which we might return to our own country; and that we wished him to intercede in our behalf with the commander in chief, that we might have permission to purchase horses and mules among them, for this purpose. He promised to do this, and returned to his apartment.

The amount of his promise was, that he would reflect upon the subject, and in the course of four days write to his commander, from whom he might expect an answer in a fortnight.—When we sounded him as to the probability of such a request being granted, he answered with apparent conviction, that he had no doubt that it would be in our favour. As our hopes were intensely fixed upon this issue, we awaited this answer with great anxiety. The commander at this time was at the port of San Diego. During this period of our suspense, we had full liberty to hunt deer in the woods, and gather honey from the blossoms of the *mascal*, which grows plentifully on the sea shore. Every thing in this strange and charming country being new, we were continually contemplating curiosities of every sort, which quieted our solicitude, and kept alive the interest of our attention.

We used to station ourselves on the high pinnacles of the cliffs, on which this vast sea pours its tides, and the retreating or advancing tide showed us the strange sea monsters of that ocean, such as seals, sea otters, sea elephants, whales, sharks, sword fish, and various other unshapely sea dwellers. Then we walked on the beach, and examined the infinite variety of sea shells, all new and strange to us.

Thus we amused ourselves, and strove to kill the time until the 20th, when the answer of the commander arrived, which explained itself at once, by a guard of soldiers, with orders to conduct us to the port of San Diego, where he then resided. We were ordered to be in immediate readiness to start for that port. This gave us unmingled satisfaction, for we had an undoubting confidence, that when we should really have attained the presence of an officer whom we supposed a gentleman, and acting independently of the authority of others, he would make no difficulty in granting a request so reasonable as ours. We started on the 2nd, guarded by sixteen soldiers and a corporal. They were all on horseback, and allowed us occasionally to ride, when they saw us much fatigued. Our first day's journey was a north course, over very rough mountains, and yet, notwithstanding this, we made twenty-five miles distance on our way.

At night we arrived at another mission, situated like the former, on a charming plain. The mission is called St. Thomas. These wise and holy men mean to make sure of the rich and pleasant things of the earth, as well as the kingdom of heaven. They have large plantations, with splendid orchards and vineyards. The priest who presides over this establishment, told me that he had a thousand Indians under his care. During every week in the year, they kill thirty beeves for the subsistence of the mission. The hides and tallow they sell to vessels that visit their coast, in exchange for such goods as they need.

151

On the following morning, we started early down this valley, which led us to the sea shore, along which we travelled the remainder of the day. This beautiful plain skirts the sea shore, and extends back from it about four miles. This was literally covered with horses and cattle belonging to the mission. The eye was lost beyond this handsome plain in contemplating an immeasurable range of mountains, which we were told thronged with wild horses and cattle, which often descend from their mountains to the plains, and entice away the domesticated cattle with them. The wild oats and clover grow spontaneously, and in great luxuriance, and were now knee high. In the evening we arrived at the port of Todos Santos, and there passed the night. Early on the 23rd, we marched on. This day we travelled over some tracts that were very rough, and arrived at a mission situated immediately on the sea board, called St. Michael. Like the rest, it was surrounded with splendid orchards, vineyards and fields; and was, for soil, climate and position, all that could be wished.

The old superintending priest of the establishment showed himself very friendly, and equally inquisitive. He invited us to sup with him, an invitation we should not be very likely to refuse. We sat down to a large table, elegantly furnished with various dishes of the country, all as usual highly seasoned. Above all, the supply of wines was various and abundant. The priest said grace at the close, when fire and cigars were brought in by the attendants, and we began to smoke. We sat and smoked, and drank wine, until 12 o'clock. The priest informed us that the population of his mission was twelve hundred souls, and the weekly consumption, fifty beeves, and a corresponding amount of grain. The mission possessed three thousand head of domesticated and tamed horses and mules. From the droves which I saw in the plains, I should not think this an extravagant estimation. In the morning he presented my father a saddle mule, which he accepted, and we started.

This day's travel still carried us directly along the verge of the sea shore, and over a plain equally rich and beautiful with that of the preceding day. We amused ourselves with noting the spouting of the huge whales, which seemed playing near the strand for our especial amusement. We saw other marine animals and curiosities to keep our interest in the journey alive. In the evening we arrived at a ranch, called Buenos Aguos, or Good Water, where we encamped for the night.

We started early on the 25th, purchasing a sheep of a shepherd, for which we paid him a knife. At this ranch they kept thirty thousand head of sheep, belonging to the mission which we had left. We crossed a point of the mountain that made into the water's edge. On the opposite side of this mountain was another ranch, where we staid the night. This ranch is for the purposes of herding horses and cattle, of which they have vast numbers. On the 26th, our plain lay outstretched before us as beautiful as ever. In the evening we came in sight of San Diego, the place where we were bound.

In this port was one merchant vessel, which we were told was from the United States, the ship *Franklin*, of Boston. We had then arrived within about a league of the port. The corporal who had charge of us here, came and requested us to give up our arms, informing us, it was the customary request to all strangers; and that it was expected that our arms would be deposited in the guardhouse before we could speak with the commander, or general. We replied, that we were both able and disposed to carry our arms to the guardhouse ourselves, and deposit them there if such was our pleasure, at our own choice. He replied that we could not be allowed to do this, for that we were considered as prisoners, and under his charge; and that he should become responsible in his own person, if he should allow us to appear before the general, bearing our own arms. This he spoke with a countenance of seriousness, which induced us to think that he desired no more in this request than the performance of his duty.

We therefore gave him up our rifles, not thinking that this was the last time we should have the pleasure of shouldering these trusty friends. Having unburdened ourselves of our defence, we marched on again, and arrived, much fatigued, at the town at 3 o'clock in the evening. Our arms were stacked on the side of the guard house, and we threw our fatigued bodies as near them as we could, on the ground.

An officer was dispatched to the general to inform him of our arrival, and to know whether we could have an immediate audience or not? In a short time the officer returned with an answer for us, that we must remain where we were until morning, when the general would give us a hearing. We were still sanguine in seeing only omens of good. We forgot our past troubles, opened our bosom to hope, and resigned ourselves to profound sleep. It is true, innumerable droves of fleas performed their evolutions, and bit all their pleasure upon our bodies.— But so entire was our repose, that we scarcely turned for the night. No dreams of what was in reserve for us the following day floated across our minds; though in the morning my body was as spotted as though I had the measles, and my shirt specked with innumerable stains of blood, let by the ingenious lancets of these same Spanish fleas.

On the 27th, at eight a.m., we were ushered into the general's office, with our hats in our hands, and he began his string of interrogations. The first question was, who we were? We answered, Americans. He proceeded to ask us, how we came on the coast, what was our object, and had we a passport? In answer to these questions we again went over the story of our misfortunes. We then gave him the passport which we had received from the governor of Santa Fé. He examined this instrument, and with a sinister and malicious smile, observed, that he believed nothing of all this, but considered us worse than thieves and murderers; in fact, that he held us to be spies for the old Spaniards, and that our business was to lurk about the country, that we might inspect the weak and defenceless points of the frontiers, and point them out to the Spaniards, in order that they might introduce their troops into the country; but that he would utterly detect us, and prevent our designs.—This last remark he uttered with a look of vengeance; and then reperused the passport, which he tore in pieces, saying, it was no passport, but a vile forgery of our own contrivance.

Though amazed and confounded at such an unexpected charge, we firmly asserted our innocence in regard to any of the charges brought against us. We informed him that we were born and bred thorough and full blooded republicans; and that there was not a man of us who would not prefer to die, rather than to be the spies and instruments of the Spanish king, or any other king; and that but a few years since, we had all been engaged in fighting the forces of a king, allied with savages, and sent against the country of our home; and that on this very expedition we had been engaged in a great many battles with the Indians, hostile to his people, redeeming their captives, and punishing their robberies and murders. In distress, and in want of everything from the robbery of these hostile Indians, we had taken refuge in his country, and claimed its protection.

We told him we considered it an unworthy return for such general deportment, and such particular services to their country, that we should be viewed as spies, and treated as prisoners. He stopped us in the midst of our plea, apparently through fear that representations, which must have carried conviction to his prejudiced mind, might tend to soften his obdurate heart, and unnerve his purpose towards us. He told us he did not wish to hear any more of our long speeches, which he considered no better than lies; for that if we had been true and *bona fide* citizens of the United States, we should not have left our country without a passport, and the certificate of our chief magistrate. We replied that the laws of our country did not require that honest, common citizens, should carry passports; that it did not interfere with the individual business and pursuits of private individuals; that such persons went abroad and returned unnoted by the government; and in all well regulated states, sufficiently protected by the proof that they were citizens of the United States; but that there were in our country two classes of people, for whom passports were necessary, slaves and soldiers; that for the slave it was necessary to have one, to certify that he was travelling with the knowledge and permission of his master; and for the soldier, to show that he was on furlough, or otherwise abroad with the permission of his officer. As we spoke this with emphasis, and firmness, he told us that he had had enough of our falsehoods, and begged us to be quiet. He ordered us to be remanded to our prison, and was immediately obeyed.

As we were driven out of his office, my father, who was exceedingly exasperated, observed, 'my boys, as soon as we arrive in the guard house, let us seize our arms and redress ourselves, or die in the attempt; for it seems to me that these scoundrels mean to murder us.' We all unanimously agreed to this advice, and walked back with a willing mind, and an alert step. But our last hope of redressing ourselves, and obtaining our liberty was soon extinguished. On entering the guard house, our arms had been removed we knew not where. They had even the impudence to search our persons and to take from us even our pocket knives. The orderly sergeant then told us, that he was under the necessity of placing us in separate apartments. This last declaration seemed the death stroke to us all. Affliction and mutual suffering and danger had endeared us to each other, and this separation seemed like rending our hearts.

Overcome by the suddenness of the blow, I threw my arms round the neck of my father, burst into tears, and exclaimed, 'that I foresaw, that the parting would be forever.' Though my father seemed subdued, and absorbed in meditation, he reproved this expression of my feelings, as weak and unmanly. The sergeant having observed my grief, asked me, pointing to him, if that was my father? When he learned that it was, he showed himself in some degree affected, and remarked, that it seemed cruel to separate father and child, and that he would go and explain the relationship to the general, and see if he could not obtain permission for us to remain together. On this he set off for the general's office, leaving me in the agony of suspense, and the rest gazing at each other in mute consternation and astonishment. The sergeant returned, informing me, that instead of being softened, the general had only been exasperated, and had in nothing relaxed his orders, which were, that we must immediately be put in separate confinement. He accordingly ordered some soldiers to assist in locking us up.

We embraced each other, and followed our conductors to our separate prisons. I can affirm, that I had only wished to live, to sustain the increasing age and infirmities of my father. When I shook hands with him, and we were torn in sunder, I will say nothing of my feelings, for words would have no power to describe them. As I entered my desolate apartment, the sergeant seemed really affected, and assured me, that neither my companions nor myself should suffer any want of food or drink, as far as he could prevent it, for that he did not consider us guilty, nor worthy of such treatment.

My prison was a cell eight or ten feet square, with walls and floor of stone. A door with iron bars an inch square crossed over each other, like the bars of window sashes, and it grated on its iron hinges, as it opened to receive me. Over the external front of this prison was inscribed in capital letters *Destinacion de la Cattivo*. Our blankets were given us to lie upon. My father had a small package of medicines which he gave in charge to the sergeant, binding him on his word of honour not to part with it to any one. My door was locked, and I was left to reflect upon our position and my past misfortunes; and to survey the dreary walls of my prison.

Here, I thought, was my everlasting abode. Liberty is dear to every one, but doubly dear to one, who had been from infancy accustomed to free range, and to be guided by his own will. Put a man, who has ranged the prairies, and exulted in the wilderness, as I have for years, in a prison, to let him have a full taste of the blessings of freedom, and the horror of shackles and confinement! I passed the remainder of the day in fierce walking backwards and forwards over my stone floor, with no object to contemplate, but my swarthy sentinel, through the grate. He seemed to be true to his office, and fitly selected for his business, for I thought I saw him look at me through the grate with the natural exultation and joy of a bad and malicious heart in the view of misery.

When the darkness of night came to this dreary place, it was the darkness of the grave. Every ray of light was extinct. I spread my blankets on the stone floor, in hopes at least to find, for a few hours, in the oblivion of sleep, some repose from the agitation of my thoughts.

But in this hope I was disappointed. With every other friend and solace, sleep too, fled from me. My active mind ranged everywhere, and returned only to unavailing efforts to imagine the condition and feelings of my father and what would be our ultimate fate. I shut my eyes by an effort, but nature would have her way, and the eyelids would not close.

At length a glimmer of daylight, through my grate, relieved this long and painful effort to sleep. I arose, went to my grate, and took all possible survey of what I could see. Directly in front of it was the door of the general's office, and he was standing in it. I gazed on him awhile. Ah! that I had had but my trusty rifle well charged to my face! Could I but have had the pleasure of that single shot, I think I would have been willing to have purchased it by my life. But wishes are not rifle balls, and will not kill.

The church bell told eight in the morning. The drum rolled. A soldier came, and handed me in something to eat. It proved to be dried beans and corn cooked with rancid tallow! The contents were about a pint. I took it up, and brought it within the reach of my nostrils, and sat it down in unconquerable loathing. When the soldier returned in the evening to bring me more, I handed him my morning ration untasted and just as it was. He asked me in a gruff tone why I had not eaten it? I told him the smell of it was enough, and that I could not eat it. He threw the contents of the dish in my face, muttering something which amounted to saying, that it was good enough for such a brute as I was. To this I answered, that if being a brute gave claims upon that dish, I thought he had best eat it himself. On this he flung away in a passion, and returned no more that night, for which I was not sorry. Had the food even been fit to eat, my thoughts were too dark and my mind too much agitated to allow me appetite. In fact, I felt myself becoming sick.

At night I was visited by the sergeant, who asked me about my health and spirits in a tone and manner, that indicated real kindness of feeling. I trusted in the reality of his sympathy, and told him, I was not well. He then questioned me, if I had eaten anything? I told him no, and explained to him the double reason, why I had eaten nothing. He answered that he would remove one of the causes, by sending me something good. I then asked him if he had seen my father? He said he had, though he had been unable to hold any conversation with him, for want of his understanding Spanish. I thanked him for this manifestation of friendship, and he left me. In a short time he returned with two well cooked and seasoned dishes. I begged him to take it first to my father, and when he had eaten what he wished, he might bring the remainder to me, and I would share it among my companions. He assured me that my father was served with the same kind of food, and that my companions should not be forgotten in the distribution.

While I was eating, he remained with me, and asked me, if I had a mother, and brothers, and sisters in my own country? My heart was full, as I answered him. He proceeded to question me, how long it had been since I had seen them or heard from them, and in what I had been occupied, during my long absence from my country? My misfortunes appeared to affect him. When I had finished eating, he enquired how I had passed the preceding night? In all his questions, he displayed true humanity and tenderness of heart. When he left me, he affectionately wished me goodnight. This night passed as sleepless and uncomfortable as the preceding one. Next day the kind sergeant brought my dinner again, though from anxiety and growing indisposition I was unable to eat. At night he came again with my supper, and to my surprise accompanied by his sister, a young lady of great personal beauty. Her first enquiry was that of a kind and affectionate nature, and concerned my father. She enquired about my age, and all the circumstances that induced me to leave my country?

I took leave to intimate in my answer, my extreme anxiety to see my relatives, and return to my country, and in particular, that it was like depriving me of life, in this strange land, and in prison, to separate me from my old and infirm father. She assured me that she would pray for our salvation, and attempt to intercede with the general in our behalf, and that while we remained in prison, she would allow us to suffer nothing, which her power, means or influence could supply. She then wished me a goodnight, and departed. I know not what is the influence of the ministration of a kind spirit, like hers, but this night my sleep was sound and dreamless.

She frequently repeated these kind visits, and redeemed to the letter all her pledges of kindness. For I suffered for nothing in regard to food or drink. A bed was provided for me, and even a change of clothing. This undeviating kindness greatly endeared her to me. About this time, Captain John Bradshaw, of the ship *Franklin*, and Rufus Perkins, his supercargo, asked leave of the general, to come and visit us. The general denied them. But Captain Bradshaw, like a true hearted American, disregarded the little brief authority of this miserable republican despot, and fearless of danger and the consequences, came to see me without leave. When I spoke to him about our buried furs, he asked me about the chances and the means we had to bring them in? And whether we were disposed to make the effort, and if we succeeded, to sell them to him? The prisoners, as he separately applied to them, one and all assured him, that nothing would give them more pleasure. He assured us, that he would leave nothing in his power undone, in making efforts to deliver us from our confinement. We thanked him for this proffered friendship, and he departed.

His first efforts in our favour were directed to gaining the friendship of the general, in order to soften his feelings in regard to us. But in this he entirely failed. He then adopted an innocent stratagem, which was more successful. He informed the general that he had business with a Spanish merchant in port, which he could not transact for want of some one who could speak the language fluently, who would interpret for him, that he understood that one of the American prisoners could speak the language perfectly well, and that if he would allow that prisoner to come and interpret for him a few hours, he would bind himself in a bond to any amount, that the prisoner at the expiration of his services, would return voluntarily to his prison. To this the general gave his consent. Captain Bradshaw came to my prison, and I was permitted by the general's order to leave my prison.

When I went abroad, Captain Bradshaw conducted me to the office of an old captain, who had charge of the arms. We begged him to intercede with the general to obtain his permission, that we might go out and bring in our furs. We informed him, that Captain Bradshaw and the supercargo, Rufus Perkins, would be our security in any amount that the general was disposed to name, that we would return, and surrender ourselves to him, at the close of the expedition. He was at once satisfied of our honour and integrity, and that we were by no means those spies, whom the general took us for, and he promised to use all his influence with the general, to persuade him to dispatch us for our furs.

We assured him, that in addition to our other proofs, that we were *bona fide* Americans, and true republicans, we had documents under the proper signature of the President of the United States, which we hoped, would be sufficient to satisfy him, and every one, who we were. He asked to see those papers, of which I spoke. I told him they were my father's commission of first lieutenant in the ranging service, during the late war with England, and an honourable discharge at the close of the war. He promised to communicate this information to the general, and departed, proposing to return in half an hour. During this interval, we walked to my father's cell, and I had the satisfaction of speaking with him through the grates. He asked me if I had been visited by a beautiful young lady? When I assented, he replied, that this charming young woman, as a ministering angel, had also visited his cell with every sort of kindness and relief, which she had extended to each one of our companions. I had the satisfaction afterwards, of speaking with each one of our companions. I need not add, how much delighted we were to speak with one another once more. From these visits I returned to the office of the captain of arms.

We found him waiting with the most painful intelligence. Nothing could move the general, to allow us to go out and bring in our furs. He expressed a wish, notwithstanding, to see the commission of which I had spoken, and that I should return to my cell. I gave the papers to Captain Bradshaw, requesting him to return them to my father, after the general should have examined them. This he promised, and I took my leave of him, returning to my dreary prison, less buoyant and more completely desponding of my liberty than ever.

In a few moments Captain Bradshaw and Perkins came again to my cell, and said that the general had no faith in our papers, and could not be softened by any entreaty, to give us our liberty. As he said this, the sentinel came up, and stopped him short in his conversation, and ordered them off affirming, that it was the general's express command, that he should not be allowed to see or speak with me again. They however pledged their honour as they left me, that whenever an occasion offered, they would yield us all the assistance in their power, and wishing me better fortune, they departed.

A fortnight elapsed in this miserable prison, during which I had no other consolation, than the visits of the young lady, and even these, such was the strictness of the general's orders, were like all angel visits, *few and far between.* At length a note was presented me by the sergeant, from my father. What a note! I appeal to the heart of every good son to understand what passed within me. This note was written on a piece of paste board torn from his hat. The characters were almost illegible, for they were written with a stick, and the ink was blood, drawn from his aged veins! He informed me that he was very ill, and without any hope of recovery, that he had but one wish on this side the grave, and that was, to see me once more before he died. He begged me to spare no entreaties, that the general would grant me permission to come and see him a last time; but, that if this permission could not be obtained, to be assured, that he loved me, and remembered me affectionately, in death.

This letter pierced me to the heart. Oh, could I have flown through my prison walls! Had I possessed the strength of the giants, how soon would I have levelled them, even had I drawn down destruction on my own head in doing it. But I could own nothing in my favour, but a fierce and self devouring will. In hopes that the heart of the general was not all adamant, I entreated the sergeant to go and inform him of my father's illness, and his desire to see me once more, and to try to gain permission that I might have leave to attend upon him, or if that might not be, to visit him once more, according to his wish. He went in compliance with my entreaties, and in a few minutes returned with a dejected countenance, from which I at once inferred what was the fate of my application. His voice faltered as he related that the general absolutely refused this request. Oh God! of what stuff are some hearts made! and this was a republican officer! What nameless tortures and miseries do not Americans suffer in foreign climes from those miserable despots who first injure and oppress, and then hate the victims of their oppression, as judging their hearts by their own, and thinking that their victims must be full of purposes of revenge.

The honest and kind hearted sergeant hesitated not to express manly and natural indignation, in view of this inhuman brutality of the general, in refusing a favour, called for by the simplest dictates of humanity, a favor too, in the granting which there could be neither difficulty nor danger. All he could do in the case he promised to do, which was to see that my father should want no sort of nourishment, or aid which he could render him. I tried to thank him, but my case was not of a kind to be alleviated by this sort of consolation.

When I thought of our expectations of relief, when we threw ourselves in the power of these vile people, when I took into view our innocence of even the suspicion of a charge that could be brought against us, when I thought of their duplicity of disarming us, and their infamous oppression as soon as we were in their power, and more than all, when I thought of this last brutal cruelty and insult, my whole heart and nature rose in one mingled feeling of rage, wounded affection, and the indignation of despair. The image of my venerable father, suffering and dying unsolaced and unrelieved, and with not a person, who spoke his language, to close his eyes, and I so near him, was before me wherever I turned my eyes.

What a horrible night ensued at the close of this day! As the light was fading, the excellent young lady presented herself at my grate. She repeated all that her brother had related to me, in regard to the cruel refusal of the general. While she discussed this subject, the tears fell from her eyes, and I had the consolation to know, that one person at least felt real sympathy for my distress. She added, in faltering tones, that she was well aware that in a case like this words were of but little avail, but that I might be assured of the kindest attention to all the wants of my father, that she could relieve; and that if it was the will of God, to take him out of this world of sorrow and change, that he should be buried decently and as if he were her own father. Judge what I must have felt towards this noble minded and kind hearted young lady! As she withdrew, my prayers at this time were hearty, if never before, that God would reward her a thousand fold in all good things, for her sympathy with our sufferings.

Thus passed away these days of agony and suspense. The young lady visited me as often as it was understood the general's orders would permit, that is, once in two or three days, bringing me food and drink, of which in the present state of my thoughts, I had little need. In fact, I had become so emaciated and feeble that I could hardly travel across my prison floor. But no grief arrests the flight of time, and the twenty-fourth of April came, in which the sergeant visited me and in a manner of mingled kindness and firmness told me that my father was no more. At these tidings, simple truth calls on me to declare, my heart felt relieved. I am a hunter, and not a person to analyze the feelings of poor human nature. My father now was gone, gone where the voice of the oppressor is no more heard. Since the death of my mother, I have reason to think, that life had been to him one long burden. He had been set free from it all, and set free too, from the cruelty of this vile people, and the still viler general. I felt weak, and exhausted myself, and I expected to rejoin him in a few days, never to be separated from him. Life was a burden of which I longed to be relieved.

After I had given vent to natural feelings on this occasion, the sergeant asked me touching the manner in which we bury our dead in our country? I informed him. He then observed that the reason why he asked that question was, that his sister wished, that my father's body might be interred in a manner conformable to my wishes. I could only thank him for all this kindness and humanity to me, as he left me. I passed the remainder of this day in the indulgence of such reflections as I have no wish to describe, even had I the power.

At night the sergeant's sister again visited my prison. She seemed neither able nor disposed to enter upon the subject before us, and reluctant to call up the circumstance of my father's death to my thoughts. At length she presented me with a complete suit of black, and begged that I would wear it on the following day at my father's funeral. I observed, in astonishment, that she could not doubt what a melancholy satisfaction it would be to me to follow the remains of my father to the grave, but that between me and that satisfaction were the walls of my prison, through which I could not break. She remarked, that by dint of importunity, she had prevailed on the general to allow me to attend the funeral.

The fair young lady then undertook the duties of minister and philosopher, counselling me not to grieve for that, for which there is no remedy, proving to me that it was the will of God, that he should thus obtain deliverance from prison, and all the evils of this transitory life, and abundance of common place language of this sort, very similar to what is held in my own country on like occasions. Having finished her kindly intended chapter of consolations, she wished me a goodnight and left me to my own thoughts. The night I spent in walking the floor of my prison.

At eight in the morning, a file of six soldiers appeared at the door of my prison. It was opened, and I once more breathed the fresh air! The earth and the sky seemed a new region.—The glare of light dazzled my eyes, and dizzied my head. I reeled as I walked. A lieutenant conducted the ceremonies: and when I arrived at the grave he ordered the crowd to give way, that I might see the coffin let down, and the grave filled. I advanced to the edge of the grave, and caught a glimpse of the coffin that contained the remains of the brave hunter and ranger. The coffin was covered with black. No prayers were said. I had scarce time to draw a second breath, before the grave was half filled with earth. I was led back to my prison, the young lady walking by my side in tears. I would gladly have found relief for my own oppressed heart in tears, if they would have flowed. But the sources were dried, and tears would not come to my relief. When I arrived at the prison, such a horrid revulsion came over me at the thoughts of entering that dreary place again, that I am sure I should have preferred to have been shot, rather than enter it again. But I recovered myself by reflecting that my health was rapidly declining, and that I should be able in a short time to escape from the oppressor and the prison walls, and rejoin my father, and be at rest.

This thought composed me, and I heard the key turn upon me

BURIAL OF MR. PATTIE

with a calm and tranquilized mind. I lay down upon my bed, and passed many hours in the oblivion of sleep. The customary habit of sleep during the night returned to me; and my strength and appetite began to return with it. I felt an irresistible propensity to resume my former habit of smoking. I named my inclination to my friend the sergeant. He was kind enough to furnish me cigars. This was a new resource to aid me in killing the time. Apart from the soothing sensation of smoking, I amused myself for hours in watching the curling of my smoke from the cigar. Those who have always been free, cannot imagine the corroding torments of thoughts preying upon the bosom of the prisoner, who has neither friend to converse with, books to read, or occupation to fill his hours.

On the 27th of June, Captain Bradshaw's vessel was seized, on the charge of smuggling. There were other American vessels in this port at the same time, the names of the captains of which, as far as I can recollect, were Seth Rogers, Aaron W. Williams, and H. Cunningham. These gentlemen, jointly with their supercargoes, sent me five ounces of gold, advising me to keep this money secret from the knowledge of the Spaniards, and preserve it as a resource for my companions and myself, in case of emergencies.

About this time the general received several packages of letters in English, the contents of which, not understanding the language, he could not make out. There was no regular translator at hand; and he sent orders to the sergeant to have me conducted to the office for that purpose. When I entered the office he asked me if I could read writing? When I told him yes, he procured a seat, and bade me sit down. He then presented me a letter in English, requesting me to translate it into Spanish. Though I put forth no claims on the score of scholarship, I perfectly comprehended the meaning of the words in both languages. I accomplished the translation in the best manner in my power; and he was pleased entirely to approve it. He proceeded to ask me a great many questions relative to my travels through the Mexican country; how long I had been absent from my own country, and what had been my occupation, during that absence? To all which questions I returned satisfactory answers. When he bade the guard return me to prison, he informed me that he should probably call for me again.

I returned to my prison somewhat cheered in spirits. I foresaw that he would often have occasion for my services as a translator, and if I showed an obliging disposition, and rendered myself useful, I hoped to obtain enlargement for myself and my companions. As I expected,

I was summoned to his office for several days in succession. On my entering the office he began to assume the habit of saluting me kindly, giving me a seat, enquiring after my health, and showing me the other customary civilities. When I found him in his best humour, I generally took occasion remotely to hint at the case of our being detained as prisoners. I tried, gently and soothingly, to convince him of the oppression and injustice of treating the innocent citizens of a sister republic, as if they were spies. He generally showed a disposition to evade the subject; or alleged as a reason for what he had done, that he regretted exceedingly that circumstances on our part seemed so suspicious, that, obliged as he was, to execute the laws of his country, he felt himself compelled to act as he had done; that it was far from his disposition to desire to punish any one unjustly, and without cause; and that he would be glad if we could produce any substantial evidence to acquit us from the suspicion of being spies.

Though, as a true and honest man, I knew that every word he pronounced was a vile and deceitful lie, yet such is the power of the oppressor, I swallowed my rising words, and dissembled a sort of satisfaction. Waiving the further discussion of our imprisonment, I again recurred to the subject of permission to bring in our furs, persuading him, if he had any doubts about our good faith in returning to this place, to send soldiers to guard us; assuring him, that on obtaining our furs we would pay the soldiers, and indemnify him for any other expense he might incur on the occasion; and that, moreover, we would feel ourselves as grateful to him as if he had bestowed upon us the value of the furs in money. He heard me to the close, and listened with attention; and though he said he could not at present give his consent, he promised that he would deliberate upon the subject, and in the course of a week, let me know the result of his resolution. He then bade his soldiers remand me to prison. I begged him to allow me to communicate this conversation to my companions. This he refused, and I re-entered my prison.

From these repeated interviews, I began to acquaint myself with his interior character. I perceived, that, like most arbitrary and cruel men, he was fickle and infirm of purpose. I determined to take advantage of that weakness in his character by seeming submissive to his wishes, and striving to conform as far as I could to his capricious wishes; and more than all, to seize the right occasions to tease him with importunities for our liberty, and permission to bring in our furs. Four days elapsed before I had another opportunity of seeing him. During this time I had finished the translation of a number of letters, some of which were from Captain Bradshaw, and related to the detention of his ship and cargo, and himself. When I had finished these translations, and was readmitted to his presence, I asked him if he had come to any determination in regard to letting us go to bring in our furs? He answered in his surliest tone, no! How different were my reflections on returning to my prison from those with which I had left it! How earnestly I wished that he and I had been together in the wild woods, and I armed with my rifle!

I formed a firm purpose to translate no more letters for him. I found that I had gained nothing by this sort of service; nor even by dissembling a general disposition to serve him. I was anxious for another request to translate, that I might have the pleasure of refusing him, and of telling him to his face that though I was his prisoner, I was not his slave. But it was three days before he sent for me again. At their expiration I was summoned to his office, and he offered me a seat, according to former custom. When I was seated, with a smiling countenance he handed me a packet of letters, and bade me translate them. I took one, opened it, and carelessly perused a few lines, and returning the packet back, rose from my seat, and told him I wished to return to my prison; and bowing, I moved towards the door. He darted a glance at me resembling that of an enraged wild beast; and in a voice, not unlike the growl of a wounded, grizzly bear, asked me why I did not put myself to the translation of the letters?

Assuming a manner and tone as surly as his own, I told him my reasons were, that I did not choose to labour voluntarily for an oppressor and enemy; and that I had come to the determination to do it no longer. At this he struck me over the head such a blow with the flat of his sword, as well nigh dropped me on the floor; and ordered the soldiers to return me to prison, where he said I should lay and rot. The moment I recovered from the stunning effect of the blow I sprang toward him; but was immediately seized by the guards, and dragged to the door; he, the while, muttered abundance of the curses which his language supplies. In return, I begged him to consider how much it was like an officer and gentleman to beat an unarmed prisoner in his power, but that if I only had a sword to meet him upon equal terms, I could easily kill as many such dastards as he was, as could come at me. He bade me be silent, and the soldiers to take me off. They shoved me violently on before them to prison. When it closed upon me I never expected to see the sun rise and set again.

Here I remained a week without seeing even the young lady, who was justly so dear to my heart. She was debarred by the general's orders not only from visiting me, but even sending me provisions! I was again reduced to the fare of corn boiled in spoiled tallow, which was brought me twice a day. At this juncture came on Captain Bradshaw's trial. The declaration of the captain, supercargo and crew was to be taken, and all the parties separately interrogated by a Spaniard. Not an individual of them could speak a word of Spanish, except the captain, and he was not allowed to translate in his own case. The general supposed that by interrogating the parties separately, he should be able to gain some advantage from the contradictions of the testimony, and some positive proof of smuggling. Captain Bradshaw being denied the privilege of interpreting for his crew, requested the general to procure some one who might be allowed to perform that office for him.

The general told him that I was capable of the office, if I could be gained to the humour; but that he would as willingly deal with a devil, as with me, when out of humour. Captain Bradshaw asked him if he might be allowed to converse with me on the subject? He consented, and Captain Bradshaw came to my prison. In reference to the above information, he asked me what had taken place between me and the general which had so exasperated him against me? I related all the circumstances of our last interview. He laughed heartily at my defiance of the general. I was ready, of course, to render any service by which I could oblige Captain Bradshaw. He returned to the general, and informed him that I was ready to undertake to translate or interpret in his case.

In a short time my door was opened, and I was once more conducted to the office of the general. Captain Bradshaw was sitting there in waiting. The general asked me if I had so far changed my mind, as to be willing to translate and interpret again? I told him I was always ready to perform that office for a *gentleman*. I placed such an emphasis on the word gentleman, as I purposed, should inform him, that I intended that appellation for the captain, and not for him. Whether he really misunderstood me, or dissembled the appearance of misunderstanding me, I know not. He only named an hour, in which he should call on me for that service, cautioning me to act in the business with truth and good faith. I told him that my countrymen in that respect, had greatly the disadvantage of his people; for that it was our weakness, not to know how to say anything but the truth. At this he smiled, ordering me back to prison, until I should be called for next day.

At eight the next morning, I was again summoned to his office, where he proceeded, through me, to question Captain Bradshaw touching the different ports at which he had traded, and what was his cargo, when he left the U.S.? He added a great many other questions in relation to the voyage, irrelevant to the purposes of this journal. The clerk on this occasion was an Indian, and a quick and elegant writer. Captain Bradshaw produced his bill of lading, and the other usual documents of clearing out a ship; all which I was obliged to translate. They being matters out of the line of my pursuits, and I making no pretensions to accurate acquaintance with either language, the translation, of course, occupied no inconsiderable time. It was nearly twelve, when he bade us withdraw, with orders to meet him again at his office at two in the afternoon. Captain B. accompanied me to prison, and as we went on, requested me to make the testimonies of his crew as nearly correspond, and substantiate each other, as possible; for that some of them were angry with him, and would strive to give testimony calculated to condemn him. I assured him that I would do any thing to serve him, that I could in honour. I entered my prison, and slept soundly, until the bells struck two.

I was then reconducted to the general's office; where he continued to interrogate Captain Bradshaw, until three. The supercargo, Mr. R. Perkins, was then called upon to produce his manifesto, and cautioned to declare the truth, in relation to the subject in question. This manifesto differed in no essential respect from the account of the captain. At sunset they were dismissed, and I remanded to my prison. Day after day the same task was imposed, and the same labours devolved upon me. I at length summoned courage to resume the old question of permission to go out and bring in our furs. To my surprise he remarked, that as soon as he had finished taking all the evidence in relation to Captain Bradshaw's ship and cargo, he would not only allow us to go, but would send soldiers to prevent the Indians from molesting us.

I informed him, that his intended kindness would be unavailing to us, if he did not allow us to depart before the month of August; for that in that month the melting of the snow on the mountains at the sources of Red River caused it to overflow, and that our furs were buried in the bottom, so that the river, in overflowing, would spoil them. He replied, that it was out of his power to grant the consent at this time, which was the 19th of July.

On the 28th he had finished taking all the depositions, and I again asked him for permission to go and bring in our furs. He still started delays, alleging that he had made no arrangements for that purpose yet. Captain Bradshaw was present, and asked him to allow me to stay with him on board his vessel, promising that he would be accountable for me. To my astonishment the general consented. I repaired to the house of the young lady, who had been so kind to me. She received me with open arms, and manifested the most unequivocal delight. She congratulated me on being once more free from my dismal prison, and asked me a thousand questions. The captain and myself spent the evening with her; and at its close, I repaired with him on board his beautiful ship, the first sea vessel I had ever been on board.

It may be imagined what a spectacle of interest and eager curiosity the interior of this ship, the rigging, masts, awning, in short, every thing appertaining to it, would be to a person raised as I had been, and of a mind naturally inquisitive. What a new set of people were the sailors! How amusing and strange their dialect! They heartily shook me by the hand, and commenced describing the several punishments they would inflict upon the general, if they had him in their power. Among the different inflictions purposed, none seemed to please them better, than the idea of tarring and feathering him, all which I would gladly have seen him endure, but the worst of it was, after all, the general was not in their power.

I spent the greater part of the night with the captain and supercargo, conversing about the oppressions and cruelties of the general, and the death of my father, for, during the time of his sickness, Captain Bradshaw had sailed to Monte el Rey, and had not returned, until after his death. He intended, he said, if his vessel was condemned, to slip his anchors, and run out of the harbour, at the risk of being sunk, as he passed the fort. He promised me, if I would take passage with him, that I should fare as he did, and that, when we should arrive at Boston, he would obtain me some situation, in which I could procure a subsistence. I thanked him for his very kind offer, but remarked, that my companions had suffered a great deal with me, that we had had many trials together, and had hazarded our lives for each other, and that now I would suffer any thing rather than desert them, and leave them in prison, probably, to have their sufferings enhanced, in consequence of my desertion.

In the morning we all three went on shore together, and took breakfast at the house of my friend, the brother of the young lady. We passed from breakfast, to the office of the general. I asked leave of him to visit my companions in prison. His countenance became red with anger, and he ordered the guard to search me, and take me to prison. I perceived that he thought I had arms concealed about me, and assured him I had none. This did not hinder the guard from searching me, before they put me in prison.

I heard no more from him, and remained shut up in prison until the 28th of August. On that day the general ordered me again to be conducted to his office, where, according to his request, I translated some letters for him. When I had finished, he asked me if I still had an inclination to go for my furs? I replied, that I had reason to suppose that they had been covered before this time, with the waters of Red River, and were all spoiled; but that nevertheless, I should be glad to be certain about it, and at least we should be able to bring in our traps. He asked me what adequate security I could give for our good behaviour, and the certainty of our return, provided he should allow us the use of our arms for self-defence? I replied, that I knew no one, who could give the security required, but that the soldiers he would send with us, would be his security for our return; but that it was out of the question to think of sending us on a trip, so dangerous under any circumstances, without allowing us to go armed. He remanded me to prison, saying, that he would reflect upon it, and let me know the result of his reflections in the morning.

I reflected as I walked to prison, that I could have procured the security of Captain Bradshaw, merely for the asking. But I knew the character of my companions, and was so well aware, how they would feel when all should be once free again, and well armed, that I dared not bind any one in security for us. Such had been the extent of the injuries we had suffered, and so sweet is revenge, and so delightful liberty, when estimated by the bondage we had endured, that I was convinced that Mexico could not array force enough to bring us back alive. I foresaw that the general would send no more than ten or twelve soldiers with us. I knew that it would be no more than an amusement to rise upon them, take their horses for our own riding, flea some of them of their skins, to show them that we knew how to inflict torture, and send the rest back to the general on foot. Knowing that the temptation to some retaliation of this sort would be irresistible, I was determined that no one of my countrymen should be left amenable to the laws on our account. Such thoughts passed through my mind as I told the general, I could offer him no security.

Next morning, immediately after eight, I was allowed to walk to the general's office without being guarded. What a fond feeling came back to my heart with this small boon of liberty! How much I was exalted in my own thoughts, that I could walk fifty yards entrusted with my own safe keeping! When I entered the general's office, he saluted me with ceremonious politeness. '*Buenas dias, don Santiago,*' said he, and showed me to a seat. He proceeded to make known his pleasure, in respect to me and my companions. In the first place he told us, we were all to be allowed the use of our arms, in the next place, that he would send fifteen of his soldiers with us; and in the third place, that we should all be allowed a week, in which to exercise ourselves, before we set out on our expedition. All this good fortune delighted us, and was more almost, than we would have dared to wish.

My companions, in an ecstasy of satisfaction, soon joined us from their prisons. We met with as much affection and gladness of heart, as if we had been brothers. They looked more like persons emancipated from the prison of the grave, than human beings; and I am perfectly aware, that my spectre like visage must have been equally a spectacle to them. We had the privilege of walking in the vicinity of the port, accompanied by a guard of soldiers. Our only immediate restriction was the necessity of returning to our guard house to sleep at night. In this way our time passed pleasantly.

On the 3rd of September, the general sent for me to his office. When I entered, he presented me a note, and bade me accompany a soldier to a mission at the distance of thirty miles, where he stated I was to deliver this note to a priest, and that he perhaps would be able to furnish us with horses and mules for our expedition to bring in our furs. I started with the soldier, each of us well mounted. The note was unsealed, and I read it of course. The contents were anything, rather than encouraging. It contained no demand for the horses, as I had hoped. It simply stated to the priest, what sort of person the general supposed me to be, that we had furs buried on Red River, and wished horses on which to ride out and bring them in, and that if the priest felt disposed to hire his horses to us, he would send soldiers with us to bring us back.

Discouraging as the note was, we pushed ahead with it, and arrived at the priest's mission some time before night. I handed the note to the old priest, who was a very grave looking personage. He read the note, and then asked me to come in and take some wine with him, of which they have great plenty. I followed him into a large parlour, richly adorned with paintings of saints, and several sideboards, abundantly stored with wines, which I took it for granted, were not

172

unacceptable to the holy man. The glass ware, the decorations of the parlour, and the arrangement of every thing showed me at a glance, that this priest was a man of taste and fashion. So I was on my guard not to let any of my hunting phrases and backwood's dialect escape me. He asked me a great many questions about the circumstances of my passage across the continent, to all which I responded in as choice and studied words as I could command. He then asked me how many beasts we should want? I replied that there were seven of us, and that we should each need a pack mule, and a horse to ride upon, which would be fourteen in all.

He then asked how many days it would require to go, and return? I answered, that this was a point upon which I could not pronounce with certainty, since I was unacquainted with the road, and accidents might change the issue. He then proposed to charge what was tantamount to 25 cents of our money a day for each mule, that carried a saddle, during the expedition, longer or shorter. To this I consented, and he drew an article of agreement to that effect. He then wrote a note to send by me to the general, in reply to his. By this time the sun was setting, and the church bells began to strike. On this he knelt, and commenced his prayers. He was repeating the Lord's prayer. According to the customs of his church, when he had commenced a member of a sentence, I finished it, by way of response. Such are their modes of repeating their prayers, when there are two or more in company.

When we had finished, he turned to me, and asked me why I had prayed? I answered for the salvation of my soul. He said, that it had a Christian appearance, but that he had been informed, that the people of our country did not believe that man had a soul, or that there is a Saviour. I assured him, that he had been entirely misinformed, for that we had churches on every side through all the land, and that the people read the Scriptures, and believed all that was taught in the Gospel, according to their understanding of it.

But he continued, 'your people do not believe in the immaculate conception of the Virgin Mary.' I replied, that what the general faith of the people upon this point was, I could not say, and that for myself, I did not pretend to have sufficiently studied the Scriptures, to decide upon such points. My assumed modesty soothed him, and he told me, that it was evident, I had not studied the Scriptures, for that if I had, I could not be in doubt about such obvious articles of faith. I acquiesced in his supposition, that I had not studied the Scriptures, remarking, that I was aware that they contained many mysteries, about which the people in my country entertained various opinions. He said that he was truly sorry, that I was not more conversant with the Scriptures, for that if I had been, I could not have been led astray by the Protestants. His time, however, he added was now too limited to enlighten me, but he laughed, as he said he hoped to have the pleasure of baptising me on my return. To this I replied with a smile, for the truth was, I was fearful of disgusting him, and breaking off the bargain. Glad was I, when he dismissed this subject, and began to chat about other matters. We had an excellent supper, and I was shown to my bed.

In the morning I took leave of the old father, and arrived on the following evening at San Diego. My companions were delighted with the apparent complete success of my mission. The general informed us, that we should have permission to start on the 6th, and that our beasts would be ready for an early start on that day. On the evening of the 5th, he called us to his office, and asked us, how many days we thought the expedition would require? We informed him, as near as we could conjecture. He then said, that he could not spare any soldiers to accompany us. We answered, that it was a point of indifference to us, whether he did or not. 'To insure your return however,' he rejoined, 'I shall retain one of you as a hostage for the return of the rest,' and pointing to me, he informed me, 'that I was the selected hostage,' and that I must remain in prison, during their absence, and that if they did not return, it would convince him, that we were spies, and that in consequence he would cause me to be executed.

At this horrible sentence, breaking upon us in the sanguine rapture of confidence, we all gazed at each other in the consternation of despair. Some of our company remarked, that they had better abandon the expedition altogether, than leave me behind. Others stood in mute indecision. We had all in truth confidently anticipated never to return to this place again. My indignation, meanwhile, had mounted to such a pitch, as wholly to absorb all sense of personal danger, or care about myself. It seemed as if Providence had put the unrelenting seal of disappointment to every plan I attempted to devise. I told them to go, and not allow my detention to dishearten, or detain them, for that I had no fear of any thing, the general could inflict, that I had little left, but life to relinquish, and that their refusal to go, as things now were, would be taken for ample proofs, that we were spies, and would ensure our condemnation and the conviction, that we never had intended to return.

On this they all agreed to go, and began to pledge their honour and everything sacred, that they would return, if life was spared them. I told them to follow their own inclinations, as to returning, for that I would as willingly be buried by the side of my father, as anyone else; that, however, I did not believe the laws of the country would bear the general out, in putting me to death. The general now bade us arrange everything to start early in the morning. I was again locked up in my prison, though my companions spent the greater part of the night in conversing with me. In the morning, when they were ready to start, they came and shook hands with me.

When the Dutchman, as good hearted a fellow as ever lived, took my hand he burst into tears, and said, 'goot py Jim, if I ever does come back, I will bring an army *mit* me, and take yours and your daddy's bones from dis tammed country, for it is worse as hell.' I should have laughed heartily at him, had not his tears prevented me, for I knew, that they came from his heart. Mounting their mules they now set off. Their only arms were old Spanish muskets, which, when fired, I would almost as soon have stood before as behind. Under such circumstances, knowing, that they would be obliged to pass through numbers of hostile tribes of Indians, I was very doubtful of their return.

On the 8th, Captain Bradshaw came to my prison, and asked me, why I was in prison, and my companions at liberty? I told him the whole story. When he had heard it, he expressed doubts in regard to their returning. I replied to him, that I was not at all in doubt of their return, if they lived. He then told me, that he intended to go to the general, and demand his papers on the 11th, and if they were not given up to him, he would cut cable, and run out in spite of any one, adding his advice to me, which was, that I should write to the consul at Wahu and inform him of my imprisonment. He seemed to think, I might thus obtain my release. Mr. R. Perkins would undertake, he said, to place it in the hands of the consul, as he was acquainted with him. I answered, that I had neither ink nor paper. He said I should have some in a few minutes, and took leave of me.

A soldier soon entered with writing materials, and I wrote my letter to Mr. Jones, for that was the name of the consul, stating every circumstance relative to our imprisonment, and the death of my father, giving the names of all our party, and begging him, if it was not in his power to obtain our freedom, that he would inform our government of our situation. I supposed it was in his power to grant my first request, placed as he was, in the midst of a foreign nation.

On the 11th, at the request of the general, I was conducted to his office, to serve as interpreter for the captain and Mr. Perkins. The papers were now demanded by them. The general refused to comply with the demand, and told them, that both the vessel and cargo were condemned, but that if they would discharge the cargo, and deliver it to him, he would allow them to clear the vessel, to go and seek redress, wherever they pleased. The captain's answer to this was, that it was not in his power to do so, and that the laws of his country would hang him, if he thus gave up his ship and cargo at the request of an individual. The general now became enraged, and repeating the words, at the request of an individual, added, the ship and cargo have both been lawfully condemned, and if they are not given up peaceably, I have soldiers enough to take the ship, and every thing belonging to it.

In reply the captain remarked, that he came to trade on the coast, and not to fight, that if he was disposed to seize the vessel or cargo, he had nothing to say farther, than that he should not aid, or advance in any shape the unlading of the vessel himself, and taking up his hat walked away. I asked permission of the general to go to Miss. Peaks, to get a change of clothing, which was granted. He, however, told me to be in haste. My principal business there was to give my letter to Mr. Perkins, for I knew that Captain Bradshaw, would set sail with the first breeze, of which he could avail himself. I found both the gentlemen in the house, when I entered. I was assured by Mr. Perkins, that he would give the letter to the consul, and endeavour to interest him in my behalf. I thanked him, and was upon the point of taking leave, when Captain Bradshaw asked me to take a note from him to the general, and to tell him that he would like to have an answer, and would wait an hour for it. I took the note and went to the general's office, gave him the note and told him what the captain had said. He bade me sit down, after he had read the note, for a few minutes. I obeyed, and he passed into the adjoining room, and ordered his porter to call the ensign Ramirez.

The porter hastened to execute his commission, and in a few minutes the ensign entered. The general and ensign then began to converse, drawing near the door, behind which I was seated. I heard distinctly the former tell the latter, that Captain Bradshaw, and Mr. Perkins, were both at Peak's awaiting an answer from him, and that he would send me to tell them that he was engaged at present, but at the expiration of an hour and a half they should have their answer through me. Meantime he, the ensign, was to provide a guard of soldiers, with which to take them prisoners, and then the vessel and cargo would be sure. All this, as I have said, I heard distinctly. He then came in, and told me to go and inform them, as he told the ensign, he should direct me. I hastened to Captain Bradshaw, and told him what I had heard from the general concerning him. I advised him to go to the vessel immediately, for that the ensign and guard would soon be upon the spot. Both he and Mr. Perkins went directly to the vessel, and I returned to the general, to inform him that I had delivered his message. He then ordered me to return to prison. It was now three o'clock.

In a few hours the ensign returned from the pursuit of Captain Bradshaw, and as he passed the prison on his way to the general's office he shook his sword at me with vengeance in his face, saying, 'Oh! you traitor!' I inferred from this, that he supposed I had informed the captain of the projected attempt to take him prisoner. My situation now seemed to me desperate. I thought more of my comrades than myself, for I could not expect to live. Concluding that I should soon be executed, I feared, that when they returned, they would be put to death also. In a few minutes I was summoned to the general's office. I expected to hear my sentence.

When I entered the general bade me stand by the door, near a large table, at which several of his clerks were seated writing, and he then gravely asked me if I had overheard the conversation which took place between himself and the ensign, after he had read the note brought by me to him from Captain Bradshaw? I replied that I did not see the ensign at that time, and furthermore could not say positively, whether he had held any conversation with the ensign, since my arrival on the coast or not. The general proceeded to question me, as to the fact of my having advised the captain to go on board his ship, and if I knew the motives, which induced him to do so, after saying that he would wait for an answer to his note.

He tried to extort an answer from me such as he wished, threatening me with death if I did not relate the truth. I regarded all this as no more than the threats of an old woman, and went on to state what was most likely to be favourable to my cause. I was now remanded to prison with the assurance, that if found guilty, death would be my doom.

A few days only elapsed before, the breeze serving, the captain slipped anchor, and ran out of the port. He was compelled to perform this under a heavy shower of cannon balls poured forth from the fort, within two hundred yards of which he was obliged to pass. When he came opposite it, he hove to, and gave them a broadside in return, which frightened the poor engineers from their guns. His escape from the port was made without suffering any serious injury on his part. Their shots entered the hull of the vessel, and the sails were considerably cut by the grape. I was greatly rejoiced when I heard of their escape from these thieves. The general pretended great disgust at the cowardly conduct of the engineers, but, I believe, had he been there, he would have run too. I have no faith in the courage of these people, except where they have greatly the advantage, or can kill in the dark, without danger to themselves. This in my view is the amount of a Spaniard's bravery.

But to return to myself, I remained in prison, until a sufficient time had elapsed, as I thought, for the return of my companions. I still did not entirely despair of seeing them; but the Spaniards came daily and hourly to my prison with delighted countenances to tell me that my companions had deserted me, and that the general would soon have me executed. Some consoled me with the information, that at such an hour or day, I was to be taken out, and burnt alive; and others, that I was to be stationed at a certain distance, and shot at, like a target, or hung. These unfeeling wretches thus harassed and tormented me, until the arrival of my companions on the 30th Sept. put an end to their taunts, with regard to their desertion of me. They brought no fur however, it having been all spoiled as I had expected, by an overflow of the river. Our traps which they did bring, were sold, and a part of the proceeds paid to the old priest for the hire of the mules.

I have failed to remark, that my comrades had returned with the loss of two of their number, one of whom we learned, had married in New Mexico. When the party reached the river, these two concluded that rather than return to prison, they would run the risk of being killed by the Indians, or of being starved to death; and set forth on their perilous journey through the wilderness to New Mexico on foot. The probability of their reaching the point of their destination was very slight, it being a great distance and through great dangers. Happily for us, their not returning, did not appear to strengthen the general, in his opinion of our being spies. I had the pleasure of conversing with my companions an hour, or more, after which they were again disarmed, and all of us returned to our separate places of confinement.

I had now no prospect before me, but that of lingering out a miserable and useless life in my present situation; as I was convinced, that the only inducement, which operated in the general's mind, to allow a part of us to go in search of our property was the hope of taking a quantity of furs and other valuables from us. I was thankful that he obtained nothing but the traps, which, as he knew no more how to use, than a blind horse, could be of no utility to him. This feeling may seem a poor gratification, but it was certainly a natural one. In this condition we remained for months, never seeing the outside of our prison, deprived of the pleasure we had received from the visits of the charitable young lady, formerly allowed entrance to us, and the advantage we had derived from the generous nourishment she so kindly furnished us, and compelled by hunger to eat the food set before us by our jailors; and confined principally to dried beans, or corn boiled in water, and then fried in spoiled tallow.

At length the smallpox began to rage on the upper part of the coast, carrying off the inhabitants by hundreds. Letters from the distressed people were continually arriving, praying the general to devise some means to put a stop to the disease, which seemed to threaten the country with destruction. The general was thus beset by petitions for several weeks, before he could offer a shadow of relief for them. He was much alarmed, fearing that the disorder might extend its ravages to that part of the coast where he resided.

One day the soldiers, through mere inquisitiveness, asked the Dutchman if he knew any remedy for the complaint? He answered that he did; but that he had none of the article that constituted the remedy. He added, however, that he thought that my father had brought some of it with him, as he recollected his having vaccinated the people at the copper mines. This conversation was communicated to the general immediately, who sent a sergeant to me to inquire if I had any of the remedy spoken of by the Dutchman, as brought by my father? I answered in the affirmative; I then showed him where I had been vaccinated on the right arm, and assured him that it had effectually protected me from the smallpox. Upon his demand whether I knew the method of applying it, I again answered in the affirmative; but when he asked me to show him the remedy, and let him have it to apply to his own arm, as he was fearful of losing his life from the spread of this dreadful disease, I told him I would not.

This sergeant, who wished the matter, was my friend, and brother of the charitable young lady who had procured my father's burial, and for whom I would have sacrificed my life. But thinking this my only chance for regaining liberty, I refused it to him, saying, that I would neither show it to anyone, nor apply it, unless my liberty and that of my companions was rendered secure; and that in sustaining this resolution I would sacrifice my life. I also mentioned that I must be paid, over and above my liberty. My object in this, was to influence the fears of the general. If he acceded to my proposition, my friend and his sister would share the benefit in common with others. If I granted the request of the sergeant to inoculate him, I might lose my advantage; but my gratitude decided me against allowing himself and his sister to be exposed to an imminent danger, which I could avert. I told him that if he would pledge himself, solemnly, for his own part, and that of his sister, that he would not communicate the matter to another individual, I would secretly vaccinate them. He replied that I need not fear his betraying me, as he would much rather aid me in my design, which he thought excellent, and likely to accomplish my wishes. He then left me to communicate the result of our conversation to the general.

This incident, so important in its influence upon my fortunes, occurred December 20th. The sergeant had not been absent more than a half hour, when he returned and told me that the general said he would give me a passport for a year, if I would vaccinate all the people on the coast; and furthermore, if I conducted properly during that period, that he would at the expiration of it, pay me for my services, and give me my liberty. His countenance was bright with delight, as he related this to me, not dreaming that I could refuse what seemed to him so good an offer.

When I repeated, in reply, my resolution not to vaccinate anyone, except on the conditions I had stated, and added that I would not agree to any terms without an audience from the general, his pleasure vanished, giving place to gloom as he told me he did not think the general would accede to the proposal to set my companions and myself at liberty upon parole for one year, for any consideration; but that, if I persisted in my refusal, he feared I should incur some violent punishment, and perhaps death. My answer was, that in my present situation I did not dread death. I then requested him to tell the general I wished to talk with him personally upon the subject.

He went, and in a few minutes returned with orders to conduct me to the general's office. Upon my arrival there, the general questioned me with regard to the efficacy of the remedy of which he had been much informed in the same manner as I have related in the conversation between the sergeant and myself; and he then repeated the same terms for the matter and the application of it, that he had transmitted me through my friend, to which I replied as before. When I had finished, he asked me in a surly manner, what my own terms were? I told him, as I had done the sergeant, that I would vaccinate all the inhabitants on the coast, provided he would allow myself and companions to leave our prison on parole for one year, with liberty to travel up or down the coast, in order to find some occupation, by which we could obtain food and clothing.

Upon hearing this his rage burst forth. He told me I was a devil; and that if I did not choose to take the offer he had made, he would compel me to perform its conditions, or put me to death. I replied, that he could take my life; but that it was beyond his power to compel me to execute his commands, adding, that life or liberty would be no object to me, if my companions were denied the enjoyment of them with me. They had had the alternative in their power of leaving me in prison to suffer alone, or returning to share my captivity, and had chosen the latter; I concluded by saying, that rather than accept of liberty while they remained in prison, I would undergo all the torments his *Excellency* could devise. He said he might as well let loose so many wolves to ravage his country, as give myself and companions the liberty I required; adding, that he gave me twenty-four hours to reflect on the alternative of his wrath, or my liberty upon the conditions he had proposed. I was now remanded to prison.

As I walked out, I remarked to the general, that my resolution was fixed beyond the possibility of change. He made no reply, and I proceeded to prison. The soldiers who accompanied me, tried to induce me to conform to the general's wishes, saying, that he was a terrible man when enraged. I made them no answer, and entered my prison, where I remained until 8 o'clock the next day; when I was again escorted to the office, and asked by the general, what security I would give for the good behaviour of myself and companions, if he let us out on parole for one year? I told him I would give none, for no one here knew me. He then ordered me back to prison, where he said I should lay and rot, calling me a *carracho picaro*, and similar names, which I did not regard. I walked to my prison as undauntedly as I could. I now felt somewhat encouraged; for I perceived he was not inflexible in his resolutions, and by adhering firmly to mine, I hoped finally to conquer him.

In the course of the night he received a letter containing information of the death of one of his priests, and that great numbers were ill of the smallpox. Early in the morning of the 23rd I received a summons to attend him at the usual place. When I arrived, he said he wanted to see my papers, that is, those I had mentioned as being my father's commission, and his discharge from the service of a ranger. I told him they were at Miss Peak's, which was the name of the young lady who had been so kind to me. He sent a soldier for them, who soon returned with them. I translated them to him. He said that was a sufficient proof of my being an American; and asked if my companions could produce proofs of their belonging to the same country? I replied that I did not know.

He sent orders for them to come to the office; and before their arrival, told me that all he now wanted, was proof that they were Americans, to let us go on a parole, as all Americans were tolerated in his country. My opinion with regard to his motive in the case was, that he was less unwilling to grant our liberty, as the payment for my services in spreading the vaccine disease, now that he knew we had no property for him to extort from us.

He talked, too, about rendering himself liable to suffer the rigor of the laws of his country, should he set us free, without our establishing the fact of our being Americans.

My companions entered: I was glad to see them. Their beards were long, and they were haggard and much reduced in flesh. I gave them to understand what was wanting, and they readily produced some old black papers, furnishing in themselves proof of any thing else, as much as of their owners being American citizens. I, however, so interpreted them, that they established the point with the general. I believe he had as firmly credited this fact from the first hour he saw us, as now. He concluded to let us out a week upon trial, before he gave us freedom on parole, although he compelled me to engage to vaccinate all the people in the fort. He then directed us to endeavour to find some employment around the fort, which would procure us food, and to return every night to the guard house to sleep. The guard bell now tolled eight o'clock, and according to the permission given, we walked in the direction of our inclinations.

I went directly to Miss Peak's, who was much astonished, and apparently delighted to see me at liberty. She had expected, she said, every day to see me on my way to be shot, or hung. The manifestation of kindness and benevolence to us having been forbidden by our jailors, she now indemnified her humanity and good feeling by telling me how much she had regretted not being allowed to send me proper food, asking me if I was not hungry? and proceeding, before I could answer, to spread a table with every thing good, of which I partook plentifully; after which we had a pleasant conversation together. My enjoyment of my fortunate change of situation was, however, mingled with uncertainty, as to the length of its duration. I felt that I was still in the lion's jaws, which might close upon me from the first impulse of petulance or anger.

I therefore, endeavoured to devise some way of availing myself of my momentary freedom, to place myself beyond the possibility of losing it again. That one which suggested itself to me, was to prevail upon the officer, who had our rifles in charge to allow us possession of them for a short time, to clean them. When we should once more have them in our hands, I hoped we would have resolution to retain them, until death rendered them useless to us. I went to my companions, and imparted my plan to them. They agreed with me upon all points. The only difficulty now was, to lay our hands upon our arms. I went directly to the apartment of the officer, in whose care they were, one of the best hearted Spaniards I have ever seen. I appealed to his goodness of heart in order to obtain my purpose, telling him, that we only wanted the rifles a few minutes, in order to rub off the rust, and dirt, which must have accumulated upon them. I told him after this was done, they should be returned to him. He did not answer for some minutes; and then said, that if he complied with my request, and was discovered by the general to have done so, he should be punished.

I replied that there was no danger of an act of this kind, a mere kindness of this sort being known by any, but those immediately concerned; concluding by slipping ten dollars in silver, which had been given me by Captain Bradshaw, into his hand. He then handed me the rifles, and all belonging to them, through a back door, cautioning me not to let my having them in possession be known. I answered, that I would be upon my guard. I was now joined by my companions. We found an old and unoccupied house, into which we entered, and soon put our guns in order, and charged them well, resolving never to give them into the hands of a Spaniard again. We had been so treacherously dealt with by these people, that we did not consider it any great breach of honour to fail in our promise of returning our arms, particularly as the officer had taken my money.

We then concluded to conceal our rifles in a thicket near at hand, and to keep our pistols, which the officer had also given us as a part of our arms, concealed around our persons. At night we went to the guard house to sleep, as we had been commanded to do. The officer who gave me the rifles, came to me, and asked why I had not returned the arms according to promise? I told him that I had not finished cleaning them, and repeated, that the general should not know I had them. He charged me to fulfil my former promise of returning the arms on the succeeding morning. I satisfied him, thinking as before, that it made no great difference what is said to such persons, in a position like ours.

Early the next morning we met a countryman by the name of James Lang, who had come upon the coast to smuggle, and to kill sea otters for their skins, which are very valuable. He was now here secretly, to enquire if sea otters were to be found in abundance higher up the coast; and to obtain information on some other points connected with his pursuits. He told us he had a boat distant eighty miles down the coast, with men in search of otters, and proposed that we should accompany him to it, offering to furnish everything required for this species of hunting, and give us half of whatever we caught, adding, that when his brig returned from the Gallipagos islands, where it had gone in search of tortoise shell, he would give us a free passage to our own country.

We all considered this an offer advantageous to us, as it held out the prospect of our being enabled to obtain something in the way of gain, after which a way would be open for our return to our homes, and we agreed to meet him on a certain day at Todos Santos, in English All Saints. This took place on the 24th. Our new friend set off to rejoin his companions, and we fell to consultation upon the best method of conducting in our present circumstances. We did not wish to do anything, that would render us amenable to the laws of the country, should we be detected in our attempt to escape. We were consequently precluded from relying on horses to aid us in hastening beyond the reach of pursuers.

The night was chosen, as the time for our experiment; but in the course of an hour after this determination was made, all my companions excepting one, receded from it, pronouncing the plan of running off without any cover for our intentions, not a good one. They proposed instead of it, that we should ask permission of the general to go a hunting, assigning as our reason for this request, that we were barefoot, and wanted to kill some deer in order to obtain their skins to dress, to make us *moccasins*. I consented to this plan, and to try its efficacy immediately, I went to the general's office. It was late, but I related my errand. He asked me, where I could get arms, to kill deer with? I replied, that if he would not allow us to use our own arms, we could borrow some. He refused the permission, I had asked of him.

184

On Christmas night, the one among my companions, whom I have mentioned, as agreeing with me, in regard to the original plan for our escape, set off with me at 12 o'clock, while the people, who were all Catholics, were engaged in their devotions at church. We were obliged to leave our comrades, as they would not accompany us in our enterprise. We travelled entirely by night, and reached the before mentioned place of rendezvous on the 28th. We found Mr. Lang and his men in confinement, and his boat taken by the Spaniards. We gained this information in the night, without committing ourselves. We retreated to the woods, in which we remained concealed through the day. At night our necessities compelled us to enter a house, in order to obtain some food. It was occupied by a widow and her two daughters. They gave us bread, milk and cheese, treating us with great kindness. We spent a week passing the day in the woods, and going to this friendly house to get food in the night; in the hope of hearing of some vessel, by means of which we might escape from this hated coast. But no such good fortune awaited us.

We then concluded to return, and see our comrades, whom we supposed to be again in prison; although we were determined never again to be confined there ourselves alive, with our own consent. So we walked back to San Diego, killing some deer by the way, the skins of which we carried to the fort. To our great admiration and surprise, we found our companions at liberty. They informed us, that the general was exceedingly anxious for my return, and that our arms had not been demanded, although the officer, through whose means we obtained them, had been placed under guard.

I felt grieved by the latter part of this information, as I had deceived the unfortunate man, when he intended to do me a kindness, of the utmost importance to my interests, as I viewed it. He would probably, be severely punished. But I nevertheless was firm in my purpose to retain my arms. It was late in the day; but the companion of my flight and myself proceeded to present ourselves before the general, leaving our rifles concealed in a safe place. Our pistols we carried in our bosoms, determined not to be taken to prison without offering resistance.

The general appeared much surprised to see us, and asked where we had been? I told him, that we had been out upon a hunting expedition; upon which he wished to know if we had killed anything? We answered in the affirmative. He then looked serious, and demanded of me, if I was not aware that it was wrong to go off, without taking leave of him? My reply was, that I did; and that he refused it to me; and that then I concluded to go without permission, knowing it could not be a crime. His next question was, how I obtained my arms? I told him the truth with regard to this point. The succeeding demand was, why I did not return them, according to my promise? To which I replied, that I did not intend to return them from the first; and I now declared that they should never be taken from me for the time to come, while I drew my breath. He smiled, and said he did not want them; but that I must begin to vaccinate the people of the garrison; for that he wished me to go up the coast soon to practice vaccination there.

On the 18th of January, 1829, I began to vaccinate; and by the 16th of February had vaccinated all the people belonging to the fort, and the Indian inhabitants of the mission of San Diego, three miles north of the former place. It is situated in a valley between two mountains. A stream runs through the valley, from which ships obtain fresh water. An abundance of grain is raised at this mission. Fruit of all kinds, growing in a temperate climate, is also plentiful. The climate is delightfully equal. The husbandman here does not think of his fields being moistened by the falling rain. He digs ditches around them, in which water is conveyed from a stream, sufficient to cover the ground, whenever the moisture is required. Rains seldom fall in the summer or autumn. The rainy season commences in October; and continues until the last of December, and sometimes even through January; by which time the grass, clover and wild oats are knee high. When the rain does come, it falls in torrents. The gullies made in the sides of the mountains by the rains are of an enormous size.

But to return to my own affairs. Having completed my vaccinations in this quarter, and procured a sufficient quantity of the vaccine matter to answer my purpose, I declared myself in readiness to proceed further. I communicated the matter to one thousand Spaniards and Indians in San Diego.

February 28th, the general gave us each a legal form, granting us liberty on parole for one year, at the expiration of which period it was in his power to remand us to prison, if he did not incline to grant us our freedom. He likewise gave me a letter to the priests along the coast, containing the information that I was to vaccinate all the inhabitants upon the coast, and an order providing for me all necessary supplies of food and horses for my journey. These were to be furnished me by the people, among whom I found myself cast. They were, also, directed to treat me with respect, and indemnify me for my services, as

far as they thought proper. The latter charge did not strike me agreeably; for I foresaw, that upon such conditions my services would not
be worth one cent to me. However, the prospect of one whole year's
liberty was so delightful, that I concluded to trust in Providence, and
the generosity of the stranger, and think no more of the matter. With
these feelings I set forth to the next mission, at which I had already
been. It was called San Luis.

I reached it in the evening. I found an old priest, who seemed glad
to see me. I gave him the general's letter. After he had read it, he said,
with regard to that part of it which spoke of payment, that I had better
take certificates from the priests of each mission, as I advanced up the
coast, stating that I had vaccinated their inhabitants; and that when I
arrived at the upper mission, where one of the high dignitaries of the
church resided, I should receive my recompense for the whole. Seeing
nothing at all singular in this advice, I concluded to adopt it.

In the morning I entered on the performance of my duty. My
subjects were Indians, the missions being entirely composed of them,
with the exception of the priests, who are the rulers. The number of
natives in this mission was three thousand, nine hundred and four. I
took the old priest's certificate, as had been recommended by him,
when I had completed my task. This is said to be the largest, most
flourishing, and every way the most important mission on the coast.
For its consumption fifty beeves are killed weekly. The hides and tallow are sold to ships for goods, and other articles for the use of the
Indians, who are better dressed in general, than the Spaniards. All the
income of the mission is placed in the hands of the priests, who give
out clothing and food, according as it is required. They are also self
constituted guardians of the female part of the mission, shutting up
under lock and key, one hour after supper, all those, whose husbands
are absent, and all young women and girls above nine years of age.

During the day, they are entrusted to the care of the matrons. Notwithstanding this, all the precautions taken by the vigilant fathers of
the church are found insufficient. I saw women in irons for miscon-
duct, and men in the stocks. The former are expected to remain a
widow six months after the death of a husband, after which period
they may marry again. The priests appoint officers to superintend
the natives, while they are at work, from among themselves. They are
called *alcaides*, and are very rigid in exacting the performance of the
allotted tasks, applying the rod to those who fall short of the portion
of labour assigned them. They are taught in the different trades; some

of them being blacksmiths, others carpenters and shoe-makers. Those, trained to the knowledge of music, both vocal and instrumental, are intended for the service of the church. The women and girls sew, knit, and spin wool upon a large wheel, which is woven into blankets by the men. The *alcaides*, after finishing the business of the day, give an account of it to the priest, and then kiss his hand, before they withdraw to their *wigwams*, to pass the night. This mission is composed of parts of five different tribes, who speak different languages.

The greater part of these Indians were brought from their native mountains against their own inclinations, and by compulsion; and then baptised; which act was as little voluntary on their part, as the former had been. After these preliminaries, they had been put to work, as converted Indians.

The next mission on my way was that, called St. John the Baptist. The mountains here approach so near the ocean, as to leave only room enough for the location of the mission. The waves dash upon the shore immediately in front of it. The priest, who presides over this mission, was in the habit of indulging his love of wine and stronger liquors to such a degree, as to be often intoxicated. The church had been shattered by an earthquake. Between twenty and thirty of the Indians, men, women and children, had been suddenly destroyed by the falling of the church bells upon them. After communicating the vaccine matter to 600 natives, I left this place, where mountains rose behind to shelter it; and the sea stretched out its boundless expanse before it.

Continuing my route I reached my next point of destination. This establishment was called the mission of St. Gabriel. Here I vaccinated 960 individuals. The course from the mission of St. John the Baptist to this place led me from the sea-shore, a distance of from eighteen to twenty miles. Those, who selected the position of this mission, followed the receding mountains. It extends from their foot, having in front a large tract of country showing small barren hills, and yet affording pasturage for herds of cattle so numerous, that their number is unknown even to the all surveying and systematic priests. In this species of riches St. Gabriel exceeds all the other establishments on the coast. The sides of the mountains here are covered with a growth of live oak and pine. The chain to which these mountains belong, extends along the whole length of the coast. The fort St. Peter stands on the sea coast, parallel to this mission.

My next advance was to a small town, inhabited by Spaniards, called the town of The Angels. The houses have flat roofs, covered with bituminous pitch, brought from a place within four miles of the town, where this article boils up from the earth. As the liquid rises, hollow bubbles like a shell of a large size, are formed. When they burst, the noise is heard distinctly in the town. The material is obtained by breaking off portions, that have become hard, with an axe, or something of the kind. The large pieces thus separated, are laid on the roof, previously covered with earth, through which the pitch cannot penetrate, when it is rendered liquid again by the heat of the sun. In this place I vaccinated 2,500 persons.

From this place I went to the mission of St. Ferdinand, where I communicated the matter to 967 subjects. St. Ferdinand is thirty miles east of the coast, and a fine place in point of position.

The mission of St. Buenaventura succeeded. Not long previous to my arrival here, two priests had eloped from the establishment, taking with them what gold and silver they could lay their hands upon. They chose an American vessel, in which to make their escape. I practised my new calling upon 1000 persons in this mission.

The next point I reached was the fort of St. Barbara. I found several vessels lying here. I went on board of them, and spent some pleasant evenings in company with the commanders. I enjoyed the contrast of such society with that of the priests and Indians, among whom I had lately been. This place has a garrison of fifty or sixty soldiers. The mission lies a half a mile N. W. of the fort. It is situated on the summit of a hill, and affords a fine view of the great deep. Many are the hours I passed during this long and lonely journey, through a country every way strange and foreign to me, in looking on the ceaseless motion of its waves. The great *Leviathan* too played therein. I have often watched him, as he threw spouts of water into the air, and moved his huge body through the liquid surface. My subjects here amounted to 2600. They were principally Indians.

The next mission on my route was that called St. Enos. I vaccinated 900 of its inhabitants, and proceeded to St. Cruz, where I operated upon 650. My next advance was to St. Luis Obispes. Here I found 800 subjects. The mission of St. Michael followed in order. In it I vaccinated 1850 persons. My next theatre of operations was at St. John Bapistrano. 900 was the number that received vaccination here. Thence I went to La Solada, and vaccinated 1685, and then proceeded to St. Carlos, and communicated the matter to 800.

From the latter mission I passed on to the fort of Monte el Rey, where is a garrison of a hundred soldiers. I found here 500 persons to vaccinate. The name of this place in English signifies the King's Mount or Hill. Forests spread around Monte el Rey for miles in all directions, composed of thick clusters of pines and live oaks. Numberless grey bears find their home, and range in these deep woods. They are frequently known to attack men. The Spaniards take great numbers of them by stratagem, killing an old horse in the neighbourhood of their places of resort. They erect a scaffold near the dead animal, upon which they place themselves during the night, armed with a gun or lance. When the bear approaches to eat, they either shoot it, or pierce it with the lance from their elevated position.

Notwithstanding all their precautions, however, they are sometimes caught by the wounded animal; and after a man has once wrestled with a bear, he will not be likely to desire to make a second trial of the same gymnastic exercise. Such, at any rate, is the opinion I have heard those express, who have had the good fortune to come off alive from a contest of this kind. I do not speak for myself in this matter, as I never came so near as to take the *close hug* with one in my life; though to escape it, I once came near breaking my neck down a precipice.

From Monte el Rey I advanced to the mission of St. Anthony, which lies thirty miles E. from the coast. In it I found one thousand persons to inoculate. I had now reached the region of small pox, several cases of it having occurred in this mission. The ruling priest of this establishment informed me, that he did not consider it either necessary or advisable for me to proceed farther for the purpose of inoculating the inhabitants of the country, as the small pox had prevailed universally through its whole remaining extent. As I had heard, while in San Diego, great numbers had been carried off by it. I then told him that I wished to see the church officer who had been described to me by the first priest whom I had seen on my way up the coast. He furnished me a horse, and I set off for the port of San Francisco, vaccinating those whom I found on the way who had not had the smallpox.

I reached the above mentioned place, on the twentieth of June, 1829. Finding the person of whom I was in search, I presented him all the certificates of the priests of the missions in which I had vaccinated, and the letter of the general. I had inoculated in all twenty-two thousand persons. After he had finished the perusal of these papers, he asked me, what I thought my services were worth? I replied, that I should leave that point entirely in his judgment and decision. He then remarked, that he must have some time to reflect upon the subject, and that I must spend a week or two with him. I consented willingly to this proposal, as I was desirous of crossing the bay of San Francisco to the Russian settlement, called the Bodego.

I proceeded to carry my wish into execution on the 23rd, accompanied by two Coriac Indians, whose occupation was the killing of sea otters for the Russians, who hire them into their service. Those who pursue this employment, have water crafts made of the sea lions' skins, in the shape of a canoe. Over this spreads a top, completely covered in such a manner as to preclude the possibility of the entrance of any water. An opening is left at the bow and stern, over which the person who has entered draws a covering of the same material with that of the boat, which fastens firmly over the aperture in such a manner, as to make this part entirely water proof, as any other portion of the boat. Two persons generally occupy it. No position can be more secure than theirs, from all the dangers of the sea. The waves dash over them harmless. The occupants are stationed, one at the bow, and the other at the stern; the latter guides the boat, while the other is provided with a spear, which he darts into the otter whenever he comes within its reach. Great numbers are thus taken.

But to return to myself: We crossed the bay, which is about three miles in width. It is made by the entrance of a considerable river, called by the Spaniards Rio de San Francisco. After we reached the north shore, we travelled through a beautiful country, with a rich soil, well watered and timbered, and reached the Russian settlement in the night, having come a distance of thirty miles. As our journey had been made on foot, and we had eaten nothing, I was exceedingly fatigued and hungry. I accompanied my fellow travellers, who belonged here, to their *wigwams*, where I obtained some food, and a seal skin to sleep upon. Early in the morning I arose, and learning from one of my late companions where was the dwelling of the commander of the place, I proceeded towards it.

I had become acquainted with this person while I was vaccinating the inhabitants of San Diego. He came there in a brig, and insisted upon my promising him that I would come and communicate the remedy to the people of his establishments, offering to recompense me for my services. I agreed to do what he wished, should it be in my power. Accordingly, finding that the Spaniard did not intend to keep a strict guard over my movements, I availed myself of this opportunity of fulfilling the expressed wish of Don Seraldo, for so was he called. I reached the place pointed out to me by the friendly Indian, and was received by the above mentioned gentleman with the warmest expressions of kindness and friendship. He said that so long a time had elapsed since he saw me, he was afraid I had forgotten our conversation together, and that circumstances had rendered my coming to him impossible. He had suffered greatly from the fear that the small pox would spread among his people, before he should be enabled to prevent danger from it, through the means of the kine pox.

After breakfast, he circulated an order among the people, for all who wished to be provided with a safe guard against the terrible malady that had approached them so near, to come to his door. In a few hours I began my operations; and continued to be constantly occupied for three days, vaccinating during this period fifteen hundred individuals. I reminded them all that they must return on the fourth day, provided no signs of the complaint appeared; and that they were not to rub, or roughly touch the spot, should the vaccine matter have proper effect.

This done, Don Seraldo offered to accompany me through the fort and around the settlement, in order to show me the position, and every thing which might be new and interesting to me. Its situation is one of the most beautiful that I ever beheld, or that the imagination can conceive. The fort stands on the brow of a handsome hill, about two hundred feet above the level of the sea. This hill is surrounded on all sides for two miles with a charming plain. A lofty mountain whose sides present the noblest depth of forest, raises a summit, glittering with perpetual ice and snow on one hand, and on the other the level surface is lost in the waves of the sea. Clear cold streams pour down the mountain, unceasingly from different points, and glide through the plain, imparting moisture and verdure. The same multitudes of domestic animals, that are every where seen in this country, graze around in the pastures. They find abundant pasturage in the wild oats, which grow spontaneously upon this coast. Very little attention is paid to cultivation, where so many advantages are united to favour it. The amount of produce of any kind raised is small, and the inhabitants depend for bread entirely upon the Spaniards.

I remained in this delightful place one week. At the expiration of this time Don Seraldo gave me one hundred dollars, as payment for my services, and then mounted me upon a horse and conducted me back to the bay himself, and remained on the shore, until he saw me safe upon the other side.

I soon saw myself again in the presence of the Spanish priest, from whom I was to receive my recompense for the services performed on my long tour. He was not aware where I had been, until I informed him. When I had told him, he asked me what Don Seraldo had paid me? I stated this matter as it was. He then demanded of me, how I liked the coast of California? I answered, that I very much admired the appearance of the country. His next question was, how I would like the idea of living in it? It would be agreeable to me, I returned, were it subject to any other form of government. He proceeded to question me upon the ground of my objections to the present form of government? I was careful not to satisfy him on this point.

He then handed me a written piece of paper, the translation of which is as follows:

I certify, that James O. Pattie has vaccinated all the Indians and whites on this coast, and to recompense him for the same, I give the said James O. Pattie my obligation for one thousand head of cattle, and land to pasture them; that is, 500 cows and 500 mules. This he is to receive after he becomes a Catholic, and a subject of this government. Given in the mission of St. Francisco on the 8th of July, in the year 1829.

John Cabortes

When I had read this, without making use of any figure of speech, I was struck dumb. My anger choked me. As I was well aware of the fact, that this man had it in his power to hang me if I insulted him, and that here there was no law to give me redress, and compel him to pay me justly for my services, I said nothing for some time, but stood looking him full in the face. I cannot judge whether he read my displeasure, and burning feelings in my countenance, as I thus eyed him, and would have sought to pacify me, or not; but before I made a movement of any kind, he spoke, saying, 'you look displeased, sir.'

Prudential considerations were sufficient to withhold me no longer, and I answered in a short manner, that I felt at that moment as though I should rejoice to find myself once more in a country where I should be justly dealt by. He asked me, what I meant when I spoke of being justly dealt by? I told him what my meaning was, and wished to be in my own country, where there are laws to compel a man to pay another what he justly owes him, without his having the power to attach to the debt, as a condition upon which the payment is to depend, the submission to, and gratification of, any of his whimsical desires.

Upon this the priest's tone became loud and angry as he said, 'then you regard my proposing that you should become a Catholic, as the expression of an unjust and whimsical desire!' I told him 'yes, that I did; and that I would not change my present opinions for all the money his mission was worth; and moreover, that before I would consent to be adopted into the society and companionship of such a band of murderers and robbers, as I deemed were to be found along this coast, for the pitiful amount of one thousand head of cattle, I would suffer death.'

When I had thus given honest and plain utterance to the feelings, which swelled within me, the priest ordered me to leave his house. I walked out quickly, and possessed myself of my rifle, as I did not know, but some of his attendants at hand might be set upon me; for if the comparison be allowable the priests of this country have the people as much and entirely under their control and command, as the people of our own country have a good bidable dog. For fear they should come barking at me, I hastened away, and proceeded to a ranch, where I procured a horse for three dollars, which I mounted, and took the route for Monte el Rey. I did not stop, nor stay on my journey to this place. I found upon my arrival there, an American vessel in port, just ready to sail, and on the point of departure.

Meeting the captain on shore, I made the necessary arrangements with him for accompanying him, and we went on board together. The anchor was now weighed, and we set sail. In the course of an hour, I was thoroughly sick, and so continued for one week. I do not know any word, that explains my feelings in this case so well as that of heart sickness. I ate nothing, or little all this time; but after I recovered, my appetite returned in tenfold strength, and I never enjoyed better health in my life. We continued at sea for several months, sailing from one port to another, and finally returned to that of Monte el Rey, from which we had set sail.

It was now the 6th of January, 1830, and I felt anxious to hear something in relation to my companions, from whom I had so long been separated. I accordingly went on shore, where I met with a great number of acquaintances, both Americans and English. The latter informed me, that there was a revolution in the country, a part of the inhabitants having revolted against the constituted authorities. The revolted party seemed at present likely to gain the ascendency. They had promised the English and Americans the same privileges, and liberty in regard to the trade on the coast, that belonged to the native citizens, upon the condition, that these people aided them in their attempt to gain their freedom, by imparting advice and funds.

This information gladdened my very heart. I do not know, if the feeling be not wrong; but I instantly thought of the unspeakable pleasure I should enjoy at seeing the general, who had imprisoned me, and treated me so little like a man and a Christian, in fetters himself. Under the influence of these feelings, I readily and cheerfully appropriated a part of my little store to their use, I would fain have accompanied them in hopes to have one shot at the general with my rifle. But the persuasions of my countrymen to the contrary prevailed with me. They assigned, as reasons for their advice, that it was enough to give counsel and funds at first, and that the better plan would be, to see how they managed their own affairs, before we committed ourselves, by taking an active part in them, as they had been found to be a treacherous people to deal with.

On the 8th of the month, General Joachim Solis placed himself at the head of one hundred and fifty soldiers well armed, and began his march from Monte el Rey to the fort of St. Francisco. He was accompanied by two cannon, which, he said, he should make thunder, if the fort was not quietly given up to him. General Solis had been transferred from a command in the city of Mexico to take command of the insurgents, as soon as they should have formed themselves into something like an organized party, and have come to a head. He had left Monte el Rey with such a force as circumstances enabled him to collect, recruiting upon his route, and inducing all to join him, whom he could influence by fair words and promises.

As has been said, he threatened the fort of St. Francisco with a bloody contest, in case they resisted his wishes. He carried with him written addresses to the inhabitants, in which those, who would range themselves under his standard, were offered every thing that renders life desirable. They all flocked round him, giving in their adhesion. When he reached the fort, he sent in his propositions, which were acceded to, as soon as read by the majority. The minority were principally officers. They were all imprisoned by General Solis, as soon as he obtained possession of the place. He then proceeded to make laws, by which the inhabitants were to be governed, and placed the fort in the hands of those, upon whom, he thought he could depend.—These arrangements being all made, he began his return to Monte el Rey, highly delighted with his success.

There now seemed little doubt of his obtaining possession of the whole coast in the course of a few months. He remained at Monte el

Rey increasing his force, and drilling the new recruits, until the 28th of March, when he again marched at the head of two hundred soldiers. The present object of attack was Santa Barbara, where the commander under the old regime was stationed. The latter was General Echedio, my old acquaintance of San Diego, for whom I bore such good will. He was not in the least aware of the visit intended him by General Solis; the latter having prevented any tidings upon the subject reaching him, by posting sentinels thickly for some distance upon the road, that lay between them, to intercept and stop any one passing up or down.

The insurgent general had as yet succeeded in his plans; and was so elated with the prospect of surprising General Echedio, and completely dispossessing him of his power, and consequently having all in his own hands, that he did not consider it necessary any longer to conceal his real character. The professions of the kind purposes of the insurgent towards the English and Americans will be recollected; and also, that it was at a time when application was made by these Spaniards to them for aid. The tone was now changed. Threats were now made, with regard to the future treatment, which we, unfortunate foreigners, might expect, as soon as General Solis became master of the coast.

We learned this through a Mexican Spaniard, whose daughter Captain Cooper had married. This old gentleman was told by the general, that he intended either to compel every American and Englishman to swear allegiance to the government, which should be established, or drive them from the country. This information was, however, not communicated to us, until the general had departed. We held a consultation upon the subject, to devise some means, which should render him incapable of carrying his good intentions towards us into effect. No other expedient suggested itself to us, but that of sending General Echedio information of the proposed attack, in time to enable him to be prepared for it. We agreed upon this, and a letter was written, stating what we deemed the points most necessary for him to know.

The signatures of some of the principal men of the place were affixed to it; for those who think alike upon important points soon understand one another; and the character of Solis had not been unveiled to us alone. It was important, that General Echedio should attach consequence to our letter, and the information, it contained, would come upon him so entirely by surprise, that he might very naturally entertain doubts of its correctness. I added my name to those of the party to which I belonged. The object now was to have our document conveyed safely into the hands of General Echedio. We sent a runner with two good horses and instructions, how to pass the army of Solis in the night undiscovered.

All proceedings had been conducted with so much secrecy and caution, that the matter so far rested entirely with ourselves. We occasionally heard the citizens around us express dislike towards the insurgent general; but as they did not seem inclined to carry their opinions into action, we concluded these were only remarks made to draw out our thoughts, and took no notice of them. From after circumstances I believe, that the number of his enemies exceeded that of his friends; and that the remarks, of which I have spoken, were made in truth and sincerity. Meanwhile we impatiently awaited some opportunity of operating to the disadvantage of the general, and to hear what had taken place between him and General Echedio.

A messenger arrived on the 12th of April with the information, that the commander of the insurgents had ranged his men for three days in succession before the fort upon the plain. A continual firing had been kept up on both sides, during the three days, at the expiration of which General Solis, having expended his ammunition, and consumed his provisions, was compelled to withdraw, having sustained no loss, except that of one horse from a sustained action of three days! The spirit with which the contest was conducted may be inferred from a fact, related to me. The cannon balls discharged from the fort upon the enemy were discharged with so little force, that persons arrested them in their course, without sustaining any injury by so doing, at the point, where in the common order of things, they must have inflicted death.

Upon the reception of this news, we joined in the prevalent expression of opinion around us. The name and fame of General Solis was exalted to the skies. All the florid comparisons, usual upon such occasions, were put in requisition, and all the changes were sung upon his various characteristics wit, honour and courage. The point was carried so far as to bring him within some degrees of relationship to a supernatural being. Then the unbounded skill he displayed in marshalling his force, and his extreme care to prevent the useless waste of his men's lives were expatiated upon, and placed in the strongest light. The climax of his excellence was his having retreated without the loss of a man. This was the burden of our theme to his friends, that is, the fifty soldiers, in whose charge he had left the command of the fort.

197

The Captain Cooper, of whom I have spoken, looked rather deeper into things, than those around him; and consequently knew the most effectual means of operating upon the inefficient machines, in the form of men, which it was necessary for our present purpose, to remove out of the way for a time. Accordingly he rolled out a barrel of good old rum, inviting all the friends of the good and great General Solis to come, and drink his health. The summons was readily obeyed by them. Being somewhat elevated in spirit by the proceedings of their noble general, previous to swallowing the genuine inspiration of joy, the feeling afterwards swelled to an extent, that burst all bounds, and finally left them prostrate and powerless. We, like good Christians, with the help of some of the inhabitants, conveyed them into some strong houses, which stood near, while they remained in their helpless condition, locking the doors safely, that no harm might come to them. In our pity and care for them, we proposed, that they should remain, until they felt that violent excitements are injurious, from the natural reaction of things. We now proceeded to circulate another set of views, and opinions among the inhabitants in the vicinity of the fort; and such was our success in the business of indoctrination, that we soon counted all their votes on our side.

General Solis was now pitched down the depths, as heartily as he had before been exalted to the heights. 'Huzza for General Echedio and the Americans!' was the prevailing cry.

The next movement was to make out a list of our names, and appoint officers. Our number including Scotch, Irish, English, Dutch and Americans, amounted to thirty-nine. The number of Americans, however, being the greatest, our party received the designation of American. Captain Cooper was our commanding officer. We now marched up to the castle, which is situated on the brink of a precipice, overlooking the sea, and found four brass field pieces, mounted on carriages. These we concluded to carry with us to the fort. The remainder placed so as to command a sweep of the surface of water below, and the surrounding ground, we spiked fearing, if they fell into the hands of Solis, that he might break down our walls with them. This done, we went to the magazine, and broke it open, taking what powder and ball we wanted.

We then posted sentinels for miles along the road, to which we knew Solis was hastening in order to prevent news of our proceedings from reaching him, before it was convenient for us, that he should know them. We were aware of his intention to return here to recruit again, and it was our wish to surprise him by an unexpected reception, and thus obtain an advantage, which should counterbalance his superiority of numbers. In so doing, we only availed ourselves of the precedent, he had given us, in his management with regard to General Echedio. He had not derived benefit from his plan, in consequence of his too great confidence of success, which led him to discover his real feelings towards our people.

We hoped to avail ourselves of what was wise in his plan, and profit by his mistakes. We shut up all the people, both men and women, in the fort at night, that it might be out of their power to attempt to make their way, under the cover of darkness, through our line of sentinels, to give information, should the inclination be felt. Our precautions were not taken through fear of him, should he even come upon us, prepared to encounter us as enemies: but from the wish to take both himself and army prisoners. Should they learn what we had done, we feared, they would pass on to St. Francisco, to recruit, and thus escape us.

Our designs were successful; for in a few days General Solis and his men appeared in sight of the first of our sentinels, who quickly transmitted this information to us. Our preparations for receiving him were soon made, with a proper regard to politeness. A regale of music from air instruments, called cannons, was in readiness to incline him to the right view of the scene before him, should he seem not likely to conform to our wish, which was, simply, that he should surrender to us without making any difficulty.

Our fortification was in the form of a square, with only one entrance. From each side of this entrance a wall projected at right angles from it fifty yards. The Spaniards call them wings; and it seems to me a significant and fitting name for them. We intended to allow the approaching party to advance between these walls, before we began our part. Our cannons were charged with grape and balls, and placed in a position to produce an effect between the walls. Every man was now at his post, and General Solis approaching within sight of the fort, a small cannon which accompanied him was discharged by way of salute. No answer was returned to him. The piece was reloaded, and his fife and drum began a lively air, and the whole body moved in a quick step towards the fort, entering the space between the wings, of which I have spoken. This was no sooner done than our matches were in readiness for instant operation.

Captain Cooper commanded them to surrender. He was immediately obeyed by the soldiers, who threw down their arms, aware that death would be the penalty of their refusal. The general and six of his mounted officers fled, directing their course to St. Francisco. Six of our party were soon on horseback with our rifles, and in pursuit of them. I had been appointed orderly sergeant, and was one of the six. We carried orders from the principal Spanish civil officer, who was in the fort, and had taken an active part in all our proceedings, to bring the general back with us, either dead or alive. The commands of our military commander, Captain Cooper, spoke the same language.

I confess that I wanted to have a shot at the fugitive, and took pleasure in the pursuit. We went at full speed, for our horses were good and fresh. Those belonging to the party we were so desirous to overtake, would of course be somewhat weary, and jaded by their long journey. We had not galloped many miles, before we perceived them in advance of us. As soon as we were within hearing distance of each other, I called upon them to surrender. They replied by wheeling their horses and firing at us, and then striking their spurs into their horses' sides, to urge them onward. We followed, producing more effect with our spurs than they had done, and calling upon them again to surrender, or we should fire, and give no quarter. They at length reined up, and six dismounted and laid down their arms.

The seventh remained on horse back, and as we came up, fired, wounding one of our number slightly in the right arm. He then turned to resume his flight; but his horse had not made the second spring, before our guns brought the hero from his saddle. Four of our balls had passed through his body. The whole number being now assembled together, victors and vanquished, General Solis offered me his sword. I refused it, but told him, that himself and his officers must accompany me in my return to the fort. He consented to this with a countenance so expressive of dejection, that I pitied him, notwithstanding I knew him to be a bad man, and destitute of all principle.

The man who had lost his life through his obstinacy, was bound upon his horse, and the others having remounted theirs, we set out upon our return. Our captives were all disarmed except General Solis, who was allowed to retain his sword. We reached the fort three hours before sunset. The general and his men were dismounted, and irons put upon their legs, after which they were locked up with those who had forgotten themselves in their joy at the good fortune of their poor general.

These events occurred on the 18th of March. On the 20th the civil officer of whom I have before spoken, together with Captain Cooper, despatched a messenger to General Echedio, who was still in Santa Barbara with written intelligence of what we had accomplished. It was stated that the Americans were the originators of the whole matter, and that their flag was waving in the breeze over Monte el Rey, where it would remain, until His Excellency came himself to take charge of the place; and he was requested to hasten his departure, as they who had obtained possession were anxious to be relieved from the care and responsibility they found imposed upon them.

We were very well aware that he would receive our information with unmingled pleasure, as he expected Solis would return in a short time to Santa Barbara, to give him another battle. It was said, that upon the reception of the letter he was as much rejoiced as though he had been requested to come and take charge of a kingdom. As soon as he could make the necessary arrangements he came to Monte el Rey, where he arrived on the 29th. We gave the command of the place up to him; but before he would suffer our flag to be taken down, he had thirty guns discharged in honour of it. He then requested a list of our names, saying, that if we would accept it, he would give each one of us the right of citizenship in his country. A splendid dinner was made by him for our party.

On the night of the 29th a vessel arrived in the port. In the morning it was found to be a brig belonging to the American consul at Macho, John W. Jones, Esq., who was on board of it. This was the same person to whom I wrote when in prison at San Diego by Mr. Perkins. I met with him, and had the melancholy pleasure of relating to him in person my sufferings and imprisonment, and everything, in short, that had happened to me during my stay in this country. This took place in my first interview with him. He advised me to make out a correct statement of the value of the furs I had lost by the general's detention of me, and also of the length of time I had been imprisoned, and to take it with me to the city of Mexico, where the American minister resided, and place it in his hands. It was probable, the consul continued, that he would be able to compel the Mexican government to indemnify me for the loss of property I had sustained, and for the injustice of my imprisonment.

The probability of my success was not slight, provided I could establish the truth of my statement, by obtaining the testimony of those who were eye witnesses of the facts. I informed the consul that I had not means to enable me to reach the city of Mexico. A gentleman who was present during this conversation, after hearing my last remark, mentioned that he was then on his way to that place, and that if I would accompany him he would pay my expenses; and if circumstances should happen to induce me to think of returning thence to the United States, I should do so free of expense. I expressed my thanks for this offer, and said that if I succeeded in recovering only a portion of what I had lost I would repay the money thus kindly expended in my behalf; but the obligation of gratitude imposed by such an act, it would be impossible for me to repay.

In conformity to Mr. Jones' advice and instruction, I sat myself down to make out an account for the inspection of the American minister. When I had completed it, I obtained the signatures, of some of the first among the inhabitants of Monte el Rey, and that of the civil officer before mentioned, testifying as to the truth of what I said, so far as the circumstances narrated had come under their observation. The general having received the list of our names, which he had requested, he now desired, that we might all come to his office, and receive the right of citizenship from his hand, as a reward for what we had done. I put my paper in my pocket, and proceeded with my companions and Mr. Jones to the indicated place. The general had been much surprised to find my name in the list furnished him; but as I entered the room, he arose hastily from his seat and shook my hand in a friendly manner, after which I introduced him to the consul. He seemed surprised as he heard the name of this gentleman, but said nothing.

After pointing us to seats, he walked out of the room, saying he should return in a few moments. I concluded, that he thought, I had brought the consul, or that he had accompanied me for the purpose of questioning him on the subject of my imprisonment and that of my companions. He returned, as soon as he had promised, having some papers in his hand. After he had seated himself, he began to interrogate me with regard to what had happened to me, during the long time that had elapsed since he had last seen me, adding, that he did not expect ever to have met me again; but was happy to see me a citizen of his country. My answer in reply to the last part of his remarks was short. I told him, he had not yet enjoyed anything from that source, and with my consent never should.

He looked very serious upon this manifestation of firmness, or whatever it may be called on my part, and requested to know my objections to being a citizen of the country?

I replied that it was simply having been reared in a country where

202

I could pass from one town to another, without the protection of a passport, which instead of affording real protection, subjected me to the examination of every petty officer, near whom I passed, and that I should not willingly remain, where such was the order of things. Besides, I added, I was liable to be thrown into prison like a criminal, at the caprice of one clothed with a little authority, if I failed to show a passport, which I might either lose accidentally, or in some way, for which I might not have been in the least in fault.

The general, in reply, asked me if in my country a foreigner was permitted to travel to and fro, without first presenting to the properly constituted authorities of our government, proof from those among the officers of his own government appointed for that purpose, of his being a person of good character, who might safely be allowed to traverse the country? I told him I had once attempted to satisfy him on that head, and he very abruptly and decidedly contradicted my account; and that now I did not feel in the least compelled, or inclined to enter upon the matter a second time. All which I desired of him, and that I did not earnestly desire, was, that he would give me a passport to travel into my own country by the way of the city of Mexico. If I could once more place my foot upon its free soil, and enjoy the priceless blessings of its liberty, which my unfortunate father, of whom I could never cease to think, and who had died in his prison, assisted in maintaining, I should be satisfied.

While I thus spoke, he gazed steadily in my face. His swarthy complexion grew pale. He read in my countenance a strong expression of deep feeling, awakened by the nature of the remembrances associated with him. He felt that there was something fearful in the harvest of bitterness which the oppressor reaps in return for his injuries and cruelties. I thought, he feared, if he did not grant my request for a pass, that I might carry into execution the purposes of vengeance; to which I used to give utterance in my burning indignation at his conduct at the time of my father's death. Whenever I saw him pass my prison I seized the opportunity to tell him, that if my time for redress ever came, he would find me as unflinching in my vengeance as he had been in his injuries. I only expressed the truth with regard to my feelings at the time, and even now I owe it to candor and honesty to acknowledge, that I could have seen him at the moment of this conversation suffer any infliction without pity.

He did not hesitate to give the pass I desired; but asked me what business led me out of my way to the United States around by the city of Mexico? My direct course, he remarked, lay in a straight direction through New Mexico. For reply, I drew out of my pocket the paper I had written before coming to his office, and read it to him, telling him that was the business which led me to the city of Mexico. I then asked him if all the facts there stated were not true? His answer was in the affirmative; 'but,' added he, 'you will not be able to recover any thing, as I acted in conformity to the laws of my country. If you will remain in this country I will give you something handsome to begin with.' I assured him that I would not stay, but I wished him to show me the laws which allowed, or justified him in imprisoning myself and my companions for entering a country as we did, compelled by misfortunes such as ours.

In return, he said he had no laws to show, but those which recommended him to take up and imprison those whom he deemed conspirators against his country. 'What marks of our being conspirators did you discover in us,' rejoined I, 'which warranted your imprisoning us? I am aware of none, unless it be the evidence furnished by our countenances and apparel, that we had undergone the extreme of misfortune and distress, which had come upon us without any agency on our part, and as inevitable evils to which every human being is liable. We were led by the hope of obtaining relief, to seek refuge in your protection. In confirmation of our own relation, did not our papers prove that we were Americans, and that we had received legal permission from the very government under which we then were, to trade in the country? The printed declaration to this effect, given us by the governor of Santa Fé, which we showed you, you tore in pieces before us, declaring it was neither a license nor a passport.' The general replied, that he did tear up a paper given him by us, but that in fact it was neither a passport nor a license.

'Now sir,' said I, 'I am happy that it is in my power to prove, in the presence of the American consul, the truth of what I have said with regard to the license.' I then produced another copy of the paper torn up by him, which had been given my father by the governor of Santa Fé, at the same time with the former. He looked at it, and said nothing more, except that I might go on, and try what I could do in the way of recovering what I had lost.

The consul and myself now left him, and returned to Captain Cooper's. The consul laughed at me about my quarrel with the general. In a few moments the latter appeared among us, and the remainder of the day passed away cheerfully in drinking toasts. When the general rose to take leave of us, he requested the consul to call upon him at his office; as he wanted to converse with him upon business. The consul went, according to request, and the general contracted with him for the transportation of General Solis, and sixteen other prisoners to San Blas, on board his vessel, whence they were to be carried to the city of Mexico.

The 7th of May was fixed for the departure of the brig, as the general required some time for making necessary arrangements, and preparing documents to accompany the transmission of the prisoners. When I heard that this delay was unavoidable, I went to the general and returned my passport, telling him I should want another, when the vessel was ready to sail, as I intended to proceed in it as far as San Blas. He consented to give me one, and then joked with me about the honour, I should enjoy, of accompanying General Solis. I replied in the same strain, and left him.

Captain William H. Hinkley and myself went to the mission of San Carlos, where we spent three days. During the whole time, we did little beside express our astonishment at what we saw. We had fallen upon the festival days of some saint, and the services performed in his honour all passed under our eyes. They were not a few, nor wanting in variety, as this was a noted festival. Our admiration, however, was principally excited by the contest between grizzly bears and bulls, which constitutes one of the exhibitions of these people.

Five large grey bears had been caught, and fastened in a pen built for the purpose of confining the bulls, during a bull-baiting. One of the latter animals, held by ropes, was brought to the spot by men on horseback, and thrown down. A bear was then drawn up to him, and they were fastened together by a rope about fifteen feet in length, in such a manner, that they could not separate from each other. One end of it is tied around one of the forefeet of the bull, and the other around one of the hind feet of the bear. The two were then left to spring upon their feet. As soon as this movement is made, the bull makes at the bear, very often deciding the fate of the ferocious animal in this first act. If the bull fails in goring the bear, the fierce animal seizes him and tears him to death. Fourteen of the latter lost their lives, before the five bears were destroyed.

To Captain Hinkley this was a sight of novel and absorbing interest. It had less of novelty for me, as since I had been on the coast, I had often seen similar combats, and in fact worse, having been present when men entered the enclosure to encounter the powerful bull in his wild and untamed fierceness. These unfortunate persons are armed with a small sword, with which they sometimes succeed in saving their own lives at the expense of that of the animal.

I once saw the man fall in one of these horrible shows; they are conducted in the following manner: the man enters to the bull with the weapon, of which he avails himself, in the right hand, and in the left a small red flag, fastened to a staff about three feet in length. He whistles, or makes some other noise, to attract the attention of the animal, upon hearing which the bull comes towards him with the speed of fury. The man stands firm, with the flag dangling before him, to receive this terrible onset. When the bull makes the last spring towards him, he dexterously evades it, by throwing his body from behind the flag to one side, at the same time thrusting his sword into the animal's side. If this blow is properly directed, blood gushes from the mouth and nostrils of the bull, and he falls dead. A second blow in this case is seldom required.

Another mode of killing these animals is by men on horseback, with a spear, which they dart into his neck, immediately behind the horns. The horse is often killed by the bull. When the animal chances to prefer running from the fight to engaging in it, he is killed by the horseman, by being thrown heels over head. This is accomplished by catching hold of the tail of the bull in the full speed of pursuit, and giving a turn around the head of the saddle, in such a manner, that they are enabled to throw the animal into any posture they choose.

After we returned to the fort, it took us some time to relate what we had seen, to the consul. Feeling it necessary to do something towards supporting myself, during the remaining time of my stay in this part of the country, I took my rifle, and joined a Portuguese in the attempt to kill otters along the coast. We hunted up and down the coast, a distance of forty miles, killing sixteen otters in ten days. We sold their skins, some as high as seventy-five dollars, and none under twenty-five. Three hundred dollars fell to my share from the avails of our trip. Captain Cooper was exceedingly desirous to purchase my rifle, now that I should not be likely to make use of it, as I was soon to proceed on my journey to the city of Mexico. I presented it to him, for I could not think of bartering for money, what I regarded, as a tried friend, that had afforded me the means of subsistence and protection for so long a time. My conscience would have reproached me, as though I had been guilty of an act of ingratitude.

The period of my departure from this coast was now close at hand,

and my thoughts naturally took a retrospect of the whole time, I had spent upon it. The misery and suffering of various kinds, that I had endured in some portions of it, had not been able to prevent me from feeling, and acknowledging, that this country is more calculated to charm the eye, than any one I have ever seen. Those, who traverse it, if they have any capability whatever of perceiving, and admiring the beautiful and sublime in scenery, must be constantly excited to wonder and praise. It is no less remarkable for uniting the advantages of healthfulness, a good soil, a temperate climate, and yet one of exceeding mildness, a happy mixture of level and elevated ground, and vicinity to the sea. Its inhabitants are equally calculated to excite dislike, and even the stronger feelings of disgust and hatred.

The priests are omnipotent, and all things are subject to their power. Two thirds of the population are native Indians under the immediate charge of these spiritual rulers in the numerous missions. It is a well known fact, that nothing is more entirely opposite to the nature of a savage, than labour. In order to keep them at their daily tasks, the most rigid and unremitting supervision is exercised. No bondage can be more complete, than that under which they live. The compulsion laid upon them has, however, led them at times to rebel, and endeavour to escape from their yoke. They have seized upon arms, murdered the priests, and destroyed the buildings of the missions, by preconcerted stratagem, in several instances. When their work of destruction and retribution was accomplished, they fled to the mountains, and subsisted on the flesh of wild horses which are there found in innumerable droves. To prevent the recurrence of similar events, the priests have passed laws, prohibiting an Indian the use or possession of any weapon whatever, under the penalty of a severe punishment.

On the 25th I addressed the companions of my former journeyings and imprisonment in San Diego by letter. They had remained in the town of Angels, during the months which had elapsed since my separation from them, after our receiving liberty upon parole. I had kept up a constant correspondence with them in this interval. My objects at present were to inform them of my proposed departure for my native country, and request them, if they should be called upon so to do, to state every thing relative to our imprisonment and loss of property, exactly as it took place. I closed, by telling them, they might expect a letter from me upon my arrival in the city of Mexico.

On the 8th of May I applied for my passport, which was readily given me, and taking leave of the general and my friends, I entered the vessel, in which I was to proceed to San Blas, at 8 o'clock in the morning. The sails of the brig, which was called the *Volunteer*, were soon set, and speeding us upon our way. The green water turned white, as it met the advance of our prow, and behind us we left a smooth belt of water, affording a singular contrast to the waves around. I watched the disappearance of this single smooth spot, as it was lost in the surrounding billows, when the influence of the movement of our vessel ceased, as a spectacle to be contemplated by a land's man with interest. But no feeling of gratification operated in the minds of the poor prisoners in the hold. They were ironed separately, and then all fastened to a long bar of iron. They were soon heard mingling prayers and groans, interrupted only by the violent vomiting produced by sea sickness. In addition to this misery, when fear found entrance into their thoughts during the intervals of the cessation of extreme sickness, it seemed to them, as if every surge the vessel made must be its last. In this miserable condition they remained, until the 19th, when we arrived at San Blas. The prisoners here were delivered into the charge of the commanding officer of the place.

Captain Hinkley, his mate, Henry Vinal, and myself disembarked at this place, in order to commence our journey over land to Mexico. The necessary arrangements for our undertaking occupied us three days. We found the season warm on our arrival here. Watermelons were abundant, and also green corn, and a great variety of ripe fruit. Two crops of corn and wheat are raised in the year. A precipice was shown me, over which, I was told, the Mexicans threw three old priests at the commencement of the revolt against the king of Spain.—This port is the centre of considerable business in the seasons of spring and fall. During the summer, the inhabitants are compelled to leave it, as the air becomes infected by the exhalations, arising from the surrounding swamps. Myriads of mosquitoes and other small insects fill the air at the same time, uniting with the former cause to render the place uninhabitable.

Great quantities of salt are made upon the flats in the vicinity of San Blas. I did not inform myself accurately, with regard to the manner, in which it is made; but as I was passing by one day, where the preparation of it was carried on, I observed what struck me as being both curious and novel. The earth was laid off in square beds. Around their edges dirt was heaped up, as though the bed, which I have mentioned, was intended to be covered with water.

We began our journey well armed, as we had been informed that we should, in all probability, find abundant occasion to use our arms, as we advanced. Our progress was slow, as we conformed to the directions given us, and kept a constant look out for robbers, of whom there are said to be thousands upon this route.

On the 25th we reached a small town called Tipi, where we remained one day to rest from our fatigue, and then set off again for Guadalaxara, distant eight days' journey. Our path led us through a beautiful country, a great portion of which was under cultivation. Occasionally we passed through small villages. Beggars were to be seen standing at the corners of all the streets, and along the highways. They take a station by the road side, having a dog or child by them, to lead them into the road when they see a traveller approaching. They stand until the person reaches the spot upon which they are, when they ask alms for the sake of a saint, whose image is worn suspended around their neck, or tied around the wrist. This circumstance of begging for the saint, and not for themselves, struck me as a new expedient in the art of begging. At first we gave a trifle to the poor saint. As we went on we found them so numerous that it became necessary for us to husband our alms, and we finally came to the conclusion that the large brotherhood of beggars could occasionally diversify their mode of life by a dexterous management of their fingers, and shut our purses to the demands of the saints. The country for some time before we drew near Guadalaxara, was rather barren, although its immediate vicinity is delightful.

We reached that city on the 2nd of June, and spent three days in it. It is situated upon a fine plain, which is overspread by the same numbers of domestic animals that I had seen in New Mexico and California. The city is walled in, with gates at the different entrances. These gates are strongly guarded, and no one is allowed to enter them until they have been searched, in order to ascertain if they carry any smuggled goods about them. The same precaution is used when any one passes out of the city. A passport must be shown for the person, his horse, and arms, and a statement from the principal peace officer, of the number of trunks with which he set out upon his journey, and their contents. This caution is to prevent smuggling; but it does not effect the purpose, as there is more contraband trade here, than in any place I was ever in before. I was not able to ascertain the number of inhabitants of this city. The silver mines of Guanaxuato are near Guadalaxara. They are carried on at present by an English company. The evening before our departure we went to the theatre. The actresses appeared young and beautiful, and danced and sung charmingly.

The 5th day of June we resumed our journey to the city of Mexico. Again we travelled through a charming country, tolerably thickly settled. On our way we fell in company with an officer belonging to the service of the country. He had ten soldiers with him. Upon his demanding to see our passports we showed them to him, though he had no authority to make such a demand. After he had finished their perusal he returned them with such an indifferent air, that I could not resist an inclination to ask him some questions that might perhaps have seemed rude. I first asked him what post he filled in the army? He answered, with great civility, he was first lieutenant. I then requested to know, to what part of the country he was travelling? He said, still in a very civil manner, that he had had the command of some troops in Guanaxuato, but was now on his way to the city of Mexico, to take charge of the 6th regiment, which was ordered to the province of Texas, to find out among the Americans there, those who had refused obedience to the Mexican laws.

He added, that when he succeeded in finding them, he would soon learn them to behave well. The last remark was made in rather a contemptuous tone of voice, and with something like an implied insult to me. This warmed my blood, and I replied in a tone not so gentle as prudence might have counselled a stranger in a foreign land to have adopted, that if himself and his men did not conduct themselves properly when they were among the Americans, the latter would soon despatch them to another country, which they had not yet seen; as the Americans were not Mexicans, to stand at the corner of a house, and hide their guns behind the side of it, while they looked another way, and pulled the trigger.

At this he flew into a passion. I did not try to irritate him any further, and he rode on and left us. We pursued our way slowly, and stopped for the night at Aguabuena, a small town on the way. We put up at a house, a sort of *posada*, built for lodging travellers.—Twenty-five cents is the price for the use of a room for one night. It is seldom that any person is found about such an establishment to take charge of it but an old key bearer. Provisions must be sought elsewhere. It is not often necessary to go further than the street, where, at any hour in the day until ten o'clock at night, men and women are engaged in crying different kinds of eatables. We generally purchased our food of them. After we had finished our supper two English gentlemen entered, who were on their way to the city of Mexico. We concluded to travel together, as our point of destination was the same, and we should be more able to resist any adversaries we might encounter; this country being, as I have before mentioned, infested with robbers and thieves, although we had not yet fallen in with any.

These gentlemen informed us that the greatest catholic festival of the whole year was close at hand. If we could reach the city of Mexico before its celebration, we should see something that would repay us for hastening our journey. As we were desirous to lose the sight of nothing curious, we proceeded as fast as circumstances would permit, and reached the city on the 10th, late in the evening, and put up at an inn kept by an Englishman, although, as in the other towns in which we had been, we were obliged to seek food elsewhere, the only accommodation at the inn being beds to sleep in, and liquors to drink. We found supper in a coffee house.

We were awakened early in the morning by the ringing of bells. As we stepped into the street we met three biers carried by some men guarded by soldiers. Blood was dropping from each bier. The bearers begged money to pay the expenses of burying the bodies. I afterwards learned that these persons were murdered on the night of our arrival, upon the Alameda, a promenade north of the city, in one of the suburbs. We visited this place, and found it covered with thousands of people, some walking, and others sitting on the seats placed around this public pleasure ground. Small parties are sheltered from view by thickets of a growth, like that in our country, used for hedges. The open surface is surrounded by a hedge of the same shrub. These partially concealed parties are usually composed of men and women of the lowest orders, engaged in card playing.

Such are to be seen at any hour of the day, occupied in a way which is most likely to terminate the meeting in an affray, and perhaps murder. Blood is frequently shed, and I judged from what I saw of the order of things, that the accounts of the numerous assassinations committed among this populace, were not exaggerated. One of the characteristics of this people is jealousy. Notwithstanding the danger really to be apprehended from visiting this place after certain hours, my two companions and myself spent several evenings in it without being molested in the slightest degree. But one evening as we were returning to our lodgings, we were compelled to kneel with our white pantaloons upon the dirty street, while the host was passing. We took care afterwards to step into a house in time to avoid the troublesome necessity.

We attended a bull baiting, and some other exhibitions for the amusement of the people. Being one evening at the theatre, I had the misfortune to lose my watch from my pocket, without being aware when it was taken. It would have been useless for me to have thought of looking around for it, as I stood in the midst of such a crowd that it was almost an impossibility to move.

The accounts of this city which I had met with in books led me to expect to find it placed in the midst of a lake, or surrounded by a sheet of water. To satisfy myself with regard to the truth of this representation, I mounted a horse, and made the circuit of the city, visiting some villages that lay within a league of it. I found no lake; but the land is low and flat. A canal is cut through it, for the purpose of carrying off the water that descends from the mountains upon the level surface, which has the appearance of having been formerly covered with water. A mountain which is visible from the city, presents a circular summit, one part of which is covered with snow throughout the year: upon the other is the crater of a volcano, which is continually sending up proof of the existence of an unceasing fire within.

Early upon the first day of my arrival in this city, I waited upon Mr. Butler, the American *charge d'affairs*. After I had made myself known to him he showed me a communication from President Jackson to the president of this country, the purport of which was, to request the latter to set at liberty some Americans, imprisoned upon the coast of California. I then handed him the statement I had made according to the advice of Mr. Jones. He asked me many questions relative to the losses I had sustained, which I answered, and then took my leave.

A number of coaches were to leave the city for Vera Cruz on the 18th of June. My companions and myself took places in one of them. On the 15th I again called upon Mr. Butler to obtain a passport to Vera Cruz, where I intended to embark for America. He took me to the palace of the president, in order that I might get my passport. This circumstance was agreeable to me, as I was desirous to see this person, of whom I had heard so much. Upon arriving at the palace I found it a splendid building, although much shattered by the balls discharged at it by the former President Guerero, who is now flying from one place to another with a few followers, spreading destruction to the extent of his power. A soldier led me into the presence of the president. He was walking to and fro when I entered the room, apparently in deep meditation.

Several clerks were present, engaged in writing. He received me politely, bowing as I advanced, and bade me sit down. In answer to his inquiry what I wished of him? I told my errand. He then asked me from what direction I came? I replied, from California. 'California!' said he, repeating the word with an air of interest. I answered again, that I left that part of the country when I began my present journey. 'You must have been there then,' rejoined he, 'when the late revolution took place, of which I have but a short time since received information.' I remarked, that I was upon the spot where it occurred, and that I took my departure from the coast in the same vessel that brought sixteen of the captives taken in the course of its progress, and that I disembarked at St. Blas at the same time that they were taken from the vessel.

He resumed the conversation by saying, 'you were probably one of the Americans who, I am told, assisted in subduing the revolted party.' I told him, he was correct in his opinion; and by so doing I had had the good fortune to gain my liberty. His countenance expressed surprise at the conclusion of my remark; and he proceeded to ask me, what meaning I had, in saying that I had thus regained my own liberty? I then related my story; upon which he said he had understood that General Echedio had acted contrary to the laws, in several instances, and that, in consequence, he had ordered him to Mexico to answer for his conduct. I was surprised at the condescension of the president in thus expressing to me any part of his intentions with regard to such a person. I accounted for it by supposing that he wished to have it generally understood, that he did not approve of the unjust and cruel treatment which the Americans had received.

The president appeared to me to be a man of plain and gentlemanly manners, possessing great talent. In this I express no more than my individual opinion; to which I must add that I do not consider myself competent to judge of such points, only for myself. He gave me a passport, and I returned to Mr. Butler's office, who informed me that he wished me to take a very fine horse to Vera Cruz, for the American consul at that place. He said that I would find it pleasant to vary my mode of travelling, by occasionally riding the horse. I readily consented to his wish, requesting him to have the horse taken to the place from which the coach would set off, early in the morning, when I would take charge of it. I now took leave of Mr. Butler and proceeded to my lodgings.

I found both my companions busily engaged in packing, and arranging for departure. I immediately entered upon the same employment. I had two trunks; one I filled with such articles as I should require upon my journey; and in another I placed such as I should not be likely to use, and a great many curiosities which I had collected during my long wanderings. The latter trunk I did not calculate to open until I reached my native land.

At 8 o'clock on the morning of the 16th our coach left the city, in company with two others. We were eight in number, including the coachman. Three of the party were ladies. One was a Frenchwoman, a married lady travelling without her husband. Another was a Spanish woman, who had married a wealthy Irishman, and was accompanied by her husband. The third was the wife of a Mexican officer, also one of the eight. This gentleman was an inveterate enemy of the displaced President General Guerero. We journeyed on very amicably together, without meeting with the slightest disturbance, until the second day, when, about three o'clock in the afternoon, we were met by a company of fifty men, all well mounted and armed. At first sight of them we had supposed them to be a party which had been sent from the city in search of some highwaymen who had committed murder and robbery upon the road on which we were travelling, a few days previous to our departure.

A few minutes served to show us our mistake.—They surrounded the coaches, commanding the drivers to halt, and announcing themselves as followers of General Guerero. They demanded money, of which they stated that they were in great need. The tone of this demand was, however, humble, such as beggars would use. While they addressed us in this manner, they contrived to place themselves among and around the persons of our party in such a way as to obtain entire command of us. The instant they had completed this purpose, they presented their spears and muskets, and demanded our arms. We resigned them without offering an objection, as we saw clearly, that opposition would be unavailing. They now proceeded to take from us what they thought proper. I was allowed to retain my trunk of clothing for my journey. The Mexican officer was sitting by his wife in the coach. Some of the soldiers seized him, and dragged him from his almost distracted wife out of the carriage. His fate was summarily decided, and he was hung upon a tree.

When this dreadful business was terminated, we were ordered to drive on. We gladly hastened from such a scene of horror. But the agony of the unfortunate wife was an impressive memorial to remind us of the nature of the late occurrence, had we needed any other than our own remembrances. We left this afflicted lady at Xalapa, in the care of her relations. A great quantity of *jalap*, which is so much used in medicine, is obtained from this place. After leaving Xalapa, we advanced through a beautiful country. We passed many small towns on this part of our route.

Our course had been a continued descent, after crossing the mountain sixteen miles from the city of Mexico. The road is excellent, being paved for the most part. It is cut through points of mountains in several places. This work must have been attended with immense labor and expense.

We reached Vera Cruz on the 24th. On the 27th Captain Hinkley and his mate embarked for New York. I remained with the consul Mr. Stone, until the 18th of July. A vessel being in readiness to sail for New Orleans at this time, I was desirous to avail myself of the opportunity to return to the United States. Mr. Stone and some others presented me money sufficient to pay my passage to the point to which the vessel was bound. It was very painful to me to incur this debt of gratitude, as I could not even venture to hope that it would be in my power to repay it, either in money or benefits of any kind. The prospect, which the future offered me, was dark. It seemed as if misfortune had set her seal upon all that concerned my destiny. I accepted this offering of kindness and benevolence with thanks direct from my heart, and went on board the vessel.

It would be idle for me to attempt to describe the feelings that swelled my heart, as the sails filled to bear me from the shores of a country, where I had seen and suffered so much. My dreams of success in those points considered most important by my fellow men, were vanished forever. After all my endurance of toil, hunger, thirst and imprisonment, after encountering the fiercest wild beasts in their deserts, and fiercer men, after tracing streams before unmeasured and unvisited by any of my own race to their source, over rugged and pathless mountains, subject to every species of danger, want and misery for seven years, it seemed hard to be indebted to charity, however kind and considerate it might be, for the means of returning to my native land.

As we sped on our way, I turned to look at the land I was leaving, and endeavoured to withdraw my thoughts from the painful train into which they had fallen. Vera Cruz is the best fortified port I have ever seen. The town is walled in, and well guarded on every side with heavy cannon. The part of the wall extending along the water's edge,

215

is surmounted by guns pointing so as completely to command the shipping in the harbour. A reef of rocks arises at the distance of half a mile from the shore opposite the city, and continues visible for several miles in a south direction, joining the mainland seven or eight miles southwest of Vera Cruz. A fort stands upon that part of the reef which fronts the town. Ships in leaving or entering the harbour are obliged to pass between the fort and the town.

We reached New Orleans on the first of August, although the wind had not been entirely favourable. It blew a stiff breeze from a direction which compelled us to run within five points and a half of the wind. As I approached the spot where my foot would again press its native soil, my imagination transported me over the long course of river which yet lay between me, and all I had left in the world to love. I cannot express the delight which thrilled and softened my heart, as I fancied myself entering my home; for it was the home I had known and loved when my mother lived, and we were happy that rose to my view. Fancy could not present another to me. There were my brothers and sisters, as I had been used to see them. The pleasant shade of the trees lay upon the turf before the door of our dwelling. The paths around were the same, over which I had so often bounded with the elastic step of childhood, enjoying a happy existence. Years and change have no place in such meditations.

We landed, and I stood upon the shore. I was aroused by the approach of an Englishman, one of my fellow passengers, to a sense of my real position. He asked me if I had taken a passage in a steamboat for Louisville? I immediately answered in the negative. He then said he had bespoken one in the Cora; and as I had not chosen any other, he would be glad if I would go on in the same one with him, and thus continue our companionship as long as possible. So saying he took me by the arm to lead me in the direction of the boat of which he spoke, that we might choose our births. As we advanced together, it occurred to me to ask the price of a passage to Louisville? I was answered, forty dollars. Upon hearing this I stopped, and told my companion I could not take a birth just then, at the same time putting my hand in my pocket to ascertain if the state of my funds would permit me to do so at all.

The Englishman seeing my embarrassment, and conjecturing rightly its origin, instantly remarked, that the passage money was not to be paid until the boat arrived at Louisville. I was ashamed to own my poverty, and invented an excuse to hide it, telling him, that I had an engagement at that time, but would walk with him in the evening to see about the passage. He left me in consequence. I then discovered, that so far from being able to take a cabin passage I had not money enough to pay for one on the deck.

I re-entered the vessel in which I had arrived. As I approached the captain I saw him point me out to a person conversing with him, and heard him say, 'there is the young man I have been mentioning to you. He speaks Spanish, and will probably engage with you.' When I was near enough he introduced me to the stranger, whom he called Captain Vion. The latter addressed a few remarks to me, and then requested me to accompany him into his vessel. I consented and followed him on board. He then told me, that he wished to engage a person to accompany him to Vera Cruz, and aid in disposing of his vessel and cargo; and asked if I was inclined to go with him for such a purpose? I said, in reply, that it would depend entirely upon the recompense he offered for the services to be performed. He remarked, that he would give a certain *per cent* upon the brig and cargo, in case it was sold. I partly agreed to his proposal, but told him that I could not decide finally upon it until I had considered the matter. He then requested me to come to him the next day at 12 o'clock, when I would find him at dinner.

I left him, after promising to do so, and wandered about looking at the city until evening, when I met the Englishman from whom I had parted in the morning. He said he would now accompany me to the steam boat, that we might choose our births according to our engagement. I had no longer any excuse to offer, and was compelled to acknowledge that the contents of my purse were not sufficient to justify me in contracting a debt of forty dollars. I added, that I had an idea of returning to Vera Cruz. He replied, that in regard to the passage money I need have no uneasiness, nor hesitate to go on board, as he would defray my expenses as far as I chose to go. In respect to my plan of returning to Vera Cruz, he said that it would be exceedingly unwise for me to carry it into execution; as the yellow fever would be raging by the time I reached the city, and that it was most likely I should fall a victim to it.

I had, however, determined in my own mind that I would run the risk, rather than ask or receive aid from a person to whom I was comparatively unknown, and accordingly I refused his kindly proffered assistance, telling him at the same time, that I felt as grateful to him as though I had accepted his offered kindness, and that I would have availed myself of his benevolent intentions towards me, had he been a resident of my country; but as I knew him to be a traveller in a foreign land, who might need all his funds, he must excuse me. He then asked me if I had no acquaintance in New Orleans, of whom I could obtain the money as a loan? I replied, that I did not know an individual in the city; but if I carried my plan of returning to Vera Cruz into execution, I should probably be enabled to proceed to my friends without depending on any one. Upon this we separated, and each went to his lodging.

At ten the succeeding morning my English friend came to my boarding house, accompanied by Judge Johnston, who accosted me with a manner of paternal kindness, enquiring of me how long I had been absent from my country and relations? I naturally enquired in turn, if he was in any way acquainted with them? He replied, that he was; and advised me to ascend the river, and visit them. I expressed to him how pleasant it would be to me to visit them, but assured him that it was out of my power to enjoy that pleasure at present. He enquired why? I avoided a direct answer, and remarked, that I proposed returning to Vera Cruz. He not only urged strong objections to this, but offered to pay my passage up the river. It may be easily imagined how I felt in view of such an offer from this generous and respectable stranger. I thankfully accepted it, only assuring him that I should repay him as soon as it was in my power. He replied that it was a matter of no consequence. He advised me to go on board the steam boat and choose my birth, alleging, that he had business in the city which would not allow him to accompany me on board.

My English friend seemed highly gratified by this good fortune of mine, and went with me on board the steam boat, where I chose a birth. The name of this gentleman was Perry, and he was one of the two whom I have already mentioned, who had travelled in company with me from the city of Guadalaxara to Mexico. On the fourth, at nine in the morning, the starting bell rung on the steam boat, and Judge Johnston, Mr. Perry and myself went on board. This was the first steam boat on which I had ever been. Scarcely was the interior of the first ship I was ever on board at San Diego, a spectacle of more exciting interest. How much more delighted was I to see her stem the mighty current of the Mississippi.

As I remarked the plantations, bends and forests sinking in the distance behind me, I felt that I was rapidly nearing home; and at every advance my anxiety to see my relations once more, increased. To the many enquiries, made by Judge Johnston, touching the interior of the continent where I had been wandering, I am sure I must have given very unsatisfactory answers, much as I wished to oblige him. My thoughts dwelt with such constant and intense solicitude upon home, that I felt myself unable to frame answers to questions upon any other subjects. Home did I say? I have none. My father and mother sleep— widely separated from each other. They left nine orphans without resources to breast this stormy and mutable world. I, who ought to supply the place of a parent to them, shall carry to them nothing but poverty, and the withering remembrances of an unhappy wanderer, upon whom misfortune seems to have stamped her inexorable seal.

I parted with Judge Johnston at Cincinnati, who gave me a line of introduction to Mr. Flint, for which I felt under renewed obligations to him, hoping it would be of service to me. I left Cincinnati; and on the 30th of August arrived at the end of my journey. I have had too much of real incident and affliction to be a dealer in romance; and yet I should do injustice to my feelings, if I closed this journal without a record of my sensations on reaching home. I have still before me, unchanged by all, that I have seen, and suffered, the picture of the abode of my infant days and juvenile remembrances. But the present reality is all as much changed, as my heart. I meet my neighbours, and school fellows, as I approach the home of my grandfather.—They neither recognise me, nor I them. I look for the deep grove, so faithfully remaining in my memory, and the stream that murmured through it. The woods are levelled by the axe. The stream, no longer protected by the deep shade, has almost run dry. A storm has swept away the noble trees, that had been spared for shade. The fruit trees are decayed.

I was first met by my grandmother. She is tottering under the burden and decline of old age, and the sight of me only recalls the painful remembrance of my father, worn out by the torture of his oppressors, and buried in the distant land of strangers and enemies. I could hardly have remembered my grandfather, the once vigorous and undaunted hunter. With a feeble and tremulous voice, he repeats enquiry upon enquiry, touching the fate of my father? I look round for the dear band of brothers and sisters. But one of the numerous group remains, and he too young to know me; though I see enough to remind me, how much he has stood in need of an efficient protector.—I hastily enquire for the rest. One is here, and another is there, and my head is confused, in listening to the names of the places of their residence. I left one sister, a child. She is married to a person I never knew; one, who, from the laws of our nature, can only regard me with the eye of a stranger. We call each other brother, but the affectionate word will not act as a key, to unlock the fountains of fraternal feeling.

They, however, kindly invite me to their home. I am impelled alike by poverty and affection, to remain with them for a time, till I can forget what has been, and weave a new web of hopes, and form a new series of plans for some pursuit in life. Alas! disappointments, such as I have encountered, are not the motives to impart vigour and firmness for new projects. The freshness, the visions, the hopes of my youthful days are all vanished, and can never return. If anyone of my years has felt, that the *fashion of this world passeth away*, and that all below the sun is vanity, it is I. If there is a lesson from my wanderings, it is one, that inculcates upon children, remaining at the paternal home in peace and privacy; one that counsels the young against wandering far away, to see the habitations, and endure the inhospitality of strangers.

Narrative of the Adventures of
Zenas Leonard 1831-1836

Contents

Preface

The title of the following work sufficiently explains itself; how-ever, before presenting it to the public, in its present form, the original publisher deems it necessary to accompany it with a few remarks explanatory of the motives which induced the author to commit his adventures to paper: Mr. Zenas Leonard (the author) is a native of Clearfield County, Pa., where his parents and other relatives still reside, (1839); and it may not be improper here to remark, that they are well known as among the most respectable inhabitants of the county. After receiving the advantages of a common English education, and being possessed of strong mental faculties and a vigorous constitution, Mr. Leonard left his parental roof in the spring of 1830, and after spending the succeeding year in a mercantile house in Pittsburg, Pa., ventured to embark in an expedition across the Rocky Mountains, in the ca-pacity of clerk to the company.

The last letter received by his parents, left him at the extreme white settlement, where they were busily occupied in making preparations for the expedition to the mountains—from whence he promised to write at short intervals; but one misfortune after another happening the company, he was deprived of all sources of communication—so that no tidings were received of him until he unexpectedly returned to the scenes of his childhood, to the house of his father, in the fall of 1835—after an absence of 5 years and 6 months! In the interval, and at various times, minors and answers to letters written by his friends to different individuals on the route up the Missouri, were received, which represented the major part of the company he was with, as hav-ing perished, and that he was not among the number who survived. The grief of his parents from that time until his joyous return, can only be imagined.

They had long mourned him as lost forever, and all hope of again meeting him this side the grave ceased to exist. The Scriptural phrase, that *"the dead's alive, and the lost is found,"* in a temporal pointer view, was never more beautifully illustrated; nor was ever grief and mourning changed to inexpressible joy and gladness more unexpectedly and triumphantly. After again mingling with his former comrades and old acquaintances, so great was the curiosity manifested by them to hear him relate his adventures, that he was continually beset by crowds of anxious inquirers wherever he happened to be.

But few were satisfied with a partial account, and finding that it would consume too much of the time he purposed spending among his former friends, ere he should again embark for the west, to repeat the whole story on every occasion, he finally yielded to the importunities of his friends to adopt Franklin's notion of *"saying grace over the whole barrel of beef at once, in order to save time,"* and he prepared a narrative of his travels for publication in the newspapers of the county, that all might have an equal opportunity to read it. It was for this purpose, and under these circumstances, that he wrote it out—but from various causes it was never published entire, until we procured the manuscript last winter and gave it to the public through the columns of a public newspaper, (the *Clearfield Republican*, editor D. W. Moore), during the past season.

The great interest the public took in it, was satisfactorily illustrated by the increase and demand for the paper in which it was published. A number of persons sent in their names as subscribers from all the adjoining counties, besides others more distant—many of whom we were unable to accommodate. From this evidence, as well as the repented solicitations from every quarter, we have been induced to reprint it, and now offer it to the public in a more convenient form. Our author kept a minute journal of every incident that occurred, but unfortunately, a part of his narrative was stolen from him by hostile Indians; still, however, he was enabled to replace the most important events, by having access to the journal kept by the commander of the expedition. His character for candour and truth, among his acquaintances, we have never heard suspected; and, indeed, among the many who heard the narrative from his own lips, we have yet to hear the first one say they disbelieve it.

At all events, in its perusal, the reader will encounter no *improbabilities*, much less *impossibilities:*—hence it is but reasonable to suppose that in traversing such a wilderness as lays west of the Rocky Mountains, such hardships, privations and dangers as those described by Mr.

Leonard, must necessarily be encountered. He remained at home but a short time, when he returned to the west, and now, (1839), resides in Jackson County, Mo., where he is surrounded with competence—being at present engaged as a merchant and trader with the different companies employed in the fur trade of the mountains.

The Original Publisher,

Narrative

Of the adventures of a company of 70 men, who left St, Louis in the spring of 1831, on an expedition to the Rocky Mountains, for the purpose of trapping for furs, and trading with the Indians, by one of the company, Mr. Zenas Leonard, of Clearfield County. Pa.—comprising a minute description of the incidents of the adventure, and a valuable history of this immense territory—not from maps and charts, but from personal observation.

The company under the command of Captains Gant and Blackwell, left St. Louis on the 24th of April, 1831. Each man was furnished with the necessary equipments for the expedition—such as traps, guns, &c.; also horses and goods of various descriptions, to trade with the Indians for furs and Buffalo robes. We continued our journey in a western direction, in the state of Missouri, on the south side of the Missouri River, through a country thinly inhabited by the whites and friendly Indians, until we arrived at Fort Osage the extreme point of the white settlement. Here we remained several days and purchased and packed up a sufficiency of provision, as we then thought; for our subsistence through the wilderness to what is called the Buffalo country; a distance of about 200 miles. From thence we proceeded up the Missouri until we arrived at the mouth of the Kansas River, where we again tarried two or three days, for the purpose of trading some goods to the Kansas Indians for corn, *moccasins*, &c.

This tribe of Indians live in small huts, built of poles, covered with straw and dirt, and in shape are similar to a potato hole. They cultivate the soil quite extensively, and raise very good corn, pumpkins, beans and other vegetables. The principal chief is called "White Ploom."— The nation is supposed to contain 800 warriors.

From thence we proceeded on our journey up the river. We found the country here beautiful indeed—abounding with the most delightful prairies, with here and there a small brook, winding its way to the river, the margins of which are adorned with the lofty Pine and Cedar tree. These prairies were completely covered with fine low grass, and decorated with beautiful flowers of various colours; and some of them are so extensive and clear of timber and brush that the eye might search in vain for an object to rest upon. I have seen beautiful and enchanting sceneries depicted by the artist, but never any thing to equal the work of rude nature in those prairies. In the spring of the year when the grass is green and the blossoms fresh, they present an appearance, which for beauty and charms, is beyond the art of man to depict.

We continued on our journey westward, up the republican fork of Kanzas River—passing through these prairies, till the 20th of June, when we happened on another tribe of Indians, called the Otoes, from whom we obtained a quantity of sweet corn and some wild turnips; we also understood from this tribe that it was much farther to the Buffalo country than we had before anticipated, and that game in that direction, was very scarce. From thence we proceeded in a N.W. direction, up the Republican Branch—finding but very little game; and on the 21st of June we killed our last beef, which was equally divided to each mess. Here we began to feel somewhat alarmed—starvation began to stare us in the face, and some of the company became refractory and were for turning back.

Stimulated, however, by the hope of reaching game in a few days, we continued in the direction of the Buffalo country. Hunters were sent out daily in quest of game, but as often returned without any. We still continued to travel—subsisting chiefly on muscles and small fish which we caught in the river; finally the captain ordered two of the best horses to be killed, to keep the company from starving, which was immediately done, and the carcasses equally distributed to each mess. We proceeded on our journey slowly—sending out hunters as usual, but without success; game appeared to become scarcer and scarcer, and in a few days our provision (if I may call it such) again exhausted. Finding it impossible, owing to the scarcity of game, to continue any further up the Republican, we concluded to leave it and steer for the headwaters of the Missouri.[1]

Accordingly we changed our direction as well as our manner of travelling. Instead of travelling in a close mat as heretofore, we now scattered over a considerable range of country for the purpose of hunt-

---

1. The River Platte is no doubt the one here referred to, and not the Missouri.

ing, leaving ten or twelve men only to bring on the pack-mules, and at night we would collect together with our game, which generally consisted of wolves, wild cats, muscles, and some times an antelope. In this way we continued our journey slowly, some of the company being half starved to death, for eight or ten days, eating at night what little game we caught through the day; at last we collected one evening, I think about the middle of July, in a barren prairie where we could not get wood enough to make a fire, much less anything to cook on it—not a mouthful of game was returned that evening.

This was a trying time indeed—despondency and horror was depicted in the countenance of every man, and the enquiry, "what shall we do," was passed from every lip. In this condition, without fire or food, we spent the night. In the morning we held a consultation to decide whether to continue in that direction or turn. We finally agreed to proceed straight ahead and by night we arrived on the banks of the River Platte, a distance of about ten miles from where we had encamped the night before, where we pitched our tents for the night. Most of our hunters had collected without game, and pronounced it very scarce, and we were about to kill another of our horses, when we saw one of our hunters approaching us with unusual rapidity, without his gun or hat and his countenance indicating great excitement. I never wish to feel more pleasure than I did as he rushed into the tent exclaiming, "I have killed two big Buck Elk!"

Early the next morning—refreshed with what meat we had obtained and animated and encouraged with the hope of obtaining plenty more, we set out with unusual fine spirits. We continued to travel up the River Platte for several days—passing through extensive barren prairies, the soil being too poor even to produce grass; and game exceedingly scarce. Some of us again became alarmed, and one morning when the roll was called it was discovered that two of the company had stolen two of the best horses and started back to the state of Missouri. This had a bad effect—it impaired that full confidence which had heretofore existed between the members of the company, but we continued up the river and in a few days arrived at the Buffalo country. After encamping, on a pleasant evening, in the latter part of July, some of the company discovered two buffalo bulls feeding in the prairie, about half a mile from camp. Four or five of us immediately mounted our horses and started to take them; but returned in a short time without success—one of the men having got his arm broken, by falling from his horse.

But the next day we happened on a large drove of these animals, and killed six or seven of them. The flesh of the buffalo is the wholesomest and most palatable of meat kind. The male of these animals are much the largest—weighing from 1000 to 1500 pounds, and may be seen in droves of hundreds feeding in the plains. We remained here several days feasting upon buffalo meat. From thence proceeded up the river; finding an abundance of game, such as buffalo, elk, deer and antelope—and killing more or less every day. On the first day of August[2] we arrived at the forks of the River Platte; and by means of boats made of buffalo skins, crossed the south Fork and continued our journey up the valley. Here the soil appeared to be very poor, producing but little grass; and in some places for three or four miles we would travel over sand plains where there was scarcely a spear of grass to be seen. Immediately on the water courses the soil is better and produces good grass.

As we travelled up the river, we occasionally came in contact with cliffs of rock and hard clay, from two to three hundred feet above the level of the plain. One of these cliffs is very peculiar in its appearance, and is known among the whites as "Chimney cliff," and among the natives as "Elk Peak." It is only about 150 yards in circumference at its basis, and about 25 at the summit; and projects into the air to the height of 300 feet. Its towering summit may be seen at the distance of 15 or 20 miles—presenting the appearance of some huge fabric that had been constructed by the art of man.

We continued to travel in a western direction—found game plenty—met with no difficulty in getting along; and on the 27th of August we arrived at the junction of the Laramies River with the River Platte—about 1200 or 1300 miles from the United States, and two or three hundred from the top of the Rocky Mountains. Here we stopped for the purpose of reconnoitring. Several scouting parties were sent out in search of beaver signs, who returned in a few days and reported that they had found beaver signs, &c. Captain Gant then gave orders to make preparations for trapping. Accordingly the company was divided into parties of from 15 to 20 men in each party, with their respective captains placed over them—and directed by Captain Gant in what direction to go. Captain Washburn ascended the Timber Fork; Captain Stephens of these companies were directed to ascend these rivers until they found beaver sufficiently plenty for trapping, or till the snow and cold weather compelled them to stop; at which event

---

2. If Leonard's dates are correct they made an extremely slow passage to this point.

they were to return to the mouth of the Laramies River, to pass the winter together.

While at this place, engaged in secreting our merchandize, which we did by digging a hole in the ground, sufficiently large to contain them, and covering them over so that the Indians might not discover them—four men (three whites and one Indian) came to our tent. This astonished us not a little, for a white man was the last of living beings that we expected to visit us in this vast wilderness—where nothing was heard from dark to day light but the fierce and terrifying growls of wild beasts, and the more shrill cries of the merciless savages. The principal of these men was a Mr. Fitzpatrick, who had been engaged in trapping along the Columbia River, on the west side of the Rocky Mountains, and was then on his way to St. Louis. He was an old hand at the business and we expected to obtain some useful information from him, but we were disappointed.

The selfishness of man is often disgraceful to human nature; and I never saw more striking evidence of this fact, than was presented in the conduct of this man Fitzpatrick. Notwithstanding we had treated him with great friendship and hospitality, merely because we were to engage in the same business with him, which he knew we never could exhaust or even impair—he refused to give us any information whatever, and appeared disposed to treat us as intruders. On the 3rd of September, Captain Blackwell, with two others, joined Fitzpatrick, and started back to the state of Missouri, for an additional supply of merchandise, and were to return in the summer of 1832.

I was one of 21 that composed the company under the command of Captain A. K. Stephens, a man well calculated to pilot or manage in case of difficulty with the Indians. He received a portion of the profits arising from the merchandise, say $2 per pound for coffee, and the same for tea, sugar, lead, powder, tobacco, allspice, pepper, &c., and for every yard of coarse cloth $10, and for fine cloth $20; this, however, is governed entirely by their value with the Indians. For twenty or thirty loads of powder you can generally get from eight to twelve dollars worth of fur.

On the 4th of September, having everything in readiness, after shaking hands all around, we separated, each party to meander the rivers that had been respectively allotted to them, with the intention, if nothing happened them, of re-assembling in the latter part of December, to spend the winter together.

Mr. Stephen's party commenced their tour up the Laramies River and continued several days without any important occurrence. Found the prairies or plains in this direction very extensive—unobstructed with timber or brush—handsomely situated, with here and there a small creek passing through them, and in some places literally covered with game, such as buffalo, white and black tailed deer, grizzly, red, and white bear, elk, prairie dog, wild goat, big horned mountain sheep, antelope, &c.

On the 20th of Sept. we stopped on the bank of a small creek, to let our horses graze, at the junction of which we seen signs of beaver. Two hunters were sent up this stream with their traps and, guns on search of beaver, who, if they should be successful in finding game, were not to return until the next day—the main body of the company to move on slowly. After travelling several miles, and hearing nothing of our hunters, we deemed it advisable to encamp for the night, which we did. About midnight we were alarmed by the report of two rifles. Supposing it to be hostile Indians, we put ourselves in an attitude of defence, as soon as possible by throwing up a fort of logs and brush, and keeping up sentinels until morning.

On the next morning, about sunrise the two hunters came in, and informed us that it was the report of their guns that had alarmed us, as they had fired them off near the spot where they had expected to find the camp, with the hope of receiving some signal. They had me-andered the creek till they came to beaver dams, where they set their traps and turned their horses out to pasture; and were busily engaged in constructing a camp to pass the night in, when they discovered, at a short distance off, a tremendous large grizzly bear, rushing upon them at a furious rate.—They immediately sprang to their rifles which were standing against a tree hard-by, one of which was single and the other double triggered; unfortunately in the hurry, the one that was accustomed to the single trigger, caught up the double triggered gun, and when the bear came upon him, not having set the trigger, he could not get his gun off; and the animal approaching within a few feet of him, he was obliged to commence beating it over the head with his gun.

Bruin, thinking this rather rough usage, turned his attention to the man with the single triggered gun, who, in trying to set the trigger (supposing he had the double triggered gun) had fired it off, and was also obliged to fall to beating the ferocious animal with his gun; finally, it left them without doing much injury, except tearing the sleeve off one of their coats and biting him through the hand. Four men were immediately despatched for the traps, who returned in the evening with seven or eight beaver. The grizzly bear is the most ferocious animal that inhabits these prairies, and are very numerous. They no sooner see you than they will make at you with open mouth. If you stand still, they will come within two or three yards of you, and stand upon their hind feet, and look you in the face, if you have fortitude enough to face them, they will turn and run off; but if you turn they will most assuredly tear you to pieces; furnishing strong proof of the fact, that no wild beast, however daring and ferocious, unless wounded, will attack the face of man.

On the morning of the 22nd Sept. we again renewed our tour travelling at the rate of 8 or 10 miles a day; catching a few beaver, as we passed along—nothing strange occurring until the 30th, when we arrived at the foot of a great mountain, through which the Laramies passes. We attempted to follow the river through the mountain, but we soon found this to be impossible, as the bluffs of huge rocks projecting several hundred feet high, closed it to the very current. We then turned down the side of the mountain, on search of a place to cross it. On the 1st day of Oct. we came to a buffalo trail crossing the mountain, and after ascending to near the summit, we encamped for the night. About midnight it commenced snowing, and continued to fall so fast that we were obliged to remain there until the morning of the 4th, when we again renewed our journey, and in the evening we arrived in the valley on the North or West side of the mountain. Here, finding no snow and beaver signs plenty, we deemed it advisable to remain a few days for the purpose of trapping, and the first night we caught 20 beaver. We remained here until the 12th, when we proceeded eight or ten miles further up the South fork of the river, and again encamped for the purpose of trapping. On the 18th, finding beaver getting rather scarce, we proceeded a few miles further up the valley, and encamped again.

This valley is supposed to be 70 or 80 miles long, and from 10 to 15 miles wide; and is enclosed on the one side by the main chain of the Rocky Mountains, and on the other by great Piney Hills, running out from the main body of the mountain, with the river Laramies passing through the centre of it, the banks of which are covered with timber, from ¼ to ½ a mile wide. Outside of this timber, the plain is completely smooth; and on a dear morning, by taking a view with a spyglass, you can see the different kinds of game that inhabit these plains, such as buffalo, bear, deer, elk, antelope, bighorn, wolves, &c.

These plains are poor, sandy and level—the grass thin and short.

Oct. 22nd. The nights getting somewhat cold, and snow falling more or less every day, we began to make preparations to return to our winter quarters, at the mouth of Laramies river; and on the 25th commenced our tour down the river. On the 28th we arrived at the mountain, that we crossed going up, but found it impossible, owing to the enormous depth of the snow to pass over it. On the morning of the 30th we started a number of men up and down the valley, on search of a place to cross the mountain, who returned the next day and reported that they had found no passing place over the mountain; when under these circumstances a majority of the company decided in favour of encamping in this valley for the winter, and when the ice melted out of the river, in the spring, commence trapping until such times as the snow melted off the mountain; when we would return to the mouth of the river, where we had secreted our goods.

On the 1st day of November we commenced travelling up the valley, on search of a suitable place to pass the winter, and on the evening of the 4th, we arrived at a large grove of Cottonwood timber, which we deemed suitable for encamping in.—Several weeks were spent in building houses, stables, &c. necessary for ourselves, and horses during the winter season.—This being done, we commenced killing buffalo, and hanging up the choice pieces to dry, so that if they should leave the valley we would have a sufficient quantity of meat to last us until spring. We also killed deer, bighorn sheep, elk, antelope, &c., and dressed the hides to make *moccasins*.

About the 1st of December finding our horses getting very poor, we thought it necessary to commence feeding them on Cottonwood bark; for which purpose each man turned out and pealed and collected a quantity of this bark, from the grove in which we were encamped for his horses; but to our utter surprise and discomfiture, on presenting it to them they would not eat it, and upon examining it by tasting, we found it to be the bitter, instead of the sweet cottonwood. Immediately upon finding we were deceived, men were despatched up and down the valley, on search of sweet cottonwood, but returned without success. Several weeks were spent in fruitless exertion to obtain feed for our horses; finally we were compelled to give it up, and agreed that our horses must all starve to death. The great depth of the snow, and the extreme coldness of the weather, soon prevented our horses from getting anything to subsist upon, and they commenced dying.

It seldom happened during all our difficulties, that my sympathies were more sensibly touched, than on viewing these starving creatures. I would willingly have divided my provision with my horses, if they would have eat it.

On New-Years day, notwithstanding our horses were nearly all dead, as being fully satisfied that the few that were yet living must die soon, we concluded to have a feast in our best style; for which purpose we made preparation by sending out four of our best hunters, to get a choice piece of meat for the occasion. These men killed ten buffalo, from which they selected one of the fattest humps they could find and brought in, and after roasting it handsomely before the fire, we all seated ourselves upon the ground, encircling, what we there called a splendid repast to dine upon. Feasting sumptuously, cracking a few jokes, taking a few rounds with our rifles, and wishing heartily for some liquor, having none at that place we spent the day.

The glorious 8th (anniversary of the Battle of New Orleans), arrived, the recollection of the achievements of which, are calculated to gladden the hearts of the American people; but it was not so glorious to us. We found our horses on that day, like Packenham's forces, well nigh defunct. Here we were in this valley, surrounded on either side by insurmountable barriers of snow, with all our merchandize and nothing to pack it upon, but two mules—all the rest of our horses being dead. For ourselves we had plenty to eat, and were growing fat and uneasy;—but how we were to extricate ourselves from this perilous situation, was a question of deep and absorbing interest to each individual. About the 10th we held a consultation, to decide what measures should be taken for our relief.

Mr. Stephens, our pilot, having been at Santa Fe, in New Mexico, some 8 or 10 years previous, informed the company that horses in that place, were very cheap; and that he was of the opinion he could take them to it, if they saw proper to follow him. It was finally agreed upon by the company, that a part of them should start for Santa Fe; but not, however, without a good deal of confusion; as many were of the opinion that the snow on the mountain in the direction of Santa Fe, would be found to be as insurmountable, as in the direction of their merchandise, and also that the distance was too great to attempt to travel on foot, at that season of the year. It appearing from the maps to be little short of 800 miles.

On the morning of the 14th, finding everything in readiness for our Santa Fe trip, we set out, each man with his bedding, rifle and nine beaver skins, packed upon his back; leaving four men only to take care of our merchandise, and the two mules. The beaver skins we took for the purpose of trading to the inhabitants of Santa Fe for horses, mules, &c. We appointed from the middle of April till the middle of may, as our time for returning; and if we did not return within that time, our four men were to wait no longer, but return to the mouth of the Laramies River, to meet the rest of the company. We continued in the direction of Santa Fe, without any extraordinary occurrence, for several days—found game plenty and but little snow, until we arrived at the foot of a great mountain, which appeared to be totally covered with snow. Here we thought it advisable to kill and jirk some buffalo meat, to eat while crossing this mountain, after which we continued our course; finding much difficulty in travelling, owing to the stormy weather and deep snow—so much so indeed, that had it not been for a path made by the buffalo bulls it would have been impossible to travel.

The channel of the river where it passed through these mountains is quite narrow in places and the banks very steep. In such places the beaver build their dams from bank to bank; and when they become old the beaver leave them and they break and overflow the ground, which then produces a kind of flag grass. In the fall of the year, the buffalo collect in such places to eat this grass, and when the snow falls too deep they retreat to the plains; and it was in these trails that we ascended the mountain.

We still continued our course along this buffalo path, which led us to the top of the mountain; nothing occurring more than it contin-ued to snow day and night. On the 25th we arrived on the top of the mountain, and wishing to take a view of the country, if it should cease snowing. In the morning it still continued to snow so rapidly that we were obliged to remain in camp all day, and about the middle of the day, we eat the last of our jirk, and that evening we were obliged to go to bed supperless.

On the 29th it still continued to snow, and having nothing to eat, we thought it high time to be making some move, for our preserva-tion, or we must perish in this lonely wilderness. The question then arose, shall we return to the valley from whence we came, or continue in the direction of Santa Fe. This question caused considerable distur-bance. Those who were in favour of going ahead, argued that it was too far back to game—that it would be impossible to return before starving to death; while those who were for returning contended that it was the height of imprudence, to proceed in the direction of Santa Fe. Accordingly we made preparations, and started. We travelled across the summit of the mountain, where we found a plain about a mile wide, which with great difficulty, owing to the fierceness of the wind, we succeeded in crossing; but when we attempted to go into the timber, on the opposite side from the mountain, we found it impossible, in consequence of the depth of the snow, and were obliged to turn back and re-cross the plain.

As we returned by the fire we had made going over the plain the first time, we halted for the purpose of mutually deciding what to do; when it was determined by the company, that we would, if possible, return to our four men and two mules. We then started on search of the buffalo path which we had followed to the top of the mountain; but owing to the strong wind, that had blew for several days, and the increased depth of the snow, it was invisible. We then attempted to travel in the snow without the path, but we found this equally as impossible, as in the direction of Santa Fe.

Here we were, in a desolate wilderness, uninhabited (at that season of the year) by even the hardy savage or wild beast—surrounded on either side by huge mountains of snow, without one mouthful to eat, save a few beaver skins—our eyes almost destroyed by the piercing wind, and our bodies at times almost buried by the flakes of snow which were driven before it. Oh I how heartily I wished myself at home; but wishing, in such a case appeared useless—action alone could save us. We had not even leather to make snow shoes, but as good fortune would have it, some of the men had the front part of their pantaloons lined with deer skin, and others had great coats of different kinds of skin, which we collected together to make snow shoes of. This appeared to present to us the only means of escape from starvation and death.

After gathering up everything of leather kind that could be found, we got to making snow shoes, and by morning each man was furnished with a pair. But what were we to subsist upon while crossing the mountain, was a painful question that agitated every bosom, and employed every tongue in company. Provision, we had none, of any description; having eaten every thing we had that could be eat with the exception of a few beaver skins, and, after having fasted several days, to attempt to travel the distance of the valley, without any thing to eat, appeared almost worse than useless. Thinking, however, that we might as well perish one place as another, and that it was the best to make an exertion to save ourselves; and after each man had selected two of the best beaver skins to eat as he travelled along, we hung the remainder upon a tree, and started to try our fortune with the snow shoes.

Owing to the softness of the snow, and the poor construction of our snow shoes, we soon found this to be a difficult and laborious mode of travelling. The first day after we started with our snow shoes we travelled but three or four miles and encamped for the night, which, for want of a good fire, we passed in the most distressing manner. Wood was plenty but we were unable to get it, and it kept one or two of the men busy to keep what little fire we had from going out as it melted the snow and sunk down.

On the morning (30th Jan.) after roasting and eating some of our beaver skins, we continued our journey through the snow. In this way we continued to travel until the first day of February, in the afternoon, when we came to where the crust on the snow was sufficiently strong to carry us. Here we could travel somewhat faster, but at the best not much faster than a man could crawl on his hands and feet, as some of the men from hunger and cold were almost insensible of their situation, and so weak that they could scarcely stand on their feet, much less walk at speed. As we approached the foot of the mountain the snow became softer and would not carry us. This caused the most resolute despair, as it was obviously impossible, owing to extreme weakness, for us to wade much further through the snow.

As we moved down the mountain plunging and falling through the snow, we approached a large spruce or cedar tree, the drooping branches of which had prevented the snow from falling to the ground about its trunk—here we halted to rest. While collected under the sheltering bows of this tree, viewing, with horrified feelings, the way-worn, and despairing countenances of each other, a Mr. Carter, a Virginian, who was probably the nighest exhausted of any of the company, burst into tears and said, "here I must die." This made a great impression upon the remainder of the company, and they all, with the exception of a Mr. Hockday and myself, despaired of going any further.

Mr. Hockday, however, after some persuasion, telling them that if they had strength to follow us we would break the road as far as possible, if not out to the valley, succeeded in getting them started once more.—Mr. Hockday was a large muscular man, as hardy as a mule and as resolute as a lion; yet kind and affectionate. He was then decidedly the stoutest man in the company, and myself, probably, the next stoutest. As for our captain, Mr. Stephens, he was amongst the weakest of the company.

We resumed our journey, and continued to crawl along through the deep snow slowly till the evening of the fourth, when we arrived in the plain at the foot of the mountain. Here we found the snow so shallow that we could dispense with the use of our snow shoes; and while in the act of taking them off some of the men discovered, at the distance of 70 or 80 yards; two animals feeding in the brush, which they supposed to be buffalo, but from blindness, caused by weakness and pine smoke, could not be positive. Mr. Hockday and I were selected to approach and kill one of the animals without regard to what they might prove to be, while the remainder of the company were to go to a neighbouring grove of timber and kindle a fire. Having used our guns as walking canes in the snow, we found them much out of order, and were obliged to draw out the old loads and put in new ones, before attempting to shoot.

After taking every precaution we deemed necessary to insure success, we started and crawled along on our hands and knees, until we approached within ten or fifteen steps of the animals, when Mr. Hockday prepared to shoot; but upon finding that he could not see the sight of the gun or hold it at arms length, forbore, and proposed to me to shoot. I accordingly fixed myself and pulled trigger. My gun missed fire! I never was so wrecked with agitation as at that moment. "There," said I, "our game is gone, and we are not able to follow it much further;" but as good fortune had it, the buffalo, (for such we had discovered them to be,) did not see nor smell us, and after raising their heads out of the snow, and looking around for a few moments for the cause of the noise, again commenced feeding. I then picked the flint of my gun, fired and broke the back of one of the buffalo, my ball not taking effect within 18 inches of where I thought I aimed.—The men in the grove of timber, on hearing the report of my rifle came staggering forth to learn the result, and when they received the heart-cheering intelligence of success they raised a shout of joy. It was amusing to witness the conduct of some of the men on this occasion. Before we had caught the buffalo they appeared scarcely able to speak—but a moment after that, were able to hollow like Indians at war.

I will not describe the scene that followed here—the reader may imagine it—an account of it would be repulsive and offensive rather than agreeable. This was the ninth day since we had eaten any thing but dried beaver skins. We remained at this place four days feasting upon the carcass of this buffalo, during which time we recruited considerably in strength and spirits, and on the 8th we resumed our journey down the river in search of our four men and two mules, and soon landed in the valley where game was plenty, and but little snow to obstruct our march.

We continued our journey, killing plenty of game and living well, without any strange occurrence until the 14th, when we halted within a short distance of our old camp, and sent two or three of our worst looking men ahead to sec whether they would be recognised by the four men. They were not known immediately on arriving at the camp, but no sooner engaged in conversation than they were recognised by the four men, and heartily welcomed back.[3]

Here we remained at our old station until the 14th of March, during which period, having plenty of good buffalo meat to eat, we regained our usual health and appearance. Anxious to be doing something, eight of us made preparations to start again to Santa Fe for horses. We were to travel south, along the foot of the mountain till we came to a certain river which heads in the mountain near where we had hung the beaver skins on the pine tree; after finding this river we were to commence trapping, and also to endeavour to get the beaver fur off the mountain into the valley. The balance of the company, 13 in number, were to remain at the camp and secrete the merchandize, and then follow us to this river, where we were to meet; and if we had succeeded in getting the beaver skins off the mountain, we were to join together and proceed in the direction of Santa Fe.

With this understanding we started, and pursued our course slowly along the base of the mountain—found game plenty—met with no obstacle to impede our march, and on the 20th we arrived on the bank of the river. After remaining here a few days the ice melted out of the creeks and we commenced and continued to trap for beaver until the 28th during which time we caught a fine quantity of fur, and built ourselves a *wigwam* after the Indian fashion. The weather continuing warm and pleasant, and having a large quantity of dried meat on hand we concluded to hide our traps, beaver skins, baggage, &c., in our *wigwam* and pack a portion of the jirked meat on our backs and make an effort to get the beaver skins off the pine tree where we had

---

3. They had been following up the Laramie River, which flows from the southwest and led them directly Into the mountains. This would have been an extremely hazardous journey at this season.

242

left them in January.

We started, and after travelling up the river along the side of the mountain for two or three days, we came in contact with huge mountains of snow and insurmountable icebergs, and were compelled to abandon our course and return back again to the plain. When we had arrived within a short distance of our *wigwam*, on our return, we discovered several trails of *moccasin* tracks in the snow. Some of the company became somewhat alarmed at these signs, supposing them to be the trails of hostile Indians—others appeared rejoiced, and said it was the remainder of our company.—The dispute was soon decided, for on arriving at our *wigwam*, we found it completely robbed of everything we had left in it—traps, blankets, beaver skins and other utensils were all gone—nothing remained but the naked frame of the little hut.—We had now nothing left to sleep on save one old blanket for each man which we had with us on the mountain, and had lost nearly all our traps.

Under these highly aggravating circumstances some of the men became desperate, declared they would retake their property or die in the attempt. For my part, I viewed the matter calmly and seriously and determined to abide the dictates of prudence only. Seeing from the trail of the Indians that they were not very numerous, and had a number of horses with them, we determined, after some controversy, to rob them of their horses, or other property commensurate to our loss. Accordingly we made preparations for our perilous adventure—we eat supper, prepared our fire arms, and a little after dark set out on search of the enemy—the night was calm and clear. We traversed the valley up and down for several hours without making any discoveries; we then ascended an adjacent hill, from the summit of which we discovered at a considerable distance a number of dim fires.

A controversy here arose amongst the men as to the expediency of attacking the Indians. It was finally decided, however, by a majority of the company; that we should attack them at all hazards. We started in the direction of the fires, and after travelling some distance, and having lost sight of the fires, some of the men again became discouraged, and strongly urged the propriety of abandoning the project; but on calling a vote a majority again decided in favour of attacking the Indians and in a few minutes after we arrived on the top of a hill, within 50 or 60 yards of the enemy's camp. Here we halted for the purpose of reconnoitring.

At this time the moon was just rising above the summit of the mountain, and casting its glimmering rays o'er the valley beneath, but did not shine on the Indian camp.—There were five fires, and the Indians appearing more numerous than we had expected to find them, we thought it advisable to be as careful and judicious about attacking them as possible. At the foot of this hill, near a large rock, we left our hats, coats and every thing that was unnecessary in action—we also designated this as a point of meeting, in case we should get separated in the skirmish; and had an understanding that but two should fire at a time, and that Captain. Stephens was to command. Mr. Hockday and I were selected to shoot first.

We then started and crawled silently along on our hands and knees until we got within eight or ten steps of one of the fires, where we laid down in the brush, with our heads close together to consult as to the most proper mode of surprising the savages, whose dusky forms were then extended in sleep around the dying embers. While in this position, some eager for the conflict, others trembling with fear, a large dog rose from one of the fires and commenced growling and barking in the most terrifying manner. The spell of silence was now broken, and an immediate and final skirmish with our enemy rendered unavoidable. Thinking ourselves rather too much exposed to the fire of the Indians we retreated fifteen or twenty steps down the bank. Some of the Indians then came to the top of the bank and commenced shooting arrows at us, and yelling at the extent of their lungs.

At this moment Mr. Stephens was heard to say in a firm tone "now is the time my boys, we must fight or die;" upon this Mr. Hockday and I fired; one of the Indians on the bank was seen to fall, and the remainder ran back to the camp. On hearing the report of our rifles the Indians, to the number of two or three hundred, rose out of the bushes and literally covered the plain, while their terrific war whoop—mingled with an occasional crack of a rifle, rendered the aspect of things more threatening than the most timid had before anticipated. We ran to our appointed place to meet, but before we had time to gather our baggage, we found ourselves completely surrounded and hemmed in on every side by the savages.

Finding that we could not escape by flight, but must fight, we ran to the top of the hill, and having sheltered ourselves as well as we could amongst the rocks, commenced yelling and firing in turn, (yelling is a very essential point in Indian warfare.) This scene was kept up for near an hour without any damage to our company, and as we supposed, but little injury to the Indians.[4] The savages seeing we were

4. We are unable to say what tribe these Indians belonged to— they were probably the Aricaras, or possibly the Arapahoes or Utes.

determined to defend ourselves to the last gave way on the opposite side of the hill from their camp, and we made our escape out of their circle, and were glad to get away with our lives, without any of our property or that of the Indians. The scenes of this night will ever be indelibly impressed upon my memory.[5]

After travelling five or six miles we came to a deep ravine or hollow—we carefully descended the precipice to the flat below, where we encamped for the night; but from fright, fatigue, cold and hunger, I could not sleep, and lay contemplating on the striking contrast between a night in the villages of Pennsylvania and one on the Rocky Mountains. In the latter, the plough-boy's whistle, the gambols of the children on the green, the lowing of the herds, and the deep tones of the evening bell, are unheard; not a sound strikes upon the ear, except perchance the distant howling of some wild beast, or war-whoop of the uncultivated savage—all was silent on this occasion save the muttering of a small brook as it wound its way through the deep cavities of the gulph down the mountain, and the gentle whispering of the breeze, as it crept through the dark pine or cedar forest, and sighed in melancholy accents; nor is it the retiring of the "god of day" to his couch in the western horizon that brings on this desolate scene—his rising in the east does not change the gloomy aspect—night and day are nearly the same in this respect.

About midnight we were alarmed by a shrill whistle on the rocks above, and supposing it to be the Indians in pursuit of us we seized our guns and ran a few rods from our fires. After waiting for some time, without hearing any more noise, one of the men ascended the precipice, and discovered that the object of our fears was a large drove of Elk. In the morning we continued to travel down this ravine,—and I was struck with the rough and picturesque appearance of the adjacent hills. On our right and left, arose like two perpendicular ramparts, to the height of near two hundred feet, two chains of mountains. Not a blade of grass, bush or plant was to be seen on these hard slopes,— huge rocks detached from the main body, supported by the recumbent weight of other unseen rocks appeared in the act of falling, and presented a frightful appearance—nothing met the eye but an inexhaustible avalanche of rocks—sombre, gray or black rocks.

If Dante had designed to picture in one of his circles the Hell of Stones, he might have taken this scene for his model.—This is

5. This engagement no doubt occurred near where the Laramie River crosses the Colorado-Wyoming line, not far from the town of Laramie, Wyoming.

one scenery in the vicinity of the Rocky Mountains; and perhaps an hour's travel would present another of a very different character—one that the artist who designed to depict the beautiful and enchanting landscape would select for a model.

After travelling some fifteen or twenty miles, we came to the trail where the main body of the Indians with whom we had the skirmish the evening before, had passed along. It was near half a mile wide, and the snow was literally trodden into the earth. I have since understood from whites who have been in the habit of trading with this nation, prior to their declaration of hostilities against the whites, that they numbered from seven to eight hundred warriors. Alarmed at this formidable appearance of the hostile Indians, we mutually declined the idea of going to Santa Fé, and turned and travelled in the direction of the main body of our company.

We continued to travel day after day, with all possible speed—occasionally killing a buffalo, a goat, or a bighorn, as we passed over the plains and prairies which were literally covered with these animals; and on the morning of the 9th of April, we arrived safe at our old camp, and were gratified to find our thirteen men and two mules in the enjoyment of good health, with plenty to eat and drink. After exchanging civilities all around, by a hearty shake of the hand, and taking some refreshment, which was immediately prepared for us, I related to the company the dismal tidings of the near approach of the hostile Indians, and the circumstances of being robbed by them, and being defeated in the attempt to retake our property. All were now satisfied of the imprudence of attempting to go to Santa Fe by this route, as well as of the necessity of devising some other method of saving our merchandise. We finally concluded to conceal our merchandise, baggage, fur, and everything that we could not pack on our backs or on the two mules, and return to our appointed winter quarters, at the mouth of the Laramies River, with the expectation of meeting Captain Gant, and obtaining some assistance from him.

On the morning of the 20th of April, having made every necessary preparation, we set out on our journey for the mouth of the Laramies River. After two days travel, we came to the foot of the mountain which we had endeavoured in vain to cross in November. The snow was still deep on the top of it; but by aid of the buffalo trails, we were enabled to scale it without much difficulty, except that our mules suffered with hunger, having had nothing to eat but pine brush. At the foot of the mountain we found abundance of sweet Cottonwood, and our mules being very fond of it, we detained two or three days to let them recruit from their suffering in crossing the mountains. This mountain and the one we left our fur on, are covered with the most splendid timber of different kinds such as fir, cedar, white pine, &c.

On the margin of the rivers and creeks in the plains, the only timber is cottonwood, under growth, willow and rose bushes; out in the middle of the plains there is none of any description. In the month of June, a person by taking a view of the country east of this mountain with a spy glass, could see nothing but a level plain extending from the foot of the mountain as far as the eye can penetrate, covered with green grass, and beautiful flowers of various descriptions; and by turning to the northwest, the eye meets nothing but a rough and dismal looking mountain, covered with snow, and presenting all the appearance of dreary winter. These plains extend to the state of Missouri, with scarce a hill or a grove of timber to interrupt the sight, and literally covered with game of almost every kind.

On the 25th we again resumed our journey down the river, and continued ahead without any difficulty—passing over nearly the same ground that we had travelled over going up the fall before; killing plenty of game—buffalo, deer, bear, bighorn, antelope, &c., and on the 20th May we landed at the mouth of the Laramies; but to our utter astonishment and discomfiture we discovered that not one of the parties had returned according to agreement.

(Here is the end of what was published before. The manuscript continues as follows:—original publisher's note and no doubt refers to this portion of the manuscript having been published some time previous, in the Clearfield Republican.*)*

After remaining here until the 29th, our commander, Mr. Stephens, and another man took the two mules, which by this time had greatly recovered from their famished state, and started in search of the other parties. In vain they travelled up and down the La Platte and its tributaries, but no traces of the lost companions could be discovered, and on the 6th of June they returned, much fatigued and disheartened. During their travels they had discovered, on some of the creeks, 60 or 70 miles from our encampment, many signs of beaver—encountered several grizzly bears, and several times narrowly escaped the Indians (Aricaras), Mr. Stephens having had several balls shot through his clothes. In this situation we remained for five or six days, when Mr. Stephens proposed that each man should go on foot, with a trap or two on his back, his blankets, together with what we could pack upon the two mules, and commence trapping on these creeks. This proposition was objected to by some of the company who were in favour of securing some of Captain Gant's merchandise, find the Indians and purchase horses of them. So many different propositions were here made, that nothing definite could be agreed upon.—Mr. Smith, Mr. Fully and myself agreed to repair to the trapping ground and commence operations, with the understanding that Captain S. should receive a certain share of the profits, as a recompense for the discovery he had made. Accordingly having every thing arranged, on the 11th we started, leaving the remainder of the company to pursue their own course.

Mr. Stephens having a part of the men indebted to him for clothing, &c., and knowing that if they remained at camp he would not be able to collect it, told them that if they would go and bring the beaver fur off the mountain, where we had left it in January last, he would ensure them an equal share of the proceeds of our trapping expedition—and they, with this understanding set out. This contract was made without any consultation having been had with us; and the men, not aware of anything but fairness on the part of Stephens in making this bargain, marched for the fur, and succeeded in getting it off the mountain into the plain, without much difficulty, packed it on their mules, together with what we had left in our winter cabins, and brought the whole to the mouth of the Laramies River.

In the meantime. Smith, Fully, and myself were busily engaged in trapping on the tributary streams of the river Platte. We encountered much difficulty and danger in this excursion, from wild beasts and hostile Indians.—One circumstance with a bear I must relate:—On a pleasant summer evening, when nothing seemed disposed to disturb the tranquillity of our forest home, we built a fire under the cliff of a large rock, on the bank of a small creek, to roast some buffalo meat.

After having cooked and eat our evening repast, I was standing close to the rock, apart from the other men ten or twelve feet,—all at once one of them jumped up and ran off, exclaiming "the bear," "the bear!" I instantly cast my eyes to the top of the precipice, where they encountered this hideous monster seated on the rock with his mouth wide open, and his eyes sparkling like fire. My whole frame shook with agitation. I knew that to attempt to run would be certain death. My gun was standing against a tree within my reach, and after calling for the aid of my companions, I raised my rifle to my face and taking deliberate aim at the most fatal spot, fired—which brought Sir Bruin to the ground.—In the meantime Smith and Fully came to my assistance, and also discharged the contents of, their rifles into his head.

In a few days afterwards we were joined by the rest of the company, who, having secreted, the fur, &c., at the mouth of the Laramies River, had come on search of us. We now, for the first time, got a knowledge of the conduct of Stephens relative to our fur. The men informed us of the contract between them and Stephens. We answered that we could agree to no such contract—that the fur belonged to us, and that we intended to keep it. They then devised other means to secure their share of 150 beaver skins, (the whole number we had caught.) Stephens then told the men that he would not be accountable for any of the fur, and the only way to obtain any of it, was to take it by force. Seeing the folly of further resistance—18 against 3—we were obliged to surrender our earnings, which they took and divided equally among themselves.

The next day we left this company at whose hands we had received such ill-treatment, and returned to the mouth of the Laramies, with the expectation of meeting Captain Gant—but we were sadly mistaken—on our arrival there no traces of Captain Gant's company could be discovered. Next day Mr. Stephens and his party also returned. After remaining here three days together, hunting fishing, and indulging in other amusements, Mr. Fitzpatrick[6] and a company of 115 men, came to our camp. He was on his way to join his company on the west side of the mountains, on the Columbia River, and to supply them with merchandise, ammunition, horses, &c. This company informed us that the firm of Gant and Blackwell had become insolvent.

At this news we all became discouraged; and finally Mr. Stephens and the whole company agreed to join in with Fitzpatrick and go with him to his rendezvous, where we were to make arrangements as to hiring, purchasing equipments, &c. Mr. Stephens took 120 beaver skins, which belonged to Captain Gant, and sold them to Fitzpatrick, which he secreted in the ground, with the intention of raising them when on his return to Missouri—in consideration of which, he was to furnish him with horses and such other equipments as he might want.

July 1st. Having made this arrangement with Mr. F., our camp was all confusion at an early hour this morning, preparing to depart for

6. Fitzpatrick was at the mouth of the Laramie about this time, not on his return from St. Louis.

the Columbia River.[7] Mr. F., took one of the fleetest and most hardy horses in his train, and set out in advance of the main body, in order to discover the disposition of the various Indian tribes through whose dominions we were to travel, and to meet us at a designated point on the head of the Columbia River. After packing up all our moveable property, we started in the course which he had taken, with a force of near 150 strong, many of whom were afraid of nothing, and anxious to meet any danger. We this day, travelled about twenty miles and encamped for the night. The weather was serene and warm, and the men all in high spirits, as we had plenty of fresh meat.

July 2nd. Early in the morning we resumed our journey—stopped in the heat of the day to rest our horses—country quite beautiful—soil rather poor, abounding with sand plains. Travelled about 15 or 20 miles and encamped for the night.

July 3rd. This day we made but little progress in travelling in consequence of a heavy fall of rain—came in contact with a large drove of buffalo, out of which our hunters succeeded in killing ten—one of the men received a bite from a snake, but as it was not of a very poisonous species, the wound soon healed, and the victim was more scared than hurt—but little variation in the scenery of the country.

July 5, 6 and 7. The weather was fair—travelled at the rate of 25 miles per day—nothing of interest occurred. The country through which we passed is rather rough, abounding with game of every description, and is remarkable for the plentitude of wild goats. I have seen the plains literally covered with them. Occasionally the men would fall to and kill them by hundreds. We also fell in with a party of Indians, but on their seeing our forces, fled, without attempting to injure us. We were unable to ascertain the name of the tribe to which they belonged.

July 8th. Early in the morning we resumed our journey, but had not proceeded far until we found ourselves in the midst of a bed of quicksand. So deep was the sand in some places that several of our horses were completely swamped in it, and it was with great difficulty that we succeeded in getting round this swamp, as it were, to continue

---

7. Leonard throughout this narrative, when speaking of the Columbia River, does not mean the present stream of this name, but the Snake River as well, thus the Columbia River as he knew it extended from the headwaters of the present Snake River, to the Pacific Ocean.

our journey. Having surmounted this difficulty, one of our men, a Mr. White, who wandered from the company, came well nigh falling a victim to the fury of a grizzly bear—having in the encounter, had one of his arms literally torn from his body, and had it not been for the timely assistance rendered by some of his companions, who afterwards killed the bear, his death would have been the inevitable consequence. This night we selected a high piece of ground for our encampment, where the wind continued to assail us most violently during the whole night. The next day we travelled about twenty miles, without meeting with any thing of consequence.

July 10th. Finding that we were making but little headway in our travelling, we resolved to increase our speed, and accordingly the whole company was on the move at an early hour this morning. We found our route beginning to grow still more obstructed by rocky cliffs, which are dispersed over this section of the mountain region for many miles, and present an appearance to the beholder similar to a meadow covered with hay-cocks. As the country continued to grow rough, game became scarce, and we began to kill such meat as we *could*, and not such as we *chose*; indeed we thought ourselves very fortunate when one of our hunters would succeed in killing a goat or an antelope—species of meat which we would not look at, when in the vicinity of deer and buffalo.

This part of the mountain is covered with beautiful timber of the best quality, such as fir, pine, cedar, &c. We only travelled about ten miles this day. On the following morning we resumed our journey, and continued to travel day after day, when, after a long and toilsome voyage, we arrived at the point on the Columbia River, designated to meet Mr. Fitzpatrick. Judge of our surprise, when on arriving here no traces of him could be discovered. In vain we searched for some clue to this, to us, melancholy circumstance. What can detain him? was the question asked by each of us.

Disappointment is heart-sickening under any circumstance, but to be disappointed under such circumstances, and in such a place, was perplexing in the extreme.—One scouting party after another were despatched to gather some tidings of the lost Fitzpatrick, but all to no purpose. Had he been destroyed by the savages? The former brilliant success of the man's intercourse with the Indians would not warrant such a belief, as he had many times previously passed over these mountains with no other companion than his trusty steed. The most natural conclusion at which to arrive, was, that the dull and cloudy weather had caused him to loose his course, and that he had become bewildered, and was yet wandering through the wilderness.

After a fruitless search of several days, we concluded to descend the river and search for the company which Mr. Fitzpatrick had left there the summer before,—where we had a faint hope that we might find Mr. F., in safety. The first day we travelled about 20 miles and encamped for the night on the bank of the river. Although we knew that we were in the vicinity of the savage Blackfeet Indians, yet but few traces of them had been discovered through the day, and we therefore retired to rest in our encampment without taking the necessary precautions for defence, in case of an attack. But it was not long before we were enabled to appreciate the consequence of our negligence, or fancied security. About midnight we were awoke from our slumbers by a furious attack by a large party of Blackfeet. They fired into our tents before we were aware of their approach. Immediately each man was on his feet, and on the look out.

After a small skirmish of random shooting, which lasted an hour or so, the Indians, finding the strength of our forces, thought it best to retire from the field, with the loss of three killed, and as we supposed, 8 or 10 wounded. The loss on our side was one man wounded in the leg, 5 horses killed, 3 wounded, and 14 stolen. The Blackfeet are a powerful nation, and are better supplied with implements of war, than almost any other tribe of this region.[8] They have always retained a most inveterate hostility to the Flatheads, against whom they wage a continual warfare, having at one time greatly reduced their strength, and on several occasions came well nigh exterminating the entire tribe. Of late years the Flatheads have been better prepared for war, and have bravely held their own. This undying hostility appears to be owing to the Blackfeet refusing to let the Flatheads hunt buffalo on the east side of the mountain.

The following morning we took up our march and continued down the river. As we travelled along we seen many fresh signs of Indians, and apprehended much danger from them, which caused us to

8. This party with whom Leonard and his companions were travelling was under the charge of William L. Sublette, who was to bring the supplies to the mountains for the use of the Rocky Mountain Fur Company. The Indians who attacked them here were the Blackfeet and the same band, or a part of them at least were at the Battle of Pierre's Hole, and came near being exterminated. The route taken by this party was the one usually followed by these parties along the Sweetwater, and through the South Pass.

labour under the most intense fear, lest we should fall into an ambush of this crafty tribe. We killed several fat deer, goats, and an antelope, and encamped on a high hill, from which we had a beautiful view of the surrounding country; where we could sec the different kinds of game traversing the plains at leisure, contented, and undisturbed, save when aroused from their lair by the sudden onset of the Indian hunter. This night we very prudently stationed a strong guard round our encampment, and were permitted to pass the night in peace, which was quite warm and pleasant. In the morning we resumed our journey, and about the middle of the day found ourselves in the vicinity of another tribe of Indians. We sent a flag to their camp, which was received in the most friendly manner. This proved to be the Flathead tribe. These Indians are more pacific and pleasing in their manners than any tribe we had yet encountered, and reside mostly on the river of that name. I will here quote the description of this tribe as given by Mr. Cox, a gentleman well acquainted with the Indian character, which fully embraces my own views:—

The Flatheads have fewer failings than any tribe I ever met with. They are honest in their dealings—brave in the field—quiet and amiable to their chiefs—fond of cleanliness, and are decided enemies to falsehood of every description.—The women are excellent wives and mothers, and their character for fidelity is so well established that we never heard of one single instance of one proving unfaithful to her husband. They are remarkably well made—rather tall—slender, and never corpulent.

The Flatheads are well accustomed to the manners and customs of the white race, and in many respects appear ambitious to follow their example.—Some years ago, they were in the habit of using a process to flatten the heads of their children, which they deemed a very essential addition to their appearance; but since they have had intercourse with the whites they have abandoned this abominable practice. The process of flattening the head is this:—

Soon after the birth of the infant, it is placed in a kind of trough and a piece of bark fastened by means of strings through the trough, and pressed hard upon the forepart of the head, which causes it to grow flat. In this painful position they are kept a year, and in some instances over a year. They are very hospitable to strangers, and are tried friends of the white people. On coming to their village a white person always receives the best to eat, drink and smoke, and are always ready to pilot the traveller through their country. In the summer season this tribe live in the buffalo country on the head of the Columbia River, where they never fail to come in contact with their cold hearted enemies, the Blackfeet, who are the most ferocious and unsparing enemy of the white men, because the Flatheads have been supplied by the whites with munitions of war. In the fall the Flatheads again return to the plains, and in the winter subsist on Salmon, roots and small game. They are always well supplied with horses, and when provision becomes scarce in one section, they pack all they have upon the backs of their horses, and remove to another.

Their houses are made of slim pine poles from 20 to 30 feet long, 12 or 15 feet apart at the bottom, and joined together at the top, forming a structure in the shape of the roof of a common dwelling house. These are covered with dressed buffalo skins sewed together. A fire is built in the middle of the cabin, and its shape forms a kind of flue or draft for the smoke—rendering this simple structure quite a comfortable habitation at the most inclement season of the year. No storm can effect them, nor no cold can reach their inmates. When moving camp these poles are taken down and one end fastened to the sides of the mule or horse and the other end dragging on the ground forming a sort of dray. The infants are put into a sack or bag, made of leather, which closes on one side by strings; this is fastened to a board near three feet long and one wide, where they are kept constantly, with the exception of an occasional dressing, &c., until a year old. To the back of this board they have a cord attached, by which they hang the sack to the saddle, whilst travelling.

After remaining here two days to observe their manners, customs, and mode of living, and getting all the information we desired, we resumed our journey, taking one of the Indians to pilot us to the station of Mr. Fitzpatrick's company.—After several days tedious and toilsome travelling, and no extraordinary occurrence, we joined the company on the 2nd of August. It was with feelings of peculiar delight that we here beheld the visages of white men, who were no less pleased to give us a welcome reception. But a melancholy gloom was visible in every countenance, when we discovered that Fitzpatrick had not arrived. Great excitement prevailed, and vigorous measures were immediately taken to rescue him, if he had not before this, as many supposed, fallen a victim to the enraged fury of the merciless savage, or the ravenous appetite of some ferocious beast of prey.

Small companies were despatched in various directions on the tributary streams of the Columbia. Diligent search was kept up for some time without success, and our search was about to be abandoned as fruitless; and indeed some of the parties had give up in despair, and returned to camp, when, a party, who had wandered into the vicinity of the Blackfeet Indians, were reconnoitring their movements in a valley from a high bluff, saw, and immediately recognised, Fitzpatrick's horse, with which the Indians were running races.—Was this calculated to inspire hope? or was it not rather an omen that our employer was destroyed by these Indians.

Vigilant search was made to make further discoveries; and, to the great joy of every man, he was at length found on the banks of the Pieres River, which forms a junction with the Columbia, near the rendezvous of Fitzpatrick's company. When found he was completely exhausted, and so much wasted in flesh, and deformed in dress, that, under other circumstances, he would not have been recognised. The poor man was reduced to a skeleton, and was almost senseless. When his deliverers spoke of taking him to camp, he scarcely seemed to comprehend their meaning. After eating some dried buffalo meat, and a little maize, he grew better, and placing him on a horse, he was safely conveyed to camp. A general rejoicing ensued, for his appearance among us again, was like that of one risen from the dead. Although I was not much attached to the man, for I could not banish from my mind the craftiness evinced by him when we first met with him on the east side of the mountains, yet I can scarcely describe my feelings of joy on beholding him safely returned. After resting a few days, and being nourished by the provender our camp would afford, he became able to relate the misfortunes which befell him in crossing the mountain, which I will give in his own words, as follows:

ADVENTURES OF FITZPATRICK.[9]

For three or four days after I left the company I travelled without any difficulty, and at great speed, but the fourth and fifth, the weather being dull and cloudy, I got strayed from my course, and soon found myself in the midst of a rough hilly country, abounding with large loose rocks which some places almost prevented me from passing at all, and covered with various kinds of timber of the most magnificent description. In passing

---

9. Leonard's account of the adventure of Fitzpatrick here given, is probably the most full and complete of any published, although many authorities mention the same and give a more or less complete account of this particular adventure.

the nights in these solitudes my rest was constantly disturbed by the dismal howl of the wolf and the fierce growl of the bear—which animals were very numerous and would frequently approach within a few steps and threaten to devour me. One day after a toilsome ride, I dismounted, turned my horse loose to graze and seated myself on a rock, with the little remaining provision I had, to refresh myself.

While thus seated resting my wearied limbs, and satisfying the gnawings of hunger, I was suddenly startled by a scrambling on the rocks immediately in my rear. I turned round and beheld a huge bear approaching me in double quick time. I instantly sprang to my feet, for I was well acquainted with his mode of warfare. I turned and faced his lordship, when he approached within about six feet of me, rose on his hind feet and most impudently stared me right in the face, for more than a minute. After discovering that I was no ways bashful, he bowed, turned and run—I did the same, and made for my horse. Bruin was not so easy fooled; he seen my retreat and gave chase. I thought I could reach my horse and mount before the bear could reach me, but the approach of the bear frightened my beast, and just as I was going to mount he sprang loose and threw me on the broad of my back. The bear was at my heels, and I thought that all chance of escape was now gone. Instantly I was again on my feet,—and, as it were, in a fit of desperation, rushed towards the bear, which, fearing, as they do, the face of man, again turned and run.—Sir Bruin stopped to secure the little morsel I had been eating, and retired a few paces to devour it.

While the bear was thus employed, I crept to my gun, keeping the rock between him and me, having reached it, took deliberate aim and killed him dead on the spot. Having secured my horse, I fell to work at the carcase of my vanquished foe, and, after cooking and eating a choice piece of his flesh, left the rest to feed his kindred. It being now near night, I travelled two or three miles further, and encamped for the night. The next morning appeared more favourable over head, and I made an early start. Being on the banks of a small creek, I concluded to follow it a while.

After winding my way through the rocks and trees, till near the middle of the day, I came to a valley which seemed to be hemmed in on every side by huge towering hills. I had not travelled far in this valley before I found myself ushered into the presence of a hostile tribe of Indians. I halted to devise some means to effect a return without being discovered; but I soon found that it was too late. Immediately in my rear was a choice set of young warriors—in front, and on both sides by high and craggy mountains. My noble steed, than him, I would defy the whole Indian world to produce a stouter, swifter, or better, was now brought to the test. He started with the velocity of the rein deer,—bounding over ditches, stones logs and brush.—Soon I began to ascend the mountain, but found it much too steep and rough.

The Indians dismounted and followed on foot. I applied the whip, but in vain. My horse was compelled to yield to exhausted nature—and I dismounted, and left my much prized animal to fall a prey to the savages. I ran up the mountain with all possible speed, but finding that I must eventually be overtaken, I secreted myself in a hole among the rocks, and closed the mouth of it with leaves and sticks. After remaining a few minutes in this subterraneous cavern, I heard the ferocious yells of triumph of my pursuers, as they captured my lamented horse.

The victory was not yet complete, although the horse was the principal prize. Some of them followed on and came close to my hiding place, passed and re-passed within reach without discovering me.

What a moment of intense anxiety was this! All chance of escape cut off. No prospect of mercy if taken! Hope began to die—and death inevitable seemed to be the very next incident that would occur. They continued their search until near sunset, for they knew that I had not reached the summit of the mountain. As they retired down the mountain, squads of four or five would frequently halt and hold a busy consultation—then suddenly return to complete their search, as if they feared that some hollow tree or rocky cavern might escape unexplored. Finally, they gave me up in despair, and retired into the valley, with my horse.

Now that I had escaped this scrutinizing search, I began to breathe more free and easy; but I was yet far from being out of danger. I was conscious that I had lost the course to the Columbia River, and could not tell how to regain it, even if I should succeed in escaping from my present perilous situation. I remained secreted in the rocks till long after dark, when I crawled out, and surveyed the country as well as the darkness of the night would permit, and finally started in the direction which I thought I would have the least chance of meeting the Indians. I had not travelled far, however, until I was again doomed to be disappointed, for I was on the very borders of their encampment. Happily the camp was all quiet, and I returned quietly to my hiding place on the mountain, hoping that on the morrow I would be able to make some new discovery by which to extricate myself from these savages—which I judged to be the merciless Blackfeet.

Early in the morning of the next day the hunt was resumed with increased vigilance; but again returned with disappointment. After the sound of their voices no longer reached me, I crawled to the mouth of the hole from which I presently beheld them running races with the horse they had taken from me. In this sport they spent the day. This village did not appear to be their permanent residence, but was handsomely situated on the banks of a small creek, and I suppose they had came here on a sporting expedition. The second night I made another effort to save myself, and gradually descended the mountain, to the creek some distance below the camp.—This I followed, until daylight again compelled me to hide myself; which I did by crawling into the brush close to the creek, where I secreted myself till darkness again gave me an opportunity to resume my journey.

During the day I seen a number of the Indians pass and repass up and down the valley, whom I supposed to be hunters. This day I again had a view of my horse under the saddle of the chief of the tribe, as I supposed; but did not attempt to rescue him. The following night I travelled a short distance down the creek when I came to where it empties into the Pieres River.[10] Here I came to my reckoning of the country, and thought that if I could escape from hunger and beasts of prey, I could manage to elude the Indians. Supposing that the Indians were not so numerous on the opposite side of the river, I resolved to cross over—for which purpose I built a raft of old logs, laid my shot-pouch, gun, blanket, &c. on it, and pushed for the oppo-

10. The river here referred to is Pierre's River which flows through Pierre's Hole or valley, and is a tributary of the Snake, on which the famous battle occurred.

site shore. After getting nearly across, the current became very rapid, and I began to descend the river at a rapid rate until I struck a rock which tore my frail craft to pieces—committing myself, gun, blanket and all to the watery element.

Being weak from hunger and exertion, it was with great difficulty that I succeeded in reaching the land, with the loss of my only companion, and my only hope in this wilderness of dangers—my gun. I stood on the bank in the midst of despair. I had no other weapon than a butcher knife to fight my way through a country swarming with savages and equally dangerous wild beasts. On my knife depended all hope of preventing starvation. The loss of my blanket was also severe, as the weather was sometimes quite cold, and I had no other clothing than a shirt and vest—having thrown the rest away when pursued by the Indians on the mountain. I followed the banks of this river for two days, subsisting upon buds, roots, weeds, &c.

On the second evening whilst digging for a sweet kind of root, in a swamp, I was alarmed by the growl of wolves, which were descending the hill to the river, about fifty yards distant. The only chance of escape now, was to climb a tree, which I did immediately. Here I was compelled to roost until daylight, in the most painful agitation. The wolves tearing up the ground and gnawing at the tree so that I sometimes feared they would cut it through. The third day I travelled with great speed, not even stopping for any thing to eat. On the fourth I happened where the wolves had killed a buffalo.—Here I satisfied my appetite by collecting all the meat that was left on the bones, made a fire by rubbing two sticks together, and cooked it. From the gluttonous fill which I took of this meat, I was enabled to travel three or four days, without any particular occurrence; but I found that the further I descended the river, the scarcer became the roots, buds, &c., on which I must depend for subsistence, and I was finally obliged to turn my attention to get something to eat, without travelling any further.

For several days I loitered about from place to place, but could find no nourishment. My body began to grow weaker and weaker, until I was no longer able to walk. Still my mind held its sway, and I was well aware how desperate was my situation. Finally loosing all prospect of getting any thing more to eat, and no hope of being found by my companions or friendly

Indians, I thought of preparing myself for death, and committed my soul to the Almighty. I have no recollection of anything that occurred after this, until I found myself in the hands of my deliverers.

The story of Fitzpatrick created much excitement in our camp. Some were determined on immediately chastising the Indians, and retaking his horse. Others, who were not friendly disposed towards Mr. F., would not credit his story. For my part I thought the man had related nothing more than the truth as to his sufferings, for nothing less could have reduced him to the condition in which he was found. In a few days all was restored to order and tranquillity, and we commenced making arrangements for trapping, &c.

The Columbia is a strong, clear and beautiful river at this point, (the junction of the Lewis River,) and is about 1000 yards wide. The Wallah Wallah empties into it about 14 miles lower down—which is rather muddy, and a very rapid stream. There was at this rendezvous at this time, about 400 white people, who lived in constant intercourse with the Flatheads and "Nez Perces," or Pierced Nose tribes, which latter consists of 1000 warriors, besides women and children, and live in the closest friendship with their neighbours, the Flatheads. They are said to act honourable in all their dealings, nor do they now practice treachery and stealing so extensively as most of the tribes below this; although, when first discovered by the whites, a *brave* was esteemed according to his success in stealing. They have now reformed, and a white man can at all times find a trusty friend in a Nez Perces.

Among the discoveries of importance which we made here was nine of Captain Gant's men, who had left us at the mouth of the Laramies. In crossing the mountain they had several encounters with the Indians, and finally lost their horses and 3 of their men. After travelling about for a number of days, under the direction of a Mr. Saunders, their leader, they came across a party belonging to this rendezvous, whom they followed, and had arrived at camp a few days before us. No important arrangement was made among the men with regard to trapping, &c., until the people gathered in from the different parts of the mountain. In the meantime 15 of us joined together, each man furnishing an equal quantity of merchandise, horses, &c., and to receive an equal share of the proceeds.

August 25th. Every thing necessary for our expedition being ready this morning, we started in a southern direction, but did not go far until we encamped for the night—thinking that if we had neglected anything which we would stand in need of, we would thus discover it. The next morning finding all things in order, we continued travelling down what is called Pieres hole,[11] or valley. This valley is situated on the river of the same name, and is from 70 to 80 miles in length, with a high mountain on the east and west—each so high that it is impossible to pass over them, and is from eight to ten miles wide. The river runs immediately through the centre, with a beautiful grove of timber along either bank; from this timber to the mountain, a distance of four or five miles, there is nothing but a smooth plain. This meadow or prairie is so perfectly level that a person may look up or down as far as the eye will reach without meeting any thing to obstruct the sight, until the earth and sky appear to meet.

After travelling a few miles this morning, some of the men, in taking a view of the country before us, discovered something like people upon horses, who appeared to be coming towards us. After continuing in the same direction for some time we came in view with the naked eye, when we halted.—They advanced towards us displaying a British flag.[12] This we could not comprehend; but on coming closer discovered them to be hostile Indians. We immediately despatched a messenger back to the rendezvous for reinforcements and prepared ourselves for defence. The Indians commenced building a fort in the timber on the bank of the river; but at the time we were not aware of what they were doing.

After waiting here a few hours we were reinforced by 200 whites, 200 Flatheads, and 300 Nez Perces Indians. The Indians with the British flag, on seeing such a number of people galloping down the plain at full speed, immediately retreated within their fort, whither they were hotly pursued. The friendly Indians soon discovered them to belong to the Blackfeet tribe, who are decidedly the most numerous and warlike tribe in the mountains, and for this reason are not disposed to have any friendly intercourse with any other nation of an inferior number, unless they are good warriors and well armed with guns, &c.

We thought we could rush right on them and drive them out of the brush into the plain and have a decisive battle at once. We advanced with all possible speed, and a full determination of success,

11. Pierre's Hole.
12. Leonard is the only authority who mentions this use of the British flag by the Blackfeet.

until we discovered their fort by receiving a most destructive fire from the enclosure. This through our ranks into complete confusion, and we all retreated into the plain, with the loss of 5 whites, 8 Flatheads and 10 Nez Perces Indians killed, besides a large number of whites and Indians wounded. The formation of their fort astonished all hands. We Had been within a few hundred yards of them all day and did not discover that they were building it. It was large enough to contain 500 warriors; and built strong enough to resist almost any attempt we might make to force it. After dressing the wounded, and having reconnoitred their fort, our forces were divided into several detachments, and sent in different directions with the intention of surrounding the fort and making them prisoners. This was done under the superintendence of Fitzpatrick, who acted as commander-in-chief.[13]

In a case of this kind any man not evincing the greatest degree of courage, and every symptom of bravery, is treated as a coward; and the person who advances first, furthest and fastest, and makes the greatest display of animal courage, soon rises in the estimation of his companions. Accordingly with the hope of gaining a little glory while an opportunity offered, though not for any electioneering purpose, as a politician in the States would do—I started into the brush, in company with two acquaintances (Smith and Kean) and two Indians. We made a circuitous route and came towards the fort from a direction which we thought we would be least expected.

We advanced closer and closer, crawling upon our hands and knees, with the intention of giving them a *select* shot; and when within about forty yards of their breastwork, one of our Indians was shot dead. At this we all lay still for some time, but Smith's foot happening to shake the weeds as he was laying on his belly, was shot through. I advanced a little further, but finding the balls to pass too quick and close, concluded to retreat. When I turned, I found that my companions had deserted me. In passing by, Smith asked me to carry him out, which met my approbation precisely, for I was glad to get out of this unpleasant situation under any pretext—provided my reputation for courage would not be questioned.

After getting him on my back, still crawling on my hands and knees, I came across Kean, lying near where the first Indian fell, who was also mortally wounded, and died soon after. I carried Smith to a place of safety and then returned to the siege. A continual fire was kept up, doing more or less execution on both sides until late in the

---

13. Other authorities state that William L. Sublette acted in this capacity.

afternoon, when we advanced to close quarters, having nothing but the thickness of their breast work between us, and having them completely surrounded on all sides to prevent any escaping. This position we maintained until sunset, in the meantime having made preparations to set fire to the fort, which was built principally of old dry logs, as soon as night would set in, and stationed men at the point where we thought they would be most likely to make the first break, for the purpose of taking them on the wing, in their flight.

Having made all these preparations, which were to put an end to all further molestation on the part of the Blackfeet, our whole scheme and contemplated victory was frustrated by a most ingenious and well executed device of the enemy. A few minutes before the torch was to be applied, our captives commenced the most tremendous yells and shouts of triumph, and menaces of defiance, which seemed to move heaven and earth. Quick as thought a report spread through all quarters, that the plain was covered with Blackfeet Indians coming to reinforce the besieged. So complete was the consternation in our ranks, created by this stratagem, that in five minutes afterwards, there was not a single white man, Flathead or Nez Perces Indian within a hundred yards of the fort.

Every man thought only of his own security, and run for life without ever looking round, which would at once have convinced him of his folly. In a short time it was ascertained that it was only a stratagem, and our men began to collect together where our baggage was. I never shall forget the scene here exhibited. The rage of some was unbounded, and approached to madness. For my own part, although I felt much regret at the result after so much toil and danger, yet I could not but give the savages credit for the skill they displayed in preserving their lives, at the very moment when desperation, as we thought, had seized the mind of each of them.

By the time we were made sensible of the full extent of our needless alarm, it had began to get dark ; and on ascertaining the extent of the injury which we received, (having lost 32 killed, principally Indians,) it was determined not to again attempt to surround the fort, which was a sore disappointment to some of the men who were keen for chastising the Indians for their trick. We then took up our march for the rendezvous; but on starting one of our party of 15 men, who had first started out the day before, could not be found. Search was made, and he was found in the brush, severely wounded.—After carrying him on a litter a few miles he died and was buried in the Indian style: —which is by digging a hole in the ground, wrapping a blanket or skin round the body, placing it in the hole, and covering it with poles and earth. This is the manner of interring the dead in this country both by the Indians and whites, except in the winter season on account of the ground being frozen, when the Indians are in the habit of wrapping their dead in buffalo robes, and laying them on poles from one tree to another, on which poles the corpse is tied with cords. The next morning we raised another war party and went back to the battleground, but no Indians could be found.—They must have left the fort in great haste for we found 42 head of horses, together with Fitzpatrick's which they had taken on the mountain, two warriors and one squaw lying dead inside of their fort, besides a large quantity of their baggage, such as furs, skins, &c.

There must have been a great number of them, from the holes they had dug in the ground around their dead horses and the edges of the fort, say from three to four hundred. I learned afterwards that the Nez Perces Indians shortly after found seven more dead Blackfeet, in some brush close by, where they had been secreted to save their scalps, which is the principal object with these Indians, in order to have their women dance. In the afternoon we returned to the rendezvous and presented Mr. Fitzpatrick with his long-lossed and highly valued horse, which seemed to compensate for all the sufferings and hardships which he had encountered. After remaining here a few days a violent dispute arose between Stephens and Fitzpatrick about the price of the horses which the latter was to give to the former for the beaver skins of Gant's which Stephens had sold to Fitzpatrick.

No person interfered, for we all knew that it was a dishonest transaction from beginning to end. Fitzpatrick having every thing in his own possession, was therefore contented and as independent as any mean man who had it in his power to make his own terms. Stephens, on the contrary, was in a bad situation—having paid before hand, and not being able to force measures, had to put up with what he could get. Finally he succeeded in hiring four men, and started back to the mouth of the Laramies to secure the fur which he had sold to Fitzpatrick. He had not left many days, however, until he was overtaken by a scouting party of those Indians we had surrounded in the fort. Two of his men were killed, (More and Foy), and himself shot through the thigh—having the two mules along, which was the balance of the original stock, one of which was killed, and the other brought back the wounded Stephens, who died in a few days afterwards from mortification taking place in the wounded leg.

A few days after this occurrence, we were visited by a party belonging to the Nor-West (Hudson Bay Company), or British trading company, from whom we were enabled to learn the way the Blackfeet Indians had got possession and fought under the British flag. It appeared by their story that these Indians some months previous, had fell on a party belonging to their company—but few of whom escaped to tell the fate of their comrades—and among the spoils which they obtained, was this flag, which they used as a signal to deceive and mislead their enemies, whom they might meet in these extensive plains.

Sept. 1st. After remaining here until today, during which time Mr. Saunders joined our company of fifteen, which made up for the one that was killed, and who was the only one besides myself, of Captain Gant's company; leaving the balance with Fitzpatrick—some hiring with their equipments which they purchased on credit.—We set to work making preparation to start the following morning, on our second attempt to reach some region where we could prosecute our business of trapping to some advantage. The conditions of our agreement were the same, as on the first expedition, *viz:*—each man to find an equal portion of traps, guns, and ammunition, and to receive an equal share of the peltries which we might catch.

On the morning of the 2nd Sept., having everything ready, we left the rendezvous, all in a fine humour. We arrived on the head waters of the Multenemough River without anything of moment occurring— where we made our fall's hunt. After travelling near 100 miles South West from the top of the mountains, or from the head of Lewis River, we got totally out of the range of the buffalo. We were told by the natives that those animals were never known further west, which is something singular, as the country is just the same, if not better as to grass. These Indians subsist principally upon salmon, and such other fish as they can catch, with the assistance of roots, buds, berries, and some small game, which they kill with the bow and arrow.

They are generally of a more swarthy nature, small and cowardly, and travel in small gangs of from four to five families—this they are compelled to do in order to keep from starvation. They are always roving from plain to plain, and from valley to valley—never remaining in one place longer than till game gets scarce. When on the move the women have to perform the most laborious part—having charge of the transportation of their baggage. While doing this, a female, the most feeble of their sex, will carry a load of perhaps a hundred weight a whole day, without manifesting the least fatigue or complaint.

This tribe, which I believe is called the Bawnack, or Shoshonies, are the most indolent, and have the least ambition of any tribe we had yet discovered. They are lazy and dirty; and only strive to get as much as will keep them from starving. They are no way ill disposed towards the whites, or at least they never disturbed us—with the exception of stealing a few of our traps.[14] We continued moving down the Multen-emough for several hundred miles, during which time we subsisted principally upon beaver, deer, and bighorn—though we still had a little jirked buffalo meat. Between trapping and trading we had made quite a profitable hunt. To get a beaver skin from these Indians worth eight or ten dollars, never cost more than an awl, a fish hook, a knife, a string of beads, or something equally as trifling.

As winter was approaching, we began to make arrangements to return to some more favourable climate, by collecting our fur, and giving each man his share of the baggage. We travelled back with great speed, and arrived in the buffalo country on the first of November, where we met with a nation of Snake Indians, with whom we made some small trades for buffalo robes and skins for the winter. The manners and customs of the Snake Indians are very similar to those of the Flatheads, with the exception of stealing, which they consider no harm. The Snake Indians, or as some call them, the Shoshonies, were once a powerful nation, possessing a glorious hunting ground on the east side of the mountains; but they, like the Flatheads, have been almost annihilated by the revengeful Blackfeet, who, being supplied with firearms were enabled to defeat all Indian opposition. Their nation has been entirely broken up and scattered throughout all this wild region. The Shoshonies are a branch of the once powerful Snake tribe, as are also the more abject and forlorn tribe of Shuckers, or more generally termed, Diggers and Root eaters, who keep in the most retired recesses of the mountains and streams, subsisting on the most unwholesome food, and living the most like animals of any race of beings.

We left the Snake Indians and took a more Southern direction to the Bear River, which empties into Big Salt Lake—followed this river for two days, and then crossed over to Weabers River. These two rivers are about the same size, say from two to three hundred yards wide,

---

14. This description is scarcely in accord with the Bannocks or Shoshones (Snakes). It seems rather to apply to the Pai-utes or Diggers (Root Diggers).

and from three to four hundred miles long.—They run South parallel with each other, and empty into the Big Salt Lake on the North side, at no great distance apart.—This lake is much larger than any other west of the mountains—supposed to be 200 miles long, and near the same in width. It is surrounded on the North, about the mouths of the rivers, by a mountainous and broken country, and on the South and West by a barren, sandy plain, in a manner incapable of vegetation. There is also a hill or peak near the centre of it so high that the snow remains on it the greater part of the year. The water is of such a brackish nature that only part of it freezes in the coldest weather of the winter season. Its briny substance prevents all vegetation within a considerable distance of the margin of the lake. The Bear and Weabers Rivers are the principal streams by which it is fed.

In the Spring of the year, when the snow and ice melts and runs down off the mountains, this lake rises very high, on account of it having no outlet; and in the fall, or latter part of summer it sinks—leaving salt one and two inches thick on some parts of its shores. It is situated on the west side of the mountains, between the waters of the Columbia and Rio Colorado, or Red River, and is called by the natives, the Great Salt Lake. The rivers which empty into this lake abound with many kinds of fish, such as trout, cat-fish, and others suitable for hook and line, particularly at their mouths. here the country is low, and small streams empties into them, the dams of the beaver causes the water to overflow its banks, and makes a swampy, marshy country for miles round. People trapping on these streams are compelled to construct canoes of bull and buffalo skins, in order to visit their traps.

On leaving this lake we continued our journey towards the head waters of the Colorado, which stream empties into the Gulf of California. After a tedious, but not unpleasant tramp of several days we came to a beautiful situation on one of the main feeders of this river, where we halted to make preparations to spend the winter—it now being about the middle of November. We had remained here but a few days, during which time we were occupied in building tents, &c, for winter, when we were visited by a party of 70 or 80 Indian warriors. These Indians manifested the best of friendship towards us, while in our camp, and said they were going to war with the Snake Indians—whose country we were now in—and they also said they belonged to the Crow nation on the East side of the mountains.

In all the intercourse had with them, while they were with us, not the least symptom of deception was discovered, and they parted with us manifesting as much regret as if we had been old acquaintances. But we were doomed to experience the faith of the Crow nation—for, on the same night of their departure, they returned and stole five of our best hunting horses. This was a serious loss to us, and a valuable prize for them—for an Indian belonging to these hunting and warring tribes is poor indeed if he is not the owner of a horse, as it is upon this animal they much depend for success in chasing the buffalo, and upon him greatly depends the fate of the battle.

Having a man in our company who had once been a captive in their village, and who could talk and understand a little of their language, we resolved at all hazards to give chase and retake our horses. We steered across the mountains towards the Southern headwaters of the Missouri River. The first stream we came to on the east side is called Bighorn River—down which stream we travelled for some days, until we came to their village situated at the mouth of Stinking river.

In this village we found a negro man, who informed us that he first came to this country with Lewis and Clark—with whom he also returned to the State of Missouri, and in a few years returned again with a Mr. Mackinney, (Kenneth MacKennie?), a trader on the Missouri River, and has remained here ever since—which is about ten or twelve years. He has acquired a correct knowledge of their manner of living, and speaks their language fluently. He has rose to be quite a considerable character, or chief, in their village; at least he assumes all the dignities of a chief, for he has four wives with whom he lives alternately. This is the custom of many of the chiefs.

After informing the negro of our stolen horses, he told us that they had them, and that the reason they were taken from us was because we were found in their enemies' country, and that they supposed we were going to trade them guns, &c. By giving the chiefs some trifling presents our horses were produced in as good trim as when they left us. (I shall say nothing more of these Indians at present, as I shall have occasion to speak of them when I again visit their village.)

About the first of January 1833, the game getting scarce in this vicinity, the Indians left us and moved down the river. We remained at this station employing our time in hunting, fishing, and such other sports as we could come at, but without any particular occurrence, until the 20th of February, when we set out on our spring hunt. We crossed the country to the River Platte without any difficulty, and continued down this stream to the junction of it and the Laramies, where we had joined Fitzpatrick's company in the previous spring, and where also we had parted with Captain Gant. On encamping for the night we found a tree off which the bark was pealed, and wrote on with a coal, that, by searching in a certain place mentioned, we would find a letter,—which we did, and found the document, written in Gant's hand, which stated that only two parties had returned, *viz*:—Washburns and his own—and also that Captain Blackwell had come up from the States with a supply of provision, merchandise, ammunition, &c.

The letter went on to detail the hardships, sufferings, and misfortunes which they had encountered, which only amounted to this: that they had lost their horses last winter, and had been to Santa Fé and purchased more—while crossing the mountain his party had accidentally met with Washburn and his company—that they then ascertained for the first, that the company was insolvent and had declined doing business in this country—and that they (Gant's party) had left this place in September last, to go and establish a trading post on the Arkansas River, with the Arpahee Indians.[15] The letter closed by stating that Stephen's party had left him and joined Fitzpatrick. 'This letter was directed to Mr. Saunders, who was in our company, and who, Gant supposed, would be the first to return.

Soon after the contents of the letter were made known to the company, some men were sent across the Laramies river to see if they could make any discoveries of importance, as we could see the remains of what we supposed to be an old encampment on its banks. These men, after searching for some time, found where several buffalo had been slaughtered, and from the manner in which it was done, it was evident that it was the work of a party of hostile Indians—and not being able to trace which direction they had steered, we were at a great loss to know what to do—having no person to act as commander. There was much difference of opinion and great contention about which way we should take. Our object was, if possible, to avoid meeting with the Indians, as our force was small, and not well prepared to encounter a band of savages defended with firearms. Finally, it was decided that we should leave the rivers and strike for the mountains—thinking this route the least dangerous.

---

15. We have no knowledge of the location of this trading-post; the only other trading-post on the Arkansas at this period was Bent's Fort established In 1829. The Arapahoes were at this time located in the eastern part of the present state of Colorado, between the Arkansas and the South Platte.

After travelling an hour or so, we suddenly met with a body of eight or ten on horse back, who we judged to be hunting—not being backward about meeting with such a number, we marched boldly towards them. On this they immediately galloped off under full speed, in the direction which we were going. Thinking the main body to be in that direction, we thought to avoid them by turning to the right and keeping near the river. We did not advance far in this direction, however, until we suddenly came upon their encampment. Being thus led into their strong hold by mere accident, we held a hurried consultation as to our own safety. Their horses and white lodges could be distinctly seen although we were some distance off, and we flattered ourselves that we had not yet been discovered by any in the village, and that we might yet escape.

With this hope we sounded a retreat and marched slowly and silently back for the purpose of sheltering ourselves with the timber, where we intended to build a fort immediately, for we knew that even if we were not discovered now, the party we first met would gave the alarm, and the chase would be commenced. In going along, juking from bluff to bluff, in order to avoid being seen, we were overtaken by a single Indian on horseback. He would ride up at full gallop within 20 or 30 steps of us, and then suddenly wheel, ride back towards the camp, and then return as before.

After repeating this several times, some of our men, when he came close, raised their guns, and he, thinking there might be danger in running away, came to us and told us that the chief had sent for us to come to his tent, to eat, smoke and be friendly. Not having confidence in his good intentions, all declined the invitation, but told the messenger that we would just retire into the timber, (where we intended to be occupied in the meantime in building a fort,) and that if the chief wished to have any thing to say to us, he could come there—for which we started into the woods, taking this fellow with us, with the intention of keeping him until the fort would be erected.

After going but a short distance our prisoner broke loose, and immediately ran onto some rising ground, where he made his horse perform many singular feats as a signal for his followers. We galloped off as fast as we could, but were soon surrounded on all sides, without any thing to shelter us, except a hole formed by the sinking of water—which are very numerous in some of these plains. Into this hole we drove our horses, and expected to reach the top in time to keep the Indians at bay, and make peace with them. Before we got our horses properly secured in this hole there was hundreds of red men standing above and eagerly looking down upon us, uttering the most terrifying yells of vengeance, brandishing their guns, bows and spears as if they would devour us.—We were in just such a situation now, as is calculated to bring on despair, with all its horrifying feelings,—each man holding his gun cocked and ready, resolved to sell his life only with the last drop of blood.—We stood in this situation, for a few minutes, waiting for them to commence, when there was one rushed into their ranks apparently much excited, who on addressing a few words to the warriors, they all put down their arms, and made signs to us to come out, that they would not molest us. This we did, but it was with a watchful, jealous eye.

The man whose timely arrival seemed to have put a stop to their designs, and who doubtless here saved our lives, now came forward and signified to us that we had better go with them to their camp, and eat, drink and smoke, and he would exert his influence not to have us hurt—which advice we accordingly followed—taking our horses with us. On arriving at their camp, we found two who could talk the Crow language. The Rickarees, (Aricaras), the nation in whose hands we now were, on being at war with the Crow nation took these two prisoners, as they told us, and adopted them as their brethren.—After manifesting a desire to be friendly with them, by smoking, &c. these Crow prisoners informed us that, had it not been for the timely arrival of the chief, when we were in the hole, we would most certainly have been cut to pieces. This is altogether probable. The feelings of every individual, as well as those of myself, when surrounded in this hole, were horrible in the extreme. The thought struck me, as I leaned against a rock, that here I must end my career. Our feelings may be imagined, but not described.

The Crow prisoners told us that the only reason they knew why the chief had interceded for us, was because he had not previously been consulted on the subject, (having been absent when we were discovered in the plain.) This chief took a particular liking for us, and seemed determined to save us from the destructive vengeance of his people. He prepared a comfortable lodge for our own accommodation, in which we slept and eat. We remained in this situation two days and part of the third night, without anything to disturb us—during which time the Crow prisoners had many questions to ask about their own people. They appeared to be well treated, but notwithstanding they were anxious to make their escape. About midnight of the third night, our friendly chief, who slept with us every night, awoke us all, and told us the horrors of our situation. He said that he had a great many bad men among his followers, and that he was unable to appease their angry nature much longer—the red man thirsts for blood—that he had succeeded in saving us thus far, through much exertion—& that now, as the whole village was wrapt in slumber, it would be a fit time for us to escape. He gave us strict orders to travel with all speed, and not to slacken our pace for two days and nights, for he said as soon as our departure would be known, we would be pursued. When our horses were brought out and all things was ready, we were escorted by the chief until daylight, when he left us and returned—manifesting the most intense anxiety for our safety. Indeed we were loth to part with this kind man, for we felt as if we were indebted to him for our lives.

After parting with the chief, we pursued our journey with great speed, until the evening of the second day, when we were obliged to stop by a snow storm, which threatened us with destruction. We here turned our panting horses loose to graze, and made preparations to pass the night—which we did undisturbed. In the morning, two of the horses were not to be found. All search was in vain, and we gave them up for lost—concluding that they had fell into the hands of our enemies, and if so, we had better be on the move, as they were doubtless close at hand; but the owner, not being satisfied, again started out.— This detained us a while longer, when, apprehending danger from the Indians, we fired two guns as a signal for him that we were going, if he was yet in hearing. We resumed our journey, and after travelling a few miles, halted for the straggler—but he never returned. or ten years since, Mr. Mackenzie[16] took a chief from three different nations (one of which was a Rickaree,) to Washington city, and while taking them back to their native wilds through Virginia, the Rickaree chief took sick and died in the city of Richmond. Mackenzie returned with the other two, Asnaboin and Mandan.

While passing the Rickaree village, (which was then situated on the Missouri River, from whence they have since removed to this country,) Mackenzie stopped and informed them of the fate of their chief—which they disbelieved, and immediately declared war against the whites. They were much enraged, and made a violent attack upon the boats containing the merchandise of Mr. Mackenzie—a great part

16. This name has heretofore been printed Mackinny—by mistake.—(Note in original.)

of which they destroyed, and have since been the cause of the death of numbers of white men.

April 10th. Having lost all hope of being rejoined by our lost man, who we concluded had been captured by the Indians, we resumed our journey with 14 men.—Beaver we found in abundance—catching more or less every day, and everything seemed to promise a profitable business, until the 7th day of May—a day which will ever be remembered by each of us. Having encamped the night previous on a small creek in the Black Hills, or on the head waters of the river Platte, without timber or any thing to shelter ourselves, in case of an attack by the Indians, within 80 or 100 yards. We this evening again turned our horses loose to graze, which is not by any means customary and much less prudent, while travelling through a country infested with hostile savages, as they are always hovering around the encampment, ready to lay hands on any thing which they fancy. But on the present occasion we thought ourselves secure, as we had not seen nor met with any Indians for several days.

On the following morning our horses were in sight on a hill a little above the encampment. About 9 o'clock three of us started to bring them down preparatory to our start. As there was no danger apprehended, neither of us took our guns. When we got to the top of the hill the horses were not to be seen—having descended the hill on the other side. The other two men soon found their horses and started with them to camp.—After searching a while I found mine with several others. The horses appeared much frightened, and I began to apprehend some danger. Whilst leading my horse towards the camp, an Indian, armed with a bow and arrow, came rushing upon me.—I made several attempts to mount, but as often failed, for as I would spring to get on he would jump from under me. The savage now approached within about fifteen steps of me, and signified that he would slay me unless I stopped and delivered up my horse. I sprang behind a bunch of bushes, which afforded me a tolerable shelter. He then made signs to me that if I would deliver myself up he would not hurt me. But this I refused.

My only weapon was a large knife, which I carried in a scabbard at my waist. I drew this out and proposed to meet him. He then gave me to understand, that if I would lay down the knife he would lay down the bow and arrow, and we would meet and be friends. This I also refused to do.—He made use of various inducements to get me from

273

behind the bush, but I heeded them not, for I knew his intention was to kill me if it was in his power. He still advanced slowly toward me. I had been in several dangerous situations with the Indians and wild beasts,—in some of which I had almost despaired. But none seemed to cause the same feeling as did my present predicament. Alone, and unarmed—my situation was distressing indeed.

I had no chance of escaping, and an immediate and cruel death I knew would be my fate if I surrendered. Whilst reflecting on what to do, and looking at him through an aperture in the bush, he shot an arrow at me, which fortunately missed its aim, and struck a branch within a few inches of my face, and fell harmless to the ground. By this time he had got quite close and being below me on the hill side, the thought struck me that I might despatch him with a stone—for which purpose I stooped down to get one, and carelessly let my body move from the shelter afforded by the brush, and at that instant I felt the pointed arrow pierce my side.

I jerked the weapon out immediately, and started to run, still holding to my horse. I expected every moment as I ran quartering past the Indian to receive another, which I most certainly would have done, if the savage had been in the possession of any more; and to run to the brush for those he had already discharged at me, would only be giving me time to escape. He then pursued me. After running a short distance I thought that my horse might be the means of saving my life, if I would leave him for the Indian, and accordingly I released my hold; but the Indian disregarded the horse and followed me.

By this time, owing to the loss of blood from my wound, and the great excitement I was under, I began to grow weak and faint, for I thought that every moment would be my last, as I heard the Indian puffing and blowing in my rear. We were now within sight of our camp, and were fortunately discovered the men then there, who immediately ran to my relief. When I seen the face of my companions, I lost all my strength and fell prostrate to the ground. The Indian, foiled in his design on my life, retreated for the purpose of making sure of my horse, but in this he was also mistaken, for in turn he was pursued by my companions as hotly as he had chased me. When my mind again resumed its sway, I found myself in the camp carefully attended by my companions.

On entering into conversation with my companions, I found that I was not the only one who had encountered the Indians. I was ignorant of any more Indians being in the neighbourhood than the one above alluded to, but it appeared by their story that, when the two men who started out with me, were returning with the horses, they came across a large body of Indians, supposed to be about 200, who, after a sharp engagement, in which one of our men, named Gillam, of Illinois, was killed, and two wounded, succeeded in taking all our horses except two.

Whilst I was listening to this lamentable story, our spies came running to the camp, bringing the unwelcome tidings that the Indians were again approaching with great speed, determined to ride over us. Each man now gathered a robe, blanket, guns, and such things as he could not do without, and carried the wounded into the brush at the foot of the hill, where we immediately commenced building a fort.

The Indians approached and surrounded our encampment very cautiously, thinking that they would take us by surprise, and capture man, beast and baggage without any difficulty—but they were outrageous when they found that there was no body at home. They made the best of their victory however, and took every thing we had left.— When they had completed the pillage, which was only done when they could no longer find anything on which to lay their hands, they started off with their booty.—After they had travelled some distance they halted and collected in a circle, within plain view of where we were, and smoked to the Sun, or Great Spirit. While going through this ceremony, some of them happened to discover us.

On this, they quit smoking, left their horses and came on foot within 30 or 40 steps of us,—but on seeing our fort, which was only partly built, they turned away and left us, without making any attack. We remained in this situation until morning—those who were able, being occupied in completing our fort. Soon after daylight the Indians again made their appearance, and approached within a stones throw of the fort, and on reconnoitring our situation they concluded that we were too well defended for them to gain any advantage over us,—and the second time they left us without giving us a chance of trying our strength.

This morning I felt very weak and feeble from my wound, and began to fear that it was more serious than was at first supposed. About 10 o'clock the company was ready for the move, and I was packed between two horses. After travelling two or three miles we halted to rest near some brush—but not without having sentinels stationed for the purpose of keeping a vigilant look-out, for we still expected an attack from the Indians. Not long after we halted our sentinels informed us that the savages were again approaching. We immediately went into the brush and commenced throwing up a fort. They this time approached very cautiously, and seemed determined to put an end to our lives. When they observed that we were defended by a breast work, they halted, reconnoitred on every side, and finally gave up and left us. These Indians who had hung round our path so long, robbed us of so much necessary property, killed one and wounded three of us, and came so nigh exterminating our whole company, we found out, belonged to the Rickaree tribe—the same who frightened us in the sink hole, on Platte River.

It was now that we had leisure to contemplate our situation. Some of us had laboured hard, encountered one danger only to be eclipsed by another. We had at times endured the most excruciating suffering from hunger and fatigue—living in constant communion with the terrors of a wilderness studded with savages and no less dangerous beasts of prey, for two long years, and now left destitute of every thing except an old greasy blanket, a rifle and a few loads of ammunition, some thousands of miles from our paternal homes. To reflect on our present situation was enough to fill every heart with all the horrors of remorse. In fact, we felt a disposition about this time to do that which would not have been right, had an opportunity afforded.

When we first embarked in this business it was with the expectation that to ensure a fortune in the fur trade only required a little perseverance and industry. We were not told that we were to be constantly annoyed by the Indians, but that it only required the observance of a peaceful disposition on our part, to secure their friendship and even support. Some of the Indians with whom we had intercourse, it is true, had been of great advantage to us in our trapping expeditions; but then it would be of short duration,—for, if they would not render themselves obnoxious by their own treachery, our friendship with them would be sure to meet with an interruption through some ingenious artifice of a neighbouring jealous tribe. Such had been the life we had led, and such the reward.[17]

Our situation was not at all suited for sober calculation. Some ap-

---

17. Such has been the experience not only of Leonard but of a great majority of the free trappers in the mountains. A large number of those who were so fortunate as to escape the Indians and the dangers of the mountains, were sure to fall victims to the heartless traders, who were sure to secure the furs for but little more than the Indians paid when they robbed the trappers. Between the hostile Indians and the wily trader the poor trapper was Indeed to be pitied. He was truly between "*the devil and the deep sea.*"

peared altogether careless what would become of them—seeming to have a willingness to turn in with and live the life of a savage, some two or three were anxious to leave the wilderness and return to the States as empty as when we left them. But this was rejected by nearly all, for we still had a distant hope of having better luck.

Some of our men were acquainted with the situation of the rendezvous of a company of traders on the headwaters of the Colorado,[18] trading under the firm of B. L. E. Bowville, and Co. and it was proposed to start for this post immediately. After much debate and persuasion, it was agreed that we should make the attempt. We got every thing ready—the wounded having entirely recovered—and started on our long and tedious journey. As we travelled along we killed plenty of various kinds of game—met with nothing to interrupt our journey, and on the 25th of July arrived at the camp of Bowville, which at this time consisted of 195 men, together with a small company belonging to Mackenzie, from the Missouri River, of 60 men. We were well received by these men, most of whom had been in the woods for several years, and experienced many hardships and privations, similar to what we had suffered. They seemed to sympathize with us about our loss, and all appeared anxious that we should turn in with them and restore our lost fortunes.

After we had become thoroughly rested from the fatigue of our long tramp to this post, most of our men hired in different ways with this company. These men had been engaged in trapping in the vicinity of this rendezvous for a long time, and had caught nearly all the beaver, and were thinking about moving to some other section of country. There was a large tract of land laying to the South West of this, extending to the Columbia River on the North, and to the Pacific ocean and Gulph of California on the West and South, which was said to abound with beaver, and otherwise suited as a trading country. As our company was now very large, the officers concluded on dividing it into three divisions. Accordingly Captain Bowville was left here with a considerable force to watch the movements of the Indians, and to do what he could at trapping, as this had been a great harbour for beaver, it was thought that there might be still some more to be caught. A Mr. Cerren, with a few men was sent back to St. Lewis, with 4000 lbs. of beaver fur, with instructions to return and meet Captain Bowville at the Great Salt Lake in the following summer, with a supply of provisions to do the company, for the two following years.

18. The headwaters of Green River, and is really the source of the Colorado.

MICHEL SYLVESTRE CERRE

The other division, under the command of a Mr. Walker, was ordered to steer through an unknown country, towards the Pacific, and if he did not find beaver, he should return to the Great S. L. in the following summer. Mr. Walker was a man well calculated to undertake a business of this kind. He was well hardened to the hardships of the wilderness—understood the character of the Indians very well—was kind and affable to his men, but at the same time at liberty to command without giving offence,—and to explore unknown regions was his chief delight. I was anxious to go to the coast of the Pacific, and for that purpose hired with Mr. Walker as clerk, for a certain sum per year, (Nidever also joined Walker's party). The 20th of Aug. (should be July 24th), was fixed as the day for each company to take its departure.

When the day arrived everything was in readiness,—each man provided with four horses, and an equal share of blankets, buffalo robes, provisions, and every article necessary for the comfort of men engaged in an expedition of this kind. As we travelled along each man appeared in better spirits, and more lively than on any other similar occasion,—and I sometimes thought that we were now on an expedition from which we would realise some profit. On the fourth day of our journey we arrived at the huts of some Bawnack Indians. These Indians appear to live very poor and in the most forlorn condition. They generally make but one visit to the buffalo country during the year, where they remain until they jirk as much meat as their females can lug home on their backs. They then quit the mountains and return to the plains, where they subsist on fish and small game the remainder of the year. They keep no horses, and are always an easy prey for other Indians provided with guns and horses.

On telling these Indians the route we intended to take, they told us we must provide ourselves with meat enough to subsist upon for many days—which we found to be very good advice. We now set to work laying in a stock of provision, and in a few days each man was provided with about 60 pounds of substantial meat, which was packed upon our horses, and we set sail in good cheer.

On the 4th of September we killed our last buffalo on the West side of the Salt Lake. We still continued along the margin of the Lake, with the intention of leaving it when we got to the extreme west side of it. About the 12th we found the country very poor, and almost without game, except goats and some few rabbits.

On the 13th we left the lake and took a westerly course into the most extensive and barren plains I ever seen. This day we came to a spring, where we found some Indians encamped, who were on their way up to the buffalo country, to lay in their winters supply of meat. These Indians appear to be more wealthy, and exercise more ingenuity in providing for themselves than those we had met with a few days ago. They have paths beat from one spring or hole of water to another, and by observing these paths, they told us, we would be enabled to find water without much trouble.

The chief of this tribe, further told us, that after travelling so many days South-west, (the course we were now about to take,) we would come to a high mountain which was covered with snow at the top the whole year round, and on each side of which we would find a large river to head, and descend into the sandy plains below, forming innumerable small lakes, and sinks into the earth and disappears. Some distance further down these plains, he said, we would come to another mountain, much larger than the first, which he had never been across. In all this space, he said, there was no game; but that near this latter mountain we would come across a tribe of poor Indians, whom he supposed would not be friendly.

On the next morning we left these Indians, and pursued our course North-west. Our men, who were in such fine spirits when we left the rendezvous, began to show symptoms of fatigue, and were no longer so full of sport. We travelled along these paths according to the directions of the Indians, now and then meeting with a few straggling natives, who were in a manner naked, on the trail of the main body to the buffalo country.—Some of these straggling Indians showed us some lumps of salt, which was the most white, clear and beautiful I ever seen.

On the 30th we arrived at a considerable hill, which, in appearance, is similar to a smooth rock,—where we encamped for the night, and let our horses loose to graze—which we thought might now be done with safety, as we were no longer beset by the murderous Rickarees. While laying about resting ourselves, some of the men observed the horses very eagerly licking the stones which lay on the surface of the ground, near the spring. This circumstance caused the men to examine the stones, which we found to be salt, and had been carried here from the hill by the Indians. Their surface was covered with moss or rust, but on breaking them, or rubbing off the rust, the salt is seen in its purity. This hill runs north and south, and is from one to three miles across, and produces no kind of vegetation, whatever except a little grass which grows in holes or gutters around its base, formed by water descending from the hill during the rainy season. This country appeared the most like a desert of any I had yet seen. It is so dry and sandy that there is scarcely any vegetation to be found—not even a spear of grass, except around the springs. The water in some of these springs, too, is so salt that it is impossible to drink it. The Indians say that it never rains, only in the spring of the year. Everything here seems to declare that, here man shall not dwell.

After travelling a few days longer through these barren plains; we came to the mountain described by the Indian as having its peak covered with snow. It presents a most singular appearance—being entirely unconnected with any other chain. It is surrounded on either side by level plains, and rises abruptly to a great height, rugged, and hard to ascend. To take a view of the surrounding country from this mountain, the eye meets with nothing but a smooth, sandy, level plain. On the whole, this mountain may be set down as one of the most remarkable phenomenas of nature. Its top is covered with the pinone (pinon) tree, bearing a kind of must, which the natives are very fond of, and which they collect for winter provision. This hill is nearly round, and looks like a hill or mound, such as may be met with in the prairies on the east side of the mountain.

Not far from our encampment we found the source of the river mentioned by the Indian, (headwaters of the Humboldt or Mary's River). After we all got tired gazing at this mountain and the adjacent curiosities, we left it and followed down the river, in order to find water and grass for our horses. On this stream we found old signs of beaver, and we supposed that, as game was scarce in this country, the Indians had caught them for provision. The natives which we occasionally met with, still continued to be of the most poor and dejected kind—being entirely naked and very filthy. We came to the hut of one of these Indians who happened to have a considerable quantity of fur collected.—At this hut we obtained a large robe composed of beaver skins fastened together, in exchange for two awls and one fish hook. This robe was worth from 30 to 40 dollars. We continued travelling down this river, now and then catching a few beaver. But, as we continued to extend our acquaintance with the natives, they began to practice their national failing of stealing.

So eager were they to possess themselves of our traps, that we were forced to quit trapping in this vicinity and make for some other quarter. The great annoyance we sustained in this respect greatly displeased some of our men, and they were for taking vengeance before we left the country—but this was not the disposition of Captain Walker. These discontents being out hunting one day, fell in with a few Indians, two or three of whom they killed, and then returned to camp, not daring to let the captain know it. The next day while hunting, they repeated the same violation—but this time not quite so successful, for the captain found it out, and immediately took measures for its effectual suppression.

At this place, all the branches of this stream is collected from the mountain into the main channel, which forms quite a large stream; and to which we gave the name of Barren River—a name which we thought would be quite appropriate, as the country, natives and every thing belonging to it, justly deserves the name.—You may travel for many days on the banks of this river, without finding a stick large enough to make a walking cane.—While we were on its margin, we were compelled to do without fire, unless we chanced to come across some drift that had collected together on the beach. As we proceeded down the river we found that the trails of the Indians began to look as if their numbers were increasing, ever since our men had killed some of their brethren. The further we descended the river, the more promising the country began to appear, although it still retained its dry, sandy nature. We had now arrived within view of a cluster of hills or mounds, which presented the appearance, from a distance, of a number of beautiful cities Built up together. Here we had the pleasure of seeing timber, which grew in very sparing quantities some places along the river beach.

On the 4th of September[19] we arrived at some lakes, formed by this river, which we supposed to be those mentioned by the Indian chief whom we met at the Great Salt Lake. Here the country is low and swampy, producing an abundance of very fine grass—which was very acceptable to our horses, as it was the first good grazing they had been in for a long time—and here, on the borders of one of these lakes, we encamped, for the purpose of spending the night, and letting our horses have their satisfaction. A little before sunset, on taking a view of the surrounding waste with a spy-glass, we discovered smoke issuing from the high grass in every direction. This was sufficient to

19. Leonard's dates are completely confused; he mentions before this that the last buffalo was killed on the 4th of September just west of Salt Lake; here he says that they are at the lakes along the Barren River on the 4th of September after travelling a month; and later he mentions that the last buffalo was killed on the 4th of August, which is probably correct and corresponds to the time they left Green River rendezvous.

convince us that we were in the midst of a large body of Indians; but as we could see no timber to go to, we concluded that it would be as well to remain in our present situation, and defend ourselves as well as we could.

We readily guessed that these Indians were in arms to revenge the death of those which our men had killed up the river; and if they could succeed in getting any advantage over us, we had no expectation that they would give us any quarter. Our first care, therefore, was to secure our horses, which we did by fastening them all together, and then hitching them to pickets drove into the ground. This done, we commenced constructing something for our own safety. The lake was immediately in our rear, and piling up all our baggage in front, we had quite a substantial breast work—which would have been as impregnable to the Indians arrow, as were the cotton-bags to the British bullets at New Orleans in 1815.

Before we had got everything completed, however, the Indians issued from their hiding places in the grass, to the number, as near as I could guess, of 800 or 900, and marched straight towards us, dancing and singing in the greatest glee. When within about 150 yards of us, they all sat down on the ground, and despatched five of their chiefs to our camp to inquire whether their people might come in and smoke with us. This request Captain Walker very prudently refused, as they evidently had no good intentions, but told them that he was willing to meet them half way between our breast work, and where their people were then sitting. This appeared to displease them very much, and they went back not the least bit pleased with the reception they had met with.

After the five deputies related the result of their visit to their constituents, a part of them rose up and signed to us,[20] (which was the only mode of communication with them) that they were coming to our camp. At this 10 or 12 of our men mounted the breast work and made signs to them that if they advanced a step further it was at the peril of their lives. They wanted to know in what way we would do it. Our guns were exhibited as the weapons of death. This they seemed to discredit and only laughed at us. They then wanted to see what effect our guns would have on some ducks that were then swimming in the lake, not far from the shore. We then fired at the ducks—thinking by this means to strike terror into the savages and drive them away. The ducks were killed, which astonished the Indians a good deal, though

20. They probably used the sign language with which all Indians are familiar.

not so much as the noise of the guns—which caused them to fall flat to the ground. After this they put up a beaver skin on a bank for us to shoot at for their gratification—when they left us for the night. This night we stationed a strong guard, but no Indians made their appearance, and were permitted to pass the night in pleasant dreams.

Early in the morning we resumed our journey along the lakes, without seeing any signs of the Indians until after sunrise, when we discovered them issuing from the high grass in front, rear, and on either side of us. This created great alarm among our men, at first, as we thought they had surrounded us on purpose, but it appeared that we had only *happened* amongst them, and they were as much frightened as us. From this we turned our course from the border of the lake into the plain. We had not travelled far until the Indians began to move after us—first in small numbers, but presently in large companies.— They did not approach near until we had travelled in this way for several hours, when they began to send small parties in advance, who would solicit us most earnestly to stop and smoke with them.

After they had repeated this several times, we began to understand their motive—which was to detain us in order to let their whole force come up and surround us, or to get into close quarters with us, when their bows and arrows would be as fatal and more effective then our firearms. We now began to be a little stern with them, and gave them to understand, that if they continued to trouble us, they would do it at their own risk. In this manner we were teased until a party of 80 or 100 came forward, who appeared more saucy and bold than any others. This greatly excited Captain Walker, who was naturally of a very cool temperament, and he gave orders for the charge, saying that there was nothing equal to a good start in such a case. This was sufficient.

A number of our men had never been engaged in any fighting with the Indians, and were anxious to try their skill. When our commander gave his consent to chastise these Indians, and give them an idea of our strength, 32 of us dismounted and prepared ourselves to give a severe blow. We tied our extra horses to some shrubs and left them with the main body of our company, and then selected each a choice steed, mounted and surrounded this party of Indians. We closed in on them and fired, leaving thirty-nine, (Nidever says thirty-three), dead on the field—which was nearly the half—the remainder were overwhelmed with dismay—running into the high grass in every direction, howling in the most lamentable manner.

Captain Walker then gave orders to some of the men to take the

Captain Joseph Reddeford Walker

bows of the fallen Indians and put the wounded out of misery. The severity with which we dealt with these Indians may be revolting to the heart of the philanthropist; but the circumstances of the case altogether atones for the cruelty. It must be borne in mind, that we were far removed from the hope of any succour in case we were surrounded, and that the country we were in was swarming with hostile savages, sufficiently numerous to devour us. Our object was to strike a decisive blow. This we did—even to a greater extent than we had intended.

These Indians [21] (Pia-utes or Root Diggers sometimes called Snake Indians), are totally naked—both male and female—with the exception of a shield of grass, which they wear around their loins. They are generally small and weak, and some of them very hairy. They subsist upon grass-seed, frogs, fish, &c.—Fish, however, are very scarce—their manner of catching which, is somewhat novel and singular. They take the leg-bone of a sandhill crane, which is generally about 18 inches long, this is fastened in the end of a pole—they then, by means of a raft made of rushes, which are very plenty—float along the surface of these lakes, and spear the fish. They exhibit great dexterity with this simple structure—sometimes killing a fish with it at a great distance. They also have a kind of hook by which they sometimes are very successful, but it does not afford them as much sport as the spear. This hook is formed of a small bone, ground down on a sand-stone, and a double beard cut in it With a flint—they then have a line made of wild flax. This line is tied nearest the beard end of the hook, by pulling the line the sharp end with the beard, catches, and turns the bone crossways in its mouth.

These lakes are all joined together by means of the river which passes from one to another, until it reaches the largest, (Humboldt), which has no outlet. The water in this lake becomes stagnant and very disagreeable—its surface being covered with a green substance, similar to a stagnant frog-pond. In warm weather there is a fly, about the size and similar to a grain of wheat, on this lake, in great numbers.— When the wind rolls the waters onto the shore, these flies are left on the beach—the female Indians then carefully gather them into baskets made of willow branches, and lay them exposed to the sun until they become perfectly dry, when they are laid away for winter provender. These flies, together with grass seed, and a few rabbits, is their principal food during the winter season.

---

21. Pia-utes or Root Diggers (Diggers) sometimes called Snake Indians.

Their habitations are formed of a round hole dug in the ground, over which sticks are placed, giving it the shape of a potato hole—this is covered with grass and earth—the door at one side and the fire at the other. They cook in a pot made of stiff mud, which they lay upon the fire and burn; but from the sandy nature of the mud, after cooking a few times, it falls to pieces, when they make a new one.

The Indians call themselves Shoshocoes; and the lakes have been named Battle Lakes.

On the 10th of October we left these Indians and built rafts out of rushes to convey us across the river, when we left the Lakes and continued our course in the direction of a large mountain, which was in sight, and which we could see was covered with snow on the summit. In the evening we encamped on the margin of a large lake formed by a river which heads in this mountain. This lake, likewise, has no outlet for the water, except that which sinks into the ground. The water in this lake is similar to lie, and tastes much like pearlash, (probably Carson Lake with its alkali waters). If this river was in the vicinity of some city, it would be of inestimable value, as it is admirably calculated to wash clothes without soap, and no doubt could be appropriated to many valuable uses.

There is also a great quantity of pumice stone floating on the surface of the water, and the shore is covered with them. The next day we travelled up this river towards the mountain, where we encamped for the night. This mountain is very high, as the snow extends down the side nearly halfway—the mountain runs North and South. In the morning we despatched hunters to the mountain on search of game and also to look out for a pass over the mountain, as our provisions were getting scarce—our dried buffalo meat being almost done.

After prowling about all day, our hunters returned in the evening, bringing the unwelcome tidings that they had not seen any signs of game in all their ramblings, and what was equally discouraging, that they had seen no practicable place for crossing the mountain. They, however, had with them a young colt and camel, (?error?) which they secured by the natives taking fright and running off, when the hunters came in sight. The next morning, having eaten the last of our dried buffalo meat, it was decided that the colt should be killed and divided equally to each man.

Our situation was growing worse every hour, and something required to be done to extricate ourselves. Our horses were reduced very much from the fatigues of our journey and light food, having travelled through a poor, sandy country extending from the buffalo country of the Rocky Mountains, to our present encampment, a distance of about 1200 miles, without encountering a single hill of any consequence, (with the exception of the one in which Barren River heads, and that we went around,) and so poor and bare that nothing can subsist on it with the exception of rabbits—these being the only game we had met with since we had left the buffalo country, with the exception of one or two antelopes. Notwithstanding these plains forbids the support of animals of every description, yet I do not believe that we passed a single day without seeing Indians, or fresh signs, and some days hundreds of them.

Today we sent out several scouting parties to search out a pass over the mountain. Captain Walker, Nidever and myself started out together. After getting part of the way up the mountain we. came to a grove of timber, where the mountain was too steep for our horses, and we left them, and travelled on foot. Nidever was separated from us, when two Indians made their appearance, but as soon as they saw us, they took to flight and run directly towards Nidever, who at once supposed they had been committing some mischief with us, fired, and, as they were running one behind the other, killed them both at one shot. After this unpleasant circumstance we went back to our horses, and from thence to camp. Mr. Nidever was very sorry when he discovered what he had done. In the evening the balance of our scouting parties returned, but none of them had killed any game. One of them had found an Indian path, which they thought led over the mountain—whereupon it was resolved that in the morning we would take this path, as it seemed to be our only prospect of preservation.

Accordingly, at an early hour the next morning we started on our journey along the foot of the mountain in search of the path discovered on the previous day, and found it. On examination we found that horses travelled it, and must of course come from the west. This gave us great encouragement, as we were very fearful we would not be able to get our horses over at all. Here we encamped for the night. In the morning we started on our toilsome journey. Ascending the mountain we found to be very difficult from the rocks and its steepness. This day we made but poor speed, and encamped on the side of the mountain.

Oct. 16. Continued our course until in the afternoon, when we arrived at what we took for the top, where we again encamped, but without anything to eat for our horses, as the ground was covered with a deep snow, which from appearance, lays on the North side of the peaks, the whole year around. These peaks are generally covered with rocks and sand,—totally incapable of vegetation; except on the South side, where grows a kind of Juniper or Gin shrub, bearing a berry tasting similar to gin. Here we passed the night without anything to eat except these gin berries, and some of the insects from the lake described above, which our men had got from the Indians. We had not suffered much from cold for several months previous to this; but this night, surrounded as we were with the everlasting snows on the summit of this mountain, the cold was felt with three fold severity.

In taking a view the next morning of the extensive plains through which we had travelled, its appearance is awfully sublime. As far as the eye can reach, you can see nothing but an unbroken level, tiresome to the eye to behold. To the east the aspect is truly wonderful. The sight meets with nothing but a poor sandy plain, extending from the base of the Rocky Mountains to the level below—interposed with several rivers winding their way, here and there forming innumerable lakes, having their margins thinly adorned with a few withering and fading Cottonwood trees—where the water ceases to flow, and sinks into the sand. But this is not all. The rivers which head in this mountain, all lead towards the east, as if to meet those from the Rocky Mountains, and likewise empty into the lakes. The next morning it was with no cheerful prospect that each man prepared himself for travelling, as we had nothing to eat worth mentioning.

As we advanced, in the hollows sometimes we would encounter prodigious quantities of snow. When we would come to such places, a certain portion of the men would be appointed alternately to go forward and break the road, to enable our horses to get through; and if any of the horses would get swamped, these same men were to get them out. In this tedious and tiresome manner we spent the whole day without going more than 8 or 10 miles. In some of these ravines where the snow is drifted from the peaks, it never entirely melts, and may be found at this season of the year, from ten to one hundred feet deep. From appearance it never melts on the top, but in warm weather the heap sinks by that part melting which lays next the ground. This day's travel was very severe on our horses, as they had not a particle to eat. They began to grow stupid and stiff, and we began to despair of getting them over the mountain.

We encamped this night on the south side of one of these peaks or ridges without anything to eat, and almost without fire. To add to the troubles and fatigues which we encountered in the day time, in getting over the rocks and through the snow, we had the mortification this evening to find that some of our men had become almost unmanageable, and were desirous of turning back and retracing our steps to the buffalo country! The voice of the majority, which always directs the movements of such a company, would not pacify them; nor had the earnest appeals of our captain any effect. The distance was too great for them to undertake without being well provided, and the only way they could be prevented, was by not letting them have any of the horses or ammunition.

Two of our horses were so much reduced that it was thought they would not be able to travel in the morning at all, whereupon it was agreed that they should be butchered for the use of the men. This gave our men fresh courage, and we went to bed this night in better spirits than we had done for a long time. Some of the men had fasted so long, and were so much in want of nourishment, that they did not know when they had satisfied the demands of nature, and eat as much and as eagerly of this black, tough, lean, horse flesh, as if it had been the choicest piece of beef steak.

In the meaning, after freely partaking of the horse meat, and sharing the remainder to each man, we renewed our journey, now and then coming onto an Indian path, but as they did not lead in the direction we were going, we did not follow them—but the most of the distance we this day travelled, we had to encounter hills, rocks and deep snows. The snow in most of the hollows we this day passed through, looks as if it had remained here all summer, as eight or ten inches from the top it was packed close and firm—the top being loose and light, having fell only a day or two previous. About the middle of the afternoon we arrived at a small lake or pond, where we concluded to encamp, as at this pond we found a small quantity of very indifferent grass, but which our horses cropped off with great eagerness. Here we spent the night, having yet seen nothing to create a hope that we had arrived near the opposite side of the mountain—and what was equally as melancholy, having yet discovered no signs of game.

The next morning we resumed our labour, fortunately finding less snow and more timber, besides a number of small lakes, and some prospect of getting into a country that produced some kind of vegetation. The timber is principally pine, cedar and red wood, mostly of a scrubby and knotty quality. After travelling a few miles further however, than any other day since we had reached the top of the mountain, we again encamped on the margin of another small lake, where we also had the good fortune to find some pasture for our horses. This evening it was again decided to kill three more of our horses which had grown entirely worthless from severe travelling and little food. The next morning several parties were despatched on search of a pass over the mountain, and to make search for game; but they all returned in the evening without finding either.

The prospect at this time began to grow somewhat gloomy and threaten us with hard times again. We were at a complete stand. No one was acquainted with the country, nor no person knew how wide the summit of this mountain was.—We had travelled for five days since we arrived at what we supposed to be the summit—were now still surrounded with snow and rugged peaks—the vigour of every man almost exhausted—nothing to give our poor horses, which were no longer any assistance to us in travelling, but a burthen, for we had to help the most of them along as we would an old and feeble man.

This mountain must be near as high as the main chain of the Rocky Mountains[22]—at least a person would judge so from the vast quantity of snow with which it is covered, and the coldness of the air. The descent from the Rocky Mountains to this is but trifling, and supposed by all the company not to be greater than we had ascended this mountain from the plain—though we had no means of ascertaining the fact. It is true, however, that the vast plain through which we had travelled was almost perfectly level, on part of which the water gradually descended to the west, and on the other towards the east.

Our situation was growing more distressing every hour, and all we now thought of, was to extricate ourselves from this inhospitable region; and, as we were perfectly aware, that to travel on foot was the only way of succeeding, we spent no time in idleness—scarcely stopping in our journey to view an occasional specimen of the wonders of nature's handiwork. We travelled a few miles every day, still on the top of the mountain, and our course continually obstructed with snow hills and rocks. Here we began to encounter in our path, many small streams which would shoot out from under these high snowbanks, and after running a short distance in deep chasms which they have through ages cut in the rocks, precipitate themselves from one lofty precipice to another, until they are exhausted in rain below.—

22. These are the Sierra Nevada Mountains, or the California Mountain of Leonard, and the Mount Joseph of Jedediah S. Smith.

Some of these precipices appeared to us to be more than a mile high, (*Yosemite Valley?*). Some of the men thought that if we could succeed in descending one of these precipices to the bottom, we might thus work our way into the valley below—but on making several attempts we found it utterly impossible for a man to descend, to say nothing of our horses.

We were then obliged to keep along the top of the dividing ridge between two of these chasms which seemed to lead pretty near in the direction we were going—which was west,—in passing over the mountain, supposing it to run north and south. In this manner we continued until the 25th, without any particular occurrence, except that of our horses dying daily—the flesh of which we preserved for food. Our course was very rough and tiresome, having to encounter one hill of snow and one ledge of rocks after another. On the 25th every man appeared to be more discouraged and down-spirited than ever, and I thought that our situation would soon be beyond hope if no prospect of getting from the mountain would now be discovered. This day we sent out several parties on discoveries, who returned in the evening without bringing the least good news, except one man, who was last coming, having separated from his companions, brought a basket full of acorns to camp.

These were the first acorns we had seen since we left the State of Missouri. These nuts our hunter had got from an Indian who had them on his back travelling as though he was on a journey across the mountain, to the East side.—When the Indian seen our hunter he dropped his basket of provision and run for life. These nuts caused no little rejoicing in our camp, not only on account of their value as food, but because they gave us the gratifying evidence that a country mild and salubrious enough to produce acorns was not far distant, which must be vastly different from any we had passed through for a long time.

We now felt agreeably surprised that we had succeeded so far and so prosperously, in a region of many miles in extent where a native Indian could find nothing to eat in traversing the same route, but acorns. These nuts are quite different from those in Missouri—being much larger and more palatable. They are from 1½ to 3 inches in length, and about ¾ in diameter, and when roasted in the ashes or broiled, are superior to any chesnuts I ever eat—(though a person subsisting upon very lean horse meat for several days is hardly capable of judging with precision in a case of this kind.)

The next morning we resumed our journey somewhat revived with the strong expectation that after a few days more tedious travelling, we would find ourselves in a country producing some kind of game by which we might recruit our languid frames, and pasture to resuscitate the famished condition of our horses. We still found snow in abundance, but our course was not so much obstructed with rocks as formerly. In two or three days we arrived at the brink of the mountain. This at first was a happy sight, but when we approached close, it seemed to be so near perpendicular that it would be folly to attempt a descent. In looking on the plain below with the naked eye, you have one of the most singular prospects in nature; from the great height of the mountain the plain presents a dim yellow appearance;—but on taking a view with the spy glass we found it to be a beautiful plain stretched out towards the west until the horizon presents a barrier to the sight. From the spot where we stood to the plain beneath, must at least be a distance of three miles, as it is almost perpendicular, a person cannot look down without feeling as if he was wafted to and fro in the air, from the giddy height.

A great many were the surmises as to the distance and direction to the nearest point of the Pacific. Captain Walker, who was a man well acquainted with geography, was of the opinion that it was not much further than we could see with the aid of our glass, as the plain had the appearance of a sea shore. Here we encamped for the night, and sent men out to discover some convenient passage down towards the plain—who returned after an absence of a few hours and reported that they had discovered a pass or Indian trail which they thought would answer our purpose, and also some signs of deer and bear, which was equally as joyful news—as we longed to have a taste of some palatable food. The next morning after pursuing our course a few miles along the edge of the mountain top we arrived at the path discovered by our men, and immediately commenced the descent, gladly leaving the cold and famished region of snow behind.

The mountain was extremely steep and difficult to descend, and the only way we could come any speed was by taking a zigzag direction, first climbing along one side and then turning to the other, until we arrived at a ledge or precipice of rocks, of great height, and extending eight or ten miles along the mountain—where we halted and sent men in each direction to ascertain if there was any possibility of getting over this obstruction. In the afternoon of the same day our men returned without finding any safe passage through the rocks—

but one man succeeded in killing a small deer, which he carried all the way to camp on his back—this was dressed, cooked and eat in less time than a hungry wolf would devour a lamb.

This was the first game larger than a rabbit we had killed since the 4th of August, when we killed the last buffalo near the Great Salt Lake, and the first we had eat since our dried meat was exhausted, (being 14 days,) during which time we lived on stale and forbidden horse flesh. I was conscious that it was not such meat as a dog would feast on, but we were driven to extremes and had either to do this or die. It was the most unwholesome as well as the most unpleasant food I ever eat or ever expect to eat—and I hope that no other person will ever be compelled to go through the same. It seemed to be the greatest cruelty to take your rifle, when your horse sinks to the ground from starvation, but still manifests a desire and willingness to follow you, to shoot him in the head and then cut him up and take such parts of their flesh as extreme hunger alone will render it possible for a human being to eat. This we done several times, and it was the only thing that saved us from death. 24 of our horses died since we arrived on top of the mountain—17 of which we eat the best parts.

When our men returned without finding any passage over the rocks, we searched for a place that was as smooth and gradual in the descent as possible, and after finding one we brought our horses, and by fastening ropes round them let them down one at a time without doing them any injury. After we got our horses and baggage all over the rocks we continued our course down the mountain, which still continued very steep and difficult. The circumstance of one of our men killing a deer greatly cheered the languid spirits of our hunters, and after we got safely over the rocks several of the men started out on search of game, although it was then near night. The main body continued on down until we arrived at some green oak bushes, where we encamped for the night, to wait for our hunters,—who returned soon after dark well paid for their labour, having killed two large black tailed deer and a black bear, and all very fat and in good eating order. This night we passed more cheerful and in better heart than any we had spent for a long time. Our meat was dressed and well cooked, and every man felt in good order to partake of it.

In descending the mountain this far we have found but little snow, and began to emerge into a country which had some signs of vegetation—having passed thro' several gloves of green oak bushes, &c. The principal timber which we came across, is Red-Wood, White Cedar and the Balsam tree. We continued down the side of the mountain at our leisure, finding the timber much larger and better, game more abundant and the soil more fertile. Here we found plenty of oak timber, bearing a large quantity of acorns, though of a different kind from those taken from the Indian on the mountain top. In the evening of the 30th we arrived at the foot or base of this mountain—having spent almost a month in crossing over.

Along the base of this mountain it is quite romantic—the soil is very productive—the timber is immensely large and plenty, and game, such as deer, elk, grizzly bear and antelopes are remarkably plenty.— From the mountain out to the plain, a distance varying from 10 to 20 miles, the timber stands as thick as it could grow, and the land is well watered by a number of small streams rising here and there along the mountain. In the last two days travelling we have found some trees of the Red-wood species, incredibly large—some of which would measure from 16 to 18 fathom round the trunk at the height of a man's head from the ground.

On the 31st we pursued our course towards the plain in a western direction.—Now, that we had reached a country thickly filled with almost all kinds of game, our men and particularly those fond of hunting, were in fine spirits. This day our company was much scattered, and we coud hardly tell which was the main body, as the men were stretched over a large space of ground, all moving within each others hearing towards the plain. After a walk of about fifteen miles we arrived at the margin of the woods, where we concluded to spend the remainder of the day and night. When our men all gathered together it was astonishing to see the quantity of game which they had collected—principally deer and bear.

Our hunters complained very much because there was no buffalo here—as killing these animals afford the hunter such fine sport: and they would not believe any thing else than that buffalo inhabited this region until they had made several unsuccessful hunts—as the climate and soil is about the same, the grass equally as good and plenty, and the prairies and forests as extensive as those of the region of the Rocky Mountains. But none of these animals have ever been found west of the Great Salt Lake, which is about three hundred miles west of the summit of the Rocky Mountains.

On the following morning we directed our course across or rather along the plain, until we came to a large river heading in the mountain and wending its way through the plain, this river presents more wonderful curiosities than any other stream we passed. Its bed lays very deep forming very high banks, even in smooth and level parts of the country; but where there is rocks its appearance is beyond doubt the most remarkable of any other water course. Some places the rocks are piled up perpendicular to such a height that a man on top, viewed from the bed of the river, does not look larger than a small child.

From the appearance of these precipices it is not exaggerating to state that they may be found from a quarter to half a mile high—and many of them no wider at the top than at the bottom. Through such places the river forces its way with great rapidity, tossing pitching and foaming to such a degree that no Indian has the courage to attempt to navigate it with his canoe.—When the water passes through these *narrows* it spreads out in a beautiful deep bay as if to repose after its turbulent dashing against the rocks immediately above, until it reaches the next rapids, when it again pitches forward, (Merced River). This plain is well watered and is quite productive, as we found a large quantity of wild pumpkins and wild oats.

This night it was decided that we should forthwith commence trapping for furs and make this expedition as profitable as possible, for, as yet we had spent much time and toil, and lost many horses, without realising any profit whatever—although every man expressed himself fully-compensated for his labour, by the many natural curiosities which we had discovered. According to the arrangements made on the evening previous, we all the next morning commenced travelling down the river at a slow gate, carefully examining for beaver signs, and recruiting our horses, which they had much need of, as we found them to be much more injured in crossing the mountains than we had at first supposed—many of them being sprained and stiffened almost beyond recovery, and certainly beyond present use. We laid up a large supply of deer, elk, and bear meat, of the best kind. These animals are the fattest of the kind I had ever eat. Here we found a large quantity of acorns, such as those taken from the Indian. These acorns compose the principal food of the wild animals in this section,—the bear, I believe, solely subsists upon them, and where acorns are scarce, the game is both poor and scarce.

The country here appears to be in many respects similar to the east side of the Rocky Mountains. The land is generally smooth and level, and the plains or prairies are very extensive, stretching towards the setting sun as far as the eye can reach; whilst a number of beautiful rivers, all heading in this rugged mountain, running parallel with each other thro' the plain, also to the west, with their banks handsomely adorned with flourishing timber of different kinds, such as blackwalnut, hickory. oak, elm, mulbery, hackberry, alder, shoemack, &c. This grove of timber may be found along the river at any point, and generally extends about four miles into the plain. Between this grove of timber, and the forest extending from the foot of the mountain, there is a level prairie of the richest soil, producing grass in abundance of the most delightful and valuable quality.

These prairies are in many places swarming with wild horses, some of which are quite docile, particularly the males, on seeing our horses. They are all very fat, and can be seen of all colors, from spotted or white, to jet black; and here, as in the land of civilization, they are the most beautiful and noble, as well as the most valuable of the whole brute creation.

Since we left the mountain we have seen many signs of Indians, such as *moccasin* tracks, and smoke rising from the prairies in different places, but as yet we had not succeeded in getting in company with any. At this season of the year, when the grass in these plains is dry, if a fire should be started it presents a spectacle truly grand—and if the flame is assisted with a favourable wind, it will advance with such speed that the wild horses and other animals are sometimes puzzled to get out of the road, and every thing looks overwhelmed with consternation. We continued travelling down the river until the 7th of November, when we arrived at five Indian huts, containing 15 or 20 Indians male and female. When they first beheld the approach of beings so mysterious as we were to them, they exhibited the most unbounded alarm and fear.

But it was not long till we succeeded in calming their terror, and convincing them that they had no reason to apprehend any danger, by showing a willingness to smoke, (this being the first token of friendship with all Indians,) which they at once understood and immediately became reconciled, and we commenced gathering all the information from them that our limited means would afford—each being entirely ignorant of the others language, and the Indians being extremely awkward both in making and understanding signs—which is the principal method of conversation with the different tribes in this region. After making many efforts to get some information from them with reference to the Big Water, white people, beaver, &c., without receiving any further satisfaction by way of answer to our inquiries, than a grunt similar to that of a hog, we concluded to spend the night with them for further trial. Towards night whilst passing through their camp, some of our men found two blankets and a knife, which convinced us at once that they had some communication with white people. When the blankets were held up to them they pronounced in tolerable distinctness, the word Spanish, and pointed to the west—from which circumstance we inferred that the Spanish settlement could not be far distant.

The next morning our Indian hosts brought some horses to the camp for the purpose of trading, which were marked with a Spanish brand. After trading for five of the best of their horses, for which we gave one yard of scarlet cloth and two knives; we left these Indians and continued down the river in search of beaver, which are very scarce. These Indians are quite small, and much darker than those of the buffalo country, as well as more indolent and slothful. They generally run naked with the exception of a few, who wear shields made of some kind of skins. Their huts are composed of dry polls or logs set upon end, and their bedding consists of grass. Their food is composed principally of horse meat and acorns—the latter are very large and of a good quality which they manufacture into a kind of mush. Their method of manufacturing this is as follows:—

They go to a large log and build a fire upon it and burn it half or two-thirds of the way through, which is done by keeping the log wet except about a foot in diameter, where the fire is kept up until the hole is deep enough, and of the proper shape. After the hole is burnt deep enough they extinguish the fire, scrape out the coals and ashes, and have a tolerably well shaped *hopper*. When this is done they get a long stone which is rounded at one end, and put the acorns in and commence mashing them fine, which is easily done as they are always previously dried by fire or the sun. The meal thus made is then taken out and mixed with water in a basket made almost watertight—which they broil by making stones red hot and throwing them into the basket. By this process they make a kind of mush with which any hungry man would be glad to satiate his appetite.

These Indians also appear very delicate and feeble—which they attribute to eating acorns. Today, whilst some of our hunters were searching for beaver signs along the river beach, they found the carcases of four Indians, two of which were partly consumed by Grizzly bears. They appeared as if they had died natural deaths, and been laid there by their friends according to their custom of disposing of the dead, as two of them were well wrapped up in beaver skins. This day our course lay through a large prairie covered with wild oats—which at this season of the year when nothing but the stock remains, has much the appearance of common oats.—This plain lays on the South side of the river, to which we gave the name of Oat Plain. The grizzly bear and wild horses appeared more numerous in the country through which we this day passed, than I had ever before known them. In the evening just before sunset we came across the carcase of another Indian, which was also partly eaten by the wild beasts.

From the numerous signs we were led to the belief that the country through which we were now travelling was thickly inhabited with Indians, but notwithstanding we kept watch both night and day we were unable to discover any but those we had left in the morning; nor could we find any of their habitations, although we would sometimes come across a trail that looked as if it was traversed by hundreds at a time. We also discovered some signs of white people, as we would occasionally come across a tree or log chopped with an axe as if done by trappers and hunters. At this place the river is from two to three hundred yards wide, as the country is generally level the water moves gently forward, being quite deep, clear and smooth, (San Joaquin, probably near its mouth).

This night we encamped on the bank of the river in a very beautiful situation. Soon after the men went to rest and the camp had became quieted, we were startled by a loud distant noise similar to that of thunder. Whilst lying close to the ground this noise could be distinctly heard for a considerable length of time without intermission. When it was at first observed some of our men were much alarmed, as they readily supposed it was occasioned by an earthquake, and they began to fear that we would all be swallowed up in the bowels of the earth; and others judged it to be the noise of a neighbouring cataract. Captain Walker, however, suggested a more plausible cause, which allayed the fears of the most timid. He supposed that the noise originated by the Pacific rolling and dashing her boisterous waves against the rocky shore. Had any of us ever before been at the coast, we would have readily accounted for the mysterious noise.

The idea of being within hearing of the *end* of the *Far West* inspired the heart of every member of our company with a patriotic feeling for his country's honour, and all were eager to loose no time until they should behold what they had heard. We felt as if all our previous hardships and privations would be adequately compensated, if we would be spared to return in safety to the homes of our kindred and have it to say that we had stood upon the extreme end of the great west. The two next days we travelled very fast, without meeting with anything to impede our progress. On the night of the 12th our men were again thrown into great consternation by the singular appearance of the heavens. Soon after dark the air appeared to be completely thickened with meteors falling towards the earth, some of which would explode in the air and others would be dashed to pieces on the ground, frightening our horses so much that it required the most active vigilance of the whole company to keep them together. This was altogether a mystery to some of the men who probably had never before seen or heard of anything of the kind, but after an explanation from Captain Walker, they were satisfied that no danger need be apprehended from the falling of the stars, as they were termed.[23]

After travelling a few miles the next morning we arrived at the head of tide water, which convinced us that the noise we had heard a few days previous was created by the ocean. We continued down the river until we arrived at the bay, (northern arm of San Francisco bay), where it mingles its water with the briny ocean. The country here lays very low, and looks as if it was subject to being overflowed. Here we found difficult travelling owing to the ground being wet and swampy. In the vicinity of this bay we found a great many Indians, who were mostly occupied in fishing—which are very plenty. These Indians appeared friendly enough, but then they manifested a kind of careless indifference, whether they treated us well or ill, that we did not like, and we therefore concluded to leave this place and make for the main coast as soon as possible,—and accordingly we started in a southern direction and after travelling a day and a half the broad Pacific burst forth to view on the 20th.

The first night we encamped quite close to the beach near a spring of delightful water. The scenes which we could now contemplate was quite different from those we had beheld and dwelt amidst for months back. Here was a smooth unbroken sheet of water stretched out far beyond the reach of the eye—altogether different from mountains, rocks, snows and the toilsome plains we had traversed. Here we occasionally found the traces of white men, and as the Indians still appeared to act so strange, we began to think that the Spaniards had the Indians under complete subjection, and that they could, if so disposed, set them on

---

23. This is the celebrated meteoric phenomenon which occurred on the night of November 12, 1833, and was observed throughout the whole of the United States, and caused much speculation among the superstitious.

us and give us trouble. It was therefore thought best to find out the whereabouts of the Spaniards and cultivate their friendship. The Indians here practice fishing to a great extent; indeed it seems to be the only thing they do.—They have many methods of catching them—but the principal process is by spearing them with bones made sharp, and some have proper instruments of Spanish manufacture, in which they are very expert.—The principal fish in the river we came down, and which has the principal Indian fisheries, are shad and salmon. We did not find out the name of this tribe, or whether they consider themselves distinct from any other tribe.

Most all of the natives we met with since crossing the last mountain, seem to belong to the same nation, as they were about the same colour and size—spoke the same language for any thing we could discover to the contrary, and all appeared equally ignorant and dilatory—and most of them entirely naked. They have no particular place of residence but claim the whole of the country stretching from the mountain to the seashore as their own. In some parts the natives raise a small quantity of corn, pumpkins, melons, &c., the soil being so very strong and mellow, that it requires but little labour to raise good crops.

21st. This morning the ocean was not so calm as it was the previous evening.—All its sleeping energies were lashed into fury, and the mountain waves of the great deep would roll and dash against the shore, producing the most deafening sound. In the course of the day a detachment of our company was despatched to make discoveries, who returned in the evening and stated that they had discovered many signs of white people, whom they supposed to be Spaniards, but they were unable to come up with them. This same party also found the carcase of a whale which was ninety feet long—the tusks weighing 4½ pounds. About noon of the third day after we arrived here, the attention of the company was directed to an object which could be dimly seen at a distance riding on the water, which was immediately judged to be a ship, but no one knew from whence it came, where it belonged or where going. It was now our curiosity to know more of this singular object and if possible to attract their attention and bring them to shore. Accordingly we fastened two white blankets together and hoisted them into the air on a pole. This had the desired effect.

It was not long until we could tell that the distance between us was fast diminishing, and our joy and surprise may be imagined when we

301

beheld the broad stripes and bright stars of the American flag waiving majestically in the air at the mast head. The ship anchored some distance from the shore and the boats were despatched to see what nation we belonged to, and what our business was. Their astonishment was equally as great as ours when they ascertained that we were children of the same nation of themselves. On making this discovery, and a signal to that effect being given by the boats, the ship fired several salutes of canon in honour of our meeting, which made the welkin ring.—On further acquaintance we ascertained this ship (the *Lagoda*) to belong to Boston, commanded by Captain Baggshaw.

After exchanging civilities by shaking hands all round, Captain Baggshaw strongly insisted on us going on board and partaking of the ships fare, stating that he had a few casks of untapped Coneac, (brandy).. This was an invitation that none of us had the least desire to refuse, and accordingly 45 of us went on board the *Lagoda*, leaving the remainder to take care of the camp, &c. When arriving on the ship Captain B., had a table spread with the choicest of liquors and best fair the ship would afford, which was immediately surrounded with hungry captains, mates, clerks, sailors and greasy trappers—after eating, the glass was passed around in quick succession, first drinking after the fashion of brave Jack Tars, and afterwards in the mountain style, mixed with something of the manners of the natives, in order to amuse the sailors.

After we got on board, the sea became very rough, causing the vessel to pitch and plunge a great deal as she lay at anchor, and consequently I was compelled to return to shore from sea sickness. The balance remained and kept up the celebration until daylight the next morning, when they all returned to land, accompanied by the ships crew to taper off on the harder fare of the trapper and hunter. The feast on the vessel was far superior to anything we could give them, although they appeared perfectly satisfied with the reception they met with from us, as it was a long time since they had tasted any fresh meat, or anything but salted victuals; and theirs was the first bread, butter, cheese, &c., that we had seen for more than two years.

After the feasting was at an end, Captain Baggshaw gave us a description of the country to enable us to lay our plans accordingly. He said the nearest settlement was the town of St. Francisco, about forty miles north of our present encampment, situated on the south side of the Francisco Bay, formed by the river which we descended, which he calls Two Laries or Bush River, (Tulare or San Joaquin River). It is about three-fourths of a mile wide at its mouth, and is considered a safe harbour for almost any quantity of vessels; and within 60 or 70 miles South of us is the town of Monterey, also Spanish, the capital of this province, and which is called Upper California. He also informed us that about 60 or 70 miles north of St. Francisco, and about 100 miles from our present position was a Russian settlement, which consists of about 150 families who settled in this country a few years ago for the purpose of catching sea otter, which are of great value, on account of the quality of the fur. They also cultivate the ground to a considerable extent.

Captain Baggshaw went and examined the carcase of the whale which our men had found, and pronounced it to be the Sperm whale, the oil of which is of the most valuable kind. He supposed it had been washed here when the sea was rough during a storm, and was unable to make its way back over the sand bars. From him we also learned some further particulars concerning the mountain which had caused us so many hardships in crossing, parts of which was visible from the ocean, particularly the snow covered peaks. This he called the California Mountain, as it runs parallel with the coast for a great distance, commencing at the mouth of the Columbia River, and extending along the coast to the mouth of Red River, or Gulf of California, forming a beautiful country from the seashore to the base of the mountain, and extending north and south a distance of about 600 or 700 miles of rich soil, well timbered and abundantly watered by innumerable small streams heading in the mountain and flowing toward the Father of Waters.

Most of this vast waste of territory belongs to the Republic of the United States. What a theme to contemplate its settlement and civilization. Will the jurisdiction of the federal government ever succeed in civilizing the thousands of savages now roaming over these plains, and her hardy freeborn population here plant their homes, build their towns and cities, and say here shall the arts and sciences of civilization take root and flourish? yes, here, even in this remote part of the great west before many years, will these hills and valleys be greeted with the enlivening sound, of the workman's hammer, and the merry whistle of the plough-boy. But this is left undone by the government, and will only be seen when too late to apply the remedy.

The Spaniards are making inroads on the South—the Russians are encroaching with impunity along the sea shore to the North, and further North-east the British are pushing their stations into the very heart of our territory, which, even at this day, more resemble military forts to resist invasion, than trading stations. Our government should be vigilant. She should assert her claim by taking possession of the whole territory as soon as possible—for we have good reason to suppose that the territory *west* of the mountain will some day be equally as important to the nation as that on the *east*.

The next day Captain Baggshaw took leave of us and started out on his trading expedition—appointing Monterey as the point where we were to meet in a few days.

The next morning after the departure of the ship, we were all in readiness to start for Monterey, the capital of the province, which lays in a southern direction. After travelling a few miles along the coast finding it very difficult in consequence of the wet, swampy ground, we found the carcase of another large fish, measuring 47 feet in length, with a horn or sword projecting from its nose 12½ inches long. As travelling so near the water still continued difficult, we here concluded to strike out into the plain, where we found much better walking, the country being quite level, soil rich, and a few Indians. Some of these natives live well, as they cultivate pumpkins, beans, and some of them Indian corn—they also raise an abundance of melons, which grow to an enormous size. But all these Indians still seemed to be very ignorant and stupid.

On the evening of the 22nd November we encamped at some rough hills near a small creek. In this neighbourhood there are a great number of these hills, all of which are well covered with excellent timber, and abounding with all kinds of game except buffalo. The most of our company had become nearly bare footed for want of *moccasins*, as we had wore out every thing of the kind in travelling from the Rocky Mountains—and, as winter was approaching, and no one knowing what kind of a reception we would meet with among the Spaniards, it was advised that we should tarry here and provide ourselves with an abundant winter supply of shoes. Accordingly, our hunters were despatched to scour these hills for the purpose of getting hides to make *moccasins*, &c., when we would be at leisure.

In the evening the hunters all returned to camp, with the tongues of 93 deer and some of the hides, and also of some wild cattle, which are likewise very numerous. They brought the tongues in order to show the number each man had killed. The wild cattle are very timorous, keeping hid pretty much all day and feed at night. They are much wilder than deer, elk, &c. Our hunters brought in some of the choice parts of the cattle they had killed, which was quite fat beef, but it was much inferior to the meat of the buffalo of the Rocky mountains. These cattle incline much to rough and hilly parts of the country, owing, it is supposed, to the Spaniards and Indians hunting them when found in the plains.

23rd. This morning we directed our course across these hills. On arriving at the foot of the hills on the South side, we found one of the horns of these cattle which measured 3½ feet on the outside or bend, and one foot in circumference at the root or thickest part. This we supposed had been the horn of an ox. These cattle are much larger and look better in their wild state than when domesticated. Their horns particularly are much larger than those of our country—but this is probably owing to the softness of the climate; as here there is no winter nor freezing weather. We continued across the plain and arrived on the banks of a small creek which empties into the sea at the distance of 7 or 8 miles, where we encamped for the night. Not long after we had halted, there was eight Spaniards arrived at our camp, from whom we found it as difficult to get information of any kind, as from most of the Indians. All our efforts to make them understand signs was unavailing, and not one of our company understood a word of Spanish.—They were fine portly looking men, but looked as if they had been cast from civilized society as long as ourselves. They remained with us all night.

24th. We set out this morning for Monterey accompanied by the Spaniards as guides, who piloted us to the house of a Mr. Gibroy, (Gilroy), who had been a brave and dutiful tar in his younger days, when he had learned to speak a little English.—From this old man we gathered much useful information as to the country, climate, people, natives, &c. Here we concluded to remain for the night. The old man showed every disposition to give us all the information he could, and treated us very kindly. We ascertained that we were within 35 miles of Monterey. In the morning we started in the direction of Monterey, intending to pass through the town of St. Juan or John which lay in the course we were going.

Here we found the travelling much easier, as we now had some kind of roads to travel on, although they were far from being wagon roads—running through an extensive prairie of rich soil, with here and there a lonely hut built near some grove of timber or brook. Towards evening we arrived at St. Juan, which we now found to be a Spanish Missionary station for the establishment of the Christian religion and civilization among the Indians.

THE OLD MISSION OF SAN JUAN BAUTISTA

Here Captain Walker deemed it prudent to halt for a few days, in order to ascertain the disposition of the people, and make further inquiries with respect to the country, &c., lest we might be considered as intruders and treated in a way that we would not much like. It was our desire to keep on peaceable terms with the Spaniards, at least no one desired to give the least offence of any kind—knowing that Spaniards and Indians had quite a different mode of carrying on a warfare. We obtained privilege from the priests to select a convenient place for grass, wood, water, &c., to pitch our encampment, and immediately commenced erecting a breast work, with which to defend ourselves in case we were attacked by Indians or anything else that chose to molest us. From information gained here, Captain Walker thought it advisable to go no further into their country, or the inhabited parts of it, owing to the difficulty in getting pasture for our horses and provisions for ourselves—as there is no preparations of any kind made for the accommodation of travellers; besides the expense of living would be much less to remain here where game was plenty and grass good.

Today Captain Walker, after getting a passport, which is necessary for a stranger to have in passing from one ward or district to another, and which must be renewed by the *alcalde* or squire in each district, took two men and started for Monterey, where he intended presenting himself to the Governor, and asking the permission of His Excellency to pass the winter in his settlements, and to inform him where we were from, our business, intensions, &c.

St. Juan or St. John is beautifully situated on the banks of a small creek in a rich level plain, about 20 miles from the coast and about the same distance from Monterey, containing from six to seven hundred inhabitants—all of whom are Indians, with the exception of the priests and 15 or 20 people, who are occupied in teaching and instructing these heathens in the ways of religion and truth ; besides giving them instructions in the art of farming and rendering the soil productive— with the hope that they will eventually succeed in. inculcating into the minds of the savages such a knowledge of agriculture as will greatly conduce to the amelioration of the red man's condition.

Their habitations are simple in construction—mostly such as may be found in the wildest parts of the mountains. But those of the missionary establishment are quite different, & plainly show the superiority of the white man over the Indian, both as regards comfort and convenience. This station much resembles a fort or garrison. The part which is called the Church, forms one side or end. The other three sides are divided into different departments like cells, each cell sheltering so many Indians, and covers near half an acre of ground, with the door of each cell opening to the inside.

These buildings are the same as if they were under one roof, with the exception of a gate at each corner of the square. The buildings are constructed of brick, the principal part of which are dried in the sun.—The walls are built thick and strong when built of this kind of brick. For rafters they use poles tolerably well shaped, and for lathing they make use of poles of a smaller size. The roof is generally composed of a kind of cane grass which is carefully laid on the rafters and then covered with earth; for which purpose they generally have the roof nearly flat in order to hold the earth. But the church, or principal building, is built of handsome brick, and is well finished, being covered with tile. For the instruction of these Indians there is four hours of each day devoted to education and prayer, and the balance of the day is occupied in teaching them the rudiments of agriculture and the mechanical arts.

The females are carefully instructed in the art of sewing, and other accomplishments of housewifery. Everything in this station is under the control and management of the priests, who exercise the authority of governor, judge, &c., being privileged to try and condemn all criminal acts.

On the first evening we spent in our new encampment, we were shown the manner in which the Spaniards take wild cattle, which was quite a different practice from that used by the Indians of the Rocky

Mountains in taking buffalo, &c. Never less than two goes at a time, who arc always on the back of their fleetest horses, each provided with a strong: cord with a noose fixed on one end. When the animal is started they give chase and the rider that overtakes the game first, throws the noose round its neck or horns, and begins to draw the noose tight. When the noose is found to be secure he gives the cord several winds round the pummel of the saddle, (which is made strong for this purpose) and stops his horse all of a sudden, which throws the animal to the ground and frequently breaks its neck. If the animal is thrown without injury, the other hunter comes forward with his noose and fastens it round its hind foot, which enables them to manage the stoutest and most ferocious bulls.

Having thus captured their object of pursuit, they sometimes have great trouble in getting them home alive. The one with the cord round the animals head goes before while he with the cord fastened to the hind foot stays in the rear. If their prisoner becomes refractory and refuses to advance, the man in the rear commences whipping, while he in front uses many devices to provoke the brute, until it in a fit of rage makes at him, when he puts off at full speed, and sometimes run two or three miles in this way without stopping. In this manner they brought a large handsome cow into our camp this evening which we purchased, and found to be good beef.

Although they exhibit a great degree of dexterity in taking these wild beasts, their mode of killing them is far different.—When they want to butcher their beef they make the horse with the noose round the neck pull a different way from the one with the noose round the foot, until the animal is thrown on the ground, when they dismount and cut its throat with large knives. They appear to do most of their work on horse-back. If they want wood they repair to the forest, ride along until they find a log to suit them, when they drop their noose round the end of it; and thus drag it to their homes. They are very expert on horseback, nor could it be otherwise, for they are constantly riding and never appear so well satisfied as when they are seated on a prancing steed.

On the first of December, Captain Walker returned from Monterey, where he had met with a hospitable reception by the governor, (Figueros), and principal people in and about the Capitol, and where he also again met with Captain Baggshaw, who served as an interpreter for Captain Walker and the governor, as he was fully capable of fulfilling such an office. With the governor, Captain Walker succeeded in every thing he desired, having obtained permission to remain in the country during the approaching winter, to hunt and kill as much game as would support our company, and to trade as much with the Spaniards as we pleased, but were forbid trapping in the Indian lands or trading with the natives.

The Spaniards manifest a warm friendship for the Indians under their jurisdiction, as those who were friendly towards us were constantly reminding us of the danger of wronging the Indians. Here we remained until about the 18th of December, without anything occurring except the daily visits we received from the Spaniards and Indians, who were curious to know how we lived, and all about us. They however, only found that we lived like they did themselves, any more than they lived in habitations built of wood, brick, mortar, &c. while we lived in huts made of skins of animals. About this time Captain Walker proposed to me to take a tramp through the settlements for the purpose of taking a view of the country, and the manners and customs of the inhabitants.

This was precisely what I had long been wanting. Accordingly, Captain W., two others and myself left the camp and steered to the south-east, intending to return through Monterey. The country through which we passed contained rich soil, tolerably well timbered, but thinly inhabited with a few Spaniards and Indians, who appeared to live there because they were not permitted to live any other place. These people, generally, are very ignorant and much more indolent— have little or no ingenuity—and only seem to enjoy themselves when engaged in the chase. This is the only occupation of the wealthier portion of Spaniards. Their habitations are built of sun-dried brick, some of which appear well enough on the outside, but the inside shows no kind of mechanism—there being no floor, partition, or work of any kind except the bare walls.

Their floors are made smooth by taking a large beetle and hammering the surface of the ground until it becomes perfectly level— thus they never fail of having a solid foundation!—They have a small fire-place in one corner of the house, with a chimney extending only a little above the mantle. Their beds and bedding generally consists of blankets spread upon a large hide layed on the ground, and after rising in the morning these beds are rolled up in one corner, where they answer the purpose of seats through the daytime. Their diet is generally composed of beans and meat made into a kind of soup, with but little bread. Most of them are entirely destitute of cooking utensils, and, were it not that they are all provided with knives, their manner of cooking and eating would be equally as inconvenient as the wildest savages of the Rocky Mountains.

But the wealthy, who, it may be supposed, constitute the aristocracy of this country, appear to live at ease, surrounded with all the comforts of life, are entirely independent and unconnected with the common people. They carry on farming to a considerable extent in some districts, the principal labour of which is done by the Indians from the missionary station. The principal productions are wheat, corn, and beans. They also have many vine-yards, and manufacture a large quantity of wine—which is their principal drink. Their mode of preparing the soil for grain is of an awkward and rather novel nature. When they want to plough, they repair to the woods and get a sapling with a knot or branch jutting out on one side, which they make sharp, hitch two or more teams of oxen to it and then proceed to score out the ground—which is generally done in wet weather, when the ground is moist. Another method, no less novel, however, is to get a crooked log, much the shape of a sled-runner, fix a piece of iron in front which answers for a coulter, then sharpening the log they make a furrow similar to the track of a sled. As a substitute for a harrow, they use a brush, and by laying a weight on it, some times scratch the ground in tolerable style. This manner of tilling the soil could not be done with such success in any other country where the soil is less mellow and tender than here.

These people have no fences round their cleared or cultivated land, although they raise an immense amount of stock, such as horses, mules and horned cattle—all of which range at large over these extensive prairies all seasons of the year, many being in a manner totally wild, so much so, that when they wish to milk a cow, they mount one of their coarsers and noose her, fasten the cord to a tree, and then tie her feet, when she is forced to be quiet. During our whole stay in this country I have never seen any thing like a stable or a barn, as a shelter for the dumb brutes—nor did I ever see any one feeding an animal, unless it was a favourite cow or horse that was sick. This, however, is not at all singular as any number of animals could subsist, and be in good order all seasons of the year, on these plains, as in many spots the grass is green the whole year round. The months of August, September and October are the least enticing to animals, as it is the warmest and driest season of the year.

As soon as August sets in the beasts inhabiting the dry prairies and hills, repair to the low wet ground, where they can get enough to subsist upon until the dry season passes away. The rainy season commences generally in the latter part of October, and continues until the first and sometimes middle of January, when the weather becomes fair and the farmers sow their grain, such as wheat and rye. During this wet weather the animals grow fat, and the inhabitants employ the principal part of this time in catching and domesticating them. This fair weather generally lasts about two months, or until the first of March, when the rain again descends and continues until about the middle of June—the grain, however, grows and ripens during the wet weather. It then keeps dry for a month or so until the farmers gather their crops—which occupies about a month, when the warm weather sets in; destroying all kinds of vegetation, giving but a poor subsistence to the dumb brutes, and to the country the appearance of an unproductive climate.

About the end of the dry season (say about the first of November) the face of nature in this country has more the appearance of spring in the United States than any other part of the year, and, as there is no winter nor freezing weather here it may be said that August, September and October, is their only winter, (to substitute *warm* for *cold*) as, at the end of this period the face of nature assumes a new dress and vegetation shoots forth precisely in the manner that it does in Pennsylvania when the frost leaves the ground in the Spring of the year.

The dry season is occupied by the inhabitants in gathering the mules into large droves and driving them off to the market at Santa Fé, a distance of 12 or 1400 miles from this part of the coast, through a wild and desert country. Here they meet with ready sale at a profitable price from the traders of Missouri, who repair to Santa Fé annually for that purpose. These traders are generally well supplied with merchandize which they exchange at Santa Fé for gold and silver, and with these Californian traders for mules and Spanish hides. The price of a mule at Santa Fé is generally from 6 to $10.—Merchandise is sold at a great advance, particularly silks, jewellery and groceries.

The principal part of their hides are sold to U. S. vessels trading on the coast. When a trading vessel anchors on the coast for the purpose of trading, the news is spread over the whole country like wild fire. The owners of cattle, who are of the wealthier class, collect together all the poorer Spaniards and Indians for the purpose of catching and butchering the cattle, in order to get their hides. This is the commencement of their sporting season. They are all mounted on their fleetest horses, and on these occasions the hunters go in pairs, one provided with a noose and the other with a spear or lance, which is used in cutting the sinews of the animals hind legs after it is noosed, which causes it to fall to the ground, after which they are easily despatched. After they strip off the hides and take out the tallow, and sometimes the choice part of the meat, the remainder of the carcase is left on the ground to be devoured by the wolves. The hides are then stretched out on the ground, and the tallow moulded into large cakes. As a compensation for their labour, the butchers, or hunters, receive one third of all the tallow they can collect. When the vessel is about leaving the coast, the hides and tallow which has been collected, is conveyed to the beach, where the hides are sold at $1.50 a piece, and the tallow at 4 cents per pound.

The greater part of this cargo is paid for in merchandize at high prices, but which is as valuable here as money itself, and much more useful. A vessel loaded with hides and tallow from this coast is of the greatest value, and has afforded an easy path to wealth for many of the American merchants.

After travelling leisurely along through their country, which still continued thinly inhabited by these people, find passing two small missionary establishments, we arrived at a small town called St. Hose, or St. Joseph, about 10 miles south of Monterey, where we arrived on the 25th of December. This is also a missionary station, (San Carlos del Carmel?), and the largest of any we had yet encountered, containing about 900 Indians, principally from the mountains. This station is constructed and managed similar to that of St. Juan, except the church, which is much larger, and built with a greater display of the arts of civilization. Here we remained for two days, employing our time in watching the proceedings of these Indians in their devotional exercises. The manoeuvres of those who have been lately converted to the Christian religion (being of the Catholic faith,) is something very singular, as they at one moment manifest the most unbounded transports of joy, and the next throw themselves into the greatest paroxysm of weeping and lamentation.—We then continued our journey and soon arrived at Monterey, which town is built on a beautiful situation on the south side of Monterey Bay—this bay being formed by Kings River. This is the Capitol of Upper, or North California, and under the government of New Mexico. The town is small containing only about 30 or 40 dwelling houses, one church, one calaboose a part of which is used as a house of justice, or in other words, a court house, where the governor transacts his public business, and a kind of a fort, built in a commanding situation on the edge of the bay, to be used in the defence of the town in case an attack should be made upon it from the sea, containing several pieces of artillery.

This bay is very deep, affording an excellent harbour for any number of vessels. The town has every natural advantage that a seaport could desire; and if a proper spirit of enterprise prevailed among the inhabitants, it might be made to flourish equal to any other town in the dominions of New Mexico. Vessels sailing along the coast of the Pacific to the north, all stop here to take in supplies, as it is the last white settlement they pass, until they reach the Russian dominions of the North-West; but as the inhabitants raise no grain only what is used for home consumption; the mariner is only enabled to supply his vessel with meat and water.—Besides the advantage the agriculturalist might derive by supplying vessels with provisions, he might be enabled to carry on a large exporting business—as the soil and climate is ever calculated to raise large crops of grain. Another prominent advantage the town of St. Joseph would have, is the facility of internal communication with the Indians now inhabiting the prairies and mountains of the interior, or the white race, who, it may reasonably be expected, will have undisputed dominion over this entire region before long.

As it is at present, there are some men here of considerable wealth, the principal part of which they have acquired by trading with vessels different kinds of peltries, such as Spanish hides, tallow, beaver, sea-otter, bear, deer and elk skins, and also horses and mules. There is also a brisk trade carried on in this place with the Sandwich Islands, about nine days sail from this port,—and which might be rendered quite lucrative. The most of the vessels, however that put into this bay are on fishing expeditions. The Sperm whale are very numerous in this part of the Pacific ocean—the oil of which affords a profitable reward to all who embark in this dangerous and toilsome business.

On the 29th some of our men arrived in St Joseph, (Monterey?), with a portion of the peltries we had collected whilst crossing the mountains, and which we exchanged with Capt Baggshaw for merchandise, such as groceries and ammunition to do us whilst on our return to Missouri the next summer. After concluding our trade with Captain Baggshaw, and spending the last day of the expiring year on land, we all resolved by invitation, to celebrate New-Years day on board the *Lagoda*, with the governor and Captain Baggshaw. The day was spent quite merrily, and the whole company manifested the best

313

possible humour each one contributing to keep up the sport by telling some mountain adventure or seafaring exploit. In the evening we ended the celebration by returning on shore and taking a few rounds with our rifles—which terminated by conclusively convincing the sailors that if they could beat us in telling "long yarns," we were more than a match for them with the rifle.

On the morning of the 2nd of January, 1834, Captain Baggshaw insisted on us again visiting his vessel, for the purpose of taking a glass, which we gladly accepted, and after shaking hands all round, and affectionately bidding farewell with our friends on board the vessel, returned to land in company with the governor, when His Excellency offered our captain a gratuity of a tract of land seven miles square if he would bring 50 families, composed of different kinds of mechanicks, and settle on it. Captain Walker was well pleased with the country, and said he had a great mind to accept the governor's offer, as he had no doubt he could in a few years amass a fortune, and be at the head of a rich and flourishing settlement; but his love for the laws and free institutions of the United States, and his hatred for those of the Spanish Government, deterred him from accepting the governor's benevolent offer—and we bid farewell to the governor and his people, well pleased with the reception we had thus far every where met with among the Spaniards.

We now left St. Joseph and returned with our merchandize, consisting principally of groceries, ammunition, &c., to our encampment, where we arrived without meeting with any difficulty; finding everything in good order, and all well except one man named Philips, who was laying in a very precarious state from wounds inflicted by a bear. It appeared that Philips had been out hunting deer, and having killed one, took out the insides and hung it upon a tree, and started to the camp to get a horse to bring it home. After travelling a mile or so, whilst ascending a hill, came suddenly upon an old bear and two cubs.—The bear immediately on seeing Philips, as is their custom, reared on her hind feet, and being very close, commenced growling most furiously.

This our hero could not brook, and fearing the consequences if he should shoot and wound her, lost his presence of mind, and started to run.—The bear immediately pursued and caught him. He now found it quite useless to attempt to get loose, and only saved his life by sinking to the ground and affecting to be dead. The bear then left him, but not without wounding him to such a degree that it was a long time before he could collect strength enough to raise to his feet. It was late at night when he reached the camp, and was so far gone, from hunger and loss of blood, that his life was despaired of at first. One of his arms was broke and his body most shockingly cut and mangled.

On our way from the capital to our camp, (*must be at Monterey not St. Joseph*), we had an opportunity of witnessing a part of the Spanish mode of gambling in this country, which was rare amusement to us. and which they call bull-bating. It is in this fashion, as near as I could understand: When a number of sporting gentlemen get together for this purpose, they repair to the prairies, all well mounted and prepared for the chase. When they come across a herd of cattle they make large bets on who shall be the first to noose one of the cattle in the drove in sight. When everything is arranged this far they all take an even start. The one that gets the rope round the animals horn or neck first claims the assistance of the rest to throw the animal to the ground—which ends the chase for this time.

As the Spaniards are generally skilled in the art of throwing the noose, the chase in a case of this kind mostly depends on the fleet-ness of the horses. When they have secured a bull in this way, they take him to a pen made strong for this purpose, where they put him in for safe-keeping, and settle the bets. Having got through with this game, to give the losers an opportunity to regain their losses, they start out on the hunt of a grizzly bear, always preferring the largest, which they capture in the same way. Taking a bear is a much more danger-ous piece of work, than any other animal, owing to their enormous strength.

It often happens that, in taking a bear, they are unhorsed; when, if alone, they are in imminent danger of being tore to pieces; but this seldom happens unless the horse is thrown, or the saddle tore loose. In taking a bear, their object is to noose him round one of the hind legs, in order to keep him from biting the cord, which they are very apt to do if fast round the neck. A single hunter can do but little with a large bear, and they are seldom attacked single handed, or without the certainty of assistance from some of their comrades. When overtaken by the foremost rider, the bear stops running and prepares for war. This man will then engage the attention of the bear by teasing him, whilst another hunter will come up in the rear of the excited animal and noose him by the hind foot; when the cord is securely fastened to the hind foot, he is generally considered safe.

It is then that their sport begins in good earnest, and the feats that are sometimes performed by the men, bear and horses, would be incredible to any person who has never seen any sport of this kind. After the bear finds himself secure and has become pretty well worried, he seats himself sullenly on the ground and lets the horse pull at the cord, stretching his leg out until the pain becomes too severe, when he will draw up his leg, horse and all, with as much apparent ease as a horse would a sleigh.

I have been told that some of the largest bears have been known to drag two horses a considerable distance in a fit of rage, in spite of all the exertions of the horses and riders to the contrary. After the bear is pretty well worried in this way, another noose is fastened round one of the fore feet or neck, when the bear will commence beating the ground with his feet and manifesting the most intense rage and anger imaginable—and in this manner they drag, whip and coax him along to the pen where the bull is confined. Their cords are made of green cow-hide, which they cut into narrow strips, hang them in the sun and rub them as they dry, making them soft and pliable, when they are platted into a rope which no weight can sever.

When the bear has arrived at the bull pen, their bets on taking him and all disputes are settled, refreshments taken, and preparations made for another scene, which is by far the most pleasing to the Spaniards. They begin to enrage the bull by pricking him with a nail fixed in the end of a stick, and when his anger has rose to the war pitch, the bear is let into the pen with the bull. The men now bet all they are worth on which will be the conqueror, and every thing manifests the greatest possible excitement. Sometimes the animals refuse to fight until they are forced to it by being tormented with the sharpened sticks, but when one receives a blow from the other, nothing can part them until one or the other falls. These fights last sometimes half an hour without relaxation. The bear is much the strongest, but it has no chance of avoiding the thrusts of the bull, in consequence of the smallness of the pen; but in an open field, a grizzly bear will conquer a bull in a few moments.

When the fight is over the conquered animal is taken out and the bets are again settled. If it is the bear that is whipped, the game is continued and the bets renewed on some person who will offer to go into the pen with the enraged bull, lay his hand on some part of his body and escape untouched. This is by far the most dangerous part of the whole play, and many lives have been lost at it; but so fond are the Spaniards of gambling, that in play a life is of but little consequence.

When the bets are all arranged, the adventurer stands at the door of the pen with his blanket in his hand, and the company is occupied in maddening the bull,—when he has become sufficiently enraged the hero steps in, when the bull will make a desperate plunge at him with his horns, which the man escapes by throwing the blanket over the face of the bull and blinding him—he then claps his hand on the designated spot, snatches the blanket off his horns and makes his escape. If he gets out without the bull striking him, he has won the stakes for all those who bet on him—which will be a profitable business for him, as he receives a certain percentage on all the money thus won.

It happened that one of these games was to be played while we were in the neighbourhood, and on being invited to attend Captain Walker, several others, and myself concluded on going to see the performance. When we reached the ground the Spaniards had the bull and the bear both secured, and were just going to set them to fighting. Presently the animals got to blows, and continued for a short time, when the bull became master and the bear was let out of the pen. The battle was very closely contested, and I never seen animals so much enraged, and fight with so much fierceness.

The bear could master the bull for a good spell, when it could get its arms around him, but the large body of the bull would prevent any serious injury, and presently the bear would be shaken to the ground, when the bull would have a chance to plunge at him with effect. It was in this manner that the bull managed to get the advantage of bruin.— After the bear was taken out, the company commenced betting on an old timeworn Spaniard who offered to go into the pen and touch the enraged animal. In a short time all the preliminaries were arranged, and the man entered the pen in the manner as described above, but unfortunately, when he went to pull his blanket off the animals head and come out, one of the beasts horns was thrust quite thro' his thigh. As soon as this happened, the Spaniards commenced plaguing the bull at the opposite side of the pen and the wounded man was suffered to crawl out in the best manner he could.

There are also many other methods of gambling practised by these people,—and vice of every description seems to be openly countenanced in some parts of the settlements, such as horse racing, card playing, and even stealing. The latter of which is carried on to a considerable extent by both male and female, and is even recognised, under some circumstances, as one of the established customs of the country. The men are always provided with dirks, which they can use with superior skill.

We remained at our old encampment near St. Juan, without meeting with any thing to disturb our situation, and on the most friendly intercourse with both Spaniards and Indians, until last night, when six of our best horses were stolen, and which we at first supposed to be the work of Indians. We had heretofore trusted everything in the fidelity of both the Spaniards and Indians, but when our horses had been thus taken from us we began to keep a sharp look out. In the morning (10th) several scouting parties were despatched on search of the stolen property, and returned in the evening with only one, after following the trail far into the Spanish settlement, which convinced us immediately that it was not the Indians but the Spaniards who had behaved so dishonourable. In the following morning Captain Walker went himself to one of the *alcaldes* or esquires for the purpose of enquiring what steps had best be taken to restore our stolen property, or how we could be recompensed.

On having an interview with the magistrate he learned a good many things more than he had formerly known—which was this, that Spaniards, whilst travelling through the country with a poor horse, was at liberty to take a good one if he could find such, no matter who it belonged to, or whether wild or tame, and continue his journey. And also, if two men set down to play at cards, and the looser thinks that his opponent has cheated or defrauded him, he is at liberty to visit his horses and help himself to such as he can, but if the owner catches him in the act, it generally ends in bloodshed.—For this and other reasons, a Spaniard is never seen away from home without his rope or cord, in order to noose anything he stands in need of.

Stealing horses is practised more than any other kind of theft, and it is not recognised as a crime, owing, probably, to the cheapness of these animals—as they can be bought at any time for from one to ten dollars. Those costing $1 are unbroke fillies, and those for $10 are first rate horses well tamed. When we became aware that such was the practice of the country, Captain Walker thought it would be the best plan for us to pack up and leave the neighbourhood, in order to avoid a difficulty with a people of a ferocious and wicked nature, at a time too, when we were not very well prepared to contend against such an enemy in their own country. Accordingly we set about purchasing provision, and the next day we were pretty well supplied with flour, corn, beans, &c.

13th. This morning everything was prepared and we took up our march in an eastern direction. We only travelled 12 or 15 miles this day and encamped for the night, which we spent without the occurrence of any thing of importance more than the recalling to mind of the scenes encountered and hardships endured by each of us in our wayfaring to this remote corner of the world.

The two following days we continued without interruption in the same direction, and encamped on the banks of a beautiful stream called Sulphur River, where we concluded to remain until in the Spring, when it would be more pleasant travelling eastward to the Rocky mountains. Our encampment is beautifully located on a rising piece of ground, with a handsome river gliding smoothly along immediately in front, an extensive oat plain stretching out as far as the eye will reach to the rear, and is about 40 miles east of St. Juan.—The banks of this river are most delightfully shaded with timber, principally oak and elm. The soil in the plain is very strong and deep, producing heavy crops of wild oats and grass—affording excellent pasture tor horses, at this season of the year.

After we had made every arrangement necessary to our comfort while we remained here, our men commenced hunting in good style—bear, elk and deer being very plenty, and the fattest we had anywhere met with. On the 20th, it being a fine day for hunting, a large portion of our sportsmen set out early in the morning bound for a general hunt, and determined to rake the whole prairie. Towards the middle of the day, two of the men came in sight of a large drove of elk, feeding in the open prairie, and as they were cautiously approaching near enough to shoot, they unexpectedly came upon five grizzly bear that were sleeping in the grass—two old ones and three cubs; the latter began to howl most piteously, which enraged the old ones, and they made at our hunters with open mouth.

But as one of them was an old practitioner in such matters, having a good gun, carrying an ounce ball, which he called "*Knock-him-stiff,*" stood quite composed (bidding his companion, who was about to run, to stand his ground) until the bear came within reach of him when he discharged it with the muzzle in her mouth—which, as our hero said, gave her a very bad cough. This inspired the other hunter with courage, and he treated the other bear in nearly the same manner. The cubs not showing any desire to depart alone, were also killed. This days hunt was exceedingly lucky, not only to these two men, but to nearly all who were out, as they all returned with heavy loads of game.

On the 25th Captain Walker started to Monterey with eight men for the purpose of laying in a larger supply of provision for us on our journey to the east, in the spring, as we began to reflect that we might fall in with some other companies on the road who would need assistance.

26th. Today about 10 o'clock, we discovered a large drove of horses passing through the plain, followed by a few people, whom we supposed to be Spaniards or Indians—but they did not appear to know that we were in the neighbourhood, and we were not anxious to let them know it for fear they might *travel* our way some time. In the evening, as some of our men who had been out hunting, were returning home, they accidentally came across a large bear laying in a hole, sound asleep. Our men were anxious to see some sport, and commenced making a noise, and even fired a gun or two without bringing her to her senses, and getting her out of the hole. They then dismounted, stationed themselves around the hole and shot her before she moved. On examination, they found her to be of the grizzly species and of the largest size; and also having two young ones in the hole with her, not larger than a common sized cat. The old one was extremely fat, and from the signs about the hole, it appeared that she must have had this as a permanent place of residence. It is the first instance I ever knew of taking a bear of this size whilst asleep.

28th. Today a party of Spaniards arrived at our encampment on search of a party of Indians who had eloped from the St. Juan Missionary station, and taken with them 300 head of horses—which we supposed to be the party seen by us on the 26th. These men stayed with us all night and the next morning some of our men joined the Spaniards in the chase, who were to get one half of the horses as a compensation for their trouble, if lucky enough to find them. These men followed the Indians to the foot of a large mountain, where they discovered several smokes rising out of the forest along the base of the mountain. In a thicket of timber, from the smoke that arose, they thought the whole Indian force was concentrated, and the Spanish and American force surrounded the spot in battle array, determined to give the offenders a severe chastisement at once. When all the preparations were made, the word to fire was given. But instead of the lamentations of wounded Indians, and the frantic prancing of frightened horses, nothing but a dead silence answered the discharge of their artillery.—They then dismounted and went into the thicket, where they found a large portion of their horses well butchered, and partly dried and a few old and feeble Indians, with some squaws and children. The Indians having killed some of the horses, were engaged in drying the meat,—but on seeing the white men approach, fled to the mountain, leaving nothing behind but what is above stated. The disappointment of the Spaniards now exceeded all bounds, and gave our men some evidence of the depravity of the Spanish character.

By way of revenge, after they found that there was no use in following the Indians into the mountain, the Spaniards fell to massacring, indiscriminately, those helpless creatures who were found in the *wigwams* with the meat, and cutting off their ears. Some of them were driven into a *wigwam*, when the door was barricaded, and a large quantity of combustible matter thrown on and around the hut, for the purpose of setting fire to it, and burning them all together. This barbarous treatment our men would not permit and they went and released the prisoners, when the Spaniards fell to work and despatched them as if they were dogs. When this tragedy was completed they all returned to our encampment on the 31st.

On their arrival at our camp, the Spaniards told me that their object in taking off the ears, was to show the priests and *alcaldes*, that they had used every effort to regain the stolen property. These people also informed me that the Indians of this country are in the habit of coming in large droves to the missionary stations, and make the most sincere professions of religion, until they gain the confidence of the priests, when they will suddenly decamp, and take off all the horses they can get, to the mountain, where they remain as long as their meat lasts—when they will send another detachment, whose duty it is to do likewise. They prefer eating domesticated horses because the act of stealing them gives their flesh a superior flavour—and it would be less trouble for them to catch wild horses, if they could thus gratify their stealing propensities.

There is supposed to be about ten Indians to one white man, or Spaniard, in this country. The population is divided or classed into three degrees, 1st. The whites or Spaniards. 2nd. The Indians; and third the offspring of a white and an Indian.—The seasons are distinguished only as wet and dry—there being no snow and very little frost. The only established religion is that of the Roman Catholic faith, which is professed by almost every Spaniard.

Today Captain Walker returned from the settlements well supplied with such articles as he was in need of—bringing with him 100 horses, 47 cow cattle, and 30 or 35 dogs, together with some flour, corn, beans, &c., suitable for our subsistence in the long journey, for which every man was now busily engaged in making preparations. Two or three days after Captain Walker returned from this expedition, we were visited by 40 or 50 Spaniards, all well mounted, and each man prepared with a noose, on their way into the neighbourhood of wild horses, for the purpose of catching some. In this company we found one of the horses which had been stolen from us before we left the settlement:—The Spaniards honourably gave him up after we proved our claim. As the manner of taking wild horses was altogether a curiosity to me, I was anxious to see the sport, and accordingly several others and myself joined the Spaniards and accompanied them. After travelling a short distance we arrived at a large pen, enclosing about three-fourths of an acre, which they call a park or corral. This pen is built quite strong, to prevent horses from breaking through.

Attached to this pen, are two wings extending to the right and left, in the shape of a V, upwards of a mile and a half in length. The wings are made by posts being set in the ground and poles tied to them with a piece of elk or horse hide, about four feet high—the neck or pen being built much higher and stronger. This pen appears as if it had been used for this purpose many years. After we halted here, the Spaniards were occupied during the remainder of the day in repairing some weak parts of the pen and wings, and in the morning all hands proceeded to drive in the horses, which was done by sending out parties in different directions, mounted upon the swiftest horses in order to outrun the wild ones and turn them in front of the pen, when the men all collect in a breast and drive them down into the pen; which answers the same purpose as a basket does a fish-dam. When the animals are all in the pen, a fence is erected across the neck to prevent the escape of any horses. The men will then dismount and pass along close to the pen for the purpose of accustoming the horses to the smell of human beings.

When this is done, four or five will enter the pen, leaving the balance on the outside to prevent them from breaking out, and with their cords noose and tie all under two or three years old. After securing 70 or 80 in this manner, all over this age were turned out,—as they are considered too hard to tame. They then blind-folded those they had taken and turned them loose with the tame horses, and they followed the same as a dog. It is in this way they always get them into the settlements, where they are divided to each man, who brands and hobbles them, and then turns them loose upon the prairie. After they have been confined in this situation two or three days, they are considered domesticated, their fetters taken off, and treated similar to the other horses.

There is another way of catching these horses, which is this: They are noosed, thrown to the ground, partly blind-folded and saddled, when some adventurous Spaniard will mount on his back, let the horse rise to his feet, and if he becomes unmanageable, they give him the whip, and run the brute until he is no longer able to keep his feet under him, after which he is generally sufficiently docile.

On the 12th we returned to our camp, when Captain Walker traded with the Spaniards for several of these horses—and in the evening they bid us farewell and continued their homeward journey.

Feb. 14th. This morning had been appointed for our departure, and accordingly every thing requisite for our comfort was in readiness, and we lazily left our camp for the east—leaving six of our company behind, all of whom are tradesmen, such as carpenters, hatters, &c. where they purposed following their occupations, which will no doubt be profitable to themselves, and of great advantage to the indolent and stupid Spaniard. The price of furniture here is exceedingly high. A rough table (more like a bench,) consisting of rough hewn boards nailed together, will cost 8 and 10 dollars. A pair of similar made bedsteads the same. Two of our men constructed a wind-mill which they sold for $110. All kinds of mechanical productions command a corresponding price.—This is partly owing to the inconvenience of getting out the stuff—there being no saw-mills in the country, the carpenter is compelled to cut out his stuff by hand; and as there are very few tools in the country, it requires great labour to manufacture a piece of work with any kind of taste.

The parting scene between the company and these six men appeared the most melancholy separation we had undergone since we left the States. On other occasions, when we had separated with a portion of our hunters, it was with the confident hope of meeting again. But these men remained with the determination of making a permanent residence in the country, and never again returning to the states; whilst the most of us were as determinedly bent on never again returning to this region—hence we parted as if we were forever afterwards to be separated by worlds. On shaking hands with these men, with whom I had been in daily intercourse for the last eighteen months, it appeared more like parting with brothers, than anything else.

Our company was now reduced to 52 men, 315 horses—and for provisions, 47 beef, and 30 dogs, together with a considerable portion of flour, Indian corn, beans, some groceries and a few other articles necessary on such an expedition. We continued up Sulphur River in an eastern direction, and for the first night encamped on the South side of this stream, after travelling not more than 12 or 15 miles.

15th. Continued our journey up Sulphur River, passing through a fine country, most of which is prairie, covered plentifully with wild oats and grass. After we had encamped this evening, two Spaniards came to our camp bringing with them 25 very fine horses, which they sold to the company, and engaged themselves to accompany us to the buffalo country. They informed us that they had deserted from the Spanish army, and that as it was the second time, if taken now, according to the Spanish military discipline, their punishment would be certain death.

We continued travelling from day to day, the country all the way being of the most enticing nature, soil very strong, timber tolerably plenty, and game in abundance. The two Spaniards we found to be of great advantage to us, as some of our horses caused us great trouble, and one of the Spaniards being an excellent rider and well acquainted with the art of noosing, would catch and bring together our horses at any time they would become separated.

About the 27th we arrived at the base of the California Mountain, having past many Indians on our way, and also finding many here.

On the 28th we continued our journey to the south along the base of the mountain in search of pasture for our cattle and a convenient pass over the mountain.—Here game is very scarce, owing to the numerous swarms of Indians scattered along in every direction. On the second of March we killed one of our beef. Pursued our course, still in a southern direction finding game rather scarce, Indians plenty, pasture improving, and vegetation of every description beginning to grow rapidly—weather showery with warm sun, until the 10th of March, when we arrived at 60 or 70 huts, containing from 250 to 300 Indians. These Indians appear quite different from those more convenient to the Spanish settlements, and call themselves Pagans, (?) their chief Capetaine, and have names for several things nearly the same as we have. Their wives they call *wifa*,—kettle, wood, and meat the same as we do.

These people seem to live poor, and are equally as indolent as any of those we had met with in the Spanish dominions. They are generally small in stature, complexion quite dark, and some quite hairy. Whilst here we killed another of our beef, and made a present of some of the beef, together with a dog and some tobacco, to these Indians. Their principal diet during this season of the year, consists of roots and weeds, amongst which is parsley, and a kind of cabbage, all of which they eat raw. In the summer they subsist principally upon acorns, at least a person would so judge to see the number of holes that are burnt into the logs for the purpose of mashing them.

When we were about leaving these Indians, their chief brought a hearty and good-looking young female to our captain and proposed to give her in exchange for an ox. Captain Walker very prudently declined the offer, telling the chief that we had a great distance to travel, and would probably be without meat half the time. We travelled along quite comfortably meeting with no unusual occurrence. The country through which we passed still continued as charming as the heart of man could desire. The Indians were quite numerous, some of whom would at times manifest the most unbounded alarm. We also passed a great number of streams flowing out of the mountain, and stretching afar towards the Pacific. The prairies were most beautifully decorated with flowers and vegetation, interspersed with splendid groves of timber along the banks of the rivers,—giving a most romantic appearance to the whole face of nature.

We at length arrived at an Indian village, the inhabitants of which seemed to be greatly alarmed on seeing us, and they immediately commenced gathering up their food and gathering in their horses— but as soon as they discovered that we were white people, they became perfectly reconciled. After we halted here we found that these people could talk the Spanish language, which we thought might be of great advantage to the company, and on inquiry ascertained that they were a tribe called the Concoas, (?) which tribe some eight or ten years since resided in the Spanish settlements at the missionary station near St. Barbara, on the coast, where they rebelled against the authority of the country, robbed the church of all its golden images and candle-sticks, and one of the priests of several thousand dollars in gold and silver, when they retreated to the spot where we found them—being at least five or six hundred miles distant from the nearest Spanish settlement.

This tribe are well acquainted with the rules of bartering for goods or anything they wish to buy—much more so than any other tribe we met with. They make regular visits to such posts where they are unknown, and also make appointments with ship-traders to meet at some designated time and place; thus they are enabled to carry on a considerable degree of commerce. They still retain several of the images which they pilfered from the church—the greater part of which is the property of the chiefs.—These people are seven or eight hundred strong, their houses are constructed of poles and covered with grass, and are tolerably well supplied with house-hold furniture which they brought with them at the time they robbed the church. They follow agricultural pursuits to some extent, raising very good crops of corn, pumpkins, melons, &c. All the outdoor labour is done by the females. They are also in the habit of making regular visits to the settlements for the purpose of stealing horses, which they kill and eat.

We passed one night with these Indians, during which time they informed us of an accessible passage over the mountain. In the morning we resumed our journey, hiring two of these Indians as pilots, to go with us across the mountain—continued all day without any interruption, and in the evening encamped at the foot of the passover.

In the morning we continued up the mountain in an eastern direction, and encamped this evening at the lower end of the snow. The next day we found the snow more plenty, and encamped without grass of any kind. We now began to apprehend hard times again. Our horses no longer resumed their march in the mornings with a playful cheerfulness, but would stumble along and go just when their riders would force them to do so. We continued travelling in this way for four days when we landed safely on the opposite side of the mountain, in a temperate climate, and among tolerable pasture, which latter was equally as gratifying to our horses as the former was to the men.

We here made our pilots presents of a horse, some tobacco, and many trifling trinkets captivating to the eye of an Indian, when they left us to return to their friends.

Our horses and cattle were pretty much fatigued, but not as much as we anticipated. The country on this side is much inferior to that on the opposite side—the soil being thin and rather sandy, producing but little grass, which was very discouraging to our stock, as they now stood in great want of strong feed. On the opposite side vegetation had been growing for several weeks—on this side, it has not started yet.

After discharging our pilots we travelled a few miles and encamped at some beautiful springs, where we concluded to spend the remainder of the day, in order to give our horses and cattle rest. Our captain here concluded on following the base of the mountain to the north until we would come to our trail when crossing to the west, or California.

May 2nd.(?) This morning we resumed our journey, every man possessed of doubtful apprehensions as to the result of this determination, as the hardships which we encountered in this region on a former occasion, were yet fresh in the minds of many of us. The country we found to be very poor, and almost entirely destitute of grass. We continued through this poor country travelling a few miles every day, or as far as the weakened state of our dumb brutes would admit of. The weather was mostly clear and otherwise beautiful, but we had quite a cold wind most all the time. Travelling along the eastern base of this mountain(California), we crossed many small rivers flowing towards the east, but emptying into lakes scattered through the plain, or desert, where the water sinks and is exhausted in the earth. This plain extends from here to the Rocky Mountains, being an almost uninterrupted level, the surface of which is covered with dry, loose sand.

In this manner we travelled along, passing such scenes as are described above, until at length we arrived at some springs which presented a really remarkable appearance, and may be called boiling, or more properly Steam Springs, situated near the base of the mountain, on or near the banks of a small river. These springs are three in number, and rise within a short distance of each other, one being much larger than the other two. The water constantly bolls as if it was in a kettle over a fire, and is so hot that if a piece of meat is put under the water at the fountain-head, it will cook in a few minutes, emitting a strong sulphurous smell—the water also tastes of sulphur.

In a clear morning the steam or smoke rising from these springs may be seen a great distance as it hangs in the air over the springs, similar to a dense sheet of fog. There is not a spear of vegetation growing within several rods of the spot, and the surface of the ground presents the appearance of one solid piece of crust, or hard baked mud. When the water empties in and mixes with the river water, it leaves an oily substance floating on the surface similar to tar or grease of any kind.

About the 25th of May, we again continued our journey, but our difficulties had been multiplying for some time, until now we found them quite formidable.—The principal part of our present difficulties arose from the scarcity of pasture for our horses and cattle. After travelling the best way we could, for a few days towards the North, we arrived at another beautiful sandy plain, or desert, stretching out to the east far beyond the reach of the eye, as level as the becalmed surface of a lake. We occasionally found the traces of Indians, but as yet, we have not been able to gain an audience with any of them, as they flee to the mountain as soon as we approach. Game being very scarce, and our cattle poor, gives us very indifferent living.

Our direct course, after reaching the eastern base of this mountain, would have been a north-east direction, but we were apprehensive of perishing for water in crossing this extensive desert—which would doubtless be the fate of any traveller who would undertake it, when it is recollected that it extends from the base of the Rocky Mountains to this mountain, a distance of several hundred miles. This being the case we were obliged to pass along the base of the mountain in a northern direction, until we would arrive at the point where we ascended the mountain when going to the coast, and then follow the same trail east towards the Rocky Mountains, or Great Salt Lake, where we expected to meet the company we had left at the latter place.

Travelling along the mountain foot, crossing one stream after another, was any thing but pleasant. Day after day we travelled in the hope each day of arriving at the desired point when we would strike off in a homeward direction. Every now and then some of the company would see a high peak or promontory, which he would think was seen by the company on a former occasion, but when we would draw near to it our pleasing anticipations would be turned into despondency; and at one time, about the middle of May, our captain was so certain that he could see a point in the distance, which he had distinctly marked as a guide on our former tramp, that he ordered the men to prepare for leaving the mountain;—this also proved to be the result of imagination only.

The next morning our captain, thinking the desert not very wide at this point, decided on striking across in a north-eastern direction, which would shorten our route considerably, if we could only be so successful as to surmount the difficulties of travelling through loose sand, without water, (as the streams descending from the mountain into the plain all sink.)

On the 16th of May, everything necessary for our dry tramp being in readiness, we started across the plain, which was done with a willing heart by almost every man, as we were all anxious to get home, and had been travelling many days without getting any nearer. The travelling in the plain, after passing the termination of the streams, we found to be extremely laborious. The sand lays quite loose, and as the wind would blow whilst driving our horses and cattle ahead of us, the sand would be raised up in such clouds that we could scarcely see them, which was very painful to our eyes. The first night in the plain we encamped at a large hole or well dug deep in the ground, which we supposed to be the work of Indians, and in which we found a small portion of stagnant water, but not half enough to slake the thirst of our numerous herd.

The next morning we resumed our toilsome march at an early hour, finding our stock suffering greatly for the want of water. This day we travelled with as much speed as possible, with the hope of finding water whereat to encamp; but at length night arrived, and the fatigues of the day obliged us to encamp without water, wood or grass. The day had been excessively warm, except when the wind would blow, and in the afternoon two of our dogs died for want of water. On examination we found that the feet of many of our dumb brutes were completely crippled by the sand.

Our situation at present seemed very critical. A dull, gloomy aspect appeared to darken the countenance of every member of the company. We were now completely surrounded with the most aggravating perplexities—having travelled two long day's journey into the plain and no idea how far yet to its termination, and from the manifestations of many of our most valuable stock, we were well convinced they could not endure these hardships much longer. To add vexation to our present difficulties, a violent altercation took place between the men as to whether we would proceed in our present direction, or turn back to the mountain.—A majority of the men were in favour of the latter, but Captain Walker, who never done anything by halves, with a few others, were of the opinion that we were halfway across, and could as easily proceed as return.

On all such disputes, on all former occasions, the majority decided on what steps should be taken; but when our captain was in the minority, and being beloved by the whole company, and being a man also who was seldom mistaken in any thing he undertook, the men were very reluctant in going contrary to his will. The dispute created much confusion in our ranks; but fortunately, about midnight the captain yielded to the wishes of his men, and as it was cool, and more pleasant travelling than in the daytime, we started back towards the mountain, intending to follow the same trail, in order to come to the hole at which we encamped on the first night in the plain.

Previous to starting, we took the hides off our dead cattle and made a kind of *moccasin* for such of our beasts as were lame, which we found to be of great advantage, as it effectually shielded their feet from the scouring effects of the sand.

Nothing happened through the night, and we moved carelessly along our trail, as we thought; but our feelings cannot be described at daylight when no signs of our former tracks could be discovered. Men were despatched in every direction on search, but all returned without any tidings with which to comfort our desponding company. The compass told which direction we should go, but otherwise we were completely bewildered. Our horses, cattle and dogs were almost exhausted this morning. The pitiful lamentations of our dogs were sufficient to melt the hardest heart.

The dumb brutes suffered more for water than food, and these dogs, when death threatened to seize them, would approach the men, look them right in the face with the countenances of a distracted person, and if no help could be afforded, would commence a piteous and lamentable howl, drop down and expire. When the day became warm we slackened our pace, and moved slowly forward, but without any hope of meeting with any water at least for a day longer. When night came we halted for a short time in order to collect the men and animals together, which were scattered in every direction for a mile in width, lest we should get separated at night, as we intended to travel on without ceasing until we would find water or arrive at the mountain.

When our forces collected together, we presented a really forlorn spectacle. At no time, either while crossing the Rocky or California Mountains, did our situation appear so desperate. We had to keep our dumb brutes constantly moving about on their feet, for if they would once lay down it would be impossible to get them up again, and we would then be compelled to leave them. Nor were the men in a much better condition. It is true, we had food, but our thirst far exceeded any description. At last it became so intense, that whenever one of our cattle or horses would die the men would immediately catch the blood and greedily swallow it down.

When our men had collected together, and rested their wearied limbs a little, our journey was resumed, finding that the cattle and horses travelled much better at night than in daylight. We advanced rapidly this evening without any interruption, until about midnight, when our horses became unmanageable, and contrary to our utmost exertions would go in a more northern direction than we desired. After several ineffectual attempts to check them, we thought perhaps it would be well enough to follow wherever they would lead. We had not followed our horses far until we discovered, to our indescribable joy, that the instinct of our horses was far more extensive and more valuable than all the foresight of the men, as we, unawares, came suddenly upon a beautiful stream of fresh water.

We now had the greatest trouble to keep our beasts from killing themselves drinking water—in which we succeeded only in part, and were thus occupied until daylight, when we counted our force for the purpose of ascertaining how much loss we sustained by undertaking to cross the desert, and found that we had lost 64 horses, 10 cows, and 15 dogs.

In order to get something to eat for our stock, and also to keep them from drinking too much water, we left this stream which had afforded such delight, before either the men or beasts had time to repose their wearied limbs. After travelling a few miles this morning we had the good luck to come across tolerable pasture and plenty of wood and water. Here we determined on staying until the next morning, for the purpose of resting our wearied stock.

This desert which had presented such an insurmountable barrier to our route, is bounded on the east by the Rocky Mountains, on the west by the California Mountain, on the North by the Columbia River, and on the south by the Red, or Colorado River. These two mighty rivers rise in the Rocky mountains adjacent to each other, and as the former flows in a N.W. and the latter in a southern direction, forms this plain in the shape of the letter A.—There are numerous small rivers rising in either mountain, winding their way far towards the centre of the plain, where they are emptied into lakes or reservoirs, and the water sinks in the sand. Further to the North where the sand is not so deep and loose, the streams rising in the *spurs* of the Rocky and those descending from the California Mountains, flow on until their waters at length mingle together in the same lakes.

The California Mountain extends from the Columbia to the Colorado River, running parallel with the coast about 150 miles distant, and 12 or 15 hundred miles in length with its peaks perpetually covered with eternal snows. There is a large number of water courses descending from this mountain on either side—those on the east side stretching out into the plain, and those on the west flow generally in a straight course until they empty into the Pacific; but in no place is there a water course through the mountain.

The next morning after finding the pasture, our herd having rested and satisfied their hunger pretty well, we resumed our journey along the edge of the plain, travelled as fast as their weakened state would admit of, still finding pasture sufficient for their subsistence, until, after several day's constant travelling, we fortunately came to our long sought for passage to the west. This was hailed with greater manifestations of joy by the company, than any circumstance that had occurred for some time, as it gave us to know where we were, and also to know when we might expect to arrive in a plentiful country of game.— Here we again layed by a day for the purpose of resting, and making preparations to follow our old trail towards the Great Salt Lake.

June 8th. This morning we left the California Mountain, and took a north-east direction, keeping our former path, many traces of which were quite visible in places. Here vegetation is growing rapidly, giving our herd abundant pasture, in consequence of which they have greatly improved in appearance, and are enabled to travel quite fast. After continuing our course in this direction for a few days without interruption, we at length arrived in the neighbourhood of the lakes at the mouth of Barren River, and which we had named Battle Lakes. All along our route from the mountain this far, we had seen a great number of Indians, but now that we had reached the vicinity of the place where we had the skirmish with the savages when going to the coast, they appeared to us in double the numbers that they did at that time; and as we were then compelled to fight them, by their movements now, we saw that this would be the only course for us to pursue.

We had used every endeavour that we could think of, to reconcile and make them friendly, but all to no purpose. We had given them one present after another—made them all the strongest manifestations of a desire for peace on our part, by promising to do battle against their enemies if required, and we found that our own safety and comfort demanded that they should be severely chastised for provoking us to such a measure. Now that we were a good deal aggravated, some of our men said hard things about what they would do if we would again come in contact with these provoking Indians; and our captain was afraid that, if once engaged, the passion of his men would become so wild that he could not call them off, whilst there was an Indian found to be slaughtered. Being thus compelled to fight, as we thought, in a good cause and in self defence, we drew up in battle array, and fell on the Indians in the wildest and most ferocious manner we could, which struck dismay throughout the whole crowd, killing 14, besides wounding a great many more as we rode right over them. Our men were soon called off, only three of whom were slightly wounded.

This decisive stroke appeared to give the Indians every satisfaction they required, as we were afterwards permitted to pass through the country without molestation. We then continued our course up Barren River, without meeting with any thing to interrupt us, until about the 20th of June, when we found that if we continued in this direction our provisions would become scarce long before we would reach the Rocky Mountains; and accordingly on the 21st our captain decided on leaving this river and taking a Northern direction for the purpose of striking the headwaters of the Columbia (Snake tributary) River, where we would find game plenty, and also beaver.

After leaving Barren River we made a quick passage across the country and the first waters we came to, was Lewis River, near its head, where we found game such as deer, elk, bear and beaver plenty. After laying in a small stock of fresh meat here, we resumed our journey towards the buffalo country. On the morning of the 3rd of July we were delighted by seeing some buffalo in company with four of our Spanish cattle that had strayed a short distance from the main body during the night, two of which our hunters killed, being the first we had seen since we left the Great Salt Lake the year before.

We travelled a short distance today when on arriving at a large spring of most delicious water situated in a beautiful grove, where we concluded to spend the National Anniversary of American Independence; and accordingly our hunters went out in the afternoon and killed several very fat buffalo, which were dressed and the choice parts prepared for a grand feast on the morrow. When the morn of the glorious fourth first dawned we gave three salutes, spent the morning in various kinds of amusement, and at noon partook of our national dinner, which was relished the better as we had a small portion of good old brandy, which we drank in a few minutes, deeply regretting that we had not a small portion of what was that day destroyed by the millions of freemen in the States.—The remainder of the day was celebrated by drinking toasts, singing songs, shooting at mark, running, jumping, and practising on our horses—having the two Spaniards still with us, who learned us many singular pranks, and were a valuable edition to our company, as they created a great deal of fun, and were always in a good humour.

July 5th. Today continued on search of Captain Bonneville, on Bear River, in finding whom we succeeded without having much difficulty, on the 12th, after travelling through a luxuriant, though rather rough country—where we again had intercourse with people of our own nation, being the first we had met with, except the crew of the *Lagoda*, since we separated from these same men at the Great Salt Lake. Here we encamped for the purpose of resting a few days, and probably remaining until we would receive supplies of provisions, merchandise, &c., from St. Lewis—spending our time in discussing the many scenes encountered by each of us, and the many hair-breadth 'scapes that such-and-such a one had made.

After remaining in this situation a few days, there arrived at our camp a company of 25 men belonging to the British North-West Fur Company, from Fort Vancouver, situated near the mouth of the Columbia River. These people informed me that the infant colony at the mouth of the Columbia River had revived, and was now increasing rapidly, under the superintendence of the British, and contained 150 families, the major part of which are English, Canadian, French and Indians, and but few Americans. They carry on agriculture to a considerable extent—the soil being very fertile, climate mild, and frost and snow but seldom known. They also have a grist and saw-mill, and are establishing an extensive fishery at the mouth of the river, for the purpose of catching salmon, as they are very abundant in this stream. They have a governor, and live under a Republican form of government. From all accounts, however, their government is not of much use, as the most unbounded freedom of action is exercised by all the members of the colony, and their government is intended more for effect with the Indians, than any advantage to the people.

About the 17th of July this party left us and continued their journey on search of the Blackfeet Indians for the purpose of trading,—after which they said it was their intention to return to the coast by the same route.

We remained here until the 20th without meeting with anything particularly, when Captain Cerrie joined us with 40 men, bringing a large supply of merchandize packed upon mules and horses from Missouri. With what we had on hand these men brought enough of merchandise and provision to supply our present company for a whole year. This party intended to return immediately to Missouri with what peltries we had on hand.

These succouring companies are always looked for with great anxiety by the people who have been in the mountains any length of time. Many are at times entirely destitute of such articles as would be of great advantage to their comfort—many expect letters or some other manifestations of remembrance from their friends—besides some, who have been strictly temperate (because they could not help it, as the supply of liquor will always be exhausted,) look forward with longing anticipations for the supply which is always sent to this country by the owners of these companies, for the purpose of selling it to the men and thus paying their wages. It is generally brought in a refined state, and is a cash article, which they retail at the enormous price of $1 per gill. Generally when a succouring company of this kind arrives at the camp of the trapper, the men get a little mellow and have a real jubilee—with the exception of a few (after the Indian fashion) who are always prevented, as they must watch the rest, and keep a look-out lest the whole company should be surprised and massacred by the Indians. Scarcely one man in ten, of those employed in this country ever think of saving a single dollar of their earnings, but spend it as fast as they can see an object to spend it for. They care not what may come to pass tomorrow—but think only of enjoying the present moment.

We now began to make the necessary arrangements for our future operations—such as dividing such men as wished to remain in the mountains, into one company, and such as wished to return to the States in another, and settling with the men for the last year's services, and hiring them for the ensuing year.

July 30th. Having every necessary arrangement completed, Mr. Cerrie returned to the State of Missouri with 45 men, and what fur, &c. we had in store. Captain Bonneville was left to make his fall hunt on the headwaters of the Columbia River, and the adjacent country with 50 men, and Captain Walker with 55 men, being the balance of our force, to cross the Rocky Mountains to the waters of the Missouri River, and then continue hunting and trading with the Indians until the month of June, 1835, when Captain Bonneville with his men would join us on the Bighorn River, at the mouth of Popoasia (Popo Agie?) Creek, which empties into the Bighorn below Wind River Mountain.

After the usual ceremony of parting on such occasions, which is performed by each one affectionately shaking hands all round—we separated, each division taking off in a separate direction. Captain Walker continued up Bear River in an eastern direction, and the first night encamped at Smith's Fork. In the morning we resumed our journey in the same direction, being the most direct route to the summit of the mountains, nothing occurring more than usual with the exception of killing any quantity of game we might think proper, until about the 8th of August, when, as the company were passing through a small prairie, we discovered a large grizzly bear laying in the shade of some brush at the edge of the woods, when four of us started for the purpose of killing him, but on coming close, the bear heard us and ran into the thicket.

We now took separate courses, intending to surround the bear and chase him out and have some sport; but one man, as we came to the thicket, acted very imprudently by dismounting and following a buffalo path into the brush, when the bear, hearing our horses on the opposite side, started out on the same path and met the man, when he attempted to avoid it by climbing a small tree, but being too closely pressed was unable to get out of the reach of the bear, and as it passed, caught him by the leg and tore the tendon of his thigh in a most shocking manner. Before we could get to his aid the bear made off and finally escaped.

Here we encamped and remained until the next day, when the wounded man expired—having bled to death from the wound, although every effort in our power was of no use. After burying this man, which was done in the customary manner of interring the dead in the mountains—having dug a deep hole in the ground, into which we deposited the body well wrapt up in blankets, and then filled up the grave, first with bark and then with earth, we continued our journey a short distance in the afternoon, and encamped on the head waters of Lewis river, and at the base of the Rocky Mountains.

Here we made preparations for our voyage across the mountains. Few that have once performed a journey across these hills will encounter them a second time with a cheerful spirit; and particularly will they dread the task if they have encountered as many hardships and perils as some of the company that now reposed at its base, silently contemplating the dreadful fatigues to be encountered until we would reach the eastern base.

In the morning at an early hour, we left the waters which empty into the Pacific, and continued our way up the mountain, which we found tolerable rough, and covered, in places, with a large quantity of snow. We travelled without ceasing, and without meeting with any interruption, until we at last arrived in the Prairies, on the east side, near the headwaters of the Yellow Stone River. On our passage across, we found several pieces of petrified wood, one of which was six or eight feet long—which our men divided amongst themselves, for the purpose of making whet-stones. Here we concluded on commencing our fall's hunt, as the beaver appeared to be quite numerous.

In the neighbourhood of the headwaters of this river, the country is generally composed of prairie hills, covered with excellent grass, and abound with plenty of game of different kinds. After trapping here a few days, we agreed to move down onto Wind River, which empties into the Bighorn, a short distance below this, and whilst leisurely travelling along one day through an extensive prairie, a large horde of buffalo were discovered at a distance making towards us with considerable speed. No one was disposed to take any notice of them, as we had plenty of provision, until we seen them advance closer and faster, as if they were going to ride right over us.

The whole drove came rushing past, at which our loose and pack horses took fright, and started in advance of the buffalo, scattering our baggage in every direction over the prairie for several miles, leaving us nothing but our riding horses. This occasioned us to encamp for the purpose of collecting our stray horses and lost baggage, which was done, with the exception of one horse and some merchandize, which we were unable to find. To see a drove of perhaps a thousand buffalo driving through a level plain as fast as their strength will permit them, is a most frightful spectacle; and then, when our horses started in advance, pitching and snorting, the scene was beyond description.

Many of our horses were severely crippled in consequence of this chase,—so much so that we were detained three days in waiting on them and repairing our injured merchandise. A few days after leaving this place we arrived, Aug. 20, on Popoasia Creek, where we found an oil spring, rising out of the earth similar to that of any other spring. After emptying into the creek, the oil can be seen floating on the surface for a considerable distance. The oil is of a dark hue when in the fountain, almost like tar, but is as thin as water. If this spring was in the States, I have no doubt the chemist might make a valuable use of it. A Mr. Bergen, belonging to our company, and who had been severely afflicted with the rheumatism, procured a phial of it, which he used,

337

and afterwards said it afforded him entire relief.

Aug. 21st. Today we continued in pursuit of beaver, which is our daily occupation, passing from one water course to another, through plains and over hills, all of which are prairie, with the exception of the base of the mountain, where there is an abundance of timber. We travelled in this manner, and spending our time mostly in this way, without meeting with any misfortunes, or any thing unusual in a backwood's life, occasionally being quite successful in catching beaver, until near the middle of October, when we arrived among the tribe of Crow Indians.

We now find the weather getting cold, with plenty of snow, frost and ice, which compels us to suspend our trapping for this season, having done a very fair business; and to increase our store of peltries, we now commenced trading with these Indians for buffalo robes, beaver fur, &c. for which purpose we intend passing the winter in this neighbourhood.

After remaining here a few days, in the meantime obtaining the principal part of the valuable peltries of the Indians, the company left them and appointed Wind River as the place to meet and resume the trading as soon as the Indians could collect a supply—leaving two men and myself among the Crows for the purpose of instigating them in the business of catching beaver and buffalo.

Nov. 1st. This morning Captain Walker and his followers left us, and continued in the direction of Wind River, there to erect a temporary trading house for the winter season, and we remained with the Indians who were engaged in collecting their winter's supply of meat, which is the custom of all tribes in a plentiful country of game, to go in bodies sufficiently large to defend themselves in case of an attack by a neighbouring hostile tribe, as there is scarcely three tribes to be found in the whole Indian country, on friendly terms with each other.

I now found myself in a situation that had charms which I had many times longed for. Ever since I engaged in the trapping business, I had occasional intercourse with the Indians, but never resided with them until now; which would afford me every opportunity to minutely observe their internal mode of living. The Crows are a powerful nation, and inhabit a rich and extensive district of country. They raise no vegetation, but entirely depend on the chase for a living. This is the situation of nearly every tribe, and when game gets scarce in one part of the country claimed by a certain tribe, they remove to another part, until after a while their game becomes scarce, when they are induced to encroach upon the territory of a neighbouring tribe, which will at once create a fearful strife, and not unfrequently ends in the total destruction of some powerful nation.

It will be recollected that I was amongst these Indians once before, when some of our horses were stolen and we followed them into the Crow village,—where we found our horses and also a negro man, in the winter of 1832-33. This man we found to be of as great advantage to us now as on former occasions, as he has become thoroughly acquainted with their language, method of transacting their public and private business, and considered of great value by the Indians. He enjoys perfect peace and satisfaction, and has everything he desires at his own command.

The Crow nation contains from 7,000 to 8,000 souls, and are divided into two divisions of an equal number in each—there being too great a number to travel together, as they could not get game in many places to supply such a force. Each division is headed by a separate chief, whose duty it is to pilot them from one hunting ground to another, and to lead his followers to battle in time of war—one of whom they call Grizzly Bear and the other, Long Haired Chief, which name he derives from the extreme length of his hair, which is no less than nine feet eleven inches long. This is the principal chief, or *sachem*, of the nation, and is quite a worthy and venerable looking old man of 75 or 80 years of age. He uses every possible precaution to preserve his hair, which is perfectly white, and has never had it cut since his infancy. He worships it as the director or guide of his fate through life—never rising or laying down without humbly and devoutly adoring this talisman, and which they term *Bah-park* (medicine.)

It is customary for every tribe of Indians in the regions of the Rocky Mountains to have some instrument or article to pay homage to and invoke, but no nation, I believe, are so devoutly attached to their talismans as the Crow nation—it is their life—their very existence. Almost every individual of the Crow tribe has something of this land, and which generally consists of a seed, a stone, a piece of wood, a bear or eagle's claw, or anything which their fancy may lead them to believe has a successful virtue, and which has been purchased of some noted warrior who has been successful in his undertakings whilst in the possession of such an article. This magical thing, whatever it may be, is carefully enveloped in a piece of skin, and then tied round their neck or body.

If an old experienced warrior gives one or two young men an article of this kind on going to war, and they happen to be successful in taking scalps or stealing horses, the whole affair is attributed to the virtue of his talisman, and he can then sell it for almost any price he demands, and if it be a precious stone, or seed, or piece of wood, all similar articles are immediately enhanced in value, and the greater the price they pay for such an article, the greater service it will be to them in the hour of need.—Some of them will even give four or five good horses for the most trifling and simple article of this kind.

Their principal wealth consists of horses, porcupine quills, and fine dressed skins, for clothing, &c. but nothing is of so much value as their idol; without which an Indian is a poor miserable drone to society, unworthy the esteem and companionship of brutes. Long-haired chief worships nothing but his hair, which is regularly combed and carefully folded up every morning into a roll about three feet long by the principal warriors of his tribe.

Their houses are composed of dressed buffalo hides and pine poles about 25 or 30 feet in length, and about three inches in diameter. These poles are stuck upon end in a circle, and all coming together at the top forms the shape of a haystack.—The buffalo robes are then cut in proper shape, sewed together and covered over their habitation. Their fire is placed in the centre of the lodge, and the poles being left apart at the top affords a very good draught for the smoke. Some of these houses are much larger than others, such as are intended for the transacting of public business. These are constructed with much care, and are quite comfortable and convenient habitations—the buffalo robes affording a sufficient shield from the effects of the cold. In their public buildings all their national affairs are discussed at stated periods by the warriors and principal men. Here they have their public smokes and public rejoicings.

This tribe is also governed by a species of police, such as having a committee of soldiers appointed for the purpose of keeping order and regulation in their village, appointing a day for a general hunt and keeping any who might be so disposed, from running ahead and chasing off the game, in order that each individual may have a fair chance to obtain an equal share of provision, with his neighbour.—These soldiers are also to observe that on such occasions their village is not left in a weak and unsafe condition by too many going to war, or to horse stealing, (which generally ends in war) at a time, and also to see that such a party is properly provided with a competent commander, and if not, it is their duty to supply the deficiency by appointing one to act in his place. If any person acts contrary to their laws, these soldiers have the liberty of punishing him for it, which is done by shaving his horses main and tail, cut up his lodge, and whip him, if not contrary to the decision of the principal chief, in whom is invested the power of vetoing every act of this executive committee, if not agreeable to his wish.

When game becomes scarce, and they are about to move to another section, every moveable article is packed upon horseback, when they travel on until they arrive in a country abounding with game.— Their children from two to three years of age, and unable to ride, are tied upon the baggage, and those younger are fastened upon a board and conveyed in manner as heretofore described. They have a sort of dray formed by these poles, which is done by fastening one end to the pack saddle, and the other end dragging on the ground, on which they place their furniture.

There is more personal ambition and rivalry existing among this tribe than any other I became acquainted with—each one trying to excel the other in merit, whilst engaged in some dangerous adventure.—Their predatory wars afford them every opportunity for this, as they are at liberty and sometimes compelled to engage in the battle's strife as soon as they are able to bend the bow or wield the tomahawk.—Their first promotion from the ranks of a private citizen, is secured by stealing a few horses and killing one or two of their enemies, when they are eligible to the title of a Small Brave. By adding so many more acts of this kind, they receive the title of a Large or Great Brave; from thence to a Little Chief, and to rise to the station of a Great Chief, they must steal such a number of horses, kill and scalp such a number of the enemy, and take so many guns or bows and arrows.

Whenever one person exceeds the existing chief in these deeds, he is installed into the office of chief of the nation, which he retains until some other ambitious, daring brave exceeds him. They always take good care, however, not to excel their present chief, old Long-hair.

This school, as it was, creates a great deal of jealousy and envy among the people, but it seldom leads to any disturbance, as the executive soldiers, or police, are always ready to chastise and punish any such conduct.

Any person not rising to either of these stations by the time he is twenty years of age, has nothing to say or do in any public business whatever, but is compelled to perform different kinds of menial labour altogether degrading to a man, as it is putting him on an equality with the squaws—which is low enough indeed in the estimation of the Indian. Such a man becomes the slave of the women, as they are at liberty to order him to do any thing they may think proper, such as carry wood, water, &c., or any drudgery that is required to be done.

After receiving the title of Little Chief they are at liberty to speak and take part in all public debates in relation to the affairs of the nation, and are exempt from all kinds of labour in going to war, which has to be done by the privates, who are generally young men, as on such occasions they have no women with them; and as they progressively rise, they are at liberty to order and command those who are beneath them. This is the principal cause of their ambition, which far exceeds description. If one of the men who has fallen into the rank of a woman, and has become tired of that occupation, he will undergo any exertion, and encounter any danger, no matter how great, in order to distinguish himself and improve his forlorn and dishonourable condition.

Soon after we took up our quarters with these Indians, I occupied my time in ascertaining their manner of taking game, which, if it is more laborious, it is more successful than the Spanish mode of taking wild horse. When their families are in want of provision, or desirous of having a hunt, one of the principal men, who might be called the *trumpeter*, will mount a horse and ride round through the encampment, village, or settlement, and publicly proclaim that on a stated day the whole tribe must be prepared for a general hunt, or *surround*. When the day arrives the village is alive betimes in the morning, and several hundred will sometimes mount their race-horses, repair to a certain designated section of country, which they are to surround. When the men have all had time to get to their allotted stations, they begin to close in, driving the game, principally buffalo, into a circle and when they are pretty well confined in the circle, they commence killing them—until which time, no man dare attempt to take any of the game. In this manner they have sometimes caught several hundred buffalo, besides many other animals, at a single surround.

When they are in a country suitable, these people will destroy the buffalo by driving a herd of some hundreds to the edge of a convenient rocky precipice, when they are forced headlong down the craggy descent. This is more dangerous than the other method, as the buffalo, unless the Indians are very numerous, will sometimes rush in a solid column through their ranks, knocking down the horses and tramping the riders under their feet.

They have another method of taking the buffalo, which is in this way:—If they know of a place at the base of some mountain that is surrounded on three sides with inaccessible precipices, and a level valley leading into it, they manage to drive the whole gang of buffalo into this neck and force them up to its termination, when they erect a strong fence across the valley, or outlet, and then butcher their prisoners at leisure.

In a place of this kind I was shewn by the chief Grizzly Bear, upwards of seven hundred buffalo skulls which he said had been caught at a single hunt, and which had taken place about four years previous.

About the 20th of November, after travelling for three or four days in pursuit of provision, we at length arrived in the vicinity of buffalo, where we pitched our tents and the Indians prepared for a general hunt. In the evening their horses were all dressed in the best style, and at an early hour the next morning four or five hundred Indians were mounted and ready for the chase.

This was a favourable opportunity for me to gratify my curiosity in seeing this kind of sport, and my companions and myself followed in the rear of the Indians.—Our hunters had not advanced far on this sporting expedition until they met with an object which entirely put them out of the notion of showing us their ability in catching buffalo, for, at some distance across the plain, along the base of some rough craggy hills, was espied a considerable body of people, who appeared to be advancing towards us. Immediately a halt was called, for the purpose of observing the movements of the strangers, and consulting on what steps should be taken. It did not require the keen eye of a Crow Indian long to tell that their visitors were Indians and belonged to their implacable enemies, the Blackfeet tribe.

This was enough. War was now their only desire, and our Indians advanced towards their enemies as fast as the speed of their horses would admit, who, being on foot, were soon overtaken and forced to ascend the rocks, which they did in safety. The Crows immediately surrounded the Blackfeet, confident of an easy victory, but when they made the attack they found that their enemy was too well prepared for defence, and they immediately despatched an express to the village for a reinforcement, of men, conscious that the Blackfeet would not attempt to leave their present position until such reinforcement would have time to arrive.

This was quite a different kind of sport from that which I expected to witness when I left the Indian camp, but one of no less interest, and far more important to me. Whilst the express was absent both parties employed their time in strengthening their positions—the Blackfeet had chosen a most fortunate spot to defend themselves, and by a little labour found themselves in a fort that might have done credit to an army of frontier regulars. It was situated on the brow of a hill, in a circle of rocks shaped similar to a horseshoe, with a ledge of rocks from three to four feet high on either side, and about ten feet, on the part reaching to the brink of the hill, with a very creditable piece of breast work built in front, composed of logs, brush and stones.

From their present situation they have a decided advantage over the Crows, and if well prepared for war, could hold out a considerable length of time, and deal destruction thick and fast on any force that might attempt to scale their fort—which looks more like the production of art than nature. Whilst the Blackfeet were assiduously engaged in defending their position, the Crows were no less idle in preparing for the attack, the destruction of which, they were determined should not be relaxed as long as there was a living Blackfoot Indian to be found in the neighbourhood. Previous to the arrival of the reinforcement, which was about ten o'clock, there had been three Crows and one Blackfoot killed, which was done at the first attack after the latter were driven into their fort.

When the express reached the Crow village every man, woman and child able to point a gun or mount a horse repaired with all speed to the scene of action, who came up uttering the most wild and piercing yells I ever heard in my life. A great deal of contention at first took place among the principal men of the Crow tribe as to the manner of attacking their enemy, who appeared to look down upon them in defiance; notwithstanding the Crows kept up a continual yelling and firing of guns, all of which was without effect. Finally they appeared to harmonise and understand each other.

As matters now seemed to indicate the approach of a crisis, I repaired to an eminence about 200 yards from the fort among some cedar trees, where I had an excellent view of all their movements. At first the Crows would approach the fort by two or three hundred in a breast, but on arriving near enough to do any execution, the fire from the fort would compel them to retreat. They then formed in a trail along the top of the ridge, and in rotation would ride at full speed past the breastwork, firing as they passed, and then throwing themselves on the side of the horse until nothing will be exposed to the enemy except one arm and one leg. This they found to be very destructive to their horses and also their men, there being now ten Crows and several horses laying dead on the field. Urged by their ill success thus far, and by the piteous lamentations of the wives, children and relatives of those who had fell, the Crow chiefs decided on suspending the attack, and determined to hold a council of war for the purpose of deciding on what measures should be adopted, in order to destroy these brave Blackfeet.

When the principal chiefs met in council, all was still except the lamentations of the bereaved, who, perhaps regret the severe penance which the customs of their people compelled them to endure for the memory of a deceased friend, and lament more on account of the prospect of trouble ahead, than for the loss which they have sustained. The chiefs held a hasty and stormy council. Some were in favour of abandoning the Blackfeet entirely, and others were determined on charging into their fort and end the battle in a total and bloody massacre. This was finally decided upon, but not until after several speeches were made for and against it, and the pipe of war smoked by each brave and chief.

As soon as this determination of the chiefs was made known the war-whoop again resounded with the most deafening roar through the plain—every voice that was able to make a noise was strained to its very utmost to increase the sound, until the very earth, trees and rocks seemed to be possessed of vocal powers. By their tremendous howling they had worked as great a change in the courage of their soldiery, as the most soul-enlivening martial music would the cowardly fears of a half-intoxicated militia company.

Now was the moment for action. Each man appeared willing to sacrifice his life if it would bring down an enemy; and in this spirit did they renew and repeat the attack on the breast-work of their enemy, but as often did they retreat with severe loss. Again and again did they return to the charge, but all was of no use—all their efforts were of no avail—confusion began to spread through their ranks—many appeared overwhelmed with despair—and the whole Crow nation was about to retreat from the field, when the negro, who has been heretofore mentioned, and who had been in company with us, advanced a few steps towards the Crows and ascended a rock from which he addressed the Crow warriors in the most earnest and impressive manner.

345

He told them that they had been here making a great noise, as if they could kill the enemy by it—that they had talked long and loud about going into the fort, and that the white men would say the Indian had a crooked tongue, when talking about his war exploits.

He told them that their hearts were small, and that they were cowardly—that they acted more like squaws than men, and were not fit to defend their hunting ground. He told them that the white men were ashamed of them and would refuse to trade with such a nation of cowards—that the Blackfeet would go home and tell their people that three thousand Crows could not take a handful of them,—that they would be laughed at, scorned, and treated with contempt by all nations wherever known—that no tribe would degrade themselves hereafter by waging war with them, and that the whole Crow nation, once so powerful, would forever after be treated as a nation of squaws.

The old negro continued in this strain until they became greatly animated, and told them that if the red-man was afraid to go amongst his enemy, he would show them that a black man was not, and he leaped from the rock on which he had been standing, and, looking neither to the right nor to the left, made for the fort as fast as he could run. The Indians guessing his purpose, and inspired by his words and fearless example, followed close to his heels, and were in the fort dealing destruction to the right and left nearly as soon as the old man.

Here now was a scene of no common occurrence. A space of ground about the size of an acre, completely crowded with hostile Indians fighting for life, with guns, bows and arrows, knives and clubs, yelling and screaming until the hair seemed to lift the caps from our heads. As soon as most of the Crows got into the fort, the Blackfeet began to make their escape out of the opposite side, over the rocks about 10 feet high. Here they found themselves no better off, as they were immediately surrounded and hemmed in on all sides by overwhelming numbers. A large number on both sides had fell in the engagement in the inside of the fort, as there the Crows had an equal chance with their enemy, but when on the outside the advantage was decidedly against them, as they were confined in a circle and cut down in a few moments.

When the Blackfeet found there was no chance of escape, and knowing that there was no prospect of mercy at the hands of their perplexed and aggravated, but victorious enemy, they fought with more than human desperation. From the time they left their fort, they kept themselves in regular order, moving forward in a solid breast, cutting their way through with their knives, until their last man fell, pierced, perhaps, with an hundred wounds.

In this massacre, if one of the Blackfeet would receive a dangerous wound he would drop to the ground, as if dead, and if his strength was not too far exhausted, he would suddenly rise to his feet and plunge his knife to the heart of an enemy who would be rushing through the crowd, and then die. This would not be done in self defence, nor with a hope of escape, but through revenge. This was truly a scene of carnage, enough to sicken the stoutest heart—but nothing at all in comparison with what took place afterwards. The Crows, when they found the enemy strewed over the field, none having escaped their vengeance, commenced a general rejoicing, after which they retired a short distance for the purpose of taking repose and some refreshments.

Although the victory was complete, the Crows paid dear for it, having lost about thirty killed, and as many more wounded, besides a great number of horses. The loss of their companions did not appear to dampen the rejoicings of the men the least bit, and indeed it would appear that the squaws should do all the mourning and lamenting, as well as all the labour. Their dead were all collected together, when the squaws went round and claimed their kindred. This was a most affecting scene—but what was it when contrasted with that enacted by the men as soon as they had rested from the toil of battle. The women would throw themselves upon the dead bodies of their husbands, brothers, &c. and there manifest the most excruciating anguish that any human being could suffer. The women were occupied in this manner when the men went to work to glut their merciless vengeance on their fallen foe.

Many of the Blackfeet who were scattered over the battleground had fallen by broken limbs or wounded in some way, and were yet writhing in agony, unable to injure anyone or help themselves in any way. All such were collected together, and then tormented in a manner too shocking to relate. These fiends would cut off their ears, nose, hands and feet, pluck out their eyes, pull out their hair, cut them open and take out part of their insides, piercing them with sharp sticks—in short, every method of inflicting pain was resorted to. In order that they might render their mode of torment still more excruciating, they would bring into the presence of the dying the bodies of those who were already dead, and then tare out their hearts, livers, and brains, and throw them in the faces of the living, cutting them to pieces, and afterwards feeding them to their dogs—accompanying the whole with the most taunting and revengeful epithets, whilst those not engaged in this fiendish work, were occupied in keeping up a constant screaming, howling and yelling.

When this torment commenced, all the sufferers who could get hold of a knife or anything with which they could take away their lives, would do so immediately. All the torment that could be inflicted by their persecutors, failed to bring a single murmur of complaint from the sufferers—nor would they signify the least symptoms of being conquered. No—not if they had been offered undisturbed liberty, would those sufferers who had lost so many of their companions, acknowledge themselves prisoners in the Crow village. Death they preferred to this, and death with indescribable horrors, did they all receive.

After they had finished tormenting the living, which was not done until there was no more to kill, they commenced cutting off the heads of the mangled bodies, which were hoisted on the ends of poles and carried about, and afterwards dashed them against trees, rocks, &c. leaving them on the plain to be devoured by wild beasts.

The men now repaired to their dead friends, where they went through various manoeuvres, as much as to say that they had revenged their death, and soon afterwards everything was on the move towards the camp, where we arrived soon after dark, not to rest, and calmly meditate on the scenes of the day, but to see further developments of the superstitious propensities of the poor neglected savage.

After arriving in the village, a part of the men commenced their public rejoicings, by beating upon drums, dancing and singing, which, together with the incessant wailings and lamentations of those who had lost relatives, gave us a night that was entirely free from repose, and averse to sober reflection. In this manner the whole night was spent, nor did the morning bring any prospect of a cessation of these singular customs.

About ten o'clock the whole tribe was engaged in performing the funeral obsequies to the remains of their deceased relatives. At an early hour the wife had seated herself by the side of her dead husband, where she would remain until it came his turn to be interred, when she would clasp the cold and lifeless form of him, whom she still seems to love, and cling to it until forced away by some of the men. Their manner of burying their dead is also most singular in some respects:

The corpse is carefully wrapped up in buffalo robes and laid into the grave, together with his talisman, and anything else to which he was attached,—and if he be a chief of some importance, his horse's tail and mane are shaved off and buried with him—these benighted Indians believing that each of these hairs will turn into a beautiful horse in the land of spirits, where they think that a horse and bow and arrow are all that a man requires to perfect his happiness and peace.

As soon as the dead were deposited in the silent tomb, the musicians collected together and marched through the camp, beating upon sticks and drums, as a signal for the mourners to fall in the rear, which they did, and the whole procession then proceeded to the top of some rising ground, not far off, where the males and females separated into different groups.—The female mourners now took the point of an arrow, which was fixed in a stick, and commenced pricking their heads, beginning at one ear and continuing round the forehead to the other, making incisions half an inch apart all round; and the men went through a similar course on their legs, arms, &c., until the blood oozed out in streams. All this performance was done without creating the least appearance of pain.

After doing this each female that had lost a near relative or particular friend, collected along a log and deliberately cut off a finger at the first joint, which was done with as much coolness as the pricking process. This is done by the males, also, except the two first fingers on the right hand, which they preserve for the purpose of bending the bow, and many of the aged females may be seen with the end off each of their fingers, and some have even taken off the second crop. Whilst this was being done by the mourners, the other Indians kept up a continual noise with their music, singing, dancing and yelling. The procession now returned to the village with the faces of all the female mourners daubed over with their own blood, which they never remove until it wears off.

Those not wishing to loose a finger are at liberty to shave off their hair close, but it is the general custom among the Crows to lose a piece of their finger. Anyone who has lost a relative is not allowed to take part in the dance or any kind of sport for 12 or 13 moons, unless one of their surviving friends take the life of an Indian belonging to the tribe that killed the mourned one—which will at once atone for all loss, and drown all grief, and she is then allowed to wash the blood from her face and resume her former standing in society. This night was spent in about the same manner as last night—some being engaged in dancing and singing, and others crying and lamenting the loss they had sustained.

Nov. 22nd. This morning the chief of the nation gave orders to move for the purpose of getting among the buffalo and other game—and also to be prepared for a national dance on their march. About ten o'clock the whole tribe was in readiness and we started in the direction of the battle ground, and on arriving there a halt was ordered for the purpose of giving the dead carcases of the Blackfeet the last evidence of the Crow's revenge—which was done by beating and mangling every piece of flesh they could find. This done, the march was resumed to a beautiful level plain, perfectly smooth and covered with short grass, for two or three miles square—where the national dance was to take place. When they had dismounted, the whole nation formed a ring, when 69 of the oldest squaws, all painted black, formed themselves in a line in the centre of the circle, each bearing a pole from 12 to 15 feet in length.

The person who struck the first blow at their late battle with the Blackfeet now commenced dancing, and was immediately followed by every young man and woman belonging to the tribe, (except the mourners, who stood silent, melancholy spectators) all clad in their best dresses, handsomely worked with porcupine quills, and their heads delightfully ornamented with magpie and pheasant tails—forming themselves in double file, and dancing round the whole circle to wild, though not irregular music—which they make by stretching a piece of buffalo skin over a hoop similar to a riddle, where it is well stretched, and then sewed together and filled with sand and left until it is dry and properly shaped, when the sand is thrown out and some pebbles or bullets put in, when it is ready for the hand of the musician—and is in shape similar to a gourd.

After dancing round the circle once or twice, they would suddenly halt; shout their terrible war-whoop—shoot off their guns, when the rattling music would again commence and they would all be engaged in the dance. Each member of the tribe, who was not mourning, from the child up to the enfeebled old man and woman took part in this exercise. After about two hours spent in this manner, they concluded their celebration by the display of an Indian battle, which was exceedingly grand, far beyond any description I had ever heard. 70 or 80 of their best warriors mounted their most active horses, one party acting the part of their enemies, the Blackfeet, each one armed with a gun, a club or lance, and some with both. They separated, one party to one side and the other to the other side of the plain, and at a given signal would advance towards each other as fast as their horses would run, firing and striking as they would pass—throwing themselves nearly under their horses, so much so, that they could fire at each other under their horse's belly. During the time they seemed to exert every nerve, yet they kept up a continual noise, by repeating the most wild and ferocious yells I ever heard. Their activity in throwing the lance is no less wonderful—being so expert in this business that they can throw it 20 or 25 yards and strike a mark the size of a man's head, whilst riding past as swift as their horses will go.

The greater part of the day was occupied in this manner, after which they took up their march towards the River No-wood, on the banks of which stream we encamped for the night. In this vicinity buffalo appeared to be quite numerous and the Indians killed several this evening. As the prospect of game appeared so good, the Indians determined on remaining here a few days for the purpose of laying in a stock of buffalo robes to trade with Captain Walker. The Indians would go out in large companies and kill a great number of these animals, when it would be the duty of the women to follow after and gather up the hides, which they would convey to the camp, and dress them ready for market. It is the duty of the squaws to dress the buffalo robes alone, which is done by stretching the hide tight on the ground and there let it dry, when they have a piece of iron or sharp stone, fixed in a stick, making a tool similar to a foot-adze, with which they cut and scrape the fleshy side until it becomes thin and smooth—after this they have a mixture composed of the brains and liver of the animal mixed together, in which they soak the hide a couple of days, when it is taken out and again stretched on the ground, where it is beat and rubbed with a paddle until it becomes perfectly soft and dry.

After catching a good many buffalo and some beaver at this place, we removed towards the point designated to meet Captain Walker and his men. On the 30th we encamped at the junction of the Bighorn and Wind Rivers. Not long after dark our encampment was surprised by a party of about fifty Blackfeet suddenly appearing among our horses for the purpose of stealing them. This created a great uproar in our camp. Every Indian was on his feet and ready for fight in an instant. The enemy was discovered too soon, and had to retreat with the loss of one man, without taking any horses at all. They were followed a great ways across the plain to the mountain, but as the night was very dark they could not be overtaken, and finally escaped. The one who had fallen was a principal chief among the Blackfeet, and had ventured too near the encampment for the purpose of choosing a valuable horse.

Here we were to have another scene of Indian exultation. On the former occasion, when the 69 Blackfeet had been killed there was too much grief mingled with the joy of the Crows to render it any thing like complete; but now it was quite different,—an enemy had fallen without costing a drop of blood on their part. On the former occasion it was joy only imitated—now it was exultation in reality. It appears natural for these Indians to exult more over the death and scalping of one enemy without the loss of one of their own—than they would to kill fifty of the enemy and lose one of their own. After those who had gave chase to the Blackfeet returned to camp, this dead Indian was taken in hands. After everyone had carefully examined him, he was taken to a tree and there suspended by the neck, when the men commenced shooting at him and the squaws piercing him with sharp sticks. This work was kept up until after midnight, when they commenced dancing and singing, yelling and shouting, which was carried far beyond that of the 21st and 22nd Nov. In this manner they spent their time until near ten o'clock, when they prepared to remove up Wind River—Which they did after all taking leave of the dead Indian by abusing it in some manner to show their spite.

We travelled up Wind River until the 4th of Dec. when we arrived at the camp of Captain Walker, whom, together with his men we found in good health and spirits. This camp is situated 60 or 70 miles east of the main chain of the Rocky Mountains, on the head waters of Wind River, which, after running 150 or 200 miles in an eastern direction, empties into the Bighorn. The Wind River valley, through which this river passes, is one of the most beautiful formations of nature. It is upwards of 20 miles wide in some places, and is as level as a floor, with the margin of the river evenly ornamented with thriving cotton wood. A great many white people pass the winters in this valley, on account of the abundance of buffalo and other game.

The first night after reaching the camp of my old companions was spent in telling and hearing told the many exploits and adventures which we had severally seen and took part in since our separation. Captain Walker and his men had passed the time without encountering any hardships, or being disturbed in any way, with the exception of a party of hostile Indians who watched their movements for some time and who at last succeeded in stealing a few of their horses.

The following day the Crow chiefs were made presents of some small articles of merchandise, when we commenced bartering with them for their furs and buffalo robes. As soon as they had sold out their present stock they left us all highly pleased with their success, and commenced hunting for more. As game was very plenty here we determined on spending the winter in this valley, where we occupied our time in hunting and trapping a little ourselves, but deriving our principal profits by trading with the Indians for robes, which they would bring into our camp as fast as they could dress them.

The daily hunting of the Indians, as well as ourselves, had thinned the buffalo pretty well, and driven them across the country onto the Platte River—in consequence of which the Indians are now (1st March, 1835) preparing to leave us and go down to the Yellow Stone River, which empties into the Missouri, where they intend spending the summer.

The Indians left with us one of their tribe who had received a stroke of the palsy, or a similar affliction, which had deprived him of speech and of the use of one-half of his body. He was a man of 30 or 35 years of age, appeared to be in good health, but was entirely helpless, one arm and one leg, being entirely numb, or dead, and beginning to decay. He was entirely speechless, and had been in this situation for four years. They told us that this man had been a great warrior, and that the morning after returning from a hard, though successful battle, he was found in his bed dead, as they supposed, and that, when about to bury him in the evening, he gave signs of remaining life—when he was conveyed back to his *wigwam* and remained there for two days and nights, when he recovered to the situation in which he was left with us. As he had been such a valuable chief, they did all in their power to restore him the use of his body, and had conveyed him about with them from place to place ever since, but had resolved to do so no longer, and therefore left him with us, telling us to do with him as we pleased—if we saw proper to take him with us well and good, if not, we might leave him to be food for the beasts of the forest.

Having concluded our winters hunt and trading with these Indians, who have left us, our men are now occupied in digging holes for the secretion of our peltries and merchandise, until we return from our spring's hunt, and when we would be joined by Captain Bonneville and his company, who was to meet us at the mouth of Popoasia Creek in June next. On the 8th I was sent by the captain to measure the size of the holes that the men were digging and whilst in one of them, taking the dimensions, with three other men, the bank caved in, covering two men entirely, another up to the shoulders, and dislocating my foot. Of the four, I was the only one that was able to get out without assistance—the others being all seated at the time the accident happened.

Help was immediately obtained, and the men extricated as soon as possible, who appeared entirely lifeless, but after rubbing and bleeding them effectually, they recovered, when the men proceeded to extricate the one whom we thought was the least injured, but whom we found to be in the most dangerous situation, as his legs and lower part of his body was completely crushed. This man, (Mr. Laront, of St. Louis, where he left a wife and four children) suffered most severely during the remainder of the day and all night, and died the next morning about sunrise.

The manner of digging these holes is upon a high dry bank, where they sink a round hole like a well, five or six feet, and then dig a chamber under ground, where the merchandise is deposited—after which the *well* part of it is filled up, and the top covered with the natural sod, and all the overpluss earth is carefully scraped up and thrown into the river, or creek, so that nothing may be left on the premises to lead to the discovery of the hidden treasure.

March 10th. Today we deposited in the cold earth the remains of our lamented companion, Mr. Laront, in the most respectable manner our means would allow, after which we resumed our business of secreting our stores. Our provisions were again growing scarce for which purpose each one is anxious to be on the move. When we first came to this place, we could stand in our encampment almost any morning and shoot down some lazy buffalo that would be lurking in the neighbourhood—but now our hunters might scour the valley a whole day and not kill as much as a rabbit.

Having every thing in readiness for removing on the morning of the 12th, Captain Walker went to the palsied Indian and told him that we were about going and were not able to take him with us. The poor Indian then, not being able to speak, made imploring signs to us to leave him as much provision as we could spare. This we done with cheerfulness, but it only consisted of the carcase of a wolf, which we placed within reach of him, when he requested that we would fasten the cabin door so as to prevent the entrance of wild beasts.

The wounded, consisting of one with a broken leg, another's back sprained, and myself my foot dislocated, were placed on a litter made of a buffalo skin, with a pole tied to each side of it and fastened between two horses. This was the most painful travelling to me, as well as to the others, that I had ever experienced,—particularly whilst passing over a rough piece of ground.

Our course led in a northern direction after reaching the Bighorn River, which we followed a few days and then crossed over to Tongue River, which stream empties into the Missouri below the mouth of the Yellowstone. Here we decided on hunting and trapping, as beaver signs were quite numerous. The ice had not entirely melted from this stream yet, but there was none left to prevent us from following our favourable pursuit. In this neighbourhood, we spent the months of April, May, and part of June, passing from one water course to another, finding plenty of beaver at each place, and some other game. During the whole time we were permitted to follow our business without any disturbance. All the wounded had completely recovered, and were enabled to make a profitable hunt—having visited, in our toilsome occupation, the headwaters of the following rivers all of which are the tributaries of the Missouri:—Tongue, Powder, Yellowstone, Little and Big Porcupine, Misscleskell, Priors, Smith's, Gallatin's, Otter, Rosebud, Clark's and Stinking Rivers.[24]

About the 10th of June we suspended our trapping and returned to Wind River, where we found Captain Bonneville and his men waiting for us according to appointment, at the mouth of Popoasia Creek.

Here we encamped for a few days, until we could collect our peltries together and make a divide—shaving sent some of our men to bring our merchandise, &c., from the place where we had deposited it, who succeeded without any difficulty, and stated that no traces of the palsied Indian we had left there could be discovered.—We now set about packing and sorting our furs, &c., and making arrangements for the ensuing year—such as paying off hands hiring them for another term, and apportioning the different companies. Captain Walker, with 59 men, was to continue trapping in this country for one year from this time, and Captain Bonneville, with the remainder, taking all the peltries we had collected, and which was packed upon horses and

---

24. Most of these rivers are tributaries of the Yellowstone, the Muscleshell is a branch of the Missouri, and the Stinking: River or Stinking Water is a branch of the Bighorn.

mules, was to go to the States, and return in the summer of 1836, with as strong a force as he could collect, and a large supply of merchandise, and meet Captain Walker in this neighbourhood.

On parting this time, many of the men were at a loss to know what to do. Many were anxious to return to the States, but feared to do so, lest the offended law might hold them responsible for misdemeanours committed previous to their embarking in the trapping business, and others could not be persuaded to do so for any price—declaring that a civilized life had no charms for them. Although I intended to return to the mountains again, I was particularly anxious to first visit the States lest I should also forget the blessings of civilized society, and was very thankful when I found myself in Captain Bonneville's company, on the march towards the rising sun.

As we travelled along we killed all the game we could, this being necessary, as provision is very scarce on the course we intended to pursue between the village of the Pawnee Indians and the white settlements. About the 25th of July we arrived on the Platte River, which we followed down until we arrived at the Pawnee village, situated about 150 miles from where the Platte River empties into the Missouri. After trading with these Indians for some corn, we left them and travelled rapidly every day until we arrived in Independence, (Mo.,) which is the extreme western white settlement, on the 29th of August, 1835—after being absent four years, four months, and five days.

LEONAUR

ALSO FROM LEONAUR

AVAILABLE IN SOFTCOVER OR HARDCOVER WITH DUST JACKET

LIFE IN THE ARMY OF NORTHERN VIRGINIA *by Carlton McCarthy*—The Observations of a Confederate Artilleryman of Cutshaw's Battalion During the American Civil War 1861-1865.

HISTORY OF THE CAVALRY OF THE ARMY OF THE POTOMAC *by Charles D. Rhodes*—Including Pope's Army of Virginia and the Cavalry Operations in West Virginia During the American Civil War.

CAMP-FIRE AND COTTON-FIELD *by Thomas W. Knox*—A New York Herald Correspondent's View of the American Civil War.

SERGEANT STILLWELL *by Leander Stillwell* —The Experiences of a Union Army Soldier of the 61st Illinois Infantry During the American Civil War.

STONEWALL'S CANNONEER *by Edward A. Moore*—Experiences with the Rockbridge Artillery, Confederate Army of Northern Virginia, During the American Civil War.

THE SIXTH CORPS *by George Stevens*—The Army of the Potomac, Union Army, During the American Civil War.

THE RAILROAD RAIDERS *by William Pittenger*—An Ohio Volunteers Recollections of the Andrews Raid to Disrupt the Confederate Railroad in Georgia During the American Civil War.

CITIZEN SOLDIER *by John Beatty*—An Account of the American Civil War by a Union Infantry Officer of Ohio Volunteers Who Became a Brigadier General.

COX: PERSONAL RECOLLECTIONS OF THE CIVIL WAR--VOLUME 1 *by Jacob Dolson Cox*—West Virginia, Kanawha Valley, Gauley Bridge, Cotton Mountain, South Mountain, Antietam, the Morgan Raid & the East Tennessee Campaign.

COX: PERSONAL RECOLLECTIONS OF THE CIVIL WAR--VOLUME 2 *by Jacob Dolson Cox*—Siege of Knoxville, East Tennessee, Atlanta Campaign, the Nashville Campaign & the North Carolina Campaign.

KERSHAW'S BRIGADE VOLUME 1 *by D. Augustus Dickert*—Manassas, Seven Pines, Sharpsburg (Antietam), Fredricksburg, Chancellorsville, Gettysburg, Chickamauga, Chattanooga, Fort Sanders & Bean Station.

KERSHAW'S BRIGADE VOLUME 2 *by D. Augustus Dickert*—At the wilderness, Cold Harbour, Petersburg, The Shenandoah Valley and Cedar Creek..

LEONAUR

ALSO FROM LEONAUR

AVAILABLE IN SOFTCOVER OR HARDCOVER WITH DUST JACKET

FARAWAY CAMPAIGN *by F. James*—Experiences of an Indian Army Cavalry Officer in Persia & Russia During the Great War.

REVOLT IN THE DESERT *by T. E. Lawrence*—An account of the experiences of one remarkable British officer's war from his own perspective.

MACHINE-GUN SQUADRON *by A. M. G.*—The 20th Machine Gunners from British Yeomanry Regiments in the Middle East Campaign of the First World War.

A GUNNER'S CRUSADE *by Antony Bluett*—The Campaign in the Desert, Palestine & Syria as Experienced by the Honourable Artillery Company During the Great War .

DESPATCH RIDER *by W. H. L. Watson*—The Experiences of a British Army Motorcycle Despatch Rider During the Opening Battles of the Great War in Europe.

TIGERS ALONG THE TIGRIS *by E. J. Thompson*—The Leicestershire Regiment in Mesopotamia During the First World War.

HEARTS & DRAGONS *by Charles R. M. F. Crutwell*—The 4th Royal Berkshire Regiment in France and Italy During the Great War, 1914-1918.

INFANTRY BRIGADE: 1914 *by John Ward*—The Diary of a Commander of the 15th Infantry Brigade, 5th Division, British Army, During the Retreat from Mons.

DOING OUR 'BIT' *by Ian Hay*—Two Classic Accounts of the Men of Kitchener's 'New Army' During the Great War including *The First 100,000 & All In It*.

AN EYE IN THE STORM *by Arthur Ruhl*—An American War Correspondent's Experiences of the First World War from the Western Front to Gallipoli-and Beyond.

STAND & FALL *by Joe Cassells*—With the Middlesex Regiment Against the Bolsheviks 1918-19.

RIFLEMAN MACGILL'S WAR *by Patrick MacGill*—A Soldier of the London Irish During the Great War in Europe including *The Amateur Army, The Red Horizon & The Great Push*.

WITH THE GUNS *by C. A. Rose & Hugh Dalton*—Two First Hand Accounts of British Gunners at War in Europe During World War 1- Three Years in France with the Guns and With the British Guns in Italy.

THE BUSH WAR DOCTOR *by Robert V. Dolbey*—The Experiences of a British Army Doctor During the East African Campaign of the First World War.

Lightning Source UK Ltd.
Milton Keynes UK
UKOW04f1959290115

245377UK00001B/48/P